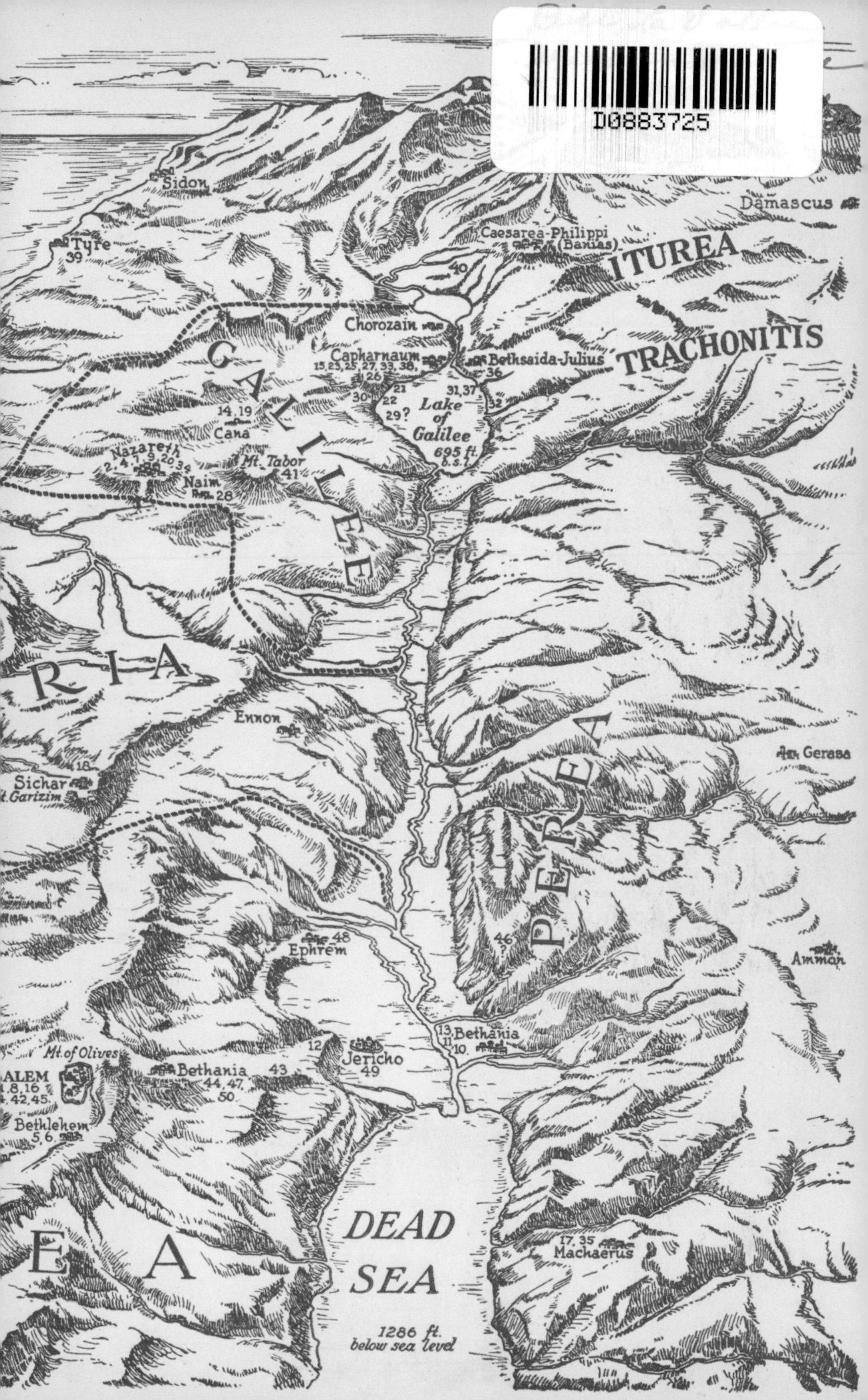

D0883725
Sidon
Tyre
39
Damascus
Caesarea-Philippi
(Banias)
40
ITUREA
TRACHONITIS
Chorozain
Capharnaum
15,23,25,27,33,38,
26
Bethsaida-Julius
36
31,37
32
21
22
30
29?
Lake of Galilee
695 ft. b.s.l.
GALILEE
14,19
Cana
Nazareth
2,4,7,9,20,34
Mt. Tabor
41
Naim
28
RIA
Ennon
18
Sichar
Gerasa
PEREA
Ephrem
48
46?
Ammon
13
11
Bethania
10
12
Jericho
49
Mt. of Olives
Bethania
43
44,47,
50
Bethlehem
5,6.
DEAD SEA
1286 ft. below sea level
17,35
Machaerus
E A

CHRIST THE LEADER

FOLLOW ME

CHRIST THE LEADER

W. H. RUSSELL, PH.D.
DEPARTMENT OF RELIGIOUS EDUCATION
THE CATHOLIC UNIVERSITY OF AMERICA

THE BRUCE PUBLISHING COMPANY
MILWAUKEE

Nihil obstat: John L. Bazinet, S.S., S.T.L.
Imprimatur: Francis J. L. Beckman, S.T.D., Archbishop of Dubuque
April 20, 1937

(Tenth Printing — 1950)

INTRODUCTION

TWO statements of our Lord determine beyond dispute the object and the motive in the teaching of religion. "You are My friends, if you *do* the things that I command you" indicates that religion is a way of living, that knowledge imparted in the classroom has for its purpose the spurring of the students to a fulfillment of the will of God. The doers of the word rather than the hearers are justified. "If you *love Me,* keep My commandments" emphasizes the motive of love that the Master would have each one of us possess. Love makes all things easy. Because the saints love God they are enabled to love men. They find no religious duty irksome. In fact, everyone feels that an obligation is more easy of accomplishment when it is to be done for someone whom he loves.

Christ is the cornerstone for any plan of teaching religion because the God-Man must be known in order to be loved. There is a growing conviction that a religion course which leaves the young untouched by the character and the words and deeds of the Nazarene lacks the element which raises the fulfillment of a religious duty to the plane of love. The teaching of religion is effective only in proportion as our Lord becomes a conscious factor in the daily decisions of the Catholic. In other words, the Person, Jesus Christ, needs to be kept constantly in the foreground in the classroom and in the home. Human minds do indeed differ in their paths of approach to God. And God's grace will often act despite our stumbling presentation of the divine message. But when Christ is loved, religion rises beyond a mere study of definitions and divisions. Newman says: "If faith is to live, it must love; it must lovingly live in the Author of faith as a true and living Being." And Newman is merely applying the rule laid down by our Lord when He said: "Learn of *Me.*" . . . "Abide in *Me* and *I* in you." The method of St.

Peter, who, in his first official teaching to the people, spoke of "Jesus of Nazareth, a Man approved of God among you," should be assurance that if we likewise make known the "power and presence of our Lord Jesus Christ," we are but continuing the apostolic tradition.

The conditions of our day suggest another urgent reason for a renewed emphasis on the life of Christ. While enlightened souls see the need of the light of revelation in the darksome discussions of life's purpose, yet, a common meeting ground between Catholics and the unchurched multitudes becomes daily more difficult. Opinions of persons are being substituted for divinely revealed truths. The existence of unchangeable, objective truth is widely denied. Self-appointed saviors have usurped the rôle of interpreters of life. Millions harbor wrong views on the nature of God and on the basis for human worth. Such a situation strengthens the shout of the materialist in his effort to shut out God from His world.

This condition calls for a reorganization in the presentation of religious truth. As hate increases, so much the more must the Catholic acquire a deeper love of Him who alone can soften hate. The unique and divine Person must be brought to the front of the stage of current life, because discussion of persons is always common ground. Erring leaders must be analyzed in the light of the truth and grace of the eternal Leader. The Church is an ominous thing to the multitudes because they no longer think of a divine founder when religion is discussed. "The world knoweth not us, because it knew not Him," says St. John. Not until they see a reflection of the character of the Nazarene in those who claim to be His followers will these multitudes come to look kindly on His organism, the Church. A better hearing for the institution results when attention is first centered on the originator of the institution.

Christ the Leader is a life of Christ applied to the teaching of religion. It is an attempt to portray His life as a dynamo which sends out energy for Christlike living. His figure is made to command attention in modern situations. A threefold method has been followed. First, sufficient comment for a Gospel passage is supplied to enable the reader to visualize the scene of the statement or of the act; second, an explanation is given of the principle implied in the narrative; third, application is made of the principle to our life of today. While alert and spiritually sensitive souls may not need much enlargement on the words of the Gospel, it is often helpful to expand the terse narrative of the Evangelists for those who have been immersed in the stream of modern confusions.

Complete commentary would have made the book too ponderous. Consequently, teachers will find it necessary and instructive to supply more details. *The Christ, the Son of God,* by Fouard, will still serve in most instances since it is widely known. For delineation of the geographic, climatic, domestic, economic, and political background *The Life of Jesus Christ* by Willam is excellent. For interpretation of the persons concerned in the Gospel story *The Public Life of Our Lord Jesus Christ* by Goodier is enlightening. In supplying these details, however, the teacher should not go too far afield from the main purpose of the book as expressed in the threefold method mentioned above. The tendency to run lightly over the Gospel sentences and to concentrate on the comments must be avoided. Students and readers should linger long on the very words of our Lord. When dealing with the comments it will be noticed that there are sometimes abrupt transitions in the paragraphs. This was made necessary by the desire to avoid expansiveness. Hence, careful attention to single sentences will often be helpful.

In the arrangement of the Gospel material I have followed mainly Lagrange's *Synopse des Quatre Évangiles*. Some Gospel passages have been omitted; and occasionally the requirements of pedagogical presentation forced a slight shifting of events. A chronological sequence has been followed, but an effort has also been made to maintain to some extent unity in each chapter. If time presses, the teacher should not hesitate to pass over now and then a section of a chapter or even a chapter. There is frequent repetition of the same thought; and the particular needs of different localities may require lengthened treatment of some chapters.

It would be advantageous for the teachers to make up their own list of questions that would be pertinent to the material of a chapter and applicable to the group in hand. The questions supplied in the book are not intended to be exhaustive. Some of them are for the purpose of testing information; many of them are judgment questions and permit of more than one conclusion. The important thing is to develop the right attitude toward God. There is some danger in refining every answer down to a mathematical point. The Pharisees did this and lost the spirit of religion. Religion is love that does not seek to measure. There are, of course, problems that require specific answers. At the same time it is necessary to develop the habit of acting on principle or of making a decision from God's viewpoint. This habit is especially difficult in our day when so much of education is statistical and quantitative. In religion God aids the individual in making a decision when He sees that the person has the right disposition.

When used in high school this book will fit best into the junior year as preparatory to the author's earlier text, *Your Religion,* which was planned for the senior year. In the college field the freshman year seems most suitable for a life of Christ. In study clubs some large maps and a few copies of the Bible should be available so that the references in the book may be studied in their background.

The author is deeply indebted to the standard lives of Christ and also to the works of Fr. Maturin on the Beatitudes and the Parables. He is likewise grateful to Rev. John L. Bazinet, S.S., for a thorough reading of the manuscript; to Dr. John M. Cooper, Dr. F. A. Mullin, and Dr. Maurice S. Sheehy of the Catholic University for suggestions; to Rev. U. M. Churchill of Columbia Academy, Dubuque, Iowa, Sr. M. Boniface of St. Ursula Academy, New York City, Sr. Giovanni of Georgian Court College, to the Sisters of Trinity College, and to other teachers who tested the manuscript, and also to numerous students who expressed their criticisms after using the work in mimeographed form. The illustrations are the work of Mr. C. J. Poiesz of Washington, D. C. Mr. J. Winnemore of Washington, D. C., and Sr. Stanisia of Chicago also contributed to the theme of the illustrations.

CONTENTS

CHRIST THE LEADER

Chapter 1

WHAT IS THE WORD?

JOHN 1: 1. In the beginning was the Word, and the Word was with God, and the Word was God. 2. The same was in the beginning with God. 3. All things were made by him: and without him was made nothing that was made. 4. In him was life, and the life was the light of men.

ABOUT the year 90 A.D. John the apostle, who had been with Christ as a beloved follower, and who was now an old man, was inspired by God to write about Jesus. Where would he begin? Since he wished to stress in his Gospel the divine nature of Jesus, he went back beyond all human ancestors. Majestically he carries us back into eternity, before the beginning of time. *In the beginning was the Word.*

The English term, *Word,* stands for the Eternal Son of God. This is a difficult thought for the beginning of a book, but we need to realize that the coming of Christ is one chapter in the long story of God's plan for man. There are previous chapters in the history of the Word. Christ has taught us that there are three equal persons in one God. We believe this because Christ told it to us. John sought for a term which would express in some way the nature of the second Person of the Trinity. In English, a word expresses our thought; hence, by calling the Son of God, "the Word," John meant that Jesus in His divine nature proceeds from the Father, or is the expression, the wisdom of the Father (Cf. Col. 1: 19; 2: 3). This Son of God, this Word, Christ in His divine nature, *was* forever. God is eternal; the Son is eternal. The Son is God. In creation, the Father works *through* the Son. Being one in nature, They are inseparable in the creative act.

Suddenly, John changes his theme to "life" and "light." These two words are repeated often in his Gospel. "Life" here means supernatural life — the divine life which we begin to share in Baptism, the life which Christ obtained for us. We do not know all about grace; we do know it is a share in God's very life. And when we have it there is a *light* in our lives. This light enables us to believe in Christ. Unbelievers remain in darkness because they do not humbly ask for the light.

John's first four verses have to do with the Son of God before His Incarnation. John wished to impress us with the sublime truth that Jesus Christ, the Man of Galilee, has a divine nature which is eternal. Divinity means the possession of the attributes or qualities of God. Christ therefore has two natures, the divine and human, united in Him. He is the God-Man. In this book we are to study Him as He appeared among men. At the outset we make our act of faith that the Word is divine, that He is God.

> JOHN 1: 5. And the light shineth in darkness, and the darkness did not comprehend it. . . . 10. He was in the world and the world was made by him, and the world knew him not. 11. He came unto his own, and his own received him not. 12. But as many as received him, he gave them power to be made the sons of God, to them that believe in his name. 13. Who are born, not of blood, nor of the will of the flesh, nor of the will of man, but of God. 14. And the Word was made flesh, and dwelt among us (and we saw his glory, the glory as it were of the only begotten of the Father), full of grace and truth.

God became Man. Christ was actually, thoroughly a Man. He took on Himself the burdens, the duties of manhood. Hunger, fatigue, failure, insults, temptations from without, ingratitude or gratitude, disloyalty or loyalty touched Him just as they affect any man. While He was a divine Person, nevertheless, His truly human will made its own decisions although they were always in conformity with the divine will. What a thought! What a privilege for the human race to have Him! Many reject Him, but we receive Him. He gives us a new life; we become children of God at Baptism. And John was a companion and an eyewitness of this Person, who is full of grace and truth, life and light, which

He imparts to us. Our greatest possessions are grace and the truths about the purpose of human life.

A GENTILE WHO WROTE ACCURATELY

LUKE 1: 1. Forasmuch as many have taken in hand to set forth in order a narration of the things that have been accomplished among us; 2. According as they have delivered them unto us, who from the beginning were eyewitnesses and ministers of the word.

We have four separate accounts of Christ's life, four Gospels. They are not biographies, for they are not complete records; they do not give all the facts about Christ. However, they are sufficient to give us a picture of His character, of the qualities of the only Person on earth who ever claimed to be God and who proved it.

Of the four Evangelists (writers of the Gospels), two, Matthew and John, were personal companions of Christ. St. Mark was St. Peter's secretary and wrote what Peter had seen and heard. St. Luke was not a Jew, but a Gentile, probably a Syrian born at Antioch. The verses above are from his Gospel.

Besides these four Gospels we have, in the New Testament, the Acts of the Apostles by Luke, fourteen letters (epistles) by St. Paul, one epistle by St. James, two by St. Peter, three by St. John, one by the apostle Jude, and the final book by St. John called the Apocalypse — twenty-seven in all. Very likely all, except the works of St. John, were written before A.D. 70.

St. Luke speaks of "many" who wrote. Some of the early writings on Christ's life have been lost. It is possible that they were not inspired accounts. Inspiration means that God caused the writers to think about writing, that He guided them while they were writing and kept them from error. The writers may or may not have been conscious of this help. Hence, God is really the author of the Bible. Inspiration is not the same as revelation. In revelation God tells man something that man did not know. Inspiration refers to the act by which God influenced a man to write what he may have already known. Since the Church was in existence before the New Testament was written, she alone could decide on what was inspired by God; and she saved these twenty-seven books of the New Testament. Without the guidance of the Church these truths would have been garbled, twisted to suit individual tastes, or lost.

Many legendary accounts of Christ's life were also written in the first and second centuries. They are called Apocryphal Gospels. They contain exaggerated and fantastic tales about our Lord. The wisdom of the Church and the reliability of the four writers of Christ's one Gospel are seen when we place an account by one of the four Evangelists alongside an Apocryphal. In a Gospel there is simple, frank, unadorned statement of the truth, told without prejudice. The Evangelists were reporters, but they did not color their report. They aimed to set down the deeds and words of Jesus and to let these facts speak for themselves. To them, whatever Christ had said or done was good.

St. Luke speaks of "eyewitnesses" as his source. He himself had never seen Christ. He was a physician (Col. 4: 14), and a very learned and noble character. He wrote in Greek, which was the language of educated people in that section of the world. Probably St. Paul converted him. St. Paul may have gone to him for treatment in sickness. At any rate, a life-long attachment sprang up between the two and Luke became Paul's companion and biographer. Probably he knew Paul before the year 50 A.D., but about that time we find him traveling over Asia Minor and Europe with the dynamic apostle.

Naturally, Luke learned much from St. Paul. He could have consulted Peter and other apostles. It is possible, but we have no direct proof, that he includes Mary, the mother of Jesus, among the eyewitnesses whom he interviewed. The accounts of the birth and the infancy — so beautifully, so simply told — his reference to Mary's presence among the first Christians (Acts 1: 14), and his courtesy for women, so evident in the pages of his Gospel, show us that, even if Luke had at his disposal an earlier written account, yet he was careful to examine all the eyewitnesses whom he could meet.

> Luke 1: 3. It seemed good to me also, having diligently attained to all things from the beginning, to write to thee in order, most excellent Theophilus, 4. That thou mayest know the verity of those words in which thou hast been instructed.

The habits of a careful historian shine forth in the pages of St. Luke. Inspiration did not relieve a writer from the labor of obtaining facts, and it did not prevent him from expressing facts in his own style. After nineteen centuries Luke looms as one of the world's great historians. His accuracy stands vindicated after skeptics have launched bitter attacks against him.

Most teaching was oral in those days. The apostles instructed orally first; the writing of the instructions came later. We do not know who Theophilus was. We can see, however, that Luke wanted his friend to know that his oral instruction had been based on facts. Through this account written for Theophilus, Luke hoped to reach pagan converts. His aim throughout the Gospel was to show the Gentiles that Christ had come for all people, not merely for the Jews.

Just as the Gospel of St. Luke strengthened and enlivened the faith of Theophilus, so our study of the life of Christ will confirm and deepen the truths which the Church has taught us. It takes time and study to develop a personal liking for the Gospels. They seem so strange at the start. The New Testament is, indeed, different from other books, because it is God's work. It is old, yes, almost 1,900 years old; still it is fresh and thrilling. Perseverance in reading it brings joy, delight, and courage. There is just one thing to keep always in mind. Here Jesus is speaking to us. We must approach this interview in the same way that we would sit on the hillside and listen to His Sermon on the Mount, or follow Him in His disputes with the Pharisees. Some passages are full of mystery; not everything will be understood. But it is a unique opportunity — to listen to what Jesus has to say to us. Close listening arouses admiration. Admiration will then grow into love and imitation. Imitation of Christ is the path to true happiness and to true greatness.

1. What is the exact meaning of the phrase *divinity of Christ?*
2. Locate these verses in the Mass: *Et Homo factus est,* and *Et Verbum caro factum est,* and show how you express belief in the Incarnation each time you genuflect at these verses.
3. What is the difference between inspiration and revelation?
4. What is there in Christ that had no beginning?
5. Look up 2 Peter 1: 16 and 1 John 1: 1–3 and note the attitude of the apostles toward teaching only the truth.
6. Aside from the fact of inspiration, what leads us to believe that we can trust St. Luke?

7. Read the story of St. Paul's conversion, Acts 9: 1–30; 22: 5–21; 26: 1–20. What bond do you think united Paul and Luke?
8. What are the Apocryphal Gospels and how do they differ from the four Gospels?
9. Read: *Paul, Hero and Saint,* by Rev. Leo Fink (Paulist Press), and *Luke, Greek Physician and Historian,* by John A. Scott (Northwestern University Library, Evanston, Ill.).
10. Find the meaning of the word *Gospel* in the dictionary.
11. What aim did St. John have in writing his Gospel? St. Luke?
12. For proofs of the reliability of the Gospels consult: *The Church and the Gospels,* by Joseph Huby, tr. by Fenton Moran (Sheed and Ward, New York); or *The Gospels — Fact, Myth, or Legend?* by J. P. Arendzen (B. Herder Book Co., St. Louis).
13. The term "hypostatic union" refers to the union of the two natures in one person. While Christ had human nature, why is it incorrect to call Him a human person?

Chapter 2

SLOWLY WAS BUILT THE STAGE

LUKE 1: 5. There was in the days of Herod, the King of Judea, a certain priest named Zachary, of the course of Abia: and his wife was of the daughters of Aaron, and her name Elizabeth. 6. And they were both just before God, walking in all the commandments and justifications of the Lord without blame. 7. And they had no son, for that Elizabeth was barren, and they both were well advanced in years.

THE Jewish religion had a priesthood. Priests offered sacrifice and performed other ceremonies. In Zachary and Elizabeth we see the better type of priesthood family — devout, simple, wholesome. Doubtless they had often thought that God was not good to them. Like every family of their race, they longed for children. Not to have children was something of a disgrace. For years they had gone childless, yet they maintained faith in God, without knowing what He had in store for them. Here is an example of trust over a long period of time.

LUKE 1: 8. And it came to pass, when he executed the priestly function in the order of his course before God, 9. According to the custom of the priestly office, it was his lot to offer incense, going into the temple of the Lord. 10. And all the multitude of the people was praying without, at the hour of incense.

To realize what Zachary was doing we must recall some Jewish history and must picture the Temple and its significance. The history of the Jews as the chosen people of God begins about 2000 B.C., under Abraham, whom God drew out of the land that is now Iraq (then called Chaldea) to be the father of the Jewish people.

For two or three centuries Abraham's descendants moved up and down what is now Palestine. God was their protector. They lived under a form of government called Theocracy, i.e., direct rule by God. Gradually the Jews became different from other people, especially by their belief in one God — monotheism.

In a period of drought, a handful of Abraham's descendants moved to Egypt. At the end of four centuries their numbers were vastly increased, but they had been reduced to slavery by Egyptian rulers. God sent Moses (roughly, fourteenth century B.C.) to be the far-famed leader of the Israelite liberation. In memory of this liberation arose their central feast of the paschal lamb (Exod. 12). Throughout the forty years of their wanderings in the Arabian desert (north of the Red Sea) many wondrous happenings impressed upon the Jews the fact that God was their protector. Manna, for instance, fell in the desert for them to eat (Exod. 16). On Mt. Sinai, near the southern end of Arabia, the Ten Commandments came to them through Moses, amid scenes of terrible grandeur (Exod. 19, 20). The Ark (small chest) of the Covenant was built according to revealed regulations (Exod. 26), in which they were to keep the Tables of the Law, the rod of Aaron, and perhaps a vessel of manna.

The appearance of Melchisedech as king and priest who offered bread and wine at the time of Abraham (Gen. 14:18) and the institution of the levitical priesthood (Exod. 28:1, 41, 43; 29:9, 39–46) at the time of Moses (and which Zachary was now continuing) was a foretaste of the priesthood of Christ.

It was only in 1017 B.C., or thereabouts, that the Jews began to center their life in what is now Jerusalem. David bought a hill, Moria, on which is a rock, almost flat, about 58 by 45 feet and 4 or 5 feet above the ground. Here he offered sacrifice (2 Kings 24: 25). Later, Solomon constructed around this rock the magnificent buildings known as the Temple, which became the center of Jewish religious life. War, some centuries later, devastated it. Another was built in the sixth century B.C., but it likewise was destroyed.

The Jewish political kingdom fell to pieces shortly after the time of Solomon. Various nations conquered the Jews. At the time of Christ, we find them ruled by the Romans, who, however, permitted Herod to be a puppet king.

What we call the Holy Land, or Palestine, is a narrow strip, in shape somewhat like the State of New Hampshire and about the same size. There were three geographical divisions in Palestine — Galilee, Samaria, and Judea. In our Lord's day the country extended east of the Jordan, which section was called Perea. Palestine of today is hilly, rocky, as it was then, and dry. Mountain ranges run north and south. Eastward from the section around Jerusalem the hills drop suddenly into a bleak desert of the Jordan valley, where the heat is intense. The Lake of Galilee is 695 feet, and the Dead Sea 1,286 feet below sea level.

As a bird would fly, it is only 32 miles from the Mediterranean up to where Jerusalem sits on its hills, 2,500 feet above sea level. The Dead Sea is about 15 miles east of the city, but roads are so winding that the distance is longer. Picture yourself on the most important hill in the city, Moria. Here was, and is today, that huge rock. As the hill slopes down to the east it meets the brook, Cedron. Crossing this, and going east, you climb Mt. Olivet, 2,665 feet above sea level. As you look back westward the entire city is below you, and you can gaze into the Temple grounds on Moria.

For a thousand years, Jews had regarded Moria as sacred. It was the hill of sacrifice and of the Temple. They even had a tradition, 2,000 years old, that Abraham had offered to sacrifice his son on this hill (Gen. 22). Our interest for the present, however, is with the third Temple built on this spot, the Temple in which Zachary was officiating. Herod had started to construct this edifice for the Jews in 18 B.C. It was not yet finished when our Lord was there, 46 years later.

A temple of those days was different from what we know as a church. It was a group of buildings, courts, and covered porches. Imagine a thick, high wall surrounding the Temple grounds, and inclosing a space equal to about three square blocks. Over 200,000 people could crowd into that area. The inside of the wall was a covered porch. On the eastern side was Solomon's porch (John 10: 23). It had four rows of white stone pillars, over forty feet high, roofed with cedar wood. A Roman fortress, Antonia, where Pilate judged Christ, was at the corner of the north and west walls.

The open spaces inside the wall were known as the Court of the Gentiles, for non-Jews could enter this court. By mounting and crossing two terraces (Court of Women and Court of Israelites) you would reach the court of the priests. Here was the famous rock, where burned sacrifices were offered. Directly west of this rock was a high porch or vestibule which led into the sanctuary or Temple proper, a rectangular hall. This sanctuary had two divisions. The first was the Holy Place. Here was a golden altar for offering incense. Here was Zachary, as we opened this chapter. A large veil, or tapestry, separated this Holy Place from the second section, the Holy of Holies — the most sacred part of the hall or sanctuary. No one, except the high priest once a year, entered the Holy of Holies. It was God's place. In Solomon's time it had contained the Ark, symbol of God's presence. The Ark had been lost or destroyed in wars, and so the Holy of Holies was now empty.

On the outside, this sanctuary was covered with gold and white stone. No wonder people gloried in its splendor. If you came up over the hills to the city, on any side, your eye caught this sanctuary, resplendent especially with the rising sun. The whole Temple grounds, but primarily this hall, was the house of God. The Temple was the one place in Palestine for sacrifice. Here came annually thousands of pilgrims at the feast of the paschal lamb. The Temple spoke to them of the past, as they re-enacted their ceremonies; it strengthened their hopes for the coming of the Messias. Christ Himself had deep respect for this Temple, yet He could not enter its sanctuary. Usually He taught down in the open Court of the Gentiles.

Let us now return to Zachary the priest. He was offering incense in the Holy Place of the sanctuary, invisible to the people outside and below. The smoke of the incense represented the prayers of the people. It was offered twice daily. Trumpets would herald his reappearance, and a hymn would be sung by all. On this day the people became uneasy. Zachary was delayed.

> Luke 1: 11. And there appeared to him an angel of the Lord, standing on the right side of the altar of incense. 12. And Zachary seeing him, was troubled, and fear fell upon him. 13. But the angel said to him: Fear not, Zachary, for thy prayer is heard; and thy wife Elizabeth shall bear thee a son, and thou shalt call his name John: 14. And thou shalt have joy and gladness, and many shall rejoice in his nativity. 15. For he shall be great before the Lord: and shall drink no wine nor strong drink; and he shall be filled with the Holy Ghost even from his mother's

womb. 16. And he shall convert many of the children of Israel to the Lord their God. 17. And he shall go before him in the spirit and power of Elias; that he may turn the hearts of the fathers unto the children, and the incredulous to the wisdom of the just, to prepare unto the Lord a perfect people.

It was nothing strange in Jewish history to have angels appear to men as messengers of God's will (Gen. 28; Num. 22: 31; Josue 5: 13–15; Tobias 12: 15–21). God had promised an angel to Moses and his people: "Take notice of him and hear his voice" (Exod. 23: 21). Presumably the angel appeared in human form. He first calmed Zachary and assured him that his visit was one of joy rather than of fear. Zachary had prayed for years, either for the coming of the Messias or for a child. He now was promised a child as a result of his prayer. This instance shows that years may sometimes elapse before our own prayers are answered.

The rejoicing would not be only individual but national. The child would become great from the viewpoint of his life of self-denial and from the abundance of grace that God would shower upon him. John the Baptist is called the precursor — he prepared the way for Christ. He put some of the spirit of Abraham, Moses, and David into those whom he converted.

Luke 1: 18. And Zachary said to the angel: Whereby shall I know this? For I am an old man, and my wife is advanced in years. 19. And the angel answering said to him: I am Gabriel, who stand before God; and am sent to speak to thee, and to bring thee these good tidings. 20. And behold, thou shalt be dumb, and shalt not be able to speak until the day wherein these things shall come to pass; because thou hast not believed my words, which shall be fulfilled in their time. 21. And the people were waiting for Zachary; and they wondered that he tarried so long in the temple. 22. And when he came out, he could not speak to them, and they understood that he had seen a vision in the temple. And he made signs to them, and remained dumb. 23. And it came to pass, after the days of his office were accomplished, he departed to his own house. 24. And after those days, Elizabeth his wife conceived, and hid herself five months, saying: 25. Thus hath the Lord dealt with me in the days wherein he hath had regard to take away my reproach among men.

Zachary's faith now became hesitant. He forgot God's power and considered only the natural difficulties in the way. His wife was too old to have children, but God could give this holy woman the power to conceive a child. Zachary should have trusted, because he could tell that the angel was from God. Nothing evil was being proposed. He had behind him centuries of tradition which told of angels appearing to the Jews.

God interferes in our lives for our own good; the devil for our harm. God can keep his promises; the devil cannot. So Zachary was to experience the power that controls angels and men. He was to be dumb, mute until the birth of the child. His hesitant faith brought him this affliction. When we refuse to trust God it is our own loss, not His (Job 13: 15). In business affairs caution is necessary; in religious matters trust in God. The Catholic Church is God's messenger to us, as Gabriel was to Zachary. Hence our faith in her teachings should never be hesitant.

From Abraham to Zachary twenty centuries rolled their course. Slowly was the stage built on which the Word was to make His appearance as the main actor in the drama of man's journey to eternity.

1. What is the main purpose of the priesthood today?
2. What are we to do when we think that God is not answering our prayers?
3. When did Elias live? What did he do?
4. Give the origin of the feast of the paschal lamb among the Jews.
5. What was the Ark of the Covenant?
6. Considered in themselves, why is the altar in a church more important than the tabernacle?
7. What does incense symbolize in the Catholic churches?
8. Why did our Lord call the Temple, "My Father's house"?
9. Show that God may have a purpose in permitting trial and sorrow to come into the lives of good people.
10. What is the purpose of gifts, acts of obedience, apologies in the home, or the writing of letters home? How can you show God, who is your Father, what your attitude toward Him is?

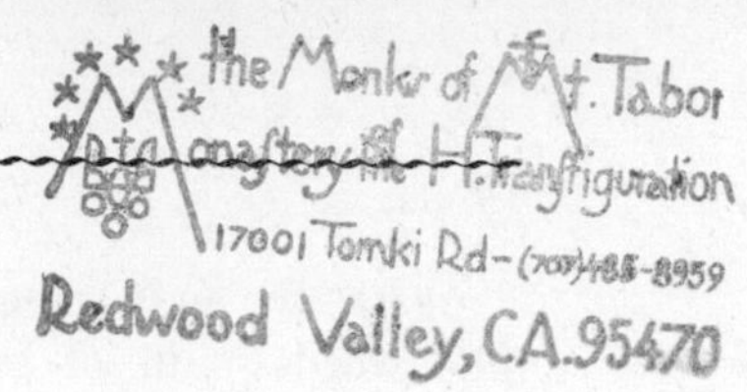

Chapter 3

WHOM GOD CHOSE TO BE THE MOTHER OF CHRIST

LUKE 1: 26. And in the sixth month, the angel Gabriel was sent from God into a city of Galilee, called Nazareth, 27. To a virgin espoused to a man whose name was Joseph, of the house of David; and the virgin's name was Mary. 28. And the angel being come in, said unto her: Hail, full of grace, the Lord is with thee: blessed art thou among women.

SIX months after his appearance to Zachary in the solitude of the sanctuary of the Temple, the same Gabriel came to a quiet country village, sixty-five miles north of Jerusalem.

Marriage customs in the East differ from ours. Usually parents arrange the marriage, but in this case it is more likely that Joseph had asked for Mary. He would have to make his wishes known to her parents. Evidently they accepted him. The espousal ceremony, which was a legal contract, was arranged. Friends and relatives of both families came together at Mary's home to act as witnesses. They were now legally married, but according to the custom of that country they would not live together for at least a year. Meanwhile, they rarely saw each other. Betrothed maidens lived in a secluded manner. Both Mary and Joseph were young when they married, for young people mature more rapidly and marry earlier in the East than in our civilization.

The Gospels tell us nothing of the early life of Mary. But if we piece together the remarks of St. Luke and St. John, we shall have plentiful proof for her high character. Our best evidence on Mary is the simple fact that God chose her to be the mother of Christ. Christ was sanctity itself. He came to make us holy. We would expect, then, that Mary would be without flaw.

Again, the first tribute to Mary's character came from heaven. The words "full of grace" mean that she had received grace abundantly. They indicate her spiritual condition at that moment. In the lives of saints such as the Little Flower and Aloysius Gonzaga, or in Margaret Sinclair and the little Guy de Fontgalland, we seem to see some of the outward effects of that invisible and mysterious thing called grace. Mary had received more than any of these young people; and she co-operated with God. She had duties to perform, just as we have. She was not only modest, pure, and trustful of God, but she was intelligent, clear-headed, and strong enough to bear the lonesome sorrows of the mother of the Crucified.

The Church uses the words "full of grace" to illustrate the doctrine of the Immaculate Conception. Human nature as it exists in people today is not the same as when God first designed it. The soul acts in two ways — it knows and it wills. It is because we have a soul that we are able to know and to will. These two faculties of the soul belong to our very nature. But if we go back to the time when God first created a soul for man, we learn that God raised man to a higher state, gave him greater gifts than were due him. As free gifts, Adam and Eve had: (*a*) sanctifying grace. This was not natural in the sense that it was due to them; it was supernatural; it raised them above the natural plane of living; it made them capable of entering into and enjoying God's very presence. (*b*) They had enlightenment of mind. He gave them the power of speech and sufficient knowledge for their state of living. (*c*) They had strength of will and control over their lower appetites. They did not experience the wild disorders that we feel in our being. (*d*) They had immunity from suffering and death. We do not know much about this condition; in some manner or other they were shielded from sickness and decay.

Of these four conditions, the last three are called preternatural gifts. They affected the body as well as the soul. They too were gifts. The important gift was grace. Man had no natural right whatever to this gift; hence we call it supernatural. And we say that man was created in a supernatural state. We do not know how long Adam and Eve lived in that happy condition, which is called the state of original justice (holiness).

By his refusal to follow God's command, Adam lost these gifts. And, since he was the head of the human race, he lost them for his descendants also. He and his descendants retained their destiny, God's presence, but had lost grace, the essential preparative for heaven. Human nature became such as we see it today. Its greatest loss was sanctifying grace. Each child is conceived without that grace which according to the original plan of God would have passed to the descendants of Adam. We call this stain, this absence of grace, original sin. It is not an actual sin on the part of the child; it is something that he inherits from the very fact of his being one of the descendants of our first parents. He inherits, not a bad human nature, but a weak one, one which lacks something.

God saw fit to make one exemption from this universal privation. From the moment that Mary's soul was created and infused into her body, she possessed grace. We call this privilege the Immaculate Conception. It is not something that took place at her birth. Even before her birth she was not in original sin. Her flesh, from which the Son of God was to take His human nature, was flesh that had never been subject to sin. Is it not fitting that God, who is Holiness, should have arranged for Christ to assume human flesh that was untainted? From the first moment of her conception, God was at work on Mary's soul, adorning it, fitting it with those qualities which make one spiritually beautiful in the eyes of God. No sinful thought ever marred Mary's character. She co-operated in the task of preparing herself to be the tabernacle of the Most High. Later we shall study what Mary's Son did to restore our destiny to us. For the present we examine how Mary handled herself in these crises of her life, for God wants modern youth to be spiritually strong and beautiful.

LUKE 1: 29. Who having heard, was troubled at his saying, and thought with herself what manner of salutation this should be.
30. And the angel said to her: Fear not, Mary, for thou hast found grace with God. 31. Behold thou shalt conceive in thy womb, and shalt bring forth a son; and thou shalt call his name Jesus. 32. He shall be great, and shall be called the Son of the Most High; and the Lord God shall give unto him the throne of David his father; and he shall reign in the house of Jacob forever.
33. And of his kingdom there shall be no end. 34. And Mary

said to the angel: How shall this be done, because I know not man? 35. And the angel answering, said to her: The Holy Ghost shall come upon thee, and the power of the Most High shall overshadow thee. And therefore also the Holy which shall be born of thee shall be called the Son of God.

A girl of high character is modest; she is prudent in the company of men. Like other girls of the East, Mary was not in the habit of being in the company of men. Yet, not the appearance of the angel, but the significance of his statement set her thinking. She thought rapidly.

Gabriel understood her perplexity. He mentioned her name, to reassure her. God was pleased with her. Her life, quiet and unobserved by the world, had been noticed by God. We shall see how she was accustomed to think things over; how she lived in the presence of God, walked and communed with Him. Thus she had prepared herself for the great task that God was to assign to her. Hundreds of thousands of Jewish women had longed and hoped that they might be the mother of the expected Messias. It is instructive to see how God passed over the great ones of the realm and went out to the country, to the quiet of rural life and chose one who had been satisfied to serve Him in the lonesome routine of a small town.

Now came the Annunciation, the truth on which we reflect as we say the first Joyful Mystery of the Rosary. Over 700 years previous to this event, Isaias had made this prophecy; "Behold a virgin shall conceive, and bear a son, and his name shall be called Emmanuel" (Isa. 7: 14). For centuries the Jews had been hoping, longing for the coming of the Messias; and now was heard the announcement to a girl that she was to be the mother of the Saviour. (The word *Jesus* means Saviour.) God was in reality to come unto His own.

* *

Describe the effects of original sin (Cf. Rom. 5: 12). Show that human nature today is not the same as when it was first created. Who was the first to honor Mary? What does this fact teach us in regard to the legitimacy of our devotions to her? What is lacking in a girl who says she could not stand the monotony of life on a farm or in a small town? Should city girls seek to train themselves to find their pleasures in their own homes? How would you describe Mary's character to a city girl who wants to be "out" every night?

* *

Note the maturing of God's plans, the centuries coming to a focus. Verses 32, 33 give the titles that had been predicted for Christ. There is a continuity in God's arrangements, but we must mount above the centuries to catch their meaning. God had told Abraham (2000 B.C.) that in his descendants all the nations of the earth would be blessed. And from that time forward, people and events in the Old Testament history pointed toward one divine event — the Incarnation. Joseph and Mary were descendants of David, whose earthly throne was a symbol of Christ's eternal Kingship over us.

Zachary had doubted that Elizabeth in her old age could give birth to a child. Mary's difficulty was moral. She had been promised in marriage; yet in her own heart she had made a vow of virginity. (This is the meaning of the words: "I know not man.") Her first thought when she heard the angel's announcement was that the Child would be conceived in a human way, through a human father. Hence she asked the angel how she could become a mother, since she had promised to remain a virgin. We do not know whether or not Mary already had the vow when she was promised in marriage or whether she had spoken to Joseph about it. It might be that her parents had arranged for her marriage without consulting her wishes. Or, it may be that since Mary had no brother, her parents arranged for the marriage in order to keep the property in the family, according to the rule shown in Numbers 36: 8. Custom among the Jews did not regard unmarried women with approval; and while yielding to the custom, which had tremendous force in that country, Mary may have told Joseph of her vow and he may have promised to respect it. In that country marriage would be a protection to her vow. In any case, Mary must have been guided by God in her decision. And now she did not hesitate to ask an intelligent question.

The angel explained that Christ was to be conceived in a virginal, supernatural, and miraculous manner. Very delicately Gabriel said that the Holy Ghost would cause the conception of the Child. Just as in the beginning, this Spirit of God moved over the waters and caused the first creation (Gen. 1: 2), so now the

Holy Ghost would work this miracle. Mary's Child was to be the Son of God made flesh. This is what we call the doctrine of the Virgin Birth of Christ, namely that He had no human father. Thus the humanity of Christ was to be without stain, since Mary was without stain of original sin. Mary was to remain a virgin and become a mother.

This is not a fairy tale, not a story invented in the first ages of Christianity. It is a real, historical fact. To those who scoff at this idea, to those who argue that many heroes of antiquity claimed a virgin birth and that the Jews or Christians borrowed the idea, we offer these considerations:

a) True, we smile at the myths which many peoples of antiquity believed. They often assigned the gods as fathers of their heroes. But in the beginning of Christianity, we are dealing with historical characters; eyewitnesses give their testimony. The period of history in which Christ lived is well known to us. Caesar had already written his commentaries; Cicero, his orations. A Roman procurator was face to face with Christ. Mary, Joseph, Peter, John, Matthew, Paul, Luke were real people, not mythological heroes. The science of archeology and objective historians have turned the laugh onto the scholars of the nineteenth century who wrote about Christ as a myth.

b) There was a vast difference between the highest moral development of the Jews and that reached by other nations. Egyptians, Greeks, Romans might wink at moral defects in their gods and goddesses, and even build up lewd stories about them. Not so the Jews. To them God was One, Just, Holy. The Jews themselves might fall low; but never could their God be immoral. He demanded that they be moral. And this commandment had an effect on their ideals and their lives. They had a high regard for married life; all young people looked forward to the married state. An unmarried mother could be stoned to death (Deut. 22: 21). Despite the prophecy of Isaias, the Jews expected that the Messias was to have a human father; and they regarded St. Joseph as the father of Christ. Hence, the Jews did not invent or borrow a tale about a virgin birth, nor would the Christians. And this high moral ideal of the nature of God is also a refutation of the theory that the Jews borrowed from Egyptians and Babylonians their idea of God, for to the minds of the Egyptians the gods were themselves immoral and sensual. Our idea of God was revealed to us, not evolved by human experience.

c) Joseph and Mary were people of very high and very strong character. Joseph knew that he was not the father of Christ. When the angel explained the origin of the Child, he assumed the task of protecting Mary and the Child. Mary and Joseph had moral ideals. And yet they both accepted the truth of the Virgin Birth. They were not people who would start a fraud.

d) Study well the character of the two men who give us the story of the Virgin Birth. (We shall deal with Matthew later.) Luke was accustomed to record only facts. He was educated, not illiterate. Modern critics admit his accuracy. Moreover, he was a physician. Physicians are not likely to believe a story about a child who had no human father; but St. Luke believed this one case in history, after he had investigated the facts and studied the characters of the eyewitnesses of Christ's life.

e) This definite statement of the angel in verse 35 must be studied in the light of Christ's later life. His sinlessness, His words, His miracles, His own claim to the title: *Son of God,* His resurrection — all prove Him to be God, and hence make it easy for us to believe in the Virgin Birth. Since the power of the supernatural is before us in the world today, the same power could work a miracle in the beginning of Christianity. Our religion is too much of a fact today to have been founded on a myth. The fundamental mistake of those who assert that Christ was only a human person with an exceptional personality, is that they do not want to admit that God could cause a miraculous conception for Christ, could send the second Person of the Trinity in the nature of man.

> LUKE 1: 36. And behold thy cousin Elizabeth, she also hath conceived a son in her old age; and this is the sixth month with her that is called barren: 37. Because no word shall be impossible with God. 38. And Mary said: Behold the handmaid of the Lord; be it done to me according to thy word. And the angel departed from her.

Mary had not asked for any sign, but Gabriel volunteered to tell her of the favor that had been granted Elizabeth, thus hinting that Mary had not doubted as did Zachary.

Verse 38 tells of the Incarnation. At that moment, when Mary gave her consent, "the Word was made Flesh." The angel courteously waited for this consent, for Mary's part was to be voluntary. God does not force us. He gives us the truth, and then He wants our mental assent. Mary could not see the future, but she was one of those whose virtue consists "in willing heroically whatever God wills." She was a meditative, calm girl, and she was not afraid of undertaking burdens for God. Her previous fidelity to graces had given her the strength, the poise, the insight for doing the right thing in an unexpected crisis. All this took place quickly and with tremendous consequences. (We also prepare ourselves for hard choices by doing the right thing daily in ordinary duties.) Wholeheartedly, she put herself in God's hands. She did not ask what she would get out of it all. And picture the problems that shot through her quick mind—how would she explain to her parents, to Joseph? Little could she know of the crucifixion. She would be His handmaid and do His will. And so she has taught us to accept with trust in God the burdens of Catholic life, to pay more attention to what God wants than to our own selfish impulses.

1. Compare the visit of Gabriel to the prophet Daniel in Dan. 9: 20–27.
2. A girl once wanted to marry a divorced man. Her mother objected. The girl replied: "I have a right to live my own life." What was missing in her attitude?
3. One boy is always regretting that he has no apparent talents, no wealth, no popularity so that he might become famous. Another boy says that he will take what God has given him, develop it for God's honor, and find his happiness in doing his work for God. Which one has the better outlook and why?
4. Show that Mary preferred to have God direct her life, rather than push herself forward into a career.
5. What is the difference between the Immaculate Conception and the Virgin Birth?
6. Show that the Virgin Birth is a fact and not a myth.
7. When did the Incarnation take place? Just what does it mean?
8. What leads you to believe that Mary was a girl of strong character?
9. Over a period of years what have the daily, private decisions to do with one's character?

Chapter 4

GLAD HEARTS SING

LUKE 1: 39. And Mary rising up in those days, went into the hill country with haste into a city of Juda. 40. And she entered into the house of Zachary, and saluted Elizabeth. 41. And it came to pass, that when Elizabeth heard the salutation of Mary, the infant leaped in her womb. And Elizabeth was filled with the Holy Ghost: 42. And she cried out with a loud voice, and said: Blessed art thou among women, and blessed is the fruit of thy womb. 43. And whence is this to me, that the mother of my Lord should come to me? 44. For behold as soon as the voice of thy salutation sounded in my ears, the infant in my womb leaped for joy. 45. And blessed art thou that hast believed, because those things shall be accomplished that were spoken to thee by the Lord.

MARY kept her secret. She said nothing to Joseph. Apparently she thought God would take care of that in time, although she realized that she would be under suspicion. She followed the hint given by the angel and sought out her cousin Elizabeth, down near Jerusalem. Perhaps she was on the road four days. It required fortitude to make this journey. Elizabeth would, however, understand the things that God had done. Mary wished also to congratulate Elizabeth. She did not sit back and wait for Elizabeth to come to her as a conceited girl might have done. Hence, true love of neighbor and humility are shown in the second Joyful Mystery of the Rosary, the Visitation.

We have often felt that it is a blessing to have certain people come into our home. Like a ray of sunshine or a vase of flowers, they brighten up the house. Moreover, here is an example of Mary's being the Mediatress of graces. Through Mary, God was to confer a favor on Elizabeth and her child. The Holy Ghost revealed to Elizabeth Mary's secret. The light that God gave Elizabeth enabled her to grasp the truth that Mary's Son was in reality God. It is a common belief that at this moment, before his birth, John the Baptist was cleansed from original sin. We shall see later how people were cured physically by the power which went out from Christ's presence. The same divine power which removes original sin when we are baptized here worked on John.

Evidently the Holy Ghost had indicated to Elizabeth the fine trust that Mary had placed in the angel. Elizabeth was touched by Mary's humility and faith. Regarding this situation only on its natural side, we see the womanly nature coming out in Elizabeth, as she recalled her husband's hesitant faith. Zachary had not been able to speak to her for six months.

> LUKE 1: 46. And Mary said: My soul doth magnify the Lord:
> 47. And my spirit hath rejoiced in God my Saviour.

Every hour, from thousands of lips there are words of praise ascending to God in the repetition of three songs of the New Testament — the *Magnificat*, the *Benedictus*, the *Nunc Dimittis*, composed by Mary, Zachary, and Simeon respectively. The Church uses these songs in what is known as the Divine Office, or the Breviary. The priest does not recite these songs for himself only; he does it in the name of all the people. The Church obliges him to praise God daily as a representative of the people who are too busy to recite these verses that are so packed with thought and meaning.

The *Magnificat* (46–55) is Mary's spontaneous, impromptu song. We believe that it was inspired; but in inspiration the individual is not simply a loud-speaker for something that comes from a higher source. Mary's personality, character, and all her past reading, memorizing, and reflecting went into the composition of the *Magnificat*. She had made herself familiar with all the history of God's dealings with the Jews; she must have known the thousand-year-old song of Anna (1 Kings 2: 1–10). She was still a young girl, yet she had an intellectual grasp of God's ancient promises to her people; and her poetic nature felt the charm of God's goodness. She made her language musical. Hers was a glad heart. The narration of great events was usually sung in those days. Memorization was thus made easier. Many people could recite by the hour from memory.

In verses 46, 47, Mary takes no credit to herself; she gives all the credit to God. She was not a self-centered girl. If we are gifted in music, or mathematics, or athletics, or personality, to whom do we give the credit? When we succeed do we give the credit to God or to ourselves? (Cf. James 1: 1–17; 1 Cor. 4: 7).

Do we find joy in the fact that Christ belongs to each one of us, that God sent Him for each of us? This fact should keep us joyful. We must, however, do some thinking and praying before we come to a realization of what we owe God. If we reflect and pray, we shall finally rejoice in the fact that God gave us our soul, with its powers of knowing and willing. Free will shows that He trusts us. And Christ is our friend, our guide on how to reach God. Christ gave us the Church in which are deposited His graces and His truths.

> LUKE 1: 48. Because he hath regarded the humility of his handmaid; for behold from henceforth all generations shall call me blessed. 49. Because he that is mighty, hath done great things to me; and holy is his name. 50. And his mercy is from generation unto generations, to them that fear him. 51. He hath shewed might in his arm: he hath scattered the proud in the conceit of their heart. 52. He hath put down the mighty from their seat, and hath exalted the humble. 53. He hath filled the hungry with good things; and the rich he hath sent empty away. 54. He hath received Israel his servant, being mindful of his mercy: 55. As he spoke to our fathers, to Abraham and to his seed for ever. 56. And Mary abode with her about three months; and she returned to her own house.

God did a great thing to us when He called us to the Catholic Faith. Mary acknowledged the low estate from which God raised her, and thus showed her humility. With the sureness of a prophet sent by God, Mary also foresaw the honor that would come to her as the mother of God. Honor to the mother is honor to the Son.

Proud people see nothing in religion. Conceit blinds them; their own confusion thwarts them. On the other hand, the Little Flower, who desired to be little and unnoticed, has been lifted up before all the world.

Cf. Gen. 3: 15. The past was known to Mary, for the Jews remained familiar with the promise made to Abraham. The *Magnificat* thus shows the inner life of the Blessed Virgin. If we do not hear much of her during the public life of our Lord, we can conclude from this hymn of hers that she had a deep appreciation of the designs of God, and followed with interest and wonderment the development of Christ along His path to the Cross.

Mary did not wait for the birth of John the Baptist. She did not wish to be in the public eye. But the three months that these two women spent together is a beautiful example of mutual trust. Elizabeth, by far the older, admired this privileged young woman and instead of being jealous, openly praised her. Mary appreciated the counsel of Elizabeth. The fact that each one put the interests of God ahead of her own personal comforts, created a bond between them. This same bond should unite young and old in our own homes. Young girls, young married women profit by the counsel of prudent, older women; older women should be charitable enough to see the good points about young girls, to rejoice with them in their achievements.

> LUKE 1: 57. Now Elizabeth's full time of being delivered was
> come, and she brought forth a son. 58. And her neighbors and
> kinsfolk heard that the Lord had shewed his great mercy toward
> her, and they congratulated with her. 59. And it came to pass
> that on the eighth day they came to circumcise the child, and they
> called him by his father's name Zachary. 60. And his mother
> answering, said: Not so; but he shall be called John. 61. And
> they said to her: There is none of thy kindred that is called by
> this name. 62. And they made signs to his father, how he would
> have him called. 63. And demanding a writing table, he wrote,
> saying: John is his name. And they all wondered. 64. And im-
> mediately his mouth was opened, and his tongue loosed, and he
> spoke, blessing God. 65. And fear came upon all their neigh-
> bors; and all these things were noised abroad over all the hill
> country of Judea: 66. And all they that had heard them laid
> them up in their heart, saying: What a one, think ye, shall this
> child be? For the hand of the Lord was with him.

The angel had prescribed this name for the child. The words: "laid them up in their heart," show us how these people, by constant repetition, kept vivid in their minds the events of the Gospel. Later, the apostles would be able to repeat word for word the sermons of Christ and to transmit them without mistake.

Luke 1: 67. And Zachary his father was filled with the Holy
Ghost; and he prophesied, saying: 68. Blessed be the Lord God
of Israel: because he hath visited and wrought the redemption of
his people: 69. And hath raised up a horn of salvation to us,
in the house of David his servant.

The *Benedictus* (68–79) was also inspired. Nevertheless, it shows the thoughts that had been running through the mind of Zachary. (Contrast his previous, hesitant faith and this tribute to God.) The *Benedictus* is a poetic song. It sums up the promises that God had made to His chosen people, praises Him for His fidelity, and predicts the future work of the child, John.

The Jews were a small group among the civilized nations at that time, but only a Jew would say, "Blessed be the Lord God," and thereby show his belief in the unity of God — one God. We are so accustomed to think of God as One that we fail to realize the change that has come over the world in two thousand years. The Mohammedans took over the idea from the Jews in the sixth century A.D., and today about half the world (Jews, Mohammedans, and all sects of Christianity) accept this belief. It was Christianity that spread the truth that all humans belong to God. He is not a national God; and of course He is more than the God of Israel. A horn denoted power, strength.

Luke 1: 70. As he spoke by the mouth of his holy prophets,
who are from the beginning: 71. Salvation from our enemies,
and from the hand of all that hate us: 72. To perform mercy
to our fathers, and to remember his holy testament, 73. The
oath, which he swore to Abraham our father, that he would grant
to us, 74. That being delivered from the hand of our enemies,
we may serve him without fear, 75. In holiness and justice before him, all our days.

Zachary knew the ancient prophecies. Most Jews thought of the coming of the Messias in a material sense, a mighty king who would fight their battles. A correct reading of the prophecies would show that under the material comparisons which were made, was also the truth that Christ's kingdom was to be spiritual (Cf. Gen. 17: 7–9; 22: 16–18). God had promised Abraham that from his descendants would come a blessing for all the world. Christ is that blessing.

Zachary shows that Christ's coming meant mercy. Those in Old Testament times were saved by faith in the Messias *to come.* Christ's re-opening of heaven to man was an act of mercy. Zachary was somewhat nationalistic; but we see the fuller meaning of the words he uttered in the fact that Christ freed us from the dominion of Satan. Religion is now not a thing of fear, like the fear that dominates superstitious people. The Faith is based on holiness, on justice, on reason. No persecution, no temptation can disturb the serenity, the peace that reigns in a person whose conscience is clear, who is in the state of grace, who is rooted in Christ. Love is the underlying motive of all the New Testament.

> LUKE 1: 76. And thou, child, shalt be called the prophet of the Highest: for thou shalt go before the face of the Lord to prepare his ways: 77. To give knowledge of salvation to his people, unto the remission of their sins: 78. Through the bowels of the mercy of our God, in which the Orient from on high hath visited us: 79. To enlighten them that sit in darkness, and in the shadow of death: to direct our feet unto the way of peace.

We should prepare the way, chiefly by good example, for the entrance of Christ into the lives of non-Catholics. Such is our obligation. Christ's coming was like the sun, rising over the darkness of the spiritual world. Many young Americans do not know Christ; many are unaware of the purpose of life. Shall it be said that we failed to instruct them? There are many who are "ever learning but never attaining to a knowledge of the truth." They are in the darkness, for they know neither Christ nor the Church. When we are tempted to sin we should remember that sin does not bring peace, or happiness, or contentment.

> LUKE 1: 80. And the child grew, and was strengthened in spirit; and was in the deserts until the day of his manifestation to Israel.

As a youth, John left his home and friends, and retired to the desert to think, to pray, to live in communion with God, to lead a life of self-denial and thus to acquire that control over himself which all Catholics should have. According to custom, no one could be a teacher or prophet till he had reached the age of thirty.

Long years did John spend alone; and yet, each one of us must learn to live alone with God at certain intervals, lest we acquire the worldling's distaste for God. Practice being alone and keeping silence during a retreat. There is a weakness in our character if we are afraid to be alone with God.

1. On what should we reflect during the second Joyful Mystery of the Rosary? Is it your practice to congratulate people when they deserve it?
2. Give one instance of Mary acting as a Mediatress of graces.
3. What are the meanings of the terms: *Magnificat* and *Benedictus?* Give the content of each.
4. Show what traits Mary and Zachary possessed, as evidenced by the songs they composed.
5. How do you account for special talents or beauty in a boy or girl? What is the true purpose of this distribution of talents?
6. What great dogmatic truth was given to the world by the Jews?
7. What might a young, married woman learn from Mary's attitude toward Elizabeth?
8. Show that deep reverence for motherhood is one of the best social assets of a community or of a nation.
9. How would you answer a student who said that he had nothing for which he felt bound to praise God?
10. Show that a true Catholic is always cheerful at heart, even if he has to pass through suffering or sorrow.
11. Do the words: praise, adoration, worship, mean the same when used in relation to God?
12. In Chapters 3 and 4 find the origin of the first part of the "Hail Mary." The Church gave us the second part.
13. What facts should we lay up in our hearts?

Chapter 5

JOSEPH, THE PRUDENT LAYMAN

MATT. 1: 18. Now the generation of Christ was in this wise.
Whereas his mother Mary was espoused to Joseph, before they
came together, she was found with child, of the Holy Ghost.
19. Whereupon Joseph her husband, being a just man, and not
willing publicly to expose her, was minded to put her away
privately. 20. But while he thought on these things, behold, the
angel of the Lord appeared to him in his sleep, saying: Joseph,
son of David, fear not to take unto thee Mary thy wife, for that
which is conceived in her, is of the Holy Ghost. 21. And she
shall bring forth a son: and thou shalt call his name Jesus. For
he shall save his people from their sins. 22. Now all this was
done that it might be fulfilled which the Lord spoke by the
prophet, saying: 23. Behold a virgin shall be with child, and
bring forth a son, and they shall call his name Emmanuel,
which being interpreted is, *God with us.*

THE place occupied by the Gospel of St. Matthew in the New Testament indicates the ancient Catholic tradition that this was the first inspired written account of Christ. Originally it was composed in Aramaic, the dialect of Hebrew spoken by our Lord and the Jews of His day. It was written before A.D. 70, the year of the destruction of Jerusalem. Probably it was written before A.D. 50. Later it was translated into Greek.

Matthew directed his Gospel to Jews. He wanted to convince them that Christ was in reality the promised Messias, that they should realize that the plans of God had matured, that the Messias had come to inaugurate a new scheme of affairs. The Temple was to yield to the Church. Matthew did not stop to arrange the details of Christ's life in chronological order; but he quotes many prophecies of the Old Testament, such as that in verse 23, to show to Christian and non-Christian Jews that Christ was the fulfillment of these prophecies.

Matthew was more than a name. He was a man, and a man's man at that. We might say that he had been a man of the streets. He not only knew Jewish history, but he knew life as it was lived by all classes of men. In the tax-gathering business which he followed, he had to be shrewd. He was, however, a diamond in the rough. And when Christ beckoned to him one day, he showed the strength of character that was hidden in him by giving up his trade immediately and following Christ. He himself tells us that he had been a Publican, one of the class despised by the blue-bloods of the Jews. Thus he shows his humility.

Matthew describes the events of the Incarnation from the viewpoint of Joseph's part in them. Perhaps he never saw St. Joseph. But the manly Matthew was drawn to the noble manhood of Joseph, and we are indebted to the first Evangelist for practically all that we know about the Patron of the Universal Church, St. Joseph. Luke, on the other hand, tells us about Mary and about the Gospel women in general. Thus we see how each Evangelist, following his own natural bent, worked out the plan of God to give us, in the four separate accounts, a unified picture of Christ. What appear to be contradictions in the four Gospels usually clear up when we examine the viewpoint from which each Evangelist was writing. There will always remain some difficulties in the Gospels which we, groping creatures, cannot solve, for we are dealing with divine mysteries; divine intelligence will always remain infinitely above human intelligence. But the marvelous thing of it all is the unified picture of Jesus which these four men record, writing from four different viewpoints. The Holy Ghost has given us an everlastingly beautiful portrayal of the God-Man, while allowing a variety in the manner of approach to the subject.

Matthew begins with the mystery of Christ's coming into the world, His miraculous conception. Here again, it is worthy of remark that both of the men who tell us about Christ's having no human father were men who knew life — Luke the physician, and Matthew the Publican. They were both accustomed to deal with hard facts. Luke accepted the fact of the miraculous conception of Christ and told it to an intelligent Gentile world;

Matthew accepted the fact and told it plainly to the Jews. Matthew implies that the second part of the Jewish marriage ceremony, reception of the bride into Joseph's home, had not yet taken place (Cf. p. 342).

Joseph was a carpenter, which means that he had to work for his living. The words, "just man," reveal much of the character of St. Joseph. "Just" means holy; it indicates that he observed to the full all Jewish laws. Certainly God had given him special graces to prepare him for his task as the protector of Mary and Jesus. Joseph placed God first in life. Religion was not merely a thing of the lips with him; it molded his thinking and acting. You have seen in your parish the same kind of honest, prudent, conscientious, and noble Catholic father or young man who, in a quiet way, without seeking publicity, lives his Catholic life, and always can be relied on to do his duty. Such was Joseph — a noble type of man.

And now he was in a quandary. Apparently Mary had not been faithful to him. And according to the Mosaic Law he had the right to repudiate her, to have her stoned to death (Deut. 22 : 24). He himself had lived a stainless life in the eyes of the Law; and he thought that Mary was also a noble creature. But, himself blameless, he was not one who was hard, unforgiving. Wherever we meet him, we shall note one fine trait in him, a quality which all husbands should possess, namely, considerateness of the feelings of others. He had to protect himself from a woman who apparently was false; but he would spare her the shame of a public exposure. What hurt him most was that Mary had offered no explanations. So, he would simply allow her to go her own way. On the other hand, we know that Mary suffered also. But she considered that the conception was God's work and that in good time He would clear up the difficulty.

Neither Joseph nor Mary acted hastily. They reflected; both were prudent. As long as he received no light from God, Joseph would act slowly. God permits us to be tried. He even allows trial and sorrow to come into the lives of young people. But He is always ready to intervene at the right time. We shall miss much of the meaning of this trial of Joseph if we fail to see that he had been accustomed to live close to God, to ask God's counsel, to think before he acted. Both of them waited to see which way the hand of God pointed before they made their decisions. True piety, deep faith, do not imply stupidity. Joseph was *thinking.* He was using his intelligence, as God wants us to do. But he was thinking of *what God wanted him to do in this case.* His prudence is different from what we often call cleverness. A prudent Catholic student will talk his problems over calmly with Christ. He will ask himself what God wants him to do in a difficulty.

God showed Joseph what to do. He sent an angel, who informed Joseph to accept Mary. She had not lost her innocence. By a miracle, by the power of God, and without the aid of man, a Child was being formed in Mary's womb. Joseph was able to distinguish this vision, which came while he slept, by the certain knowledge which the angel demonstrated. Likewise the angel had a clear knowledge of Joseph's own thoughts, of the future, even as to the name and the life-purpose of the Child. Joseph was to act as foster father, to bestow the name on the Child, to be the protector.

> MATT. 1: 24. And Joseph rising up from sleep, did as the angel of the Lord had commanded him, and took unto him his wife.
> 25. And he knew her not till she brought forth her first-born son: and he called his name Jesus.

Hitherto we have observed two qualities in Joseph — prudence and thoughtfulness. Now and hereafter he demonstrates a third trait — he was a man of obedience, of action rather than of words. We have no recorded words of his. But he was prompt when God's will became clear. Before the world, before the neighbors in Nazareth, Joseph was the father of Jesus. The Jews would have sneered at the story that Christ's conception was miraculous. After He would prove His divinity by miracles, then the secret, guarded by Mary and Joseph, could be told. Once the fact of His divine origin was made clear for future teaching, then nothing extraordinary was to happen until God willed that He should appear in public. Nazareth never knew the real beauty of the divine Flower that grew in this hamlet of flowers. In the eyes of the villagers, He was a human child, with a human father.

Joseph and Mary were two of God's choicest creatures, with the noblest of characters enhanced still more by rich graces. This is the point that the world misses. Joseph respected the vow of virginity that Mary had made. They lived as brother and sister live. They had no other children. It is necessary to know something of Jewish customs, and of the Hebrew language, to understand many words and phrases in Scripture. "First-Born" (Exod. 13: 2) was attached to a child even when there was only one child in the family because it was considered that the first-born belonged in a special manner to God. The word "till," does not imply anything for the future. It sometimes means "not at all" (Gen. 8: 7). By the word "till," Matthew implies that Joseph is not the father of this first-born child. When the phrase "brothers of the Lord" appears in Scripture, it usually means *cousins*. Neither Hebrew nor Aramaic has a word for cousin. Cousins were called "brethren." Abraham said to Lot: "Since we are brothers" (Gen. 13: 8). In reality Lot was his nephew. We know the father of John the Apostle. His name was Zebedee. Yet, on the cross Christ said to John: "Son, behold thy mother." And yet we know that John was not the real son of Mary. The tradition of Mary not having any other children, and the fact that Christ confided her to John would never have been started and believed if Mary had had other children.

We live in a day when many scoff at the idea of the Virgin Birth. But we Catholics need not be bothered much thereby. Christ once said: "If thy eye be single thy whole body will be lightsome." This means that those who have prejudices will seldom see the truth. We know that the ideals, attitudes, and beliefs of a person are influenced by the manner of life he leads. Naturally, if certain types of people do not want God, do not live virtuous lives, they may not accept the ideal that other people *do* live virtuous lives. If men accepted the divinity of Christ, logically they would have to try to lead better lives. Let the scoffer humbly learn to look at facts and he will see the truth.

LUKE 2: 1. And it came to pass that in those days there went out a decree from Caesar Augustus; that the whole world should be enrolled. 2. This enrolling was first made by Cyrinus, the governor of Syria. 3. And all went to be enrolled, every one into his own city. 4. And Joseph also went up from Galilee, out of the city of Nazareth into Judea, to the city of David, which is called Bethlehem: because he was of the house and family of David, 5. To be enrolled with Mary his espoused wife, who was with child.

The desire of the Roman emperor for a census of his provinces became the occasion for the trip of Joseph and Mary to Bethlehem. Rome unconsciously aided in the fulfillment of a prophecy (Matt. 2: 6) that Christ would be born in Bethlehem, where Joseph's ancestors had lived. Where David had herded his sheep, there came the Good Shepherd to be born, so that all sheep might find a safe sheepfold.

We can picture Joseph in the rôle of protector. Roads were rough; travel was slow; Mary needed care. In Joseph she could trust; his thoughtfulness made the fatigue seem light. Virtue in woman was safe with Joseph as protector. Joseph was poor; but we love him for the manly protection he gave to Mary and Jesus. He could not supply them with luxuries, but such things are not necessary for happiness. His manly presence was a comfort; his kindly face gave peace to the heart. We all know what a blessing it is to meet a man who is noble, thoughtful, and strong. A boy becomes noble by being thoughtful and considerate of the comfort of others.

1. Who tells us most of what we know about Mary? About Joseph?
2. What are the three qualities of Joseph that a Catholic layman should exemplify?
3. Why is it important to know the attitude of mind of an objector to any Catholic doctrine or practice?
4. What would be a good practice for a young man during the month set aside to honor St. Joseph?
5. What is the value in waiting till one had tried to determine God's will before making an important decision?
6. If you were engaged to a certain girl or to a certain boy should you keep company with another?
7. How may we develop the virtue of prudence?
8. Show the background Matthew lived in before he became an apostle. For whom did he write?
9. Name three married laymen and three laywomen who are canonized saints of the Church.
10. Would a prudent student read everything that is offered to him or her?

Chapter 6

THE HUMBLE KNOW THE REASON FOR CHRISTMAS JOY

LUKE 2: 6. And it came to pass, that when they were there, her days were accomplished, that she should be delivered. 7. And she brought forth her first-born son, and wrapped him up in swaddling clothes, and laid him in a manger, because there was no room for them in the inn.

CAN we find another historian who would relate in such simple, chaste words the greatest birth in the history of the world? One of the proofs of the truthfulness of the Gospels is the simplicity in their art of narration. They never become wordy; no personal feeling creeps into their pages. In one short statement they will express truths which have revolutionized the world, for example, verse 7, or Luke 22: 19. Had this account been invented, or had the birth been legendary, the narration of it would never have been limited to less than fifty words.

Christ's birth in a rough cave on a hillside that served ordinarily as a shelter for animals is much more than a historical fact. The manner of His coming shows what view He wants us to take toward life. His actions no less than His words have a meaning.

To be poor is to be unhappy, says the modern creed. However, this Son of God, equal to God and equipped with all the splendors of divinity, put aside His glory, concealed His power, and was born of a poor but noble mother. Poverty did not make Him unhappy; it did not prevent His rising to fame as a Man. The world could never say that His greatness was due to environment. He was a poor, unnoticed Child at His birth; and throughout His life remained detached from the desire for wealth. Thus His soul was free from wrong attachments. It is our anxiety for nice things, for wealth, for high places that prevents us from seeing God's viewpoint toward life. Greatness arises from the possession of an immortal soul, from our invitation to a life with God. We should never consider ourselves insignificant just because we are poor; nor should we be ashamed of poor parents, of homes that lack luxuries. Poverty is no bar to the development of a love for God. The poor man is rich if he knows wherein lies his true value.

Humility is a reverent acknowledgment of our dependence on the Creator and on our neighbor or parents. It is a cheerful submission to God's will and to the arrangements He has made for us in life. Pride is a refusal to submit to what God wants. Christ knew that Adam had sinned through pride; He knew that we often seek our own way instead of listening to God. Much of our unhappiness is due to a wounded pride. Christ was humble because He submitted to the life God had outlined for Him. That Infant swathed (wrapped) in a long strip of narrow linen teaches us a lesson in humility. He who is omnipotent was now helpless as a babe in His mother's arms.

The proud man wants recognition to come to himself. He attributes his talents, his success to himself. He refuses to recognize that the power of seeing, hearing, thinking, and speaking is a divine invention, not a human one. And so he takes credit to himself for his mind, his voice, and gives no credit to God. The humble man does not deny that he has talents; but he attributes his gifts to God. The good-looking girl who is humble does not deny that she is beautiful, but she gives the credit to God, and recognizes that He gave her this asset in order that she might lead others to Him. So, humility is merely a recognition of the truth. It is not servility; it is not an inferiority complex. Humility does not exclude ambition; it implies ambition to develop in such a way that God will be honored. If we have neither good looks nor talent, we have nevertheless significance and the opportunity to develop a beautiful character. Humility consists in accepting the situation and cheerfully fulfilling God's will. Christ began His life on earth by taking without complaint that which God sent to Him — poverty and neglect. He endured more than we shall ever have to suffer.

We are not sure of the exact year of Christ's birth (cf. p. 64). The important fact is to see in that birth God's great gift to man — the God-Man who lived His life in the manner God desires. The year 1 A.D. is a turning point in the world's history because the world there learned that God thought enough of mankind to come and live among men. Christ is God's gift to us on Christmas. We should give gifts to others on that day in honor of this infinite gift which came to us, to each one of us. God was good to us; we try to be good to others in order to lead them to Him. Humble people are able to see the divine in that Babe that came so humbly and meekly. If no one else seems to be good to us, at least God is good in sending this Child who grew up to be a Boy and lived as a Man in order to show us that God is interested in us and that we never need fear to approach Him. This one Christmas gift should fill our lives with joy, should make us thankful. Fundamentally our life should be cheerful because we have Christ for a Leader.

* *

What is the true significance of Christ's birth in poverty? Would a modern newspaper reporter describe this birth as St. Luke did? Give one reason for the unhappiness of many people. What event should cause the deepest joy of your life? What do many people not know in regard to the origin of the custom of giving gifts at Christmas?

* *

Luke 2: 8. And there were in the same country shepherds watching, and keeping the night watches over their flock. 9. And behold an angel of the Lord stood by them, and the brightness of God shone round about them, and they feared with a great fear. 10. And the angel said to them: Fear not; for, behold, I bring you good tidings of great joy, that shall be to all the people; 11. For this day is born to you a Saviour, who is Christ the Lord, in the city of David. 12. And this shall be a sign unto you: you shall find the infant wrapped in swaddling clothes, and laid in a manger.

Sometimes when we come home from school, or from a trip, and there is scarcely anyone there to meet us, we are disappointed. We are hurt because people do not seem to realize our importance. There was a large crowd in Bethlehem on this first Christmas night. And Jerusalem was only five miles away. But no one noticed the arrival of God; no one was there to welcome Christ. "He came unto His own and His own received Him not." Apparently only two persons were witnesses of the event, Joseph and Mary.

However, Christ never passes unnoticed. Today people in two stations in life come in greatest numbers to Him, the humble poor and the humble rich or learned. Ordinary people and truly great people have a simplicity about them which enables them to see truth. Such people obtain from God the grace to see also supernatural truth. So it was when God became Man, the poor came the first night, the learned came later.

To show His love for the poor, God chose on this night to send an announcement of the birth, not to the self-important people in Jerusalem but to the lowly shepherds. The poor are receptive of His love. If we should ever be tempted to think that God cares little for us because we are poor or because we never make the headlines, then is the time to recall this announcement of the angel. The majority of the poor are not poor because of their own faults. Our economic system of itself produces poverty, and enables the greedy to climb. And God will not revoke His plan of giving free will to man, but His choosing of the poor shepherds to receive the announcement shows us that He is watching affairs down here on earth and that the laborers who are defrauded of their hire have a final Court to which they can appeal, a Father who will welcome home those who have welcomed Him on earth.

> Luke 2: 13. And suddenly there was with the angel a multitude
> of the heavenly army, praising God, and saying: 14. Glory to
> God in the highest; and on earth peace to men of good will.
> 15. And it came to pass, after the angels departed from them
> into heaven, the shepherds said one to another; Let us go over
> to Bethlehem, and let us see this word that is come to pass,
> which the Lord hath shewed to us. 16. And they came with
> haste; and they found Mary and Joseph, and the infant lying in
> the manger. 17. And seeing, they understood of the word that
> had been spoken to them concerning this child. 18. And all that
> heard, wondered, and at those things that were told them by the
> shepherds. 19. But Mary kept all these words, pondering them
> in her heart.

Heaven sent its citizens to honor Him whom unappreciative earthlings were neglecting. So these shepherds, privileged to hear the only heavenly song ever chanted on earth, learned the twofold purpose of the Incarnation, namely, the glory of God and man's redemption. The life and death of Jesus would reflect glory on God; hence the aim of Catholic education is so to develop and live that honor will come to our Creator.

The shepherds were willing to believe God. They were probably a mile or two from the cave. Bethlehem's white limestone hills reflected the brightness of the night. The shepherds came; they saw "Omnipotence in bonds." Mary evidently was able to take care of the Child herself. How the hearts of those simple men must have thrilled! They understood. God gave them the grace to "understand." Natural learning does not always bring the ability to see God in the Child, to see divine power in the weakness of the Catholic Church. Human eyes do not see far; but the eyes of faith pierce the flesh and see what the microscope will never reveal — a soul. Just as a divine nature lay hidden in this weak Child, so a soul interpenetrates the body and makes us more than what some moderns contemptuously call "only flesh." "Simple souls whom God enlightens see far."

Mary listened to the tale of the shepherds about the angels. She was piecing together all the happenings. She was alert; she thought things over. She shows a Catholic girl how strength of character may come from meditation on the truths taught in religion class, from reflection on God's dealings with men. Great events were taking place at this time; but in the midst of them all Mary was calm, quiet, undisturbed. She was not talkative. "Her lips were as chaste as her heart," yet no detail escaped her attention. And this insight into her character, preserved by St. Luke, leads us to believe that years later she must have related these facts either to St. Luke or to someone who wrote them down, and Luke had in his hand the written document. At any rate, Luke was deeply impressed with the character of Mary. With his usual courtesy for women he likes to bring out this reflective trait in the Mother of God. Mary not only "stored up all these things in her heart"; she "pondered" them. God wanted these details preserved for our own guidance.

The girl who wishes to be truly Catholic must resolve to spend some time *alone*. Second, she must *ponder*. Instead of building dream castles, she must "store up," one by one, the points of the

Gospel story and think ("ponder") of them as she goes to school, as she works about the house, or wends her way down to the office. From the Sunday Gospels and Epistles she will carry one or two sentences as food for the week. In the third place she must be *calm,* poised. God does not have much chance to speak to the too talkative girl. She must listen, and allow the budding flowers, the sunsets, the machines, the stained-glass windows, the silent tabernacle, the sermons, and the human deeds of kindness to impart their spiritual message to her. Her chaste, alert mind will be far different from the dreamy, fickle type that never gets beyond the lurid magazine stage. She will keep the picture of Mary in her heart — Mary who was humble, quiet, intelligent, observing, and selfless.

1. Look up the origin and the meaning of the hymns, *Adeste Fideles* and *Holy Night.*
2. Write a short paragraph on the origin and the meaning of the *Gloria in excelsis* of the Mass.
3. What is the true meaning of humility?
4. Show why the acquisition of humility should put more energy and effort into one's life.
5. Show why God often grants great favors to simple and unlearned people.
6. What leads you to believe that God is interested in you as an individual?
7. Show how Mary's actions suggest a plan of character development for a Catholic girl.
8. What changes are necessary in our economic system in order to prevent poverty from increasing?
9. Memorize verse 19.
10. In the seventh or eighth century B.C., the prophet Micheas (5: 2) predicted the birth in Bethlehem of Israel's great Ruler. What is the force of this fact against efforts of unbelievers to explain away Christ as the mere product of the unsettled political conditions of that day?

Chapter 7

JOY IN THE LIVES OF OLD PEOPLE

> LUKE 2: 21. And after eight days were accomplished, that the Child should be circumcised, his name was called Jesus, which was called by the angel, before he was conceived in the womb.

SHORTLY after the birth, Joseph probably found a house in Bethlehem (Matt. 2: 11). Here in the home was performed the rite of circumcision, by which Christ was officially enrolled among the Jews. He thereby became a subject of the ancient Judaic Law, just as Baptism makes us Christians. At such a time a name was officially given to the child. Circumcision set the Jews apart from other peoples, because the ceremony had a higher meaning than the same rite among pagans. It made a Jew officially one of God's chosen people. Technically, Christ did not have to submit to this custom. However, all through His life He obeyed every prescription that God had originally given to the Hebrews. Joseph and Mary taught Him by example to fulfill Jewish regulations.

> LUKE 2: 22. And after the days of her purification, according to the law of Moses, were accomplished, they carried him to Jerusalem, to present him to the Lord.

Purification was a Mosaic regulation that concerned mothers who had recently given birth to children. It resembled our churching of women. Forty days after the birth of Jesus, Mary was required to go to the Temple for the removal of certain legal defilements (Lev. 12).

The priest who performed the ceremony in connection with the Presentation of Jesus (fourth Joyful Mystery), little realized who was before him that morning as he read the prayers. In reality, Christ was a priest, a priest sent by God, and above Jewish regulations. He was later to act as priest in offering Himself to God. But on that morning no mortal could look into the future and visualize Calvary. Only the Child was conscious of the full meaning of His presentation to the Father as a priest who would serve God faithfully. What must Mary have thought of it all? While she knew more than others, yet she could not foresee Calvary. It was God's plan to test Mary's faith as well as He tests ours. The suspense of the future must always have weighed upon her; there was so much of mystery about the Child. The greater the treasure, the greater our fear of losing it. Day by day Mary wondered what the future would hold. Even on this day she was startled.

> LUKE 2: 25. And behold there was a man in Jerusalem named
> Simeon, and this man was just and devout, waiting for the con-
> solation of Israel; and the Holy Ghost was in him. 26. And he
> had received an answer from the Holy Ghost, that he should not
> see death before he had seen the Christ of the Lord. 27. And he
> came by the Spirit into the temple. And when his parents brought
> in the child Jesus, to do for him according to the custom of the
> law, 28. He also took him in his arms, and blessed God, and
> said: 29. Now thou dost dismiss thy servant, O Lord, according
> to thy word in peace; 30. Because my eyes have seen thy sal-
> vation, 31. Which thou hast prepared before the face of all
> peoples: 32. A light to the revelation of the gentiles, and the
> glory of thy people Israel.

Official Judaism failed to see anything remarkable in this Boy. Nevertheless there were devout Jews in those days. We have seen old men, waiting for the call from God to come home, but meanwhile going to Mass or to church day by day. Their religion is a joy to them in their old age. They await the end with confidence. Such was Simeon. He had read the prophecies. Year after year he waited patiently for the coming of the Messias. God, who sees all things, rewarded this old man's faith by granting him a special light.

On this day, when the "Lord of the Temple came to the Temple of the Lord," when the throngs at the morning sacrifice had departed unaware of any great event, when the priest thought that this was but another child, when Mary and Joseph imagined they were unknown, a stranger accosted them and, paying no attention to the surprise on Mary's face and Joseph's, took the Child into his arms — an old man holding God. Men of deep faith know when God is close to them. Simeon's joy was now complete; and God wished to utter through his lips words of much significance. Simeon first voiced his *Nunc Dimittis* (29–32). It is a hymn of thanksgiving and a prediction. It has been the prayer of hundreds of thousands as they have died a holy death.

Simeon had seen the Messias. Joy lit up the evening of his life. The young have not, as a rule, been tried or tested in their faith. If they persevere, they will find that God often floods with joy the hearts of those who have passed through sorrow — joy for having overcome the allurements of the world, peace like that felt by St. Paul at the end of his long battle to win a way for Christ in the hearts of men (2 Tim. 4: 7).

Here Simeon rose above the view of the Jews of that day. They thought that the Messias would be for them only, that He would be national. Simeon foresaw that He would be international, that Christ came also for the Gentiles (all non-Jews). Simeon excluded no one from the benefits of the Incarnation. We are the Gentiles; we have that Light. As long as we keep the Faith we shall not stumble in darkness; we shall be able to say at the end, with joy of heart, our *Nunc Dimittis.*

> LUKE 2: 33. And his father and mother were wondering at those things, which were spoken concerning him. 34. And Simeon blessed them, and said to Mary his mother: Behold this child is set for the fall, and for the resurrection of many in Israel, and for a sign which shall be contradicted; 35. And thy own soul a sword shall pierce, that out of many hearts thoughts may be revealed.

Wonderment filled the minds of Joseph and Mary. In their loneliness, in the midst of strangers, they realized that God was watching them. They had been amazed that the shepherds should come; they gasped now to think that this old man not only knew the Child, but knew something of His future. Then, following this wonderment, there came a thrust at Mary's heart, like the bolt of lightning out of the dark sky. Her Child would divide the world into two camps, those for Christ and those against Him. He came from God; He is the sole Mediator between God and men. And each person must decide whether he will accept or reject Christ. God will take care in His own way of those who have not had a chance to know Christ, but with us there is no middle way. We either fall or rise in eternity according to the way we act toward Christ.

It was God's will that Mary should learn to suffer along with Christ. The sword would pierce her heart at the time of His Passion. But even before the Passion, neighbors in Nazareth would point her out as the mother of one who was hated by the Pharisees, and Joseph would not be there to protect her. She was to earn her title, Mother of Sorrows, when she stood beneath the Cross and saw what He suffered. But when Simeon uttered this prophecy, the Cross was more than thirty years away. She was even now morally strong and quietly courageous, but would not such words of Simeon's, coming from one who apparently knew, burn into the heart of this young mother? The expectancy of a great catastrophe, a great sorrow hung over her; the weight of impending disaster was hers to bear, and it was all the worse because of its indefiniteness.

The last part of verse 35 is mysterious to a certain extent. It probably means that the character, the destiny of many people is shown by the attitude they take toward Christ. And during Christ's public life Mary was hurt by the attitude of the enemies of Christ. Others say that this verse means that Mary's sorrows are the occasion of bringing some people to a belief in Christ, *ad Jesum per Mariam* ("to Jesus through Mary").

> LUKE 2: 36. And there was one Anna, a prophetess, the daughter of Phanuel, of the tribe of Aser; she was far advanced in years, and had lived with her husband seven years from her virginity. 37. And she was a widow until fourscore and four years; who departed not from the temple, by fastings and prayers serving night and day. 38. Now she, at the same hour coming in, confessed to the Lord; and spoke of him to all that looked for the redemption of Israel.

Another aged person, Anna, was to experience joy on this occasion. She was eighty-four years of age. Long had she been faithful to God. And now she had the happiness of recognizing Christ. So great was the joy of her discovery that she could not keep the news to herself; she informed others. Persevering faithfulness to Christ makes for a happy old age.

1. Is it a good thing for us to obey rules or customs even when we feel that we have a right to be exempted from them?
2. Can we in fairness ask others to keep rules that we ourselves do not follow?
3. Why do some mothers dedicate their children in a special manner to the Mother of God?
4. Show that God may choose for distinction some whom the world rejects in the distribution of its honors.
5. How may old people avoid a sour attitude toward life?
6. What is the origin and meaning of the *Nunc Dimittis?*
7. What burdens did Mary have to bear?
8. What would you consider a good practice now in order to have happiness in your old age?

Chapter 8

PROMINENT MEN CAN BE HUMBLE

MATT. 2: 1. When Jesus therefore was born in Bethlehem of Juda, in the days of king Herod, behold, there came wise men from the East to Jerusalem, 2. Saying: Where is he that is born king of the Jews? For we have seen his star in the East and are come to adore him. 3. And king Herod hearing this, was troubled, and all Jerusalem with him. 4. And assembling together all the chief priests and the scribes of the people, he inquired of them where Christ should be born. 5. But they said to him: In Bethlehem of Juda. For so it is written by the prophet: 6. And thou Bethlehem the land of Juda art not the least among the princes of Juda: for out of thee shall come forth the captain that shall rule my people Israel. 7. Then Herod, privately calling the wise men, learned diligently of them the time of the star which appeared to them; 8. And sending them into Bethlehem, said: Go and diligently inquire after the child, and when you have found him, bring me word again, that I also may come and adore him.

WE DO not know the exact time of the arrival of the Wise Men. We assume, however, that Mary and Joseph were still in Bethlehem, and that shortly after the Presentation, this visit took place. Neither do we know how many of these visitors there were, nor precisely the place from which they came, whether Persia or Arabia. They were not kings; the word *Magi* may mean either *priest* or *great*. These men were learned, perhaps priests, and their acts indicate that they were quite wealthy and in reality great of soul.

Persian and Chaldean Magi were adept in the study of the stars. The sky is very clear at night in Persia. As a class, the Magi had degenerated in the day of Christ; but it seems to be implied that these Magi of the Gospel were earnest seekers after the truth. They sought for truth in the best manner of their country, through a knowledge of the stars, through the science of their own day. God can lead men to the truth along strange paths. If science does not destroy humility in the possessor of scientific knowledge, then he may receive grace and light to see the whole truth, for a science is only a partial knowledge of the truth. Yet, just as the star pointed to God, so should science lead to the Creator.

A person can arrive at the conclusion that God exists; but to know the nature of God accurately and to know His will in our regard we need revelation. The point is that God gives this guidance to those who are humbly seeking the truth. It was because these Magi, prominent men in their field, were humble, and were willing to believe there was something behind what they saw, that God, using their own particular science, gave them the grace to see the Truth. They were the first Gentiles to come to a knowledge of God; they are our ancestors. A mysterious star led them. If they came from Persia they may have traveled from 700 to 1,000 miles, a long way, with camels making perhaps fifty miles a day through desert regions. We do not know the nature of the star. Some say there was a conjunction of planets; or, a star appearing at fixed intervals. The Gospel seems to give the impression that the star was miraculous. It was able to guide them. It went from east to west, which stars ordinarily do not do.

The star was a light leading them to a divine Light. This Light, invisible for so many centuries to the pagans, the Gentiles, now became visible to them. God had become Man. And all young people have since then a divine Leader to follow and to worship, One whose light does not dim with age. The Magi called it "His Star." They did not realize, perhaps, that grace was aiding them to expect a great King. They thought that all Jerusalem would be agog over the arrival, that everyone would be talking about the Child. They met only indifference and ignorance. (What must God think of us if we are unaware of the value of our religion and cannot enlighten the "outsiders" who are seeking for the truth?)

Herod's actions are typical of a man who has reached power or fame dishonestly, and who hears that a rival is about to expose him. Herod was a murderer, a despot detested by the people. He had killed members of his own family, lest they supplant him on his throne. And now the rumor of a Jewish king being born sent shivers of suspicion through him. The priests also were startled. These strangers were evidently prominent people; they were aware of something of which the very leaders of Jerusalem were ignorant. What must the Magi have thought when they observed this ignorance?

Herod was shrewd. He would use the apparently simple and trusting foreigners to aid him in his diabolical designs. He put on the cloak of piety to cover his plan of murder. The Magi probably had sufficient intelligence not to be deceived by this show of piety. They had undoubtedly heard of Herod's character, yet they could scarcely suspect what he now had in mind.

> MATT. 2: 9. Who having heard the king, went their way; and behold the star which they had seen in the East, went before them, until it came and stood over where the child was. 10. And seeing the star they rejoiced with exceeding great joy. 11. And entering into the house, they found the child with Mary his mother, and falling down they adored him: and opening their treasures, they offered him gifts: gold, frankincense, and myrrh. 12. And having received an answer in sleep that they should not return to Herod, they went back another way into their country.

It is not necessary to believe that the star had been continually visible all the way to Jerusalem. Evidently the star was not in appearance while they were in Jerusalem, but it was visible to them sometime before they entered Bethlehem. It had been moving; now it stood and shed its light over the house where Jesus was. Since the Jews had been unaware of the birth, God miraculously intervened for these men of deep worth, who were overjoyed at such an event.

These were the first Gentiles to make their submission to Christ. The feast celebrating the arrival of these intrepid searchers is called Epiphany. It signifies that the light of truth had come to the Gentile world. These Wise Men welcomed the light. The Light Eternal dispelled the mists of paganism and they were permitted to see God. But let us not forget their humility and their faith. In their own country these men held a high ranking. They were accustomed to court splendor and to cultured surroundings. They had expected, no doubt, to find royal glamor and protection around this King. But what a shock they received!

Their faith was put to a test. No palace, no armed guards, no servants. So inconspicuous had been the arrival of God upon earth that no one was aware of where the Infant lay. The King of kings was without pomp and power. Did these men turn back in disgust and disappointment at the poverty, the lowliness? The humility of true greatness lies in this, that they did not hesitate; they did not demand recognition of their rank; they did not ask for proof. They *believed.* It is very probable that by the word "worship," St. Matthew means the adoration that we give only to God. God had granted them special graces to begin and to persevere in their journey. Is it not fitting that He would here give them the grace to make a true, supernatural act of faith? His own received Him not; the Gentiles welcomed Him.

The Wise Men accepted Him on His own terms. They saw God in the lowliness of a Babe. Many moderns cannot find God because He does not suit their fancy. They lack the humility and courage of the Magi. Even in a worldly sense these men courted danger by going into a foreign country and acknowledging as king, one about whom the king (Herod) knew nothing. Generously they offered Him of their gifts. What meaning they attached to these three gifts is not clear to us. Perhaps gold stands as their tribute to Christ as King and the incense and myrrh as a sweet-smelling offering of adoration to Christ as God. Unconsciously, under the guidance of the Holy Ghost, they may have offered the myrrh as suggestive to us of material for Christ's later embalming.

Recall the simple, childlike faith of the shepherds. When seen in comparison with the humble faith of these great-minded men, we cannot fail to note that today the simple people and the truly great are the types that accept Christ's Church. A rich and powerful, or learned man, can have the simple faith of the Magi, provided that he be humble. Here, Learning knelt in adoration before the God who gave man the power to learn. Men of science and men of learning have much to learn from the faith of these Magi. Science cannot solve the problem of the purpose of life. Marconi, the great scientist, said: "From the time humanity began to think, it has occupied itself with the problem of its origin and its future, which is the problem of life. The inability of science to solve it is absolute. This would be truly frightening were it not for faith."

MATT. 2: 13. And after they were departed, behold an angel of the Lord appeared in sleep to Joseph, saying: Arise, and take the child and his mother, and fly into Egypt: and be there until I shall tell thee. For it will come to pass that Herod will seek the child to destroy him. 14. Who arose, and took the child and his mother by night, and retired into Egypt: and he was there until the death of Herod: 15. That it might be fulfilled which the Lord spoke by the prophet, saying: Out of Egypt have I called my son.

Virtue is wise to retire when vice sets forth. Joseph the protector was the agency through whom God foiled the designs of Herod. Again Joseph obeyed instantly. What worry, what suspense must have been his as he trod the dusty road to Egypt. We know nothing of the sojourn there. The three may have remained there two or three years. We do not know.

MATT. 2: 16. Then Herod perceiving that he was deluded by the wise men, was exceeding angry: and sending killed all the men-children that were in Bethlehem, and in all the borders thereof, from two years old and under, according to the time which he had diligently inquired of the wise men.

The real nature of Herod is shown by his ruthless killing of innocent baby boys, twenty or perhaps a few more. We shudder at the horrible crime. (What shall we think of those in our own day who kill unborn infants?) Herod's actions show us that it is futile to attempt to fight against God, against His decrees. God could not allow the crime against the Holy Innocents to remain unpunished. Neither can He forget the crimes against the innocents of our day.

MATT. 2: 19. But when Herod was dead, behold an angel of the Lord appeared in sleep to Joseph in Egypt, 20. Saying: Arise, and take the child and his mother, and go into the land of Israel. For they are dead that sought the life of the child. 21. Who arose, and took the child and his mother, and came into the land of Israel. 22. But hearing that Archelaus reigned in Judea in the room of Herod his father, he was afraid to go thither: and

being warned in sleep retired into the quarters of Galilee. 23.
And coming he dwelt in a city called Nazareth: that it might be
fulfilled which was said by the prophets: That he shall be called
a Nazarene.

Reviewing Joseph's career we find that prudence is reflected in all his actions; his considerateness of Mary and Jesus indicates his nobility; his instant obedience on all occasions was given without asking any questions, without murmuring at the difficulties. He brought them back to Nazareth; and Christ thus was to be known as the Nazarene.

1. What is the meaning of the word *Epiphany?* What special significance for us has this feast of January 6?
2. What counsel would our Lord give to a brilliant student, to a good athlete, or to a wealthy person who wished to remain humble?
3. A certain individual refuses to belong to a poor parish because he feels that it is below his social standing. What is wrong?
4. How far would you walk or travel in order to participate in the Mass on Sunday?
5. What do we need besides science to solve the purpose of life?
6. Do you think that truly great scientists lose their faith in God by delving deep into science?
7. Show why prudence is necessary in dealing with those who make a pretense of piety.
8. A lie is the saying of what is not true with the purpose of deceiving others. Show the real malice of Herod's lie.
9. Describe the main traits of St. Joseph.
10. Do you know of any outstanding men or women who possess learning, or wealth, or talent and yet are humble and devout Catholics?
11. A young man says that he gave up the Faith because he was disappointed in some Catholics whom he met. What is wrong with this reasoning?
12. What do you admire most in the Wise Men?

Chapter 9

A QUIET BOYHOOD

LUKE 2: 40. And the child grew, and waxed strong, full of wisdom; and the grace of God was in him.

THE events which we have just studied seem to have been soon forgotten by the people at large. There was so much fear of murder, bloodshed, and political disturbances during these years that the visit of the Magi passed into obscurity. The sudden disappearance of Jesus permitted the talk to die down. It was part of the plan of God that the birth being fully verified and witnessed, Jesus was not to draw too much attention to Himself for the time being. The divine splendor and heavenly accompaniments of the first few months were followed by those years of obscurity, known as the hidden life of Christ.

God became Man. And God wants us to know the manly qualities of Jesus. The human in Him is like a ladder on which we climb to an appreciation of His divinity. However, the most important truth for us to meditate upon is that, while being truly human, Jesus is in full reality God. Let us analyze further the information given to us in verse 40:

a) About sixty-five miles north of Jerusalem, as the bird flies, or over eighty by road, lies Nazareth, perched mainly on hillsides, like in an arena or bowl. The town is entirely hidden from the outside world by its encircling hills. A spring (Mary's Well) issues from the base of the hill, on the north, and supplies most of the water for the hamlet. The inhabitants must have lived on the slope of the western hill. Houses were square, built in against the hillsides, one higher than the other, with flat roofs, and without any regular arrangement. The climate was healthy, and the temperature mild in this quiet, rural community.

By climbing the hill on the west or north or east, one sees, far to the north, Mt. Hermon with its snow. On clear days the Mediterranean is visible over to the west; to the east, about fifteen miles, is the Lake of Galilee, along which went many of the great caravans which carried the goods of India down to Egypt; to the south is the level plain of Esdraelon. By walking on the ridge a mile and a half south, or going through the gully, one finds that the hills suddenly cease. Over southeast about twelve miles, rises Mount Tabor, 1,650 feet above the plain, or 1,986 feet above sea level. It stands there alone, rather round at the bottom and flat on top.

b) "The Child grew and waxed strong." Jesus learned by experience to walk and talk as other children. He was healthy, robust, and well formed in every way. He played as any healthy child plays. God did not wish Him to startle His playmates by daring deeds, although He undoubtedly was considered unusual among the children of the village. He was full of vigor, alertness, and joyfulness. Alone, or with other boys, He must have climbed the hills above the town. If their boyish wonderment was excited by the vastness of the view, He probably said not much to them of what was present to His mind concerning His future deeds in that country. His companions must have wondered at the calmness of soul that was His, as they speculated on the seemingly far-away trips they had made or would make to Jerusalem.

c) "Filled with wisdom." God is a spirit. So, in the Boy Jesus, the divinity was there but not to be seen with human eyes. Jesus was one Person, but He had two natures, divine and human. Being human, He had a human soul as we have, hence human capacity to learn and to choose. We do not know just how His infinite knowledge was related to what He learned in a human way. Just as He grew physically like other children, so He could learn in a new way, through the senses, truths already familiar to Him. As a Man we shall see Him refusing to display His divine power. He used it on occasions to do good to others. So also in His boyhood there was a reserve about Him. He submitted to being taught. He showed unusual grasp of things, but it appeared like the grasp of a very bright child.

Mary was His first teacher in a human way. No doubt she told the God-Child about God and His ancient promises to the

Jews. Jewish parents were deeply conscious of their obligation to teach religion to their children. Each home was a school. At about the age of seven Joseph began to instruct Jesus. He also taught Him carpentering. Moreover, Nazareth had a synagogue (prayer center or meeting hall). Here the people gathered on Saturday to pray and to have religion explained. Sometimes the synagogue served as a school. Along with other boys, Jesus memorized much of the Old Testament. Picture Him reading about Himself. Imagine Mary telling Him about the Messias and how her eyes would be wistfully riveted on Him as she would marvel at the perfect understanding that shone in that innocent face, those heavenly features. What answer did the listening angels hear as they watched over this Child who was "filled with wisdom"?

d) "The grace of God was upon Him." Sometimes we marvel at the brightness of children, or at the beauty of a voice, or at athletic ability. It also happens that holiness or sanctity and understanding of divine things stand out attractively in some children. They are close to God. We actually seem to see in them the effects of grace, that divine life that God can bestow on anyone but which ordinarily comes to us through the sacraments.

Jesus was infinitely holy always. In the privacy of the home Mary and Joseph were often startled at evident holiness that was reflected in His face. Three times each day set forms of prayer were repeated in the Jewish home. Religion was not a heartless, mechanical thing in the home of the Holy Family. We know that there have been young saints who liked to think of God continually. St. Thomas Aquinas as a man found difficulty in thinking about anything else but God. We could develop this habit to some extent, and still be hard-working students as Thomas was; we could still enjoy fun. Hence, Mary and Joseph must have enjoyed teaching Jesus and learning from Him. The real teacher of the Boy Jesus, however, was His Father. Jesus was always conscious of God. No matter how well Mary instructed Him, Jesus is more than the product of a good home. His human will co-operated with the suggestions of the Holy Ghost and thus He gained merit for us. In fact His whole life was one continual consecration to the task of pleasing His heavenly Father. This was His motive always, and it should be ours.

Since God became Man not only to redeem us but to show us how to live, the actions of the Boy Jesus teach us that a boy or girl can play or work and at the same time live with God. Religion is not something for Sundays only. It is a way of living; it is part of our every minute. We are to grow and wax strong; we are to be filled with the wisdom learned from Jesus; we are to develop the divine life (grace) that Jesus gives us in the sacraments. We are to keep joyful companionship with Him. Jesus the Boy is our model and our friend. A young American who was operator in a signal tower for trains in a large city, and who was always conscious of God's presence, did not make one mistake in ten years of service.

1. How do we know Jesus was a healthy Boy?
2. What leads us to believe that Mary and Joseph found it interesting to teach Jesus?
3. Describe Nazareth.
4. What is a synagogue?
5. How many natures are in Christ?
6. What is the meaning of the phrase: "Living in the presence of God"?
7. Study Francis Thompson's poem: "Little Jesus."
8. Look up Proverbs 31: 10–31, for an ideal that was held up to Jewish mothers of ancient times.
9. Read: *The Life of Guy de Fontgalland,* by G. Bernoville, trans. by D. Buckley.
10. What one motive should dominate a boy's or girl's life?
11. What leads us to believe that the people of Nazareth saw nothing miraculous in the Boy Jesus?
12. Where is Mt. Tabor? The Lake of Galilee?

Chapter 10

OBEDIENT MANHOOD

LUKE 2: 41. And his parents went every year to Jerusalem, at the solemn day of the pasch. 42. And when he was twelve years old, they going up into Jerusalem, according to the custom of the feast,

SINCE Mary accompanied Joseph each year, it is probable that Jesus also had previously been in the city. But it is not without meaning that St. Luke emphasizes this journey which took place when Jesus was twelve. Eastern children mature earlier than do those of our civilization. Jesus was now legally a man. At the beginning of his thirteenth year, a boy became subject to all the prescriptions of the Mosaic Code, such as fasting and the making of pilgrimages. (Roman boys put on the *toga virilis* at 14.) Christ would now wear on His arm and forehead certain selections from Scripture (Deut. 11: 18–20). It was at this time that a boy began the trade that he had chosen to practice.

Imagine the thoughts of Jesus on this spring day as He mingled with the joyous throng on its way to that feast which would last a week. His heart bounded as He climbed over the final hill which hid Jerusalem from view, and beheld before Him the gold and white stone of the Temple sanctuary glittering in the sunlight. There was His Father's house. It was just as when we call a church the "house of God."

LUKE 2: 43. And having fulfilled the days, when they returned, the child Jesus remained in Jerusalem; and his parents knew it not. 44. And thinking that he was in the company, they came a day's journey, and sought him among their kinsfolks and acquaintance. 45. And not finding him, they returned into Jerusalem, seeking him.

All is confusion, noise, and excitement when an Eastern caravan gets under way, for large groups of people travel together. It seems likely that Jesus chose deliberately to remain behind in Jerusalem. At nightfall of the first day His parents discovered their loss. The second day was taken up with the return trip to Jerusalem. Sharp pangs of regret shot through the soul of Mary.

> LUKE 2: 46. And it came to pass, that, after three days, they
> found him in the temple, sitting in the midst of the doctors, hear-
> ing them and asking them questions. 47. And all that heard him
> were astonished at his wisdom and his answers. 48. And seeing
> him, they wondered. And his mother said to him: Son, why hast
> thou done so to us? Behold thy father and I have sought thee
> sorrowing. 49. And he said to them: How is it that you sought
> me: did you not know that I must be about my Father's business?
> 50. And they understood not the word that he spoke unto them.

Students usually sat in circles on the floor while the teacher explained some point of religion. Young Jews had great respect for teachers. Jesus had come to listen, but He was not afraid to ask questions. There was such a depth to His answers and questions that the old men marveled. They were startled at what they thought was the comprehension of a very bright boy; but they little knew that this Boy, the subject of the prophecies, had once been visited by the Wise Men of the East and had been hounded by Herod.

Of a sudden the silence of the classroom was interrupted by the entrance of a woman and a man. They may have heard some of His answers to the old men. And what mother could keep silence after three days of absence from such a Child? The grief that she had felt came to the surface, and in a voice that had a slight reproach in it, a voice that revealed the sorrow that they had felt and the love they bore toward Him, she asked for His reasons in leaving them. The students and teachers were tense. What answer would this Child give? We are not sure that her question was asked in the presence of the group, but that is probable. And it may be that God wanted a public manifestation at this time.

His statement, His first recorded public utterance, reveals the fact that Jesus always knew who He was. He knew that His true Father was not Joseph; He knew exactly His work here on earth. At an age when other boys were thinking of their entrance upon their trade, He was thinking of His task of leading men to God. He implied that it was only natural for Him to discuss the Law and God's dealings with man.

Jesus did not intend to be rude to Mary; but He wished to take this occasion to teach us an important truth: namely, that our duty to God comes first in life. Jesus was truly human, and like other boys owed the duty of obedience to those whom God had placed over Him. But Jesus was also God, and was sent here to be our Redeemer, our Teacher. As Redeemer, He had duties to His heavenly Father. In such duties He was subject to His Father only. And so it is with us: all creatures — parents, relatives, friends, jobs, money, pleasure — have their proper use. But no creature, not even parents, must ever be placed higher than God. We owe first allegiance to Him who gave each of us an immortal soul, who adopted us at Baptism, and who, therefore, has rights over us. Gently but firmly He spoke this great truth to Mary that He owed first allegiance to His Father.

Moreover, Christ knew the future. He knew there would be critics, scoffers, who would claim that Christ imagined that He was God only after He had obtained power as a public speaker or a leader, after success had created illusions of grandeur. Christ wanted us to know that He was always conscious of His divinity, that no human teacher, no environment or success could be entirely responsible for the quality of His character.

Incidentally, the quiet determination which He showed on this occasion suggests that we ponder on what we owe to our Father. Whatever our future work may be, it must never dull the consciousness of the assignment which God has given us of molding our character so that it will be pleasing to Him. Over and above our athletics, pleasures, studies, and home duties is that ever-present obligation of becoming Christlike by taking Christ as a model for our lives.

Mary knew that Christ was divine. She guarded the secret. But she was not prepared for this strong assertion. It is doubtful if at this time she knew all that was before Him. Christ had not told her. What human person could bear up under the suspense of waiting for the treason of Judas, the denial of Peter, the scourging, the Cross? Mary and Joseph understood not the full import of His words on this occasion (neither did the learned men, evidently), because God wished them to live by faith, the same as we have to do. They were to trust God and to take what He sent day by day. They asked no further questions of Him. They only wondered. That is beautiful faith, not to inquire too much into God's affairs, not to wish to know the future, but to be loyal to Him day by day and to trust the future into His hands, to let nothing interfere with our present duty to Him, and then all will be well.

* *

What principle did Christ teach by His reply to Mary? What leads us to believe that Mary and Joseph had to live by faith, as we do? What is the test to show whether or not we actually place God first in life?

* *

> LUKE 2: 51. And he went down with them, and came to Nazareth, and was subject to them. And his mother kept all these words in her heart. 52. And Jesus advanced in wisdom and age and grace with God and men.

Having taught us that great lesson of allegiance to God, Jesus then proceeded to give us an example of the greatness of obedience. He taught always by example. He who at twelve could assume legally some independence, who had just calmly asserted that He must be loyal to God, who was conscious of the fact that He Himself was God and therefore above all men, now, as Man, humbly submitted Himself to Mary and Joseph. He obeyed cheerfully, wholeheartedly. He showed what He thought of Mary and Joseph by subjecting Himself to them. God obeyed man! What humility! He taught us that it is manly to obey lawful superiors. The more noble a young man or woman is, the more readily he or she obeys civil, ecclesiastical, and domestic superiors. He or she never gets beyond the stage or age of obedience in right and lawful matters. Stubbornness, refusal to obey, is not will power; it is hidden pride.

And Mary forgot nothing of these things. All details remained in her mind. No mother has had such harrowing conjectures of what might happen to her child. As His mother, she had had a right to ask a question. He chose not to give a clear explanation in His answer. She accepted the situation; so did Joseph. This is the last mention of him.

Once more the door closes and we are permitted no recorded view of that home life in Nazareth that went on for eighteen or twenty years more. What Luke tells us about the second period of the hidden life is almost a repetition of the first (Cf. verse 10). God certainly wishes us to learn something from this long period that Jesus spent in preparation. We of the modern age must learn that "He came to teach that continual excitement, prominent action, distinguished services, brilliant successes are not essential elements of a true and noble life, and that myriads of the beloved of God are to be found among the insignificant and obscure" (Farrar). And what we think is routine, or useless, or not practical, may, according to God's plans, be the very thing that is necessary to prepare us for some work of the future. "God is often pleased to form great souls in silence, to fashion them gradually in humility or even in suffering, and then, of a sudden, He casts them upon the field of battle where they are to glorify Him" (Le Camus).

"Jesus advanced." These key words show us that in the eyes of His neighbors He made progress. His physical growth could be observed. Outwardly His mental advancement would be as that of other young men. Outwardly He was like other men; inwardly He was different from all men. As we try to recapture some of the environment in which Jesus lived, let us recall that Christ is not the mere product of a good home; He was not the follower of any sage or great man; He was not the champion arising from the condition of the times. He willed to grow and to advance in His human nature as other men do; however, human surroundings do not explain Jesus. The divine nature in Him is fundamentally the cause of His being what He is.

EXTERIOR LIFE

a) "The Holy Family." The words are too sacred to analyze. Mary's quiet and refined influence, Joseph's daily prudence and thoughtfulness, and Christ's radiant personality make up that home. There was scant furniture. Most of the day was spent out of doors. Sublime secrets were locked in their hearts. They never boasted to their neighbors. The fact that the Nazarenes were surprised when this Man of obscurity stepped into the public gaze of all Palestine, indicates that they had known little of the hidden power of Jesus during all those years. What conversations must have brought the angels to attention in that simple abode! Often they prayed. And in the evening when darkness was settling, Mary and Joseph, as they rested from the labors of the day, often thought that heaven was close because of the peace that thrilled their hearts when the young Man spoke of God. No harsh words, no bickering, no tongue-lashing, but that indefinable happiness which comes from being close to God. We admire the apparent willingness of Mary and Joseph not to be inquisitive about His future, not to pry into what God had in store for them. They maintained a cheerful day-by-day reliance on God. Since Jesus, who is God, and who knew infinitely more than Mary or Joseph, chose to obey them, to be subject to them, we keep that same attitude toward our parents.

b) "Trade." "Is this not the carpenter?" (Mark 6: 3) Christ was a working Man. God worked. Toil, sweat, fatigue were familiar to Him. Physical labor puts one in touch with realities. Christ knew how to shape things. He who is the shaper of our souls, knew how to form well-fitting yoke for oxen. He, who later was said to do all things well, could not have been a slovenly worker. He was an expert. His hands were roughened from work. He was strong, athletic, and capable of great endurance. He had perfect health. It is wrong to think of Him as feminine in appearance. However, He was thoughtful and sympathetic, and may we not trace here some of the influence of Mary's refined character? We do not know how He looked; but it seems certain that He was strong. There is no reason to ascribe a sensuous, physical beauty to Him; neither is there evidence for any repellant quality in His physical appearance. (The picture that Isaias the prophet gave of Him centuries before He appeared, refers to the time of His Passion when He was mangled and bruised.) We do not know when Joseph died. When Christ was around thirty-three years of age the memory of Joseph was still fresh in the minds of the people, even outside of Nazareth (John 6: 42). But Jesus must have had to support Mary and Himself some years before His public life. Hence we know that He had carried the responsibility of a workman. He was a Man in the highest sense of the term.

c) "Observer of nature." We shall see later how Christ was familiar with all aspects of nature, with every type of animal and vegetable life. Nothing escaped His eye in His public life; and hence He must have spent many hours roaming the hills and observing nature around Nazareth. His language is colored with references to all phases of Palestinian life. And since He was accustomed to sleep in the open, after the world came to know Him, may we not conclude that often in these hidden years He spent lonely watches of the night on a hillside — meditating, praying, planning His work. He spent much time alone. "He was a vigorous, open-air Man."

d) "Observer of social customs." Christ studied life as it was lived around Him; He watched people at work, at play, at prayer. Business, judicial procedure, ceremonies of the court, armies, shepherds, fishermen, home life, all furnished for Him material from which He would draw comparisons for the spiritual truths He was later to teach.

INTERIOR LIFE

We are told that all of us should develop the habit of living in the presence of God. Christ did this naturally, continually. He was never alone — neither need we be. As we review His public life we note how clear He was on what He was supposed to do, how calmly determined He was in going about His task of bringing honor to His Father. Never once do we find Him hesitating for an answer in the midst of powerful enemies. He had meditated on all these things during the quiet years of His hidden life.

May we not picture Him on the bluffs in the rear of Nazareth, reflecting on the plans of God. All the past was present to Him — Adam's privileges and fall, the spreading of the human race and the gradual loss of a true knowledge of God, Abraham's selection to be the founder of a new race that would preserve the idea of One God, and then the ups and downs of this chosen people. The future was also present to Him — Peter starting the papacy in Rome, Paul converting the Gentiles and writing his Epistles. He saw Europe gradually becoming Catholic, and China being touched by faith in Him. He followed Columbus over the ocean and noted that the Cross would accompany this solid Catholic layman who wished to work for conversions. He knew that in the midst of all the modern sin, many young people would be loyal to Him and to His Church.

Despite the fact that, aside from Mary and Joseph, He experienced almost continual misunderstanding, hatred, and suspicion; despite the seeming loneliness of all the hidden years, and the burden of the approaching Calvary, there is no sign of discouragement, of the pessimist in Jesus, no bitterness in His disposition. Essentially His life was joyful because God was with Him.

The hidden years were, then, profitable to Christ. Humanly speaking, He advanced in wisdom and grace. He was not a dreamer; He was a man of action. But He spent more than thirty years in preparation for two and a half years of public life. The apparently useless practices in school and church today may be the very things that are preparing us to do real, good work later. We must, then, use our minds and wills as He did. We shall never become true Catholics unless we take the truths that Christ taught us and make them our own by *long years of meditation,* meanwhile practicing one by one the things that Christ did each day in this hidden life.

The secret of will power is to have a definite aim, like the motive of pleasing God. Character is built by our hidden, daily decisions, by continued effort to sharpen the vision of our goal. In basketball we keep on practicing day after day, so, likewise the daily practice of thinking about God, of controlling our thoughts, of doing kind deeds gradually prepares us for the day when we shall be called upon to make some important decision. For more than thirty years Christ practiced quietly, and unseen by the world, the virtues that gleamed forth in His few public years. God grants the gift of advancing in grace to those who have the courage to do their ordinary tasks in school, to perform their duties about the home, to keep at morning and night prayer. Each noble, unselfish act that we perform is an act of obedience to God. And He who was obedient Himself works with us to encourage us, to guide us. He desires that we learn from His obedience how to obey in our own lives. He who was happy and contented in those long, monotonous years has shown us how to be happy in the country, in a small town, in an obscure position.

1. Describe the life of Christ as a young Man.
2. What is the significance of St. Luke's reference to Christ at the age of twelve?
3. Should holiness, which is the same as Christlikeness, weaken or strengthen a student in sports, classes, or business?
4. Show that there is manhood or womanhood in a boy or girl who will obey willingly when he or she should do so.
5. Show that environment does not account for Christ's character.
6. Should a boy or girl feel dissatisfied if he or she must do manual labor continually?
7. How can one make his daily work serve as a prayer?
8. Show that Mary could keep a secret.
9. What may have been the purpose behind the long years of the hidden life?
10. Does the example of Christ's obedience help you in a trying situation?
11. Show how Christ exemplified this principle: "He who has never learned obedience will never know how to lead."
12. Read: *St. Aloysius Gonzaga*, by Fr. Martindale (America Press); *A Shepherd of the Far North* (*William Francis Walsh*), by R. Glady (Harr Wagner Co., 609 Mission Street, San Francisco, California).
13. Show that, humanly speaking, Christ used His time to good advantage during the hidden years.
14. What is necessary if one wishes to develop true strength of character?

Chapter 11

HE IS COMING: MAKE READY

LUKE 3: 1. Now in the fifteenth year of the reign of Tiberius Caesar, Pontius Pilate being governor of Judea, and Herod being tetrarch of Galilee, and Philip his brother tetrarch of Iturea and the country of Trachonitis, and Lysanias tetrarch of Abilina,
2. Under the high priests Annas and Caiphas, the word of the Lord was made unto John, the son of Zachary, in the desert.
3. And he came into all the country about the Jordan, preaching the baptism of penance for the remission of sins,

THE words "fifteenth year," etc., and a reference to Christ's being about the age of thirty (Luke 3 : 23), bring up the question of exact dates on which the events of Christ's life took place. We cannot at present reach an exact conclusion. The Jews were not so well equipped as we are for keeping time and recording dates and events. The Roman calendar was not the same as the Jewish. The custom of dating all events from the year of Christ's birth did not begin until the sixth century. And the monk Dionysius who made the computation placed the date of A.D. 1 from five to eight years later than He was born.

John the Baptist started to preach about September of the year 27 A.D. The fact that St. Luke refers to two high priests shows that there was corruption in religious affairs, for there should have been but one.

In the midst of such conditions, God made known to John the Baptist that he was to begin his work. He stationed himself near the river Jordan. His baptism was not like our sacrament. It was used to symbolize conversion and a reformation of life. Those who came to John and were repentant would be immersed in the river water. This immersion of itself did not blot out their sins; it did not give grace. Its purpose was to stir people to sorrow for their sins, to help them believe in the coming Christ.

> MATT. 3: 4. And the same John had his garment of camel's hair, and a leathern girdle about his loins: and his meat was locusts and wild honey. 5. Then went out to him Jerusalem and all Judea, and all the country about Jordan.

Since his early years John had lived in the desert, preparing himself to introduce Christ to the world. This was more of a hilly than a sandy desert; deep gulches, arid soil, rocky precipices stretched everywhere. Even today, except in spring, wild animals are still the main inhabitants of that gloomy region. The poor people in that country eat locusts today, a food that is not very palatable unless it is properly prepared. This shows that John was accustomed to hardship and loneliness. Only men of exceptional character could live such a life of privation. In John, we have a picture of the prophets of old who recalled the people to God. John deserves to be known as the greatest of the prophets. Stern looking, thin, unkempt, but with a piercing eye and a certain majesty of bearing, John showed the effects of his years of thought.

Why should men leave the life of a city and go out to hear this voice in the wilderness? At that time in Jerusalem, most religious teaching had degenerated into cold formalism, red tape, countless rules. The Pharisees, the leaders, emphasized details and regarded holiness as consisting in minute observance of every fine point. Over six hundred such rules confronted the conscientious Jew. John was the exact opposite of such leaders. "The bronzed countenance, the unshorn locks, the close-pressed lips, the leathern girdle, the mantle of camel's hair, would at once betoken that here at last was a man who was a man indeed in all his natural grandeur and dauntless force. . . . Men felt in him that power of mastery which is always granted to perfect self-denial. He who is superior to the common ambitions of man is superior also to their common timidities. If he have little to hope from the favor of his fellows he has little to fear from their dislike; with nothing to gain from the administration of servile flattery he has nothing to lose by the expression of just rebuke" (Farrar).

And so the merchants who were riding by with their caravans, the soldiers on the march, stopped along the Jordan and listened. They told their acquaintances in Jerusalem about this mighty torrent of denunciation. People from the countryside, leaders of religious life in the city came out to hear; for the real fact is that God had given John the grace which draws men.

> LUKE 3: 4. As it was written in the book of sayings of Isaias the prophet: A voice of one crying in the wilderness: Prepare ye the way of the Lord, make straight his paths. 5. Every valley shall be filled; and every mountain and hill shall be brought low; and the crooked shall be made straight; and the rough ways plain: 6. And all flesh shall see the salvation of God.

John was this voice in the wilderness. A comparison drawn from the physical condition of the country supplies a description of his work. Roads were seldom kept in good condition in the days of Isaias. When a king was to make a journey, workmen went ahead of him to prepare the way, to level off hills, fill valleys, and thus straighten out the roads and make them passable. John was straightening out human hearts so that Christ might enter.

> LUKE 3: 7. He said therefore to the multitudes that went forth to be baptized by him: Ye offspring of vipers, who hath shewed you to flee from the wrath to come? 8. Bring forth therefore fruits worthy of penance, and do not begin to say: We have Abraham for our father. For I say unto you, that God is able of these stones to raise up children to Abraham.

Some of the crowd were moved to penance and asked for baptism. By "offspring of vipers," John meant the leaders, the Pharisees and Sadducees, for most of them were hypocrites. The Pharisees were religious experts who set themselves up as best acquainted with the Law of Moses and most faithful in its observance. They were strict to the *n*th degree. They had the holier-than-thou appearance; they remained aloof, and scorned the common rabble. Yet the people regarded them as nationalists who were struggling for the freedom of the nation. The Sadducees were the party of the ruling priests. They were broad-minded in that they believed in mixing with the Romans, with pagan culture. They rejected many of the old beliefs of the Jews; they were what we call materialists. Frequently we shall hear Christ condemn these two classes because they sinned by excess, but in different directions. (For the time of Christ we can consider the Scribes as teachers, as professors, or theologians. They were not priests, but were attached to the Pharisees.) John condemned both of these parties because of their formalism, their external piety, their lack of sincere, humble love of God.

> LUKE 3: 10. And the people asked him, saying: What then shall we do? 11. And he answering, said to them: He that hath two coats, let him give to him that hath none; and he that hath meat, let him do in like manner. 12. And the publicans also came to be baptized, and said to him: Master, what shall we do? 13. But he said to them: Do nothing more than that which is appointed you. 14. And the soldiers also asked him, saying: And what shall we do? And he said to them: Do violence to no man; neither calumniate any man; and be content with your pay.

John's preaching was more effective with the people than with the leaders. He advised corporal works of mercy as an aid in obtaining forgiveness of sins (Cf. Tob. 12: 8–15). Publicans were the social outcasts (Matthew was one). They were often dishonest; their business of collecting taxes and exchanging Jewish money for Roman gave them opportunities to cheat. The Pharisees despised them for their very trade. Also, it is interesting to note the influence of John over the soldiers — rough, worldly-wise, sensual, yet with some good in them.

> LUKE 3: 15. And as the people were of opinion, and all were thinking in their hearts of John, that perhaps he might be the Christ: 16. John answered, saying unto all: I indeed baptize you with water; but there shall come one mightier than I, the latchet of whose shoes I am not worthy to loose: he shall baptize you with the Holy Ghost and with fire. 17. Whose fan is in his hand, and he will purge his floor, and will gather the wheat into his barn; but the chaff he will burn with unquenchable fire.

It is important to note this high regard of the common people for the honest and sincere John. The prophets had had a noble record throughout the history of the Jews; but for four hundred years no prophet had appeared. Now, hopes were afire again with expectation that John was the long-awaited Messias.

Christ was as yet unknown. John was the hero of the hour; his power was on the increase. However, he was too great a man to assume false dignities. Humbly he placed Christ far above himself. His baptism was only an external rite. It placed people in the right spirit to receive Christ. Wheat, to be threshed, was piled on a hard floor. Then, either oxen would walk over it, or it would be beaten with flails. A large fan was used to blow the chaff off to the side where it could be gathered and burned. Christ would winnow, would not be deceived, would know true contrition from hypocrisy.

1. What was the purpose of the baptism conferred by John the Baptist?
2. What was the purpose of the prophets in ancient Jewish life?
3. Contrast John with the average religious teacher of his day.
4. How would you explain John's power over the people?
5. What is the meaning of the word "precursor"?
6. Distinguish between the Pharisees, Sadducees, and Scribes.
7. Who were the Publicans?
8. Show that success did not make John the Baptist proud.
9. Do you resent correction if you know that the one giving it is living up to what he preaches?
10. What is the value of corporal works of mercy?
11. Just how would your good example to non-Catholics prepare the way for Christ's entrance into their lives?

Chapter 12

HOW TO MERIT GOD'S APPROVAL

MATT. 3: 13. Then cometh Jesus from Galilee to the Jordan unto John, to be baptized by him. 14. But John stayed him, saying: I ought to be baptized by thee, and comest thou to me?

THE peace of earth's holiest home was now to be disturbed. The hidden years had drawn to a close. Strong as was the bond between mother and Son, God decreed that it was time for His Son to bid farewell to His Mother. The shadow of Calvary was already reaching up to that haven of peace in Nazareth. From henceforth Christ would have no home, nowhere to lay His head. Apparently Mary had to remain behind for the present. She must have realized that sorrow, defeat, and hatred lay along the path that Christ would in future tread.

Within the space of four months, John had become famous. It was now the month of January of the year 28. Christ was over thirty years of age. It was the beginning of His public career. Perhaps He joined a group going south and east to the Jordan. He was under no obligation to place Himself among these penitents. However, He wished to set us an example of humility. This action fitted in with God's plan of the Innocent One taking upon Himself the guilt of the guilty. He was to be a leader who asked no exemptions from the obligations which rested upon His followers.

John had heard from his mother the facts about Jesus. However, he did not of his own power recognize Christ. The Holy Ghost seems to have enlightened John (John 1: 31–34). Most of the crowd for that day had already been baptized, and no one was aware of what was soon to happen. The keen eyes of John however, picked out this unobtrusive Stranger. Stern, fiery, dauntless had been this prophet before the high and low of Jerusalem. Now his severity melted; he knew that he was in the presence of Sanctity. He refused to act as a cleanser of One whom the Holy Ghost had assured him was God. It must have touched John to see the willingness of Christ in this matter, sinless as He was.

> MATT. 3: 15. And Jesus answering, said to him: Suffer it to be so now. For so it becometh us to fulfill all justice. Then he suffered him.

Something about that face, those eyes, convinced John that his duty was to obey. Christ told him that it was the right thing to do. Our main duty is always to do what seems to be the will of God. Perhaps John did not realize that, by thus coming to him, Christ was showing the world that John was a true prophet of God. He set His seal of approval upon the work of the Baptist. Moreover, although sin was repugnant to Christ, He acted the part of a penitent in order to show us that we should never shun any humiliating duty. If we possess some of Christ's humility, we shall, for example, never feel any sustained dislike for going to confession. God asks us to confess our sins; we do it.

> MATT. 3: 16. And Jesus being baptized, forthwith came out of the water: and lo, the heavens were opened to him: and he saw the Spirit of God descending as a dove, and coming upon him.
> 17. And behold a voice from heaven, saying: This is my beloved Son, in whom I am well pleased.

The Holy Ghost is represented by a dove, a visible symbol of the invisible Spirit of peace. Most likely the Spirit was seen only by John and Jesus. From the time of the consent of the Blessed Mary, the third Person of the Trinity had guided Christ, directed His life according to the wishes of the Father. God is indeed One; but He manifests Himself in different ways.

The work of our redemption was inaugurated at this moment. All of the Persons of the Trinity co-operated in this scene. Christ had always been God. He did not become God at this moment. But all who believe in God should see that here God solemnly presented His Son to the world as Redeemer. Now began the public entrance of Jesus on His redemptive task.

From this scene also we learn that all of Christ's actions in these hidden years had been pleasing to God. The new Adam had been loyal throughout His period of preparation. No greater praise could ever come to a young person than to hear these words spoken in his or her praise. God has given each one of us a commission, to become pleasing to Him. We have been dedicated to this one and unchangeable purpose of all Catholic education: namely, the use of our talents, our positions, our successes or failures in such a way that they will reflect honor on God our Father. Christ is our model; He gave us the example on how to acquire this quality of pleasing God.

Our Baptism is our public dedication to Christ, our enrollment under our divine Leader. In Baptism we are joined up with Christ; we are adopted by God. If we keep that baptismal promise to accept Christ fully, to adhere to Him always, then we shall merit words of approval from God. Our daily loyalty in little things, in the performance of duties that no one seems to notice, that continue year after year — these loyalties please God. We cannot all be famous or popular; but we all can be pleasing to God if we wish. Any good deed or word performed with the motive of pleasing God is a supernatural act.

1. Why did Christ come to be baptized by John?
2. How do we know that God was pleased at Christ's actions?
3. What made John the Baptist hesitate to baptize Christ?
4. Can a student become pleasing to God solely by his own efforts?
5. If we aim to "let God do it all" in the process of becoming Christlike are we really making progress?
6. What is our main duty in life?
7. What relation has Christ's submission in a rite of penance to the person who says that he, or she, does not want to go to confession because confession is humiliating?

Chapter 13

JESUS WAS TEMPTED

MATT. 4: 1. Then Jesus was led by the spirit into the desert, to be tempted by the devil.

THREE points concern us in this verse: (*a*) Jesus submitted His life to the guidance of the Holy Ghost. Jesus had free will, but to teach us always to follow God's will, He here obeyed the dictates of the Holy Ghost.

b) The existence of devils is certain. The word *demon* signifies that the devil has an intellectual and spiritual nature. The word *devil* means one who spreads false reports, who cleverly fashions evil. Christ frequently mentioned the devils. He did not accept their existence just to accommodate Himself to a superstition of the time. Satan is a reality, a fallen angel (Isa. 14: 12, 13; Luke 10: 18; 2 Pet. 2: 4; Jude 1: 6), whose aim is to prevent us from reaching heaven. Jesus being God, knew of the world of spirits, the world that we cannot see with mortal eyes. If, however, we study closely the falsehoods spread about Christ, if we analyze the worst hatred shown against the Church, we shall find reason to believe in devils. Again, if we observe the attacks often made on good people, especially the hatred against the saints, we can only conclude that the spirit of evil prompts such things.

However, not all temptations come directly from the devil. There is a triple source — the world, the flesh, the devil. The world allures many away from God; the devil need not work on them. The flesh captivates multitudes. Perhaps the majority of temptations arise from these two sources. The great hatred of the devil is against holiness. He directs his activities particularly against those who are high in sanctity; he tries especially to allure those who are leaders. To rise high in greatness of any kind, or in holiness, is to draw special attention from the evil spirit. And, even in our day, we cannot say that the influence of the devil is lacking in such dark designs as those put forth in Russia or Mexico.

c) The Holy Ghost led Christ into the desert to be tempted; God permits temptations to come to us. A temptation is a test to determine what choice we shall make. "And because thou wast acceptable to God, it was necessary that temptation should prove thee" (Tob. 12: 13). No one is excused from this trial. A person is not bad just because he or she is tempted. Temptations to hate, to steal, to become impure, to read obscene literature, to neglect prayer, Mass, and Communion may arise from our environment, our friends, ill health, our craving for recognition. If we resist and conquer we prove our worthiness to be considered friends of God.

From within, Christ was not subject to temptation. He could not be tempted by thoughts or impulses such as harass us. But since He was truly a Man, He could be tempted from without. His human nature experienced the full force of these temptations, just as we do. He did not permit His divine nature to buoy Him up so as to make victory easy. These temptations in the desert were real; He heard and realized the appeal of the devil. This attack of Satan is the greatest effort ever made by the powers of darkness. By winning over Adam, the devil cut off the entire human race from God. Christ was the new Adam, the promised Messias, come to break this hold of the devil on mankind. The devil knew Christ was a Man, was the promised Messias; but he may not have known that Christ was both God and Man.

> MATT. 4: 2. And when he had fasted forty days and forty nights, afterwards he was hungry.

To appreciate this situation, recall the previous lesson, where God the Father had publicly praised His Son. That brought joy to the heart of Christ. But the contentment of peace is often shattered by the sound of battle. We watch Jesus leave that baptismal scene of glory and depart for the solitude of the desert. Directly west of Jericho the bleak, desert hills rise sudden and steep. We know something of the heat and lonesomeness of our American desert south of Salt Lake. The desert of Palestine, a little west and north of Jericho is desolate, bare, full of precipices, and dangerous. Even today one may get lost in it. In this month of January it was dreary, wet, ugly. Jesus was a brave Man to face this lonesome vigil.

No food, no human companionship (Luke 4: 1) eased that struggle of Christ. As God He could foresee Calvary. The hatred of men, the weakness of the apostles, our own failures to be loyal to Him rose disgustingly before Him. But He laid His plan of battle. And so earnest was His prayer that perhaps it was long before hunger and physical weakness made themselves felt.

This forty-day retreat was the immediate preparation for the two and a half years of public life. We learn here the value of retreats. With Christ as a companion during days of silence we have an opportunity to chart courses of action, to analyze our probable temptations. Just as Jesus, during these days, counted the cost of offering His life for us, so we need to reflect on what we shall have to suffer in order to be thoroughly Catholic. We are not obligated to fast to the extent Christ did; we must learn to do penance, to plan on how to please Him. Then we shall not be so fretful about our eating; we shall be more inclined to pray as He did.

> MATT. 4: 3. And the tempter coming said to him: If thou be the Son of God, command that these stones be made bread. 4. Who answered and said: It is written: Not in bread alone doth man live, but in every word that proceedeth from the mouth of God.

The devil knew Christ was hungry. His purpose in this battle was to lead Christ into a false step, to trick Him, to induce Him to do something different from what the Holy Ghost would suggest. Man has a right to food. And if these desert stones had been whipped by the winds into loaflike shapes, what was more plausible, more fitting for God to do than to turn them into bread! By his "if," the devil may have intended to taunt Christ. But, though Jesus was hungry and weak, His Father's wish was that He should fast, that He should not yet work miracles. Christ's duty at that moment was to trust His Father, to wait for the Father to provide. The devil suggested that He should use His own power, instead of waiting for God's good time.

Instantly Christ retorted that the really important food (for the soul) is obedience to God's word. Christ did not come to bring food for our bodies, but for our souls, and to do His Father's will. Later, Christ did not refuse to supply food for those in need of it. But here, since the invitation was from a bad source, since it was for a selfish use of power, since it was intended to trick Him into breaking away from the guidance of the Holy Ghost, He refused utterly to show off.

The point for us in this first temptation is to avoid the inclination to *sensuality,* which is a wrong use of things that please the senses. God gave us our senses and our appetites. They are good in themselves, but they must be regulated by reason and by God's law. Material things are necessary to us, but fulfillment of material needs does not necessarily lead to happiness. Happiness is found by relying on God's word as a guide on proper use of the senses, the appetites. The example of Christ resolutely refusing to satisfy the apparently innocent suggestion of the devil calls loudly to us to guard against a wrong use of the pleasures of the flesh, and to refuse to seek only material comfort.

> MATT. 4: 5. Then the devil took him up into the holy city, and set him upon the pinnacle of the temple, 6. And said to him: If thou be the Son of God, cast thyself down, for it is written: That he hath given his angels charge over thee, and in their hands shall they bear thee up, lest perhaps thou dash thy foot against a stone. 7. Jesus said to him: It is written again: Thou shalt not tempt the Lord thy God.

It is likely that the devil appeared in human form. But we do not know whether God permitted the devil to take Christ physically to the Temple, or whether this was merely a picture placed before the imagination of Christ. In any case, the temptation was a real fact. It was an invitation to the sin of *presumption.* Christ had answered the devil with Scripture in the first case; now the devil seeks to back his invitation with Scripture, with the very word of God, as do many men, who take a text and pervert its true sense. Satan's argument was that if Christ threw Himself off the Temple and was unhurt, then the people would accept Him as Messias. But presumption is an insult to God, asking Him to protect or forgive us while we deliberately defy His commands. Christ tells us that we must ask only for what is right and just.

Sometimes a young man or woman is asked to jump off the heights of virtue — just for a thrill, or to be "one of the crowd." The excuses offered by the tempter are manifold — that one will not get caught, that all the others do it, that a sin is forgiven in the next confession. It is presumption to argue that one can "get away with it." Presumption stirs the wrath of God. It is wrong also to ask God to make up for our laziness, our lack of prudent foresight. If a saint were to neglect his teeth, he would be subject to toothache just the same as anyone else. We sometimes rashly get ourselves into a jam and then blame God if He does not get us out of it. God's help comes only if we employ common sense and prudence and do those things which He expects us to do. A boy who is lazy during the school year and then prays for success in examination will receive very little help from God. And just as Satan may have been trying to find out if Christ was really divine, so those who tempt us to sins of presumption may be trying to test our loyalty to God. Also, we must note the subtle effort of Satan to make Christ attract attention to Himself rather than to His Father. It is the same as when we seek to be praised by others instead of giving the praise to God.

> MATT. 4: 8. Again the devil took him up into a very high mountain, and shewed him all the kingdoms of the world, and the glory of them, 9. And said to him: All these will I give thee, if falling down thou wilt adore me. 10. Then Jesus saith to him: Begone, Satan: for it is written: The Lord thy God shalt thou adore, and him only shalt thou serve.

This last temptation is the most subtle of those recorded. The devil may have known that Christ had been promised a kingdom. He certainly suspected that Christ had within Him unusual powers. And he may have thought that, since Christ was innocent and inexperienced in things of this world, he could play upon this inexperience and upon the human craving for fame, power, wealth. He drew a picture of Egyptian wonders, Grecian loveliness, Roman power, and the wealth of the Indian princes. As a picture such a scene was attractive. And the devil promised all of that to Christ — Christ, the unknown, lonely, weak, friendless Man of the forty-day fast. But note: it was promised on one condition — that this Man would adore the devil, would sell His soul to the prince of evil, would choose Satan in preference to God the Father. What an important word is that small "if." Here was the crucial test of the new Adam. The original Adam and Eve had listened to the devil thousands of years previous to this time; now the devil sought to deceive the new Adam. How his words must have shocked Christ! Christ was the highest of holy souls and now He was tempted to sell His soul. Vice assaulted Sanctity.

The Light of the world was here battling alone against the prince of the kingdom of darkness. It was a bitter, relentless, and cleverly worded attempt to deceive. For the devil is the father of lies. He cannot dispose of the things of this world; he can only promise, draw pictures, allure. At that very moment when he spoke of the glory of these kingdoms, Tiberius was emperor in Rome. Power, wealth, splendor, and luxury were his. And yet he was called "confessedly the most gloomy of mankind" (Tac. *Ann.* 6: 6). We owe thanks to Christ for showing us how to tear the mask off of the temptations of life, and to say, as He said with firmness: "Begone, Satan." Christ recognized the emptiness of the promise and established the principle that God alone is to be adored.

We naturally desire fame, wealth, and popularity. Sometimes they are promised to us *under certain conditions.* We hear of others who have wealth, good times, success. The desire grows in us of obtaining these things. Then we learn that they often are to be obtained at the price of breaking some principle, or of selling our souls. A girl is told that she will be popular if she allows certain liberties; a young man is promised a rich reward if he enters into a shady deal. The third temptation of Christ teaches us to examine carefully the promises that are made to us, the alluring pictures that come before our imaginations. They who give up their religion just to get ahead in the social or business world are in reality adoring the devil. Never sacrifice principle just to gain power or popularity. In fact, we must each examine our dominant ambitions from time to time to see if we are tending to forget God and to worship the devil. The things for which we strive habitually may become gods to us.

In these three temptations to *sensuality*, to *presumption*, and to *pride of power* Christ teaches us to attack firmly those suggestions of the devil, or of his agents, which would influence us to spurn God. The appeal of temptation is often plausible, innocent-looking; it comes often at our weakest moment, when we are tired, oppressed, discouraged; and it attacks our weakest point of character, our poverty, our vanity, our ambitions.

This whole scene teaches us:

a) That temptation in itself is no sin; both good and bad people are tempted. The sin lies in the consent, in our will.

b) Intelligent examination of the source and motive of the temptation is essential. Does the proposition seem to come from God, or from the world, the flesh, and the devil?

c) Previous loyalties (daily prayer, daily self-control) develop in us a sensitiveness, a clearness of conscience by which we readily detect the approach of temptation and recognize it as such. We must develop this sensitiveness in regard to honesty, purity, humility, loyalty, and truthfulness.

d) Not to hesitate; to act with decision, as Christ did. Do not play with temptation, or tell yourself that you will permit it to remain for a few minutes.

e) A previously arranged plan of action helps us to act with decision at the moment of trial. "Begone, Satan," shows that Christ had not been taken unaware.

f) Temptation, trial, sorrow, have value for our spiritual development (Cf. Tob. 12: 7–9; Acts 9: 16; 2 Cor. 12: 7–9).

g) God will help at the proper time (Cf. 1 Cor. 10: 13; Heb. 2: 18).

h) A good practice in all temptations is to ask ourselves: What would Christ or Mary do if He or she were in our situation?

> MATT. 4: 11. Then the devil left him; and behold angels came and ministered to him.

The devil failed in his taunts, his empty promises. He attempted to induce Christ to exchange His loyalty to His Father for worldly promises. In each case Christ left the devil no crumb of victory, no wiser on the true, divine nature of the Man whom he tempted. The devil would return later to the fight, when Christ would be weak from scourging and apparent defeat. But at this moment the devil was completely baffled. He had employed his most insidious means; he had failed. And now the divine majesty of infinite holiness caused Satan to flee in terror. What strength in those two words: "Begone, Satan." They showed the devil that Christ recognized him for what he was. Vice is a coward in the face of indignant, manly virtue. A young Catholic statesman, with little money but a lot of honesty, was promised a chance to run for a high office if he would permit a wealthy man, who had little virtue, to run with him. The whole future of this young man was at stake. He was threatened with being dropped from the ticket unless he ran with this man. But indignantly he thundered *NO!* He stood alone; weaker men fell away from him. But he ran, and he won; and his record was clear. As Satan fled in fury from Christ, angels came to feed Him. God aids those who remain obedient to His will. Having "conquered Satan himself, Jesus came out of the desert to conquer him among men."

1. What reasons have we for believing that devils actually exist?
2. What leads us to believe that no one is free from temptation?
3. Do all temptations come directly from the devil?
4. In what way was Christ subject to temptation?
5. What do we mean when we say that Christ came to destroy the hold of Satan on the human race?
6. What qualities in Christ's character are shown by His withdrawal into the desert? What is the value of retreats?
7. Explain the nature of each of the temptations of Christ.
8. Why is the devil called the father of lies?
9. Name eight practical conclusions in regard to temptation.
10. Explain the meaning of James 1: 12, 13.
11. Read the life of the *Curé of Ars* by K. O'Meara (Ave Maria Press) or, by H. Ghéon (Sheed and Ward), and *St. Anthony the Hermit,* by St. Athanasius, trans. by J. McLaughlin (Benziger), to see how the devil sometimes works visibly against the saints.
12. Does the fact that Christ went through the lonely vigil of forty days and the temptations bring Him closer to you?

Chapter 14

AN INTRODUCTION

> JOHN 1: 15. John beareth witness of him, and crieth out, saying: This was he of whom I spoke: He that shall come after me, is preferred before me: because he was before me.

WE RETURN now to John the Baptist, the witness of the Light, the man sent by God to introduce Christ to the world. While Christ was in the desert, the Baptist tried to convince his audience that Jesus was eternal and hence was greater in dignity and prior in time to himself.

> JOHN 1: 16. And of his fullness we all have received, and grace for grace. 17. For the law was given by Moses; grace and truth came by Jesus Christ. 18. No man hath seen God at any time: the only begotten Son who is in the bosom of the Father, he hath declared him.

The Baptist did not speak these words. They are comments added by John the apostle when he wrote this Gospel. The Jews had lived under the written Law given to them by God through Moses. The Law was the means by which the Jews preserved the truth of monotheism through fourteen centuries while other nations languished in idolatry. The truths which Christ brought to us are, however, more complete than those delivered to the Jews. We still use some of the Law (the Commandments); and the Church dispenses to us the grace and truth brought by Christ. No man has ever seen God. It was some visible representation which Moses saw in the Old Testament times (Exod. 19: 9). But Christ, being divine Himself, knows who God is and what He is like. Christ has revealed to us what kind of person God is. If we wish to learn something about God, we must listen to what Christ has told us; for it is eternal, unchangeable truth, and can be had only from Christ and the Church.

JOHN 1: 19. And this is the testimony of John, when the Jews sent from Jerusalem priests and Levites to him, to ask him: Who art thou? 20. And he confessed, and did not deny: and he confessed: I am not the Christ. 21. And they asked him: What then? Art thou Elias? And he said: I am not. Art thou the prophet? And he answered: No. 22. They said therefore unto him: Who art thou, that we may give an answer to them that sent us? What sayest thou of thyself? 23. He said: I am the voice of one crying in the wilderness: Make straight the way of the Lord, as said the prophet Isaias.

In Jewish society religious leaders were also the political leaders. These men began to feel concerned about the growing power of the preacher by the Jordan. Since he had no commission from them to teach religious truth, they sent out an investigating committee to make inquiries as to who he was. John knew the rumors circulating about his being the expected Messias. He denied the rumors. Neither would he consent to be called Elias, who, according to a prophecy in Malachias (4: 5), was to return before the "dreadful day of the Lord." But since they had to bring an answer back to their superiors, they asked what he had to say for himself. He was merely a "voice" for someone else.

JOHN 1: 24. And they that were sent, were of the Pharisees. 25. And they asked him, and said to him: Why then dost thou baptize, if thou be not Christ, nor Elias, nor the prophet? 26. John answered them, saying: I baptize with water; but there hath stood one in the midst of you, whom you know not. 27. The same is he that shall come after me, who is preferred before me: the latchet of whose shoe I am not worthy to loose. 28. These things were done in Bethania, beyond the Jordan, where John was baptizing.

John saw that they were really not interested so much in the Messias as in the petty question of teaching without their permission. He drew them back to the one point that they should be considering, namely, that the Messias was in their midst; and he chided them for their ignorance. It was a custom for servants to remove the sandals from the feet of their masters when these latter entered a home. So humble was John that he did not consider himself worthy to do this servile task for Christ. This Bethania was on the eastern side of the Jordan.

* *

Show that John the Baptist did not seek to exalt himself. What are the two important things we have obtained through Christ? How do we know what God is like?

* *

JOHN 1: 29. The next day, John saw Jesus coming to him, and he saith: Behold the Lamb of God, behold him who taketh away the sin of the world.

The day after the visit of the committee, John was startled by the figure of a Man approaching. The scene of the baptism of Christ came back to him. He had probably been puzzled at the disappearance of Christ a month and a half previous; now here He was again. Christ was alone, probably showing the signs of His recent fast. John called his followers to attention. He uttered a sentence which is the most perfect picture of this strange, lonesome Man that could be painted at that time— the *Lamb of God*. No better introduction could have been given. The mention of the word *lamb* brought before their minds not merely a meek creature, but also a victim, an offering made to God in the sacrifices. Each Jew knew that the blood of a lamb had once saved their forefathers from destruction in Egypt (Exod. 12: 1–14). God's plans mature slowly. The paschal lamb was a symbol, a prefigure of the Lamb that was to come. After the lapse of centuries, the divine Lamb had appeared who was to offer Himself that others might be saved. John, in a single, prophetic flash understood that Christ was to become our Redeemer by His sacrifice on Calvary.

JOHN 1: 30. This is he, of whom I said: After me there cometh a man, who is preferred before me: because he was before me.
31. And I knew him not, but that he may be made manifest in Israel, therefore am I come baptizing with water. 32. And John gave testimony, saying: I saw the Spirit coming down, as a dove from heaven, and he remained upon him. 33. And I knew him not; but he who sent me to baptize with water, said to me: He upon whom thou shalt see the Spirit descending, and remaining

upon him, he it is that baptizeth with the Holy Ghost. 34. And
I saw, and I gave testimony, that this is the Son of God.

While the disciples were listening, their master related how he had not known Christ as God, but that he had been enlightened when he saw heaven pay its tribute to the lowly Nazarene. From the time of that vision, John could think of nothing else; he gave witness to (spoke the truth about) Christ whenever he had the chance.

Again Christ passed on. Among those followers of John, to whom Christ had been pointed out, was the man who later wrote this Gospel. John the apostle was an eyewitness when Christ was called the Lamb of God. What were his thoughts as he watched the receding Figure? On what did he reflect during the night that followed? The Baptist had said that this Man was the Son of God; but very likely the full meaning of that term escaped even the keenest followers of John.

JOHN 1: 35. The next day again John stood, and two of his
disciples. 36. And beholding Jesus walking, he saith: Behold
the Lamb of God. 37. And the two disciples heard him speak,
and they followed Jesus.

John the apostle now gives in his own words the story of his first meeting with Christ. He and Andrew were two of the followers of John the Baptist. Again they had their attention drawn to that mysterious Stranger. From the Baptist came that laconic statement, full of mystery, full of suggestion. This was the second time in two days that he repeated it. It was a hint; delicately John was telling these two disciples that Jesus was the Man for them to follow. A struggle undoubtedly went on within their breasts. They were attached to John; they knew little of the Stranger. Yet, they felt a pull on their hearts to follow Him. It was like the scene in many a home when a boy announces that he is going to leave those whom he loves to serve One who is love itself, or when a girl announces that she is going to enter the convent. It was a manly thing in the Baptist to permit his followers to attach themselves to Jesus; it is a mark of nobility in parents not to hinder their children from answering the call to go to the service of Christ. But that was John's task, to prepare men for Christ. And so he permitted two of his best students to transfer their allegiance to the Lamb of God.

JOHN 1: 38. And Jesus turning, and seeing them following him,
saith to them: What seek you? Who said to him: Rabbi (which
is to say, being interpreted, Master), where dwellest thou?
39. He saith to them: Come and see. They came, and saw where
he abode, and they stayed with him that day: now it was about
the tenth hour.

The two must have been somewhat perturbed at the question. It is a rule with Christ to test the faith of those who come to Him. We must "seek" Christ if we are to develop into true Catholics. Christ does not dwell in cheap literature, in lewd shows, in low conversations, in gawdy palaces. The fact that the young men here used the term *Rabbi* (Master) shows that the very presence of Jesus drew from them a term of reverence. They rejoiced at His answer: "Come and see"—an invitation and a test. Christ leaves us free to accept or to reject. He does not make the path too easy at the start. He came on earth in order that we might seek Him; and He is found only by those who seek. The fact that our parents were good Catholics is not a sign that we shall be the same unless we seek personally to know Him. If Christ sees that we are anxious to develop, to learn, then He invites us to come closer to Him. If we accept the "come," the first grace, then other graces will be given later by which we shall "see" the marvelous privilege that is ours of being friends of Jesus. That was the experience of these first students of Christ.

John the Baptist undoubtedly felt some sadness, mingled with a deeper joy, as he watched these noble two disappear into the distance, going with Christ to that "abode," a cave or the shelter of some leafy bush. It was four o'clock. We do not know what they talked about. "Presence alone often says more than long discourses: a master mind, living, intelligent, and loving is able, even in silence, to exercise influence on and to take captive those who are near" (Didon). It is difficult for any young person to know Christ and not to love Him. These young men loved Him forevermore, just from that one visit.

JOHN 1: 40. And Andrew, the brother of Simon Peter, was one
of the two who had heard of John, and followed him. 41. He
findeth first his brother Simon, and saith to him: We have found
the Messias, which is, being interpreted, the Christ. 42. And he
brought him to Jesus. And Jesus looking upon him, said: Thou

art Simon the son of Jona: thou shalt be called Cephas, which is interpreted Peter.

Andrew could not keep the good news to himself. His eagerness to tell his brother, Simon, gives some hint of the hopes that burned in pious Jewish hearts at that time. The Baptist had attracted these men from the north. All of the apostles, except Judas, were Galileans. John introduced some very good men to our Lord. And there are many honest people outside the Church today; they long for the truth; we should be anxious to tell them what we find in Christ.

In verse 42 we have the first glimpse into the plan of Christ for His Church. Who would have guessed that in this ardent, impetuous, kindly, wholehearted but unstable brother of Andrew, Christ saw material for a future pope. He read Simon's character in an instant. He saw that the virtues outweighed the faults. What a meeting that was! Those eyes of the lonely Nazarene looked right into the soul of Simon; and for once in his life Simon was too overwhelmed to make any remarks. Humanly speaking, we might say that Jesus ran a risk in attaching to the lovable but somewhat weak Simon, the name, Peter, which means rock (a symbol for stability). The power of grace to aid a willing and humble person is well exemplified in St. Peter. He founded the papacy, which is a symbol of supernatural strength. And the primacy of Peter was hinted at in this very first meeting. Only later did Peter realize what Christ meant when He conferred this name on him; only later could he appreciate the love and care with which Christ shielded him during two and a half years.

John 1: 43. On the following day, he would go forth into Galilee, and he findeth Philip. And Jesus saith to him: Follow me. 44. Now Philip was of Bethsaida, the city of Andrew and Peter.

The scene shifts now. Christ went northward. He had been away from Galilee for more than two months. On the way he met another future apostle, Philip. He was a quiet, humble sort of person who never pushed himself forward. Christ handled him differently from the others. He realized that Philip needed encouragement, hence He said: "Follow Me." In those simple words He won the "meekest of the future twelve apostles." This fact gives us a clue to the marvelous personality that Christ possessed, to the drawing power that went out from Him when He chose to use it. Philip received no warning; yet he accepted. And sometimes in our day a boy or girl will suddenly realize that Christ is calling. A vocation sometimes comes without previous warning.

> JOHN 1: 45. Philip findeth Nathanael, and saith to him: We
> have found him of whom Moses in the law, and the prophets did
> write, Jesus the son of Joseph of Nazareth. 46. And Nathanael
> said to him: Can any thing of good come from Nazareth?
> Philip saith to him: Come and see. 47. Jesus saw Nathanael
> coming to him, and he saith of him: Behold an Israelite indeed,
> in whom there is no guile. 48. Nathanael saith to him: Whence
> knowest thou me? Jesus answered, and said to him: Before that
> Philip called thee, when thou wast under the fig tree, I saw thee.
> 49. Nathanael answered him, and said: Rabbi, thou art the Son
> of God, thou art the king of Israel. 50. Jesus answered, and
> said to him: Because I said unto thee: I saw thee under the fig
> tree, thou believest: greater things than these shalt thou see.
> 51. And he saith to him: Amen, amen I say to you, you shall
> see the heaven opened, and the angels of God ascending and
> descending upon the Son of man.

Like Andrew, Philip became enthusiastic. Nathanael (Bartholomew), who lived in Cana and not far from Nazareth, evidently did not have a high regard for the town of Nazareth, consequently he was rather cold toward Philip's enthusiasm. (This shows how little was known of Christ's real nature during the hidden years of His life.) Philip was probably pitied by Nathanael for being so unintelligent as to believe that a prophet could arise from an insignificant, boorish community like Nazareth. Philip was willing to allow the very presence of Jesus to work its effect on high-spirited Nathanael. As the two of them approached Christ, the latter casually remarked to some near Him, within the hearing of Nathanael, that he (Nathanael) was a true man, frank and honest. The compliment startled Nathanael. He had come to size up Christ. Instead, he himself underwent a scrutiny. With a sort of superior tone he asked Christ how He knew him. He had been reading or meditating under the shade of a tree, and apparently he had been far from Christ. Now he was subdued.

As is often the case when a strong character "sees the light," he gave himself heart and soul to the Nazarene. It is difficult to determine the full meaning that he intended behind the term, "Son of God"; but it is certain that he was won over to our Lord. To a Jew the opening of heaven signified the assistance of God coming to man (Gen. 28: 10–15).

Our Lord often called Himself the Son of Man. He probably intended to show His close relation to us, that He is a true member of the human race. It was an act of humility for one who was divine thus to associate Himself with mankind. Students need never feel that Christ is too far above them to be approached. He became Man for this very reason, that we might call Him *Friend.* The most significant aspect of the attachment of these first few apostles to Jesus is that He won them by His very personality and character. The change in the attitude of Nathanael was rapid. No miracle had been worked. Thus does Jesus influence those who come close to Him.

Christ now had five followers, though they were not yet selected as continuous companions. They went back to their work. It is very instructive to study His method in choosing these men. He knew how to adapt Himself to each type. Most of them were fishermen. A fisherman knows how to wait, to be patient. "He lays down his net and leaves the rest to God." So, Christ's priests must be patient, willing to do their best and to leave the results to God. Moreover, Christ brought these men out of obscurity into the limelight of the world's stage. They were willing though slow students. By the very fact of making us Catholics, God has called us to a new life, not to worldly prominence, perhaps, but to significance in the kingdom of God. He expects us to make good, to be conscious of our obligations as Catholics, as His personal representatives in this modern world, a world which we are supposed to lead to Christ. By a Christlike life we introduce Christ to many who are ignorant of Him. The words, "Follow Me," still echo across the centuries. Christ continues to call young men and women to enter the priesthood or religious life and to carry on His work. The call is addressed to the Nathanaels as well as to the Philips, to the Peters and Johns and Andrews, to the Marys and the Marthas.

(This is not the appointing of these men as apostles - later.)

1. If you were the captain of a team and a younger member was gradually getting ahead of you in fame, would you aid that member to gain more fame?
2. Give the origin and the meaning of the *Agnus Dei, qui tollis peccata mundi* of the Mass.
3. One mother tries to push her girl into the convent; another tries by every means possible to prevent her girl from becoming a nun. What is wrong in both cases?
4. What is the meaning of the word "redemption" in our religion?
5. Show that God calls the young to the priesthood and convent in different ways.
6. What thought is suggested by Andrew's actions after he had met our Lord?
7. How is a boy to find out if he has the qualifications to become a priest or a brother?
8. Show that St. Peter's life is a good example of what grace may aid us to do.
9. What was it in Christ that so attracted strong, clean, energetic men?
10. What is the meaning of the word *Peter* or *Cephas?*
11. Can a student who has serious faults become a saint?
12. A student refuses to read any Catholic literature but feeds his mind on the attacks made against religion and the Church. Gradually he begins to complain that he cannot "see" anything in the Church. Can he honestly say that he is seeking the truth?

Chapter 15

"YOU ARE CORDIALLY INVITED"

JOHN 2: 1. And the third day, there was a marriage in Cana of Galilee: and the mother of Jesus was there. 2. And Jesus also was invited, and his disciples, to the marriage.

IT WAS now springtime, perhaps late March. Jesus and the disciples may have gone to Nazareth, or Mary may have sent word that she was going to the marriage and that Jesus was also invited. Evidently Christ was invited because of Mary. He was still the Man without fame. However, in the East the wedding is the outstanding event of a man's life, and he generously invites as many as possible for that ceremony, which has many attractive features.

At the outset we note a marked contrast between John's stern, unrelenting life of solitude and Christ's contact with people. "It was His intention to enter among the joys of the world to sanctify them, among its pleasures to make them wholesome, among sinners to convert them" (Le Camus). Christ is not a kill-joy. But that does not mean that He approves the types of pleasures that are often held before the young people of today. Family pleasures and wholesome fun were found at this marriage feast. Our own homes should be the scenes of our parties. He wants fun to be clean. Any pleasure that does not stain a clean conscience is permissible. Our rule is: not to indulge in pleasures of which Christ would be ashamed or to which we could not invite Him. We should recall that "though burdened with the high commission of the Messias, He retained a vivid interest in all things human" (Geikie).

JOHN 2: 3. And the wine failing, the mother of Jesus saith to him: They have no wine. 4. And Jesus saith to her: Woman, what is that to me and to thee? My hour is not yet come. 5. His mother saith to the waiters: Whatsoever he shall say to you, do ye.

Wedding feasts might last a week; this young couple may have been poor. And nothing is more embarrassing in the East than to fail to provide for guests. Mary, with her motherly heart, foresaw the plight of the hosts. She was alert to the needs of others. Patiently through the years of the hidden life she had refused to ask divine favors from her Son. But now His public life was beginning. In true, womanly fashion she did not ask outright; she made known to Him a need. She hinted that He had power to relieve the situation. Divine though He is, she did not hesitate to approach Him in the matter of human happiness.

His reply seems harsh. In reality, there is no disrespect in it (Cf. John 19: 26; Matt. 15: 28). In the original language the word *woman,* as here used, does not bear any reproof or severity. Here, just as in the Temple, Christ wished to establish the principle that governed His life — in working miracles He followed the will of His heavenly Father. He did not say that Mary had done anything wrong in asking; but He stated that every action of ours must be guided by the will of God. There are sometimes higher considerations to be followed than even the wishes of our mothers. Christ had as yet no indication from His Father that He should begin working miracles. But, since He is God, as well as the Redeemer sent by the Father, He could grant the petition for Mary. And Mary understood. She told the waiters to do whatever Christ should tell them. Evidently they knew her better than they knew Him at this time.

John 2: 6. Now there were set there six waterpots of stone, according to the manner of the purifying of the Jews, containing two or three measures apiece. 7. Jesus saith to them: Fill the waterpots with water. And they filled them up to the brim. 8. And Jesus saith to them: Draw out now, and carry to the chief steward of the feast. And they carried it. 9. And when the chief steward had tasted the water made wine, and knew not whence it was but the waiters knew who had drawn the water; the chief steward calleth the bridegroom. 10. And saith to him: Every man at first setteth forth good wine, and when men have well drunk, then that which is worse. But thou hast kept the good wine until now.

Water was carried from a common well to the homes. The numerous ceremonial washings among the Jews necessitated, in the home, large jars for the water. Extra large jars may have been provided to care for the needs of the number of guests. We are not certain, but these six jars may have held almost a hundred gallons. The jars were so full that anyone could see the contents. Astonished, the servants obeyed Him. The quality of the wine was excellent. There was no deception. Picture the relief of the bridegroom and the humility of Christ in remaining in the background, for the chief steward gave the credit to the bridegroom.

In the desert Christ refused the devil because He would have been using His divine powers for His own satisfaction and without the authorization of His Father. But to work a miracle for others is unselfish; and His heart always warmed to human needs. To be taunted by the devil is one thing; to be asked by His Mother is another.

When we reflect on the unexpected blessing that Christ added to this marriage feast, the question arises of the Catholic ideal of marriage in Christ. Is He to be cordially invited to your wedding? A man and woman before marriage may take a selfish view and think of themselves only, may imagine that marriage is a private affair. Christ made it a holy affair. They unite for the purpose of co-operating with God in the rearing of children who will reflect honor on God. That is why marriage is a sacred thing—it means co-partnership with God. Marriage as Christ instituted it means that at a Catholic wedding the young couple receive a sacrament, that is, grace and help from God to assist them in the process of developing Christlike children, and also to aid them in becoming holy themselves. If Christ rules the home, happiness will normally be found in the home. Just as His presence brought joy to this young couple, so too His aid, His grace will sweeten the home where He is invited to abide. What a noble career marriage is when viewed as a joint project with God, an undertaking rendered difficult in the case of a mixed marriage.

JOHN 2: **11.** This beginning of miracles did Jesus in Cana of Galilee; and manifested his glory, and his disciples believed in him. 12. After this he went down to Capharnaum, he and his mother, and his brethren, and his disciples: and they remained there not many days.

Christ's miracles were open, visible, evident. Never did He perform them for selfish reasons, but rather to relieve suffering humanity and to lead men to God. His miracles were always good deeds, with no trace of trickery.

This first miracle brought the Nazarene definitely out on the public stage of life. He showed Himself to be in sympathy with the simple joys of honest people. Nathanael was already seeing marvels. "His miracles declare His might; and in these flashes of power He stands forth revealed, as in the fierce white glare of the lightning, the almighty Son of God" (Pascal). Must not Mary have been thrilled also — she who had believed and waited for this manifestation of His divine nature? The journey to Capharnaum, which was on the lake, was a joyful one. The "brethren" spoken of here may have been children of a brother of Joseph, or of Mary's sister

1. Contrast the beginnings of Christ's ministry with John the Baptist's.
2. What reasons have we for believing that God does not seek to take joy out of the lives of people?
3. May a man or woman marry without thought of the future religious training of the children that come into the home?
4. If a person lives in a home where there is continual quarreling and unhappiness, what might he do to help the situation?
5. Would Christ be at the ceremony if a young Catholic couple refused to be married before a priest?
6. Have we any solid reasons for believing that Mary will intercede for us to God?
7. What mistake does a person make if he imagines that God is not interested in him?
8. What principle did Christ teach us by refusing to use His power at the suggestion of the devil and by using it at the petition of Mary for human needs?
9. How and why is marriage more than a private affair?
10. Why would a real Catholic, in our present marriage customs, refuse to have the wedding in the evening, since there is a special nuptial Mass?
11. Look up the character of the parents of the Little Flower.
12. When the husband earns enough to support a family, why is it wrong for the wife to seek work outside the home?

Chapter 16

CHRISTLIKENESS INCLUDES HONESTY AND JUSTICE

> JOHN 2: 13. And the pasch of the Jews was at hand, and Jesus went up to Jerusalem.

THE Pasch (Hebrew word meaning *passover*) was one of the three annual feasts that drew Jews from everywhere to Jerusalem. It was celebrated in memory of that time in Egypt when the destroying angel killed the first-born of the Egyptians but *passed over* those Jewish homes that had doorposts sprinkled with the blood of a lamb (Exod. 12: 14).

> JOHN 2: 14. And he found in the temple them that sold oxen and sheep and doves, and the changers of money sitting. 15. And when he had made, as it were, a scourge of little cords, he drove them all out of the temple, the sheep also and the oxen, and the money of the changers he poured out, and the tables he overthrew. 16. And to them that sold doves he said: Take these things hence, and make not the house of my Father a house of traffic. 17. And his disciples remembered, that it was written: The zeal of thy house hath eaten me up.

Thousands of sheep and oxen were required for the sacrifices. The poor could offer doves. And each Israelite had to pay a Temple tax, and only Temple coins could be offered, not foreign money. All of this commerce should have been handled outside the Temple walls, for the outer wall was supposed to separate God's holy place from the world. But underneath the splendid colonnades and in the open court of the Gentiles, a regular market had been established. Greed had crept close to the Holy of Holies.

In the midst of this shouting, bleating, bellowing, and general din, Christ arrived through one of the gates. He glanced around.

The divine energy of that Presence was let loose. The devil, John the Baptist, the five disciples, and the waiters at the marriage had felt Christ's eyes upon them and had obeyed. Outwardly He was still the meek, lowly Nazarene. Suddenly He became the indignant Christ. Here is an example of how strong meekness can be. He was a total stranger to this hardened crew, but fear filled them as they saw Him twist cords into a whip. "Men, sheep, and cattle broke and fled." There was a pell-mell rush to escape from one lone Figure who had justice in His heart and who hated iniquity. Of a sudden, however, He became gentle. The poor people who were selling doves were less at fault. He did not scatter them; He asked them to leave.

Christ merely stood for justice to God, for respect and reverence for holy places. He did not think of Himself, but of honor due to the things of God. It was sacrilegious to make a trading mart out of the Temple. The manner in which He treated the money-changers leads us to believe that their work was not even honest. This was, then, a case of righteous anger — anger at sin, at lack of reverence, and at greed. To be indignant at what is wrong is not a sin; in fact, it is a virtue. What made those traffickers in greed cringe before a just wrath? "Because sin is weakness; because there is in the world nothing so abject as a guilty conscience, nothing so invincible as the sweeping tide of a Godlike indignation against all that is base and wrong. . . . Because Vice cannot stand for one moment before Virtue's uplifted arm" (Farrar).

Jesus also showed strength of character, which means love of truth, of justice, of decency. Our civilization tends to produce "yes" men. We are afraid of losing popularity or our jobs if we launch forth in indignation against abuses. And yet, Christ expects us to stand always for honesty and for justice, and to enter into those movements which will bring social justice to the common men and women. We have much to learn from the *strong* Christ as well as from the meek Christ. This action of Christ gives the lie to the Communistic calumny that religion is the opium of the people. There is social injustice in the eastern hemisphere, but Communism did not arise there. It borrowed its vitality against social injustice from the craving for justice that Christ aroused in the western world.

We reverence a church because it is a place of holy sacrifice and the house of God. It is the center of parish activities. We were baptized in a church; there we first told our serious faults to the priest; there we offer, as a gift to God the Father, Christ's Body and Blood, and receive Communion, which unites us to Christ and increases our capacity to enjoy and understand God's presence; there we hear the words that Christ spoke to His followers; there many of this class will pledge their troth in marriage; there we may go at any time and converse with Him who asks us always to be reverent toward holy places, holy things, holy people.

> JOHN 2: 18. The Jews, therefore, answered, and said to him:
> What sign dost thou shew unto us, seeing thou dost these things?
> 19. Jesus answered, and said to them: Destroy this temple, and
> in three days I will raise it up. 20. The Jews then said: Six and
> forty years was this temple in building; and wilt thou raise it
> up in three days? 21. But he spoke of the temple of his body.
> 22. When therefore he was risen again from the dead, his dis-
> ciples remembered that he had said this, and they believed the
> scripture, and the word that Jesus had said.

From the terraces above, the priests also had been attracted to the confusion. They were the guardians of the Temple; by their connivance these abuses were tolerated. They became jealous and resentful. They approached Christ, towering with rage. But one look from Him and their knees shook. They did not dare accuse Him of wrong, so they meekly asked why He did it. Christ gave them an answer that they never forgot. He was not confronted with honest inquirers, hence His statement is somewhat obscure. Had they really been looking for the truth they would have understood, for Christ probably used a gesture when He said: "Destroy this temple." He pointed to Himself. He was predicting His own resurrection. It was a bold, a confident statement. In their blindness, they read a false meaning into His words. We know that they caught something of the true meaning (Matt. 27: 63), but they preferred now to conclude that He lacked appreciation of this marvelous Temple which had been forty-six years in the building and was not yet finished.

> JOHN 2: 23. Now when he was at Jerusalem, at the pasch, upon
> the festival day, many believed in his name, seeing his signs

which he did. 24. But Jesus did not trust himself unto them for that he knew all men, 25. And because he needed not that any should give testimony of man; for he knew what was in man.

Christ made a deep impression in this first public appearance in Jerusalem. Yet He understood fully the type of people with whom He had to deal in the city itself. One thing that we shall always observe in Him is His judgment, His perfect insight into character. Power, which is very intoxicating and more deadly so than drink, was never able to turn the head of our Lord. He never was deceived, even when most popular. He knew that He would have to bear the cross alone. A leader must, indeed, often live a lonesome life. He must work with men, and yet not be deceived by them. St. Augustine wrote: "It is one thing to love men, and another thing to set one's hopes in man; and the difference is so great that God commands the former and forbids the latter." Our Lord's actions in this scene in the Temple show that He used His power for God's honor; and throughout His life He used it to aid people; but in all that time He knew that He would be rejected. He teaches us to be Christlike in our actions and to do good deeds to others and yet never to become sour, cynical, pessimistic, or discouraged. Even our friends may deceive us; but we must continue in acts of goodness and kindness and remain cheerful because we are working for God, not for popularity.

1. When may one become indignant or angry?
2. What is the origin and meaning of the word *Pasch*?
3. Have you any obligation to aid in keeping corruption out of your city, your state, or national governments?
4. Can there be any such thing as *"honest graft"*?
5. Answer the calumny that Christianity teaches us to submit meekly to social injustice, or that it permits us to condone those who exploit the poor.
6. What is the reason for the reverence we should maintain in churches?
7. How can we avoid becoming "yes" men?
8. What conclusion do you draw from the fact that Christ always was aware of the real enmity that some men bore Him and yet He continued to be good to all men?
9. How would you refute the argument of an agitator that the person who prays is weak?

10. Show that Christ intends that we should use common sense and prudence in our dealing with others at the same time that we practice childlike faith toward God.
11. A non-Catholic boy once said that he went to Mass with a Catholic girl and that as soon as they were in the pew she seemed to forget that he was there and to give all her attention to the Mass. Show why the girl did the right thing.

Work for God not man – never depend upon admiration of people etc. Must show courage, stand upon 2 feet. Sacerdotal dignity of priesthood. (don't want to hurt anyone's feelings!)

Christ was kindness itself to all men – his kindness didn't depend upon thoughts of people but upon love of God. the father

Chapter 17

BIRTH FROM ABOVE

JOHN 3: 1. And there was a man of the Pharisees, named Nicodemus, a ruler of the Jews. 2. This man came to Jesus by night, and said to him: Rabbi, we know that thou art come a teacher from God; for no man can do these signs which thou dost, unless God be with him.

AS A class the Pharisees were hypocritical. But honest and sincere individuals will be found in every class and in every creed. Nicodemus was one of these. He was powerful and well educated. He was a member of the Sanhedrin, which was a sort of Supreme Court, composed of seventy-two members.

Some time must have elapsed between the Temple cleansing and this visit, because all were talking about Christ. It was already socially dangerous for any outstanding Jew to espouse the cause of this Galilean. But Nicodemus was stirred; grace was touching him. The deeds of Christ impressed him. Yet, he was timid. He had what we call human respect. He was afraid to be seen with the Nazarene. However, he *did come*. This man of influence, of education, this "master in Israel" came to one who was not a graduate of the higher Jewish schools. To appreciate his effort, recall the difficulties that confront converts when they realize that the Catholic religion is the one true faith. Their friends, their position, and their inherited prejudices rise up and place a thousand obstacles in the way. So it was with Nicodemus, yet he paid Christ a very high compliment: "teacher from God." In reality He is. When we wish to find out something about God, we look at Christ. Christ interprets God to us and explains the nature of God, for Christ is God as well as Man.

JOHN 3: 3. Jesus answered, and said to him: Amen, amen I say to thee, unless a man be born again, he cannot see the kingdom of God. 4. Nicodemus saith to him: How can a man be born when he is old? Can he enter a second time into his mother's womb, and be born again?

We would expect Christ to be overjoyed at the fact that a prominent man had come to Him. But no, He passed over the compliment and stunned His visitor with a mysterious proposition. No bowing down, no cringing before this man of learning, but like an arrow from the bow came the sharp truth that set at naught all the learning of this Pharisee.

We must ponder long this important truth of being "born again." The birth we receive from our parents is natural; before we can enter the supernatural state we must receive something from above. A new, higher life must come to us. Talent, business ability, eloquence, personality — all these things are natural in us; but even their possession in a high degree does not enable a person to believe in Christ and in the Church. Nicodemus missed the point. Learning did not suffice for the grasp of a supernatural truth. Nicodemus could think of only a second physical and natural birth.

JOHN 3: 5. Jesus answered: Amen, amen I say to thee, unless a man be born again of water and the Holy Ghost, he cannot enter into the kingdom of God. 6. That which is born of the flesh, is flesh; and that which is born of the Spirit, is spirit. 7. Wonder not that I said to thee: You must be born again. 8. The spirit breatheth where he will; and thou hearest his voice, but thou knowest not whence he cometh, and whither he goeth: so is every one that is born of the Spirit.

Christ was patient with His new student. He taught him the meaning of Baptism. We saw (p. 14) what Adam and Eve lost when they sinned. Grace is a sharing in the very life of God. It is ability to know Him as He knows Himself. Grace is thus a new life, a supernatural life, created by God and given to men. Christ came to re-establish this life of grace, this supernatural life in men. Therefore, when Jesus told Nicodemus that we must be born of water and the Spirit, He was teaching the necessity of Baptism. The external sign of each sacrament signifies (and produces) what is going on interiorly. The pouring of water with the proper intention actually cleanses the soul of the inherited guilt, and together with that grace comes the Holy Ghost. "A new God-given and Godlike life is superadded to our natural life. By this very life we are born to God even as the child to its parent." Hence Baptism is a rebirth, a being born from above. We are elevated, joined to the life that Christ came to establish. We become in the full sense adopted children of God. We are not born Catholics; we become such at Baptism. We thus receive status or prominence which is far more enduring than the status men think they receive by joining some new movement or a club.

A gust of wind is invisible to us. So in Baptism, the coming of grace and the coming of the Holy Ghost are invisible. By faith in Christ's word we know that the effects are there. Our ability today to believe in, hope in, and love God is due to this grace which came at Baptism. In a child this supernatural life has to be nourished and developed. It can be permitted to die out, and it can be withdrawn from adults, for it is all a free gift from God; it is not due to us. It is a priceless gift; it gives us a right to call God our Father; it gives us membership with all those joined to Christ. We actually become the Temples of God, for even here on earth the presence of grace is accompanied by the indwelling of the Trinity in us. The deeper our faith, hope, and love, the more shall we enjoy God even here on earth. It is our privilege and duty to live as God-bearers, a fact which makes life glorious and cheerful.

JOHN 3: 9. Nicodemus answered, and said to him: How can
these things be done? 10. Jesus answered, and said to him:
Art thou a master in Israel, and knowest not these things? 11.
Amen, amen, I say to thee, that we speak what we know, and we
testify what we have seen, and you receive not our testimony.
12. If I have spoken to you earthly things, and you believe not;
how will you believe, if I shall speak to you heavenly things?
13. And no man hath ascended into heaven, but he that descended from heaven, the Son of man who is in heaven. 14. And
as Moses lifted up the serpent in the desert, so must the Son of
man be lifted up: 15. That whosoever believeth in him, may
not perish, but may have life everlasting.

Nicodemus was still bewildered — heavy with learning but unable to see the truth. His attitude is repeated in many non-Catholics of today — they attempt to size up the Catholic Church by a human measuring rod. If they were really humble, if they but realized that no human can measure God, if they would reflect that not learning but rather life from above (grace) enables people to believe in the Church, then they would receive light. As Newman says: "Not the keenest eye can see in the dark. Now, though your mind be the eye, the grace of God is the light; and you will as easily exercise your eyes in this sensible world without the sun as you will be able to exercise your mind in the spiritual world without a parallel gift from without." God does indeed expect us to acquire learning. And when He sees honest effort on our part, He gives the grace of belief. While some people want God to bow down before them, Catholics, on the other hand, sometimes expect God to save them without effort on their part. Both extremes are wrong.

Christ had personal experience of everything He taught about God. He did not have to experiment. He alone of all our teachers came from heaven. No scientist, no writer, no human leader has ever been to eternity and returned. Christ has told us all that it is necessary to know. When we believe in Him, we have accurate knowledge. He teaches the inspiring fact of the immortality of the human soul — life everlasting.

> JOHN 3: 16. For God so loved the world, as to give his only-begotten Son; that whosoever believeth in him, may not perish, but may have life everlasting. 17. For God sent not his Son into the world to judge the world, but that the world may be saved by him.

Each individual is worth while; no one is insignificant; no one can truthfully say that God is not interested in Him. God not only gives a soul to each individual, He sent Christ for each one of us. That is what St. John the apostle tells us in these verses, for Christ had ceased speaking. No matter how hard and difficult life may become, it will always remain true that the best description of God is one word — *love.* This love is shown not only by Christ's coming, but also by God's adoption of us at Baptism. God was generous in sending Christ to be our Saviour. It is a startling and strengthening fact that Christ came for each human individual (whosoever), for each unbeliever as well as for ourselves.

1. What type of people of our day resemble Nicodemus?
2. Prove that you cannot reach heaven without a rebirth.
3. What is the meaning of the phrase "birth from above"?
4. Is it necessary to have wide learning in order to appreciate the Catholic religion?
5. What is the reason for sponsors at baptism?
6. Why not wait until one becomes of age before administering Baptism? Does the board of health permit parents to put off vaccination until the children are of age?
7. How may one be saved who has never had a chance to be baptized?
8. What mistake do men of learning often make when they examine the Church?
9. What is meant by life on a supernatural level?
10. How do you account for the fact that some can believe in the Catholic Church and others apparently cannot?
11. How do you know that God is interested in you personally?
12. Memorize verse 16.
13. What is human respect? Show how Cardinal Newman, G. K. Chesterton, Mother Seton, and Joyce Kilmer overcame it and entered the Church.
14. Show that Christ is not too far above the young to be imitated by them.
15. In what sense is God our Father?

Chapter 18

HOW TO CURB JEALOUSY

JOHN 3: 22. After these things Jesus and his disciples came into the land of Judea; and there he abode with them, and baptized. 23. And John also was baptizing in Ennon near Salim; because there was much water there; and they came and were baptized. 24. For John was not yet cast into prison.

PROBABLY, but we are not sure, Jesus now toured the section south of Jerusalem. Followers were coming to His banner, and He instructed them. These followers baptized others, just as did John. This was not sacramental Baptism. It was still a sign of willingness to do penance, a token of attachment to Christ. "Do penance for the kingdom of God is at hand" (Matt. 4: 17). Meanwhile, John was farther north, along the Jordan.

JOHN 3: 25. And there arose a question between some of John's disciples and the Jews concerning purification: 26. And they came to John, and said to him: Rabbi, he that was with thee beyond the Jordan, to whom thou gavest testimony, behold he baptizeth, and all men come to him. 27. John answered and said: A man cannot receive anything, unless it be given him from heaven. 28. You yourselves do bear me witness, that I said: I am not Christ, but that I am sent before him. 29. He that hath the bride, is the bridegroom: but the friend of the bridegroom, who standeth and heareth him, rejoiceth with joy because of the bridegroom's voice. This my joy therefore is fulfilled. 30. He must increase, but I must decrease.

A man who had seen or heard of the baptism conferred by the followers of Christ now met some of John's disciples and perhaps jeered at these latter. The disciples were hurt. They complained to John that Christ would outdo him in popularity. They thought that Christ should be subordinate to John. We should not blame them too much for this jealousy. In their own minds they aimed to be loyal to the Baptist. The great John showed them, and us, how to curb jealousy and how to prevent the rising power of one of our rivals from causing jealousy in our own lives and thus blinding us to the truth. He was too noble to be jealous.

Very seldom do powerful men know when to step out of power. Tyrants attempt to muzzle or to slay rivals to their position. John, revered as he was, calmly told his disciples that Christ would not have this personal magnetism unless God had given it to Him. He repeated that his task was to introduce Christ to the world. He took a figure of speech from the marriage customs of the time. The friend of the bridegroom arranged all the details. He carried the first proposal from the groom to the girl or her parents. And just as the friend of the bridegroom was glad to do this service, so John found his joy in working for Christ. Our chief joy in life should come, not when we are honored, but when we see God honored. Our happiness should be found in bringing others to Christ. Instead of being jealous of beauty, talent, or success in others we should rejoice that they have this opportunity to render high honor to God, who gave them these things. Edification means the habit of seeing the good points in others and trying to imitate them. The student who is edified by goodness, success, popularity, or beauty in others is learning the secret of happiness because jealousy will find no place in him.

We cannot admire John too highly for his willingness to see Christ increase and himself decrease. He believed in the Providence of God, that is, that God permits things to happen to us for our own betterment. If later in life we see others "increase" and ourselves "decrease" God expects us not to be jealous, but to be edified and to regard the fact as part of God's plan for us. Hence we gain strength to curb jealousy by seeing correctly our relation to God. If He gives superior gifts to others, that is their responsibility. God has a purpose in permitting opportunities to come to them that may not come to us. We find our happiness in accepting His arrangements. We will serve Him as best we can according to our situation and will please Him by helping others to succeed.

MARK 6: 17. For Herod himself had sent and apprehended John, and bound him in prison for the sake of Herodias, the wife of Philip his brother, because he had married her. 18. For John said to Herod: It is not lawful for thee to have thy brother's wife. 19. Now Herodias laid snares for him: and was desirous to put him to death, and could not. 20. For Herod feared John, knowing him to be a just and holy man: and kept him, and when he heard him, did many things; and he heard him willingly.

Shortly after John the Baptist had paid his tribute to Christ, he was imprisoned, probably in May of the year 28. This Herod Antipas was a son of the Herod who was ruling when Christ was born. Philip was a half-brother of this Herod Antipas, and Herodias was the wife of Philip. Herod, however, took her from his brother. John proclaimed aloud this sin. The wrath of Herodias was aroused. She was beautiful, fiery, and desirous of power. Now her ambition was to ensnare John to his death. She succeeded in persuading Herod to imprison John, but Herod was afraid as yet to put him to death. Consequently he languished in a dungeon. Meanwhile, jealousy gnawed at the heart of Herodias and later led her into murder. A woman's hatred for a just man was finally to win against morally weak Herod.

At times it is our duty openly to denounce a scandalous situation. It is no excuse to say that nothing can be done about a bad situation. John's example teaches us to cry out against open injustice, public sin, and bold corruption.

1. What is meant by saying that one should take edification as well as give it?
2. Show why a jealous or suspicious person can have little peace of mind.
3. Make a study of one of your "pet peeves" to see if it is based on wrong information or blind prejudice.
4. What do you find to be the best method of fighting against jealousy?
5. Seek in history the incident of Stanton's jeering at Lincoln in a trial at Pittsburgh, and then compare Lincoln's magnanimity in placing Stanton in his cabinet. Then study the generosity of Grant to Lee at the surrender of Appomattox Court House. What two virtues would you say that Lincoln and Grant exemplified in these cases?

6. Show how John the Baptist is an example of the saying: "Too noble to be jealous."
7. Show that one weak spot in a person's character may entrap him into the performance of a heinous crime.

Chapter 19

THE WELL FROM WHICH WE DRAW GRACE

John 4: 1. When Jesus therefore understood that the pharisees had heard that Jesus maketh more disciples, and baptizeth more than John, 2. (Though Jesus himself did not baptize, but his disciples,) 3. He left Judea, and went again into Galilee. 4. And he was of necessity to pass through Samaria. 5. He cometh therefore to a city of Samaria, which is called Sichar, near the land which Jacob gave to his son Joseph. 6. Now Jacob's well was there. Jesus therefore being wearied with his journey, sat thus on the well. It was about the sixth hour.

WE ARE not certain of the length of time that Jesus remained in Judea after His appearance in Jerusalem in April A.D. 28. It is probable that His public ministry was of two years and four months' duration. If so, this trip through Samaria was in May of the year 28. He did not wish to detract from the work of John, so He quietly retired from the scene.

Samaria was the smallest of the three geographical divisions of Palestine. Centuries before, early leaders of the Jews had made this scene hallowed. Jacob and Joseph were beloved heroes of history. But during the exile of the Jews in Babylonia (sixth century B.C.), the Gentiles had intermarried with these Samaritans. Hence a bitter feud sprang up between the Samaritans and the returned exiles of the Judean and Galilean sections. The Samaritans were not allowed to take part in the rebuilding of the Temple of Jerusalem. They were considered heretics. They built their own temple, and thus added fire to the hatred between them and the remaining Jews.

It is important to understand this hatred in order to appreciate Christ's charity. He sat near the famous well that Jacob had built. It is still there. Originally it was perhaps a hundred feet deep. It is a blessing, because the whole countryside, except the well, dries up in the hot months. Water becomes scarce. It is an unwritten law to give water to strangers (Cf. Gen. 33: 19; Josue 24: 32). Jesus sought the shade. The time was noon, when the heat is intense. Jesus was tired. This sole Gospel reference to fatigue shows that Christ was truly human, that He knew the weariness and sweat of toil.

> JOHN 4: 7. There cometh a woman of Samaria, to draw water. Jesus saith to her: Give me to drink. 8. For his disciples were gone into the city to buy meats. 9. Then that Samaritan woman saith to him: How dost thou, being a Jew, ask of me to drink, who am a Samaritan woman? For the Jews do not communicate with the Samaritans.

Usually women came for water in the cool of the evening. But this woman probably wished to avoid the throng that gathered there morning and evening. She was not of good reputation; she would be shunned by the others. But God does not shun sinners. Christ came to save. She observed Him and recognized Him to be a Jew because of His dress. She filled her water pot, which she carried on her head. And then came the voice, which once heard is never forgotten: "Give Me to drink." Sometimes He asks a personal service from us as a condition on which depends a great grace. She was surprised, not at the request for water, but that a Jew would speak to her. Christ here rose above all national prejudices. Jews did not greet women in public; the rabbis, official teachers, would not even teach women. There was a saying: "Burn the Law rather than teach it to a woman." Christ not only talked to a Samaritan, but taught a woman, a public sinner and perhaps an illiterate creature. He could break a custom which was based on snobbery or prejudice.

> JOHN 4: 10. Jesus answered, and said to her: If thou didst know the gift of God, and who he is that saith to thee: Give me to drink; thou perhaps wouldst have asked of him, and he would have given thee living water. 11. The woman saith to him: Sir, thou hast nothing wherein to draw, and the well is deep; from whence then hast thou living water? 12. Art thou greater than our father Jacob, who gave us the well, and drank thereof himself, and his children, and his cattle?

living water means running water (spring) more desireable than well-water.

Some weeks previous He had given to a scholar truths which baffled him; now He came down to the level of this rustic woman. He adjusted His teaching to the occasion and to her background. He started with the natural and led up to the supernatural. He tried to make things with which she was familiar suggest higher, nobler truths. She missed the point. Living water meant spring water as opposed to stagnant or cistern water. The gift of God means grace; it is supernatural life. Just as this woman thought that because Christ lacked a jar He could not give her water, so many today think material things, such as money, food, or clothing, are the only means for getting the most out of life. Actually we need grace; and the only well where these living waters, this supernatural life can be obtained is Christ. The woman made the mistake of not seeing the spiritual meaning of Christ's remarks; the world makes the mistake of judging the Church by her material equipment. Her value, her riches lie in the living waters which Christ has placed at her disposal. Through the Church we are made "partakers of His holiness." If non-Catholics would pray for this "gift of God," they would see the Catholic Faith in a better light.

JOHN 4: 13. Jesus answered, and said to her: Whosoever drinketh of this water, shall thirst again; but he that shall drink of the water that I will give him, shall not thirst for ever: 14. But the water that I will give him, shall become in him a fountain of water, springing up into life everlasting. 15. The woman saith to him: Sir, give me this water, that I may not thirst, nor come hither to draw. 16. Jesus saith to her: Go, call thy husband, and come hither. 17. The woman answered, and said: I have no husband. Jesus said to her: Thou hast said well: I have no husband. 18. For thou hast had five husbands: and he whom thou now hast, is not thy husband. This thou hast said truly.

Christ was patient; He passed over her taunt and continued on the theme of grace. There is an unfailing supply of grace, of merits that Christ stored for us at Calvary. We need never be "thirsty"; we can approach the sacraments. The true Catholic is not restless, discontented. He is calm, peaceful, and not always yearning for material things which rapidly grow old. Grace gradually increases the capacity of the soul to enjoy the Faith here and to appreciate and understand God's presence when we reach heaven. The woman continued to think of natural water. She did not realize that effort on our part is necessary if we wish to receive grace.

Jesus purposely changed the conversation to show her that He knows the secrets of all human hearts. She was still ignorant of His nature, and she refused to reveal her past life to this Stranger, this Jew. But she must have blushed when she realized that her past was an open book to Him.

> JOHN 4: 19. The woman saith to him: Sir, I perceive that thou art a prophet. 20. Our fathers adored on this mountain, and you say, that at Jerusalem is the place where men must adore. 21. Jesus saith to her: Woman, believe me that the hour cometh, when you shall neither on this mountain, nor in Jerusalem, adore the Father. 22. You adore that which you know not: we adore that which we know; for salvation is of the Jews. 23. But the hour cometh, and now is, when the true adorers shall adore the Father in spirit and in truth. For the Father also seeketh such to adore Him. 24. God is a spirit; and they that adore him, must adore him in spirit and in truth.

She paid Him an honest tribute. She also attempted to change an unpleasant subject. By pointing up to the mountains and referring to the feud she tried to distract Jesus. Mt. Garizim is 800 ft. high. The ruins of the Samaritan temple there can still be seen. Both Samaritans and Jews held that there should be but one Temple, but the feud concerned the place which held this one Temple.

He told her that there was some idolatry in the Samaritan worship, and that the Messias was to come from the Jews. Then He rose above all national controversy. The Jews had lost the spirit of religion; the Samaritans had lost part of the truth. Both were to yield to the perfect religion which Christ would inaugurate. Religion must be based on truth. If Christ has told us that there are three Persons in God, then, for instance, the Unitarian religion cannot be based on truth. We have the truth, but we will not profit by being Catholics unless we also have the right spirit of religion, that is, sincerity of heart. Adoration strictly belongs to God alone. By it we acknowledge that He alone is perfect, that He has dominion over us and that we are, therefore, dependent creatures. When we consent to this truth we adore Him. We consent with our minds and desire that He be acknowledged by all. Thus we adore in spirit. The best interior adoration we can give is the consecration of ourselves to Him. Empty forms, lip service, or prayer said with no conviction are not true adoration.

Interior worship (of our minds) is, however, not sufficient. We are both body and soul. We must worship God with our bodies (a genuflection, sign of the cross), as well as with our minds. In exterior worship we give objects to God (bread and wine), but the objects given are tokens or pledges of what we feel interiorly. We give tokens of appreciation to our friends, and we give Christ's Body and Blood to God as a perfect way of adoring and of thanking Him.

> JOHN 4: 25. The woman saith to him: I know that the Messias cometh (who is called Christ); therefore, when he is come, he will tell us all things. 26. Jesus saith to her: I am he, who am speaking with thee.

Messias is a Hebrew word having the same meaning as *Christ*. This is the first clear, open statement from Christ that He is the "anointed One," the promised Messias, the fulfillment of 2,000 years of hope. The fact that He thus revealed Himself to this outcast woman proves that He has a heart of sympathy for the downtrodden, the outcasts of our own day. He sees immortal value in each individual.

> JOHN 4: 27. And immediately his disciples came; and they wondered that he talked with the woman. Yet no man said: What seeketh thou, or why talkest thou with her? 28. The woman therefore left her waterpot, and went her way into the city, and saith to the men there: 29. Come, and see a man who has told me all things whatsoever I have done. Is not he the Christ? 30. They went therefore out of the city, and came unto him.

Naturally the apostles were surprised at the ease with which Christ broke the unreasonable customs of the day. Much of the respect paid to women today is the result of this lesson that we all, poor and rich, black and white, male and female, have equal rights before God. Seeing this charity of Christ, the woman eagerly invited others to come to Him.

JOHN 4: 31. In the mean time the disciples prayed him, saying:
Rabbi, eat. 32. But he said to them: I have meat to eat, which
you know not. 33. The disciples therefore said one to another:
Hath any man brought him to eat? 34. Jesus saith to them:
My meat is to do the will of him that sent me, that I may perfect
his work. 35. Do not you say: There are yet four months, and
then the harvest cometh? Behold, I say to you, lift up your eyes,
and see the countries; for they are white already to harvest.
36. And he that reapeth receiveth wages, and gathereth fruit
unto life everlasting: that both he that soweth, and he that reapeth, may rejoice together. 37. For in this is the saying true:
That it is one man that soweth, and it is another that reapeth.
38. I have sent you to reap that in which you did not labor:
others have labored, and you have entered into their labors.

If we become interested in our work we forget about self-centered cares. "He was contemplating the truth as it came forth out of Judaism to take its flight toward the nations to transform them." He alluded to a popular proverb of that day to suggest that we help people come to God. Ordinarily six months should elapse between seedtime and harvest; but there are two seed-times in Palestine. We cannot say positively that our Lord was here in May. We are using May as the probable time, instead of January.

Christ had but one aim — to do the will of His Father. To render honor to God or to do the will of God is the same thing. The aim of Catholic education is to train a student to become such a type of athlete, lawyer, doctor, nurse, workingman, nun, priest, husband, or wife that God will be honored by the achievement. This is called a supernatural view of life. Christ is our model for learning how to use body and soul, mind and will, talent and disposition in home and school. The important truth He wishes to impress is that the spiritual harvest is always ready — there are always some who want to learn about Christ if we would tell them. Our Lord is the true sower (He gives the grace necessary for conversion). Our highest joy should consist in seeing others find Him. And we must realize that we are debtors to the past. All life is a continuity because the prophets of old did their work well. Because John the Baptist, and later the apostles, and then the faithful Catholics down through the ages worked for God, we have been enabled to enter into the Faith. The self-denials of our parents partly account for this blessing. They brought the Faith to us; now we appreciate it for what it is in itself. If the true, the real Christ be made known to people, He will be loved by many because of what He is. The human mind can always find new delight in studying and imitating Him. No person can ever drink this divine well dry.

1. What was the attitude of a Jew toward a Samaritan, and explain the reason for this attitude.
2. Explain the term *supernatural life.*
3. Why were the disciples surprised that Christ should speak with a woman?
4. Give an example of Christ's method of making a natural truth or practice suggest a spiritual truth or practice.
5. Show that a student who refuses to speak to another is not at heart a true Catholic.
6. Why is it necessary to rise above national prejudices if one wishes to be a disciple of Christ?
7. Explain why there is only one source of supernatural life.
8. Is the prayer called the "morning offering" a good act of adoration? Why?
9. What is the aim of Catholic education?
10. Explain what adoration means, strictly speaking.
11. What truth did Christ teach under the figure of "living water"?

Chapter 20

BELIEF WITHOUT MIRACLES

JOHN 4: 45. And when he was come into Galilee, the Galileans received him, having seen all the things he had done at Jerusalem on the festival day; for they also went to the festival day. 46. He came again therefore into Cana of Galilee, where he made the water wine. And there was a certain ruler, whose son was sick at Capharnaum. 47. He having heard that Jesus was come from Judea into Galilee, went to him, and prayed him to come down, and heal his son; for he was at the point of death. 48. Jesus therefore said to him: Unless you see signs and wonders, you believe not. 49. The ruler saith to him: Lord, come down before that my son die. 50. Jesus saith to him: Go thy way; thy son liveth. The man believed the word which Jesus said to him, and went his way. 51. And as he was going down, his servants met him; and they brought word, saying, that his son lived. 52. He asked therefore of them the hour wherein he grew better. And they said to him: Yesterday, at the seventh hour, the fever left him.

JESUS spent two days with the Samaritans. Then He went north. His fame was spreading. Galileans as a whole gave Him a warmer welcome than did the people around Jerusalem. He passed by Nazareth, and stopped at Cana, from which town the news spread over east to Capharnaum. The latter was on the lake, whose marshy shores often caused a fever in the residents.

The ruler regarded Jesus as one having power to cure, yet our Lord saw that he had a wrong view of why miracles are worked. Christ is primarily a healer of souls; He worked miracles on the body mainly for the purpose of proving His divinity and of arousing faith in Him as God. But this man, like many moderns who visit Lourdes, looked only to the outward healing, without catching the fact that inward healing (conversion, or renewed faith in Christ) is the real purpose of miracles. Christ taught the ruler the right kind of faith. God is truth. Christ in the very appearance of His character showed power and goodness. He did not need credentials; He could be trusted. The Samaritans had received Him without asking for miracles. Christ demands faith because God loved us before we were aware of it. He has a right to a faith that does not depend on miraculous events, a faith given because of the true character of Him who is our teacher. The official had thought that Christ's presence was necessary to effect a cure; he learned that distance does not lessen God's power. The man finally trusted Jesus and started home, a journey of twenty miles. It was afternoon when Jesus told him that his son would live. The next day, while still traveling home, he learned of the reward for his faith.

Luke 4: 15. And he taught in their synagogues, and was magnified by all. 16. And he came to Nazareth, where he was brought up: and he went into the synagogue, according to his custom, on the sabbath day; and he rose up to read. 17. And the book of Isaias the prophet was delivered unto him. And as he unfolded the book, he found the place where it was written: 18. The spirit of the Lord is upon me, wherefore he hath anointed me to preach the gospel to the poor, he hath sent me to heal the contrite of heart: 19. To preach deliverance to the captives, and sight to the blind, to set at liberty them that are bruised, to preach the acceptable year of the Lord, and the day of reward.

Synagogues served as meeting houses and as schools. A competent layman could read the Scriptures and give a sermon. Evidently our Lord went from town to town. Finally He arrived at Nazareth. Strange rumors had preceded Him. This is His first recorded return to His home town. St. Luke indicates that Nazareth was the place where He had spent all those years of hidden life. A large crowd had come; they asked Him to read. (Cf. Isa. 61: 1–2, which is a passage referring to the freeing of the Jews from their Babylonian captivity of the sixth century B.C. The same passage also fits the task that Christ had come to perform.) The acceptable year (jubilee year) occurred every fifty years, at which time slaves were freed and debts were wiped out

(Lev. 25: 8–10). Christ's coming brought freedom from the slavery of sin and restoration of the right to heaven.

> LUKE 4: 20. And when he had folded the book, he restored it to the minister, and sat down. And the eyes of all in the synagogue were fixed on him. 21. And he began to say to them: This day is fulfilled this scripture in your ears. 22. And all gave testimony to him: and they wondered at the words of grace that proceeded from his mouth, and they said: Is not this the son of Joseph? 23. And he said to them: Doubtless you will say to me this similitude: Physician, heal thyself: as great things as we have heard done in Capharnaum, do also here in thy own country.

His sitting down on a raised platform in the middle of the synagogue was a sign that He intended to preach. Breathlessly the people waited. When Christ spoke, the charm of His speech was irresistible. These crude, narrow, jealous villagers were overwhelmed by the tone of voice, the dignified bearing, the piercing eye, the spell of divine charm.

However, they soon began to reflect. He was claiming that He was the Messias, the one sent to accomplish the words of Isaias. In their minds the Messias meant the long expected liberator, who would release them from the crushing burden of Roman power. Their constant fear of drought, their sufferings under all too prevalent blindness would also be relieved when the Messias came. They imagined a life of abundance under his rule. Jesus, however, was only the carpenter's Son. It was impossible that He, one of their own, could rise above them to become the Messias! Moreover, He had slighted them by doing deeds elsewhere which He had never done at home. And now He would not work a miracle for them! Jealousy, small-town jealousy, flared up, as one might expect from the excitable, violent nature of these people. They might hear a sermon in silence, but in comments afterward they would give vent to their strong feelings. If He would work no miracles they would have revenge on Him.

Jesus read their thoughts. He knew that their worldly minds were looking for a spectacular performance. Like many of our day, they were unwilling to believe unless astounding miracles were accomplished before their eyes.

LUKE 4: 24. And he said: Amen I say to you, that no prophet
is accepted in his own country. 25. In truth I say to you, there
were many widows in the days of Elias in Israel, when heaven
was shut up three years and six months, when there was a great
famine throughout all the earth. 26. And to none of them was
Elias sent, but to Sarepta of Sidon, to a widow woman. 27. And
there were many lepers in Israel in the time of Eliseus the
prophet: and none of them was cleansed but Naaman the Syrian.
28. And all they in the synagogue, hearing these things, were
filled with anger. 29. And they rose up and thrust him out of the
city; and they brought him to the brow of the hill, whereon their
city was built, that they might cast him down headlong. 30. But
he passing through the midst of them, went his way.

Christ cited two instances of history in which prophets passed by their own people and went to the more worthy Gentiles. He knew that His neighbors resented His working miracles elsewhere after having lived so long among them without showing them His power.

He had come back to Nazareth with heart aglow at the presence of the familiar scenes of His boyhood. Momentarily His winning grace of divine presence stirred them, but the final outcome was jealousy and an attempt to push Him off a hill onto the rocks below. May we not believe that there was one who watched all this with a breaking heart? Mary had seen His power at Cana; and the neighbors had been inquisitive for many months. Henceforth the sword of sorrow would pierce her as the neighbors shunned her and sneered at her Son. Yes, Mary had to suffer.

He sought no revenge. He used omnipotence to bless, to cure, not to hurt. The evil they attempted against Him proves that He had diagnosed correctly their inner thoughts. But He forgave them. Something about His presence, His eye, His dignity overwhelmed them. Calm and serene, with the poise of a divine majesty, He passed from among them. Not a hand had power to stop Him, such was the force of His presence when He wished to use it. Perhaps He went to say good-by to His Mother, to strengthen her for rejections of the future that would be yet more brutal.

To refuse the solemn word of a friend would be an insult to Him. The Nazarenes refused to believe Christ; they thereby drove Truth from among them. We know that God is Truth; we know the character of Christ. We should believe the statements of

Christ and avoid that attitude which continually demands proofs, miracles, and signs. The modern who says: "Show me a soul, and I will believe," does not usually want proof. He would not believe even if he saw a soul or a miracle. In reality he wants God to bow down before him.

1. Why does God demand deep faith in us, or good will in a non-Catholic, before He gives light to see the real value of our religion?
2. What purpose did Christ have in His visible healings?
3. What was the jubilee year?
4. How do you explain the fact that the Nazarenes rejected Christ?
5. Why should we rejoice when one of our own succeeds?
6. Should we be willing to forgive petty jealousies among those of our own home town?
7. Show that God has a right to be believed without miraculous proofs of His existence and goodness.

Chapter 21

CHOOSING MEN TO SPREAD THE KINGDOM

LUKE 4: 31. And he went down into Capharnaum, a city of Galilee; and there he taught them on the sabbath days.
MARK 1: 22. And they were astonished at his doctrine. For he was teaching them as one having power, and not as the scribes.

CAPHARNAUM was to become "His own city" (Matt. 9: 1), the center of His activities. It was a thriving city then. Perhaps Mary accompanied Him to Capharnaum, to be with Him, and to avoid the bitterness of the Nazarenes.

On weekdays Christ spent much time by Himself. But on the Sabbath, when crowds would assemble in the synagogues, He preached. We would expect marvelous, penetrating thoughts from the God-Man. Small wonder that the people were astonished. His very words, flowing in limpid clearness and divine force, were His authority.

MATT. 4: 17. From that time Jesus began to preach, and to say: Do penance, for the kingdom of heaven is at hand.

The word *penance* is not pleasant to hear; but who has not some selfishness, some attitude which blocks the light of grace? And penance makes one conscious of the *kingdom,* which word needs an explanation.

a) The word *kingdom* before Christ came.
During long centuries the Jews had hoped that God would establish Himself among them. Captured often by surrounding nations, the Jews meditated on the prophecies concerning the redeemer and His reign. They read their own meaning into them. The phrase "kingdom of God" became a slogan, a catchword with them (Dan. 7: 27). Slogans are easily misinterpreted. The Jews wanted to triumph over their enemies, and so the majority grad-

ually built up a picture of the redeemer as a powerful, worldly ruler. They dreamed of warlike triumphs under his banner.

b) Christ's interpretation of the *kingdom*.

The people heard joyously from His lips that word *kingdom*. For more than two years He attempted to tell them its true meaning. At first they listened, because of His miracles and speeches that burned themselves into people's minds. Gradually they realized that He was rejecting the popular interpretation of the slogan. He was to be a king, yes, but with no earthly territory — a ruler of men's minds and hearts.

The word *kingdom* occurs over a hundred times in the New Testament, but not always in the same sense. Sometimes it refers to the external, visible organization of the Church. At other times it is concerned with the interior attitude of the individual toward God. Again, we may say that it means simply the state of grace. It is "Jesus known, tasted, and possessed." It is supernatural life established in us. Human beings must gain back that kind of life which Adam lost — the life of sanctifying grace. Christ came to give this life of the soul. When we accept Jesus, when we are baptized, and receive the sacraments, then the kingdom of God becomes established in us. The amount of influence Christ exerts on us, the extent to which we meditate on His words, the degree to which we co-operate with the grace — all this determines what we "see" in religion. It is very well to live an athletic life, a social life, a business, a literary life, but over and above all that another life must go on developing within us — the life of living daily for God.

> MARK 1: 16. And passing by the sea of Galilee, he saw Simon and Andrew his brother, casting nets into the sea (for they were fishermen). 17. And Jesus said to them: Come after me, and I will make you to become fishers of men. 18. And immediately leaving their nets, they followed him.

He had not yet definitely attached the disciples to Himself. They had not forgotten, however, the power of His presence. And when they saw Him along the shore of the lake they readily yielded to the "come." There was no hesitation. We admire their generosity. They abandoned their positions, which gave to them a living, to enter an uncertain future. John and James were evidently men of some standing. A future lay before them in the fishing business. Sorrowfully, perhaps, Zebedee saw his two promising sons leave him for a higher call.

How aptly Christ foretold their future work from their present occupation. The nature of the kingdom, the truth about the Catholic Church must be explained to men in every generation. The world distorts the teachings of Christ, and so He now began to make arrangements for a visible organization to explain the kingdom. Christ asks all of us to do that today. The laity can explain the purpose of life to men and women who never have occasion to come in contact with priests.

MARK 1: 29. And immediately going out of the synagogue they came into the house of Simon and Andrew, with James and John. 30. And Simon's wife's mother lay in a fit of a fever: and forthwith they tell him of her. 31. And coming to her he lifted her up, taking her by the hand; and immediately the fever left her, and she ministered unto them. 32. And when it was evening, after sunset, they brought to him all that were ill and that were possessed with devils. 33. And all the city was gathered together at the door. 34. And he healed many that were troubled with divers diseases; and he cast out many devils, and he suffered them not to speak, because they knew him. 35. And rising very early, going out, he went into a desert place: and there he prayed. 36. And Simon, and they that were with him, followed after him. 37. And when they had found him, they said to him: All seek for thee.

Quietly and early the next morning Jesus slipped away, to avoid the curious throng. He wanted time to converse with His Father. He was never too busy to pray. Even His followers could not distract Him from this habit. He probably asked them to leave Him alone, while He went to other cities. He also wants us to retire from the crowds now and then that we may enter a church and pray.

LUKE 5: 1. And it came to pass, that when the multitudes pressed upon him to hear the word of God, he stood by the lake of Genesareth, 2. And saw two ships standing by the lake: but the fishermen were gone out of them, and were washing their nets. 3. And going into one of the ships that was Simon's, he desired him to draw back a little from the land. And sitting he taught the multitudes out of the ship. 4. Now when he had ceased to speak, he said to Simon: Launch out into the deep, and let down your nets for a draught. 5. And Simon answering said to him: Master, we have labored all the night, and have taken nothing: but at thy word I will let down the net.

A few days later Christ appeared along the lake. Genesareth, Sea of Galilee, Sea of Tiberias, are names for the same lake. It is thirteen miles long and seven wide at the middle and, in places, one hundred and sixty feet deep.

His public life was now in full swing. Here in Galilee multitudes thronged about Him. Soon the hatred felt toward Him down in Jerusalem would reach up to Galilee to strike at Him. But for the time being these Northerners exulted in Him. He spoke to them in the open. Picture the boat in the placid, blue waters, and His voice rolling up along the shore, while the crowd listened in silence as He told them about His Father and about the kingdom. Christ still speaks from Peter's bark. And there are clear, strong words coming from the Pope as he teaches in Christ's name.

What a sudden shift — from preaching to fishing! The disciples had been spellbound by His sermon; and now they heard Him, who was not a fisher, give orders to expert fishermen. It was a test. It was the most unfavorable hour for fishing. As usual, Peter was outspoken. He admitted to this inexperienced Fisherman that they, the experts, had not caught anything. That admission is rather unusual in a fisherman. It seemed foolish to try again; Peter wanted it known that it was only because Christ had asked it that they would venture forth. We admire Peter's humility in obeying. Whatever God asks us to do, we should attempt, no matter whether we think the project will fail or succeed.

LUKE 5: 6. And when they had done this, they enclosed a very great multitude of fishes, and their net broke. 7. And they beckoned to their partners that were in the other ship, that they should come and help them. And they came, and filled both the ships, so that they were almost sinking.

Fishing suddenly became exciting. Christ must have had a twinkle in His eye as He watched the frantic efforts and yells of experienced fishers. In the scramble He was completely forgotten; "in moments of excitement and prosperity Jesus of Nazareth is easily ignored" (Goodier). We are prone to attribute our success to ourselves and to blame God for our failures.

> LUKE 5: 8. Which when Simon Peter saw, he fell down at Jesus' knees, saying: Depart from me, for I am a sinful man, O Lord. 9. For he was wholly astonished, and all that were with him, at the draught of the fishes which they had taken. 10. And so were also James and John the sons of Zebedee, who were Simon's partners. And Jesus saith to Simon: Fear not: from henceforth thou shalt catch men.

Noble-hearted, unselfish Peter was the first to realize that the catch was a gift from Christ. It was a reward for trust in Jesus. His first meeting with the Nazarene, the miracle of the marriage feast and the curing of his mother-in-law flashed through his mind. Underneath "the rough, outward garb of this man of Nazareth," Peter discerned something above the human, something that had its origin in the infinite holiness of God, something that was especially good to a poor fisherman, and manly Peter confessed his unworthiness to be in the presence of such Goodness. Peter was a commander, a leader. But he realized that he had certain weaknesses. The beautiful trait about him, however, was his frankness.

All in the boat heard the words of Peter. With awe they watched the future pope go down on his knees before his Lord. They liked Peter; so did Christ. Reassuringly Christ raised him up; "Fear not." Christ is patient with our faults, if we will give Him our hearts. As usual, He had a purpose behind the whole scene. He was preparing these men for the work of the priesthood and for the task of persuading men to enter the kingdom to which Christ has already called us. Christ knew the difficulties in the work. He wished to show us that without Him we shall labor all the night in vain; with Him we shall have spiritual success. Christ expects all of us to work hard, but whether worldly success or failure comes to us He wants us to continue to trust Him.

LUKE 5: 11. And having brought their ships to land, leaving all things, they followed him.

From now on, the apostles would be with Christ continually. They gave up all to go with Him. The privileged days of personal, intimate companionship with the divine Teacher had begun. From contact with the Leader they would gradually learn the nature of the kingdom.

1. When God commands a thing, why should we obey even when we can see no prospect of success?
2. What evidence have we as to the effect of Christ's sermons?
3. Describe an incident which brings out Peter's traits of character.
4. Show that Christ took time out for prayer even when He was busy.
5. How did Christ show His preference for Peter as a leader?
6. What motive should induce students to prepare for participation in the work of the Catholic Evidence Guild? In spreading books and pamphlets on religion? In advertising the Catholic radio programs?

Chapter 22

THE PHYSICIAN FOR SPIRITUAL SICKNESS

MARK 1: 40. And there came a leper to him, beseeching him, and kneeling down, said to him: if thou wilt, thou canst make me clean. 41. And Jesus having compassion on him, stretched forth his hand; and touching him, saith to him: I will. Be thou made clean. 42. And when he had spoken, immediately the leprosy departed from him, and he was made clean.

ORDINARILY lepers would not dare to approach people, for leprosy is one of the most loathsome of diseases. It is a living death. Flesh drops off the fingers; lips and nose may disappear; ulcers may cover the entire body when the disease is well advanced. No plague was more dreaded than leprosy. Lepers were social outcasts. They were banished from their homes and friends and lived in caves. They had to shout: "Unclean, unclean," if anyone ever came near them.

This man "full of leprosy," had heard of Jesus. He made bold to approach. At such an action, many rabbis would have hurled stones at him or run in horror. But Christ stopped. The man knelt while the startled disciples watched. The leper's action showed his faith. "If thou wilt, thou canst make me clean." It was a beautiful prayer. He simply put his case in Christ's hands. He showed faith and restraint.

Christ understands. The Law forbade anyone to touch a leper. Christ reached down and touched the poor man, a thing that was not necessary but which demonstrates His sympathy with those who suffer in life. He knew the leper's longing. He appreciated the delicate trust shown by the victim. Thus the leper has taught us how to pray — to leave things in God's hands and to accept whatever God wills. At the healing touch came the healing words:

"I will." God can create; He can heal miraculously, visibly, and instantaneously. Flesh, skin, health appeared. The gratitude in the upturned face of the outcast brought joy to Christ, just as it pleases Him when we show gratitude. Where He sees the proper disposition He is infinitely generous.

> Mark 1: 43. And he strictly charged him, and forthwith sent him away. 44. And he saith to him: See thou tell no one; but go, shew thyself to the high priest, and offer for thy cleansing the things that Moses commanded, for a testimony to them. 45. But he being gone out, began to publish, and to blaze abroad the word; so that he could not openly go into the city, but was without in desert places: and they flocked to him from all sides.

Christ did not linger. He passed on, after bestowing generous graces. He did not mean that the man should say nothing about the cure, for He ordered him to report to the priests as the Law required. What Christ did have in mind was to prevent added talk about His miracles. Such talk would cloud the issue about His Person, His purpose on earth. The more this popularity grew, the more Christ retired into desert places. Always in the midst of busy days He took time out to be alone with God, His Father. He refused to bask in the sunshine of popularity.

The manner in which this healing of the leper is related indicates some of the characteristic touches of St. Mark's Gospel. We are not positive that Mark ever saw Christ, but it is probable (Cf. Mark 14: 51–52). Eventually he became the secretary of St. Peter. People in Rome, who heard Peter preach, asked Mark to put in writing a summary of Peter's words. This was the human occasion for the writing of the second Gospel. Mark does not give many of the discourses of our Lord; he emphasizes the miracles. He presents a picture of Christ as Lord of all things. He adds many human touches, showing the noble manhood of Jesus. Such sentences as: "I will; be thou made clean," or, "Come apart into a desert place and rest a little. For there were many coming and going; and they had not so much as time to eat" (Mark 6: 31), show that Mark wished to portray the attractiveness of Jesus.

> Mark 2: 1. And again he entered into Capharnaum after some days. 2. And it was heard that he was in the house, and many came together, so that there was no room; no, not even at the

door; and he spoke to them the word. 3. And they came to him, bringing one sick of the palsy, who was carried by four. 4. And when they could not offer him unto him for the multitude, they uncovered the roof where he was; and opening it, they let down the bed wherein the man sick of the palsy lay. 5. And when Jesus had seen their faith, he saith to the sick of the palsy: Son, thy sins are forgiven thee.

In this city He had hitherto been welcome. It was a business center, a meeting place of the highways of trade and a fishing emporium. The rabbis had been hurt by His popularity. They thought that their authority was being undermined. So the intellectuals of Jerusalem, the religious leaders came to Capharnaum to aid in curbing our Lord (Luke 5: 17). Among the crowd that gathered in that house were spies, heresy hunters.

Often there were outside stairs to the houses. The roofs were flat and were merely covered with tiles or baked pieces of dirt. The men who thus got their friend into the presence of Jesus did not realize that they were putting Him on trial before His enemies. The faith of the people was not dampened by the hostility of their own leaders. Our Lord knew that He was being watched. Dramatic stillness settled over the crowd. No matter what interpretation the rabbis would put on this action of Jesus, He intended to reward faith. He observed the rough faces of the four — faces that reflected confidence in Him. He looked at the Scribes and Pharisees. He then turned to the paralytic, who had hoped for a physical cure. The physician for spiritual sickness had searched his soul and read his secret sins. In this case the disease was the result of a sinful life. But there was sorrow, and so Jesus pronounced the words of absolution.

MARK 2: 6. And there were some of the scribes sitting there, and thinking in their hearts: 7. Why doth this man speak thus? He blasphemeth. Who can forgive sins, but God only? 8. Which Jesus presently knowing in his spirit, that they so thought within themselves, saith to them: Why think you these things in your hearts? 9. Which is easier, to say to the sick of the palsy: Thy sins are forgiven thee: or to say: Arise, take up thy bed and walk? 10. But that you may know that the Son of man hath power on earth to forgive sins (he saith to the sick of the palsy), 11. I say to thee: Arise take up thy bed, and go into thy house. 12. And immediately he arose; and taking up his bed, went his way in the sight of all, so that all wondered and glorified God, saying: We never saw the like.

The crowd had looked for a miracle. No one expected a revelation of the cause of the disease. More astounded still were the learned doctors of the Law, who understood fully what was implied in Christ's words. They had come to judge a miracle worker; they were confronted by One who did things that only God would dare to do. It is blasphemy for a man to assume to himself one of the attributes of God. They realized that He was making Himself equal to God.

The Scribes were afraid to say anything openly because the crowd was with Christ. But He read their thoughts, just as He reads ours when we go to confession. Christ would not have thus exposed these Scribes had their attitude been an honest one. Forgiving sin is no more difficult to God than healing a disease. So now He proceeded to show them that He had a right to forgive sins. He appealed to their reason, for they were not yet as hardened in unbelief as they would be later in His public life. He, a Man in appearance, offered proof that He is God by working a miracle.

What consternation in the crowd; what joy among those who had carried the man! The cured one was so excited that he forgot to thank Christ. He was grateful, nevertheless; and the common people thanked God for such a privilege. The rabbis sulked away, embittered in defeat. Today, when a miracle is worked, for instance, at Lourdes, some believe and have their faith deepened; others seek to deny what their senses tell them.

LUKE 5: 27. And after these things he went forth, and saw a publican named Levi, sitting at the receipt of custom, and he said to him: Follow me. 28. And leaving all things, he rose up and followed him. 29. And Levi made him a great feast in his own house; and there was a great company of publicans, and of others, that were at table with them. 30. But the Pharisees and scribes murmured, saying to his disciples: Why do you eat and drink with publicans and sinners? 31. And Jesus answering, said to them: They that are whole, need not the physician: but they that are sick. 32. I came not to call the just, but sinners to penance.

While walking along the lake our Lord came to a custom house, perhaps one in which harbor dues were collected from fishermen. This Publican was a tax collector. In calling Matthew, Christ showed that He does not classify people on the basis of wealth, or talent, or social position. To Him there are only two classes — those who wish to do the will of God (rich or poor as they may be), and those who obstinately refuse to allow God in their lives.

Matthew may have had two names, or he may have changed from Levi to Matthew (Gift of God) after his selection. He had money and he had sympathy with his associates in the ill-reputed business of tax gathering. He wanted his former associates to meet Christ. Our Lord came to the feast, which may have taken place later. The Physician had come to save souls; Matthew showed his appreciation by entertaining our Lord.

To appreciate the courage of Christ in associating with outcasts we need only recall that Publicans were rated as low as the underworld characters of our own day. The "better-than-thou" type would not accept Him, yet they expressed horror at His going to those who, while not sinners in our sense of the term, had incurred some legal defilements. If occasion requires that we mingle with sinners, He expects that we be not overcome by evil but rather that we overcome evil by good. He mixed with all classes to raise all classes. He is approachable. When no one else will receive us, there is room in His heart for us.

1. Why is deliberate sin called moral leprosy?
2. What light is thrown upon the case of a sinner who is afraid to go to confession, by the courage of the leper in approaching Christ?
3. Find a scriptural prayer for one who is troubled with impure thoughts.
4. What is wrong with a student who feels that Christ is too far above him to go to Him?
5. Should we try to bring sinners to Christ to be healed?
6. Show from Scripture that Christ knows the secret views of each person, that it is senseless to try to hide a sin when going to confession.
7. Instead of the classes of people into which society divides its members today, how would Christ divide people?
8. Show that a person's position in society is not a true index to his real character.
9. Show that Christ clearly claimed to be God.

Chapter 23

REGULATIONS THAT KILL THE SPIRIT OF RELIGION

JOHN 5: 1. After these things was a festival day of the Jews, and Jesus went up to Jerusalem. 2. Now there is at Jerusalem a pond, called Probatica, which in Hebrew is named Bethsaida, having five porches. 3. In these lay a great multitude of sick, of blind, of lame, of withered, waiting for the moving of the water. . . . 5. And there was a certain man there, that had been eight and thirty years under his infirmity. 6. Him when Jesus had seen lying, and knew that he had been now a long time, he saith to him: Wilt thou be made whole? 7. The infirm man answered him: Sir, I have no man, when the water is troubled, to put me into the pond. For whilst I am coming, another goeth down before me.*

CHRIST was now in Jerusalem, but the group around the pool did not recognize Him. The man was filthy and deformed, living a miserable existence on alms. Everyone knew him. His was a celebrated case, if for no other reason than his tenacity of waiting. He was probably soured by life. Our Lord took in the whole situation. He was moved to pity by the fact that the man had long seen others get ahead of him in the struggle to bathe in the mineral waters at the proper time. As he looked up he must have noted something in Christ's face that had never been in any other visitor's countenance.

JOHN 5: 8. Jesus saith to him: Arise, take up thy bed, and walk. 9. And immediately the man was made whole: and he took up his bed, and walked. And it was the sabbath that day. 10. The Jews therefore said to him that was healed: It is the

*For omission of John 5: 4, cf. Le Camus, *The Life of Christ,* I, 334; Lebreton, *The Life and Teaching of Jesus Christ,* I, 334.

sabbath; it is not lawful for thee to take up thy bed. 11. He
answered them: He that made me whole, he said to me: Take up
thy bed, and walk. 12. They asked him therefore: Who is that
man who said to thee: Take up thy bed, and walk? 13. But he
who was healed, knew not who it was; for Jesus went aside from
the multitude standing in the place.

In the quiet of that Sabbath, divine goodness was at work. Healthful vigor, energy of mind, power to walk suddenly came to one who had been inactive since before Christ was born. And while he picked up his mattress, the Stranger slipped away; Christ never lingered for the plaudits of the crowd.

Some zealots met the man, and accused him of breaking a Sabbath commandment by merely carrying his bed. Such an accusation sounds foolish, but we must reconstruct their views. The leader, Shammai, taught that it was wrong to comfort the sick or enliven the sorrowful on the Sabbath. No one could cook anything on that day, or light a fire, or carry the least weight. The Pharisees were fanatical on such details. These leaders had made God's decree of rest mean a hundred senseless restrictions. And people were in a horrible dread of breaking these minute regulations; while the hypocritical elders invented ways of not keeping the rules themselves. Such leaders were indignant at this poor man when they should have rejoiced at the miracle. "The man who loves God and worships in truth is gentle, but he who loves himself under the cover of religion is always bitter and violent" (Didon).

John 5: 14. Afterwards, Jesus findeth him in the temple, and
saith to him: Behold thou art made whole: sin no more, lest
some worse thing happen to thee. 15. The man went his way,
and told the Jews, that it was Jesus who had made him whole.
16. Therefore did the Jews persecute Jesus, because he did these
things on the sabbath. 17. But Jesus answered them: My
Father worketh until now; and I work. 18. Hereupon therefore
the Jews sought the more to kill him, because he did not only
break the sabbath, but also said God was his Father, making
himself equal to God. 19. Then Jesus answered, and said to
them: Amen, amen, I say unto you, the Son cannot do anything
of himself, but what he seeth the Father doing: for what things
soever he doth, these the Son also doth in like manner. 20. For

the Father loveth the Son, and sheweth him all things which himself doth: and greater works than these will he shew him, that you may wonder.

Trembling, the man went to the Temple, evidently to give thanks. Christ came again to him. We learn that his disease had been the result of sin. We do not know why he told the leaders that Christ had cured him.

The leaders now had a clear case against Jesus. He had deliberately broken the Sabbath. The Sabbath observance had begun in the time of Moses as a custom which separated Jews from the remainder of the world. They were proud of this custom, but more proud of their interpretation of it. Now one of their regulations about how to keep the Sabbath had been broken. They would humiliate this upstart Galilean. Bursting with a sense of their own importance and blinded by conceit, they confronted Christ.

The Bible says God rested. This is a human way of speaking. As a matter of fact God is always active, for without His continued power all creation, ourselves included, would fall into nothingness, for we are dependent creatures.

The Jews understood, and correctly, that in His answer Christ was claiming to be equal with God. So the argument shifted from the Sabbath to the relation of Christ to the Father. They would not examine the proofs He offered. They condemned Him because their sense of self-importance was wounded. Openly, in their very stronghold He asserted His divinity. He stood alone, before a hostile, leering group of intellectuals, and taught the unity between Himself and the Father. He implied that God approved the cure He had made.

John 5: 21. For as the father raiseth up the dead, and giveth life: so the Son also giveth life to whom he will. 22. For neither doth the Father judge any man, but hath given all judgment to the Son. 23. That all men may honor the Son, as they honor the Father. He who honoreth not the Son, honoreth not the Father who hath sent him. 24. Amen, amen I say unto you, that he who heareth my word, and believeth him that sent me, hath life everlasting; and cometh not unto judgment, but is passed from death to life. 30. I cannot of myself do any thing. As I hear, so I judge: and my judgment is just; because I seek

not my own will, but the will of him that sent me. 31. If I
bear witness of myself, my witness is not true.

Christ continued to drive home His point. He can do the things that God alone does. He can raise the dead. He is to be the final judge of all men. Meanwhile, it is our duty to honor Him because the Father sent Him to us. To believe in Christ and to fulfill His commands is to be assured of a happy immortality.

So closely is Christ united with the Father that their wills are one. The closer a person comes to Christ the more will he follow this one basic rule — What does God want me to do here and now? That is holiness, to do God's will; that is successful living.

What Christ said about Himself was always true; but in Mosaic Law, according to which these leaders were pretending to judge Christ, a person's testimony about himself was not accepted.

JOHN 5: *32.* There is another that beareth witness of me; and
I know that the witness which he witnesseth of me is true. 33.
You sent to John, and he gave testimony to the truth. 34. But
I receive not testimony from man: but I say these things, that you
may be saved. 35. He was a burning and a shining light: and
you were willing for a time to rejoice in his light. 36. But I
have a greater testimony than that of John: for the works which
the Father hath given me to perfect, the works themselves which
I do, give testimony of me, that the Father hath sent me. 37.
And the Father himself who hath sent me, hath given testimony
of me: neither have you heard his voice at any time, nor seen
his shape. 38. And you have not his word abiding in you: for
whom he hath sent, him you believe not. 39. Search the scriptures, for you think in them to have life everlasting; and the
same are they that give testimony of me.

Christ now turned the tables on His accusers. As a matter of fact four witnesses bore testimony to Him: (*a*) the Baptist (32–35); (*b*) His life work; (*c*) the voice of the Father at His baptism, which they had not heard (37); (*d*) the Scriptures themselves (39).

MARK 2: *23.* And it came to pass again, as the Lord walked
through the cornfields on the sabbath, that his disciples began

to go forward, and to pluck the ears of corn. 24. And the Pharisees said to him: Behold, why do they on the sabbath day that which is not lawful? . . . 27. And he said to them: The Sabbath was made for man, not man for the sabbath. 28. Therefore the Son of man is Lord of the sabbath also.

Christ and His disciples were now, a week later, returning to Galilee. Leisurely they walked along, chatting among themselves. There were few fences in those days, so the disciples began to eat some of the grain, a thing which Mosaic Law permitted (Deut. 23: 25). Christ's every action was spied upon. His enemies followed Him like a tiger after its prey. The interpretation, which forbade a false tooth to be carried on a Sabbath, said that plucking an ear was reaping.

No Sunday law can be interpreted in a way that is harmful to man. When laws kill man's spirit they are no longer helpful. It is a law that we go to Mass every Sunday, but there are valid excuses for not going, such as sickness and distance. Yet the offering of the Mass is the greatest means we have of keeping Sunday holy. God, who is Master of the Sabbath and judge of what is good or bad on that day, intends that Sunday draw us closer to Him, instead of killing our spirit.

MARK 3: 1. And he entered again into the synagogue, and there was a man there who had a withered hand. 2. And they watched him whether he would heal on the sabbath days; that they might accuse him.

Everywhere He was watched, for the Pharisees had interpreted healing as work. His reputation for breaking such regulations had spread. The persistency with which Christ did this reveals to us how the Pharisees had reduced religion to mechanical forms. Christ's aim was to show that true religion must be in the heart, based on love of God and neighbor. Devotions and external worship are necessary, but when they degenerate, they lose the name of religion. Neither can religion be reduced to mathematics, to bargaining with God, to a superstitious belief that if we mechanically give so much to God He is bound to return so much to us. A true Catholic tries to keep self out of the picture. He thinks primarily of God's honor and his neighbor's welfare.

MARK 3: 3. And he said to the man who had the withered hand:
Stand up in the midst. 4. And he saith to them: Is it lawful to
do good on the Sabbath days or to do evil, to save life, or to
destroy? But they held their peace. 5. And looking round about
on them with anger, being grieved for the blindness of their
hearts, he saith to the man: Stretch forth thy hand. And he
stretched it forth: and his hand was restored unto him. 6. And
the Pharisees going out, immediately made a consultation with
the Herodians against him, how they might destroy him.

Jesus never feared to do a thing that was right. The audience was soon aware of a tense situation as the man stood up. Jesus put the case up to His secret accusers. They blushed with shame. They knew that the people would be on the side of Christ. They were caught. Common sense would supply the answer; but common sense was not in their possession.

Often did Christ have to endure misunderstanding and spiritual dullness. Usually He did not mind that. Now, however, He was angry, which shows us that these Pharisees were deliberately malicious in their refusal to accept the truth. Like many scoffers, they were so full of self, so conceited over their own importance as leaders of the people, that they closed their eyes to real goodness. Then Christ performed His deed of mercy, knowing that they would refuse to see the hand of God in it. The crowd was overjoyed; the Pharisees, their prestige gone, fumed and raged. They joined hands with their rivals, the Herodians, in a plot to be rid of Christ. Calvary was looming in the distance.

God intended Sunday as a day which we should sanctify by prayer, by giving our thought to Him, by meditating on our obligations to Him. It is easy to become immersed in worldly affairs, so that the thought of preparing for God's presence recedes from consciousness. He wants us on Sunday to free ourselves from weekday pursuits and to check up on our spiritual progress, to pray, to offer the Mass and to receive Communion, to read, and thus to strengthen the habit of living for Him. The Pharisaical interpretation of the Sabbath placed emphasis on externals only, and became such a burden to the individual as to prevent the lone and free flight of the soul to God. Pharisaical rules did not make people holy, but rather filled them with dread (Acts 15: 10).

The Pharisaical attitude, which was repeated in the old American blue laws for Sunday observance, has passed. A different danger confronts us now, one of laxity, of neglecting God on Sunday. God desired that the Sabbath be a day of rest. In our day, rest may often mean a change. Recreation of the proper kind is rest. If we are physically inactive during six days, physical recreation may be a good thing on Sunday. There is only one caution: to take that kind of recreation which will bring no dishonor on God.

1. Should we seek for compliments when we are successful?
2. Is God always active?
3. Show how the Pharisees were not in reality seeking God's honor.
4. Show that Christ openly, in Jerusalem, claimed to be God.
5. Just why did the leaders of Jews reject Christ?
6. Why is self-love dangerous? What prevents one who has it from realizing it?
7. Draw up a list of lawful recreations for Sunday.
8. What rule should we follow in seeking to determine what to do on Sunday?
9. Are devotions a means or an end? What is their purpose?
10. Show how Jesus had moral courage.

St John – loyal
smart (thinker)
loved by God more (the loved one)
(amiable character)
called a son of thunder

Philip – most pleasing personality

Judas – Judean, good manager —

James & John – argument over first place in kingdom.

Chapter 24

CATCHING THE SPIRIT OF THE LEADER

LUKE 6: 12. And it came to pass in those days, that he went out into a mountain to pray, and he passed the whole night in the prayer of God.

THE solitude of the hills gave Jesus companionship with His Father. After six months in public life His followers were numerous. He was gradually making known His plans for the continuance of His program. Before naming His official representatives, He wished to consult His Father. He prayed during an entire night. He talked over His plan with Him whom He sought always to please. We too should call God into consultation before any important decision. Prayer is conversation with our Leader. Since He became Man in order to teach us how to live, His action on this night tells us with whom to keep in touch.

LUKE 6: 13. And when day was come, he called unto him his disciples; and he chose twelve of them (whom also he named apostles):
MARK 3: 14. And he made that twelve should be with him, and that he might send them to preach. 15. And he gave them power to heal sicknesses and to cast out devils.

God's plan was that a visible Church should carry on this work of teaching and saving. Jesus went over in His mind the type of men He should choose to be the first bishops of the Church. Should He select learned men, wealthy men, shrewd men? No, He chose men who for the most part would co-operate with grace, men who with one exception would become saints, men who would faithfully represent Him to the world. Christ's followers were not merely to teach His doctrines; they were to be *other Christs.* They were to preach Him. "They were to keep His figure ever living before the eyes of the Church." In peaceful communion with God, at the very moment that the Pharisees were plotting to destroy Him, He was projecting the external, visible framework of that kingdom which will be life-giving and soul-elevating till earth ceases and time merges into eternity from whence it sprang. The word, *apostle,* means one who is sent. Christ Himself did the choosing. Grace for a vocation comes from Him. No one can push himself into the priesthood unless the call be given. A vocation is recognized by a feeling of dissatisfaction with worldly pleasures or by a longing to work for Christ.

Study the plan of this first seminary — personal association with the Master. His method was to be a living one. By intimate companionship with Him they were to learn His aim, absorb His teachings, copy His example. What a school that was! No rigid formalism, such as the rabbis imposed on their students, but solid piety and earnestness of heart acquired from contact with the mind and heart of Christ. Most great men either instill in us the fear of approaching too close to them, or repel us by some defect in character. Not so Christ. He became the servant of His students. He admitted them into His daily company, put up with their faults and drew them ever closer to Him. By being with Him, listening to Him, learning to love Him they caught His spirit. There is no other way to put on Christ (Rom. 13: 14).

The generous Christ gave His divine powers to His apostles. Shakespeare, Napoleon, Washington, Jefferson, Lincoln were not able to pass on their genius or power to any of their followers. Only one Man in all the world's history has done that. Christ gave them "power." There is significance in those words. Think of the power of the priest — to forgive sins, to change bread and wine into His Body and Blood.

MARK 3: 16. And to Simon he gave the name Peter: 17. And James the son of Zebedee, and John the Brother of James: and he named them Boanerges, which is, The sons of thunder: 18. And Andrew and Philip, and Bartholomew and Matthew, and Thomas and James of Alpheus, and Thaddeus, and Simon the Cananean, 19. And Judas Iscariot, who also betrayed him.

From the beginning Peter stands out as the one whom Christ intended to be the leader of the twelve. That fact was firmly fixed in the minds of the Evangelists when they later wrote the Gospels. They felt that Christ desired such a thing as the papacy. Peter was a natural leader, an executive with initiative. He had many faults. He was unstable and impetuous. But he was practical. He admired deeds more than words. He was generous and warm hearted; he was unselfish and loyal.

Of James the Greater we know very little. He has the honor of being the first martyred apostle. John, his brother, was the opposite of Peter. He was steady, tender, and mentally quick. He was given to reflection. He it was who best caught the significance of Christ's sermons and sayings. His was the love that excluded all fear, and there was no softness in his character. The very fact that Christ called these brothers "sons of thunder" shows that they had tempers and ambition. Andrew's name signifies virility. Bartholomew is another name for Nathanael. James the Less and Jude (Thaddeus) were brothers. Eleven of the twelve being from Galilee, they had the loyalty and fire of hardy people. Judas was a good manager and was made treasurer.

When chosen by Christ, Judas had defects, but so did the others. Christ chose him because he had possibilities; He selected him for what he was at that time. Instead of permitting the grace of Christ's presence to root out his faults, as others did, he allowed avarice, ambition, and jealousy to take hold of him. Judas was secretive and hid his ambitions; the others were open and frank, even in their faults. Perhaps Judas at first thought that Christ would be a mighty monarch and would reward His followers in gold and power.

If there appears to be a mystery about Christ's choice of the traitor, it is no more so than the fact that God grants great talents to some who will abuse them. Judas was responsible for the development of his character, just as we are held responsible. He could have developed differently. God's foreknowledge of our use of our lives does not determine the direction of our lives. He does not interfere with our free choice; we are the ones who decide.

Great men do not often permit their subordinates to become too prominent. Christ never crushed the individual personality of any of His apostles. He aimed to correct their defects; but He allowed each individual to perfect his own gifts. There is a vast difference between Peter and John, yet they both loved Jesus. It is a mistake if one imagines that religion crushes his personality or cramps his development. Jesus merely asks that each develop his own individual talent and use it in such a way as to bring credit on God and on the Church. And just as He was always loyal to the apostles and protected them, so likewise He is loyal to each of us, despite our faults. He is patient so long as He sees that, like Peter, we are striving to improve and that we are loyal to Him.

Nor should we forget that it was with a purpose that Christ chose men who would later be called "illiterate and ignorant men" (Acts 4: 13) by the scoffers of that day. Actually the apostles were men of intelligence. Learning and wealth are good when rightly used. But the Church's main task is to aid men to reach God's presence. For this purpose, divine power (grace) is necessary. Therefore Christ chose men who would become efficient instruments of God's grace. In other words, the Church's real strength is in the holiness of her teachings, her means of grace and her holy members. Her success will depend on the extent to which all of us become Christlike. The apostles were great men precisely because they forgot selfishness and reproduced in their own lives the qualities exemplified by our Lord. The slowness of the apostles in corresponding to the helps Christ gave them shows us that moral progress is slow. We need not be discouraged if we feel that our advance toward love of Christ seems to make little headway. What counts is our effort to catch His spirit, to have the "mind of Christ."

> Luke 6: 17. And coming down with them, he stood in a plain place, and the company of his disciples, and a very great multitude of people from all Judea and Jerusalem, and the seacoast both of Tyre and Sidon, 18. Who were come to hear him, and to be healed of their diseases. And they that were troubled with unclean spirits, were cured. 19. And all the multitude sought to touch him, for virtue went out from him, and healed all.

Study on the map the localities from which the crowd came to hear the Sermon on the Mount. It was June of 28 A.D. It was not such a crowd as one sees at Mass on Sundays. Poverty was widespread; leprosy, blindness, and other diseases were rampant. And a certain hardness toward the sufferings of others was apparent in the leaders of the day. The sympathy of Christ shines brightly by contrast.

1. Give the names of the apostles.
2. Contrast the characters of Peter and John.
3. Describe how Christ called His Father into consultation before He made important decisions.
4. What qualities does a student need in order to aid Christ in His work?
5. Describe Christ's method of training the apostles.
6. Show how each student is responsible for the direction his character takes.
7. What is wrong with an individual who says that his religion ties him down?
8. What advice would you give to a student who says that he wants to progress spiritually but that he can see no improvement in himself?

1) Peter
2) James
3) John
4) Andrew
5) Phillip
6) Barthalomew (Nathaniel)
7) Matthew
8) Thomas
9) Judas
10) James (of alphens)
11) Simon (Cananean)
12) Jude (Thaddeus)

Chapter 25

DIVINE GUIDANCE ON SPIRITUAL DEVELOPMENT AND CONTENTMENT

MATT. 5: 2. And opening his mouth he taught them, saying:

THE fifth, sixth, and seventh chapters of St. Matthew's Gospel contain what is known as the Sermon on the Mount. It may not all have been delivered on this occasion. Matthew may have grouped a number of sayings in this one section, since he did not aim to arrange events chronologically. These three chapters contain most of the Christian moral code, that is, the pattern for a truly Catholic life. Moreover, the entire three chapters seem to be summed up in the eight Beatitudes. We shall deal at some length with the Beatitudes, because they are basic rules for our development. Spiritual development means the becoming like Christ. Each student knows what physical development is, and mental development. There are also spiritual rules, which, if followed, produce a happiness which is beyond measure.

Christ came not only to redeem, but to teach and to establish a kingdom. As Catholics, we are members of that kingdom. As members we ought to exhibit contentment. The Beatitudes point out the principles of contentment in our lives; they outline the qualities by which we may acquire here on earth a foretaste of the happiness which will be ours when we reach God's presence. Each beatitude states a principle and also gives the interior result of following that principle. The Beatitudes give us eight rules for acquiring that joy of the soul which comes from checking our lower desires and permitting the Holy Ghost to work on us. They are the eight marks of the true Christian.

The Beatitudes are called paradoxes, because they appear to contradict the advice which the world usually gives for happiness. When correctly understood, however, they are found to contain the highest common sense. Christ Himself had inner contentment and happiness. He lived the Beatitudes before He preached them. He found happiness in their observance. He understands human nature. He does not need to experiment. Hence we can trust these rules which we must follow if we are to reach our goal of bringing honor to God. In the Beatitudes God is speaking to us.

MATT. 5: 3. Blessed are the poor in spirit: for theirs is the kingdom of heaven.

We hear it said that happiness is found by acquiring a large number of things, by gaining certain positions or places and by attaching ourselves to certain persons. Under things, we include money, clothes, food, cars, radios, etc. We hear it said that wealth means success and happiness because we can purchase all the things that we desire. We imagine that if we held a high position or could be in a place other than where we are, we would be happy. Always we dream that to be with certain people would bring contentment to us. Things, places, and persons may be grouped under the one heading of creatures. We feel a desire to attach ourselves to creatures in the hope of finding happiness. Is it wise to depend on that hope?

Christ said: "Blessed (happy, contented) are the poor in spirit" (spirit here stands for mind and heart). What did He mean?

a) He loved the poor. He came to bring them hope that the world cannot give them. They are the defeated, the victims. And God will be merciful to them and will reward them for their struggles to keep faith in Him.

b) He did not imply that all the poor are virtuous. Rather He wished to tell us how to accept poverty, if it comes. And the key lies in "poverty of spirit," that is, a placing of our hope in God rather than in creatures. It is no disgrace to be poor; to be rich is no proof of God's approval.

c) Hence the first beatitude lays down the principle that the secret of happiness lies in an attitude of detachment from all creatures. Man is made for God; and all creatures are means by which we may reach God. If any thing, place, or person becomes the sole object of our desire, then we are making an end out of a means, and we shall not find contentment because we shut out God. Happiness comes if we keep our hearts free from entanglement with things, places, and persons; it comes if we put God first and creatures second. Our contentment should not depend on the acquisition or the loss of fame, wealth, power, or love. Whether we possess them or not, the moment we reach the stage where they cease to disturb or disquiet us they lose their power to cause suffering. We must remain unattached to whatever we have or whatever we lack. "He could love the things that pass because His affection was set on the things that do not pass," was said of St. Thomas More.

d) Christ does not tell us to hate things, places, or persons. He does not forbid their use. He does not want us to become lazy, to cease to labor and plan. God does not excuse indolence. He knows that people cannot be happy in starvation. But He tells us to avoid overanxiety, excessive care, and intense craving for creatures. Sin consists in turning away from God and exalting things, places, persons as the highest goals of life. Jesus wants us to be intelligent enough to realize that modern talk about success and wealth as necessary conditions for happiness is not true.

e) Experience proves Christ's principle. People who make money their god, who seek only to satisfy themselves, have not been happy people. Tauler, a great German, was asked how he found God: "When I left creatures," he replied.

f) The first beatitude is, therefore, a guide to the proper use of things, places, and persons. If we do not become too attached to them, there will be room for God in our hearts and we shall be happy in the possession of Him. True poverty of spirit or detachment leaves us free to think of God, to meditate, and to pray. It means we can use or enjoy all things or creatures because we have trained ourselves to use them to lead us closer to God, who gave them to us.

g) It is wrong, therefore, to despise the poor and to look down on them. And it is blessed to seek to develop the spirit of poverty, the spirit of detachment from creatures. Christ chose to be born and to live in poverty, and He thereby gave us an example. He taught that riches are dangerous, for the "desire of money is the root of all evils," and gain is not godliness. Regard wealth, fame, talent, beauty as though they were but loaned to you to be used for God's glory. The interior peace of mind which God can give, partly here and completely hereafter, is the reward for acquiring the spirit of detachment from creatures. Membership in the Church is possession of the kingdom. Appreciation of the possible happiness as a member is up to the individual.

> MATT. 5: 4. Blessed are the meek: for they shall possess the land.

Meekness implies self-control. It comes from humility, from good judgment on when and how to act. The meek person thinks God's rights and his neighbor's more important than his own. He is willing to admit that he does not know everything; he is ready to receive correction; he is prompt to obey. Having acquired a spirit of detachment, the meek person "does not break out in brutish rage when things go badly." He has control over feelings of envy and resentment. He does not quit the team, the choir, or a committee if he is left out of a game, or if his name is accidentally omitted from a write-up. He does not attempt to dictate to God; he does not quit the Church if a priest misunderstands him.

Meekness is in reality strength. It is the calmness of a victory over selfishness and egotism. It attributes success to God more than to self. It is a restrained force which lets itself out when fighting for the rights of others, but which is calm under personal slights. The meek student is not always "standing on his rights." The violent individual devours himself and causes resentment in others; the meek person has a sense of humor; but he is not timid in a case of injustice.

The world tells us to "blow our own horn," to put up a bold front, to keep up with the Jones family, to be self-assertive, not to permit others to "run over us." Despite this advice, the second beatitude says that the meek are blessed.

We know from psychology that the self-assertive individual is frequently trying to hide his weakness by assuming importance. The facts of life indicate that ultimately it is the meek who succeed. David the meek triumphed over selfish Saul; Mary the humble maiden was selected over all others; Seward presumed that humble Lincoln had no talent, and he presumed wrongly. In our Civil War dozens of generals thought they were supreme, but we remember the gentle Lee and the quiet Grant. In the World War, General Allenby conquered Palestine, but, not wishing to raise himself to an equality with Christ who had ridden in on Palm Sunday, he walked into the city of Jerusalem. In order to win the World War for the Allies, men who had boasted that they would never bend a knee in adoration of God, were forced to give the head command to Foch, who meekly attended daily Mass and prayed to the Holy Ghost for guidance. True, self-assertive individuals have gotten ahead, but the end of their story is usually frustration in their personal disposition.

To acquire meekness a person must train himself to accept as the will of God conditions which are beyond his control. Day by day in little things he practices self-restraint; he never permits feelings of bitterness to reside in his heart. And then he learns to feel peace of mind. Others yield to him because he claims so little. When he has learned to use his powers for God and his neighbor, then God becomes his helper. Cheerfulness of disposition is the result.

> MATT. 5: 5. Blessed are they that mourn: for they shall be comforted.

Sorrow, lonesomeness, failure, disappointment, and pain come into the lives of all of us. No one escapes these trials. Some attempt to run away from suffering; some become sour and try to find release in sin; some blame God; and some become cheerful and saintly by accepting their sorrow as God's will.

We cannot explain each case of suffering or sorrow. We do know that Christ had to suffer and that God the Father loved Him. We have the word of Christ that God is good. Hence, Christ has taught us the value of accepting pain, loneliness, unpopularity, and of doing penance for our sins. No matter what the pain or sorrow that comes, the conviction must be ours that God is good. Noble souls who are rejected by the world must learn that such things may happen in order to draw them closer to God. And suffering may also be used as a means of regaining spiritual health.

Mourning, then, means regret over our own sins, our own faults, and also a cheerful acceptance of the hard things in life by offering them up to God as atonement for our own sins and for the sins of others. This is not an easy thing to do, but when we do it for Christ we experience, not pleasure indeed, but a certain joy of heart.

They who refuse to see the hand of God in their defeats and failures and pains will never find contentment. Christ tells us that instead of grumbling and complaining, we should accept the unavoidable pains of life, trust God's arrangements, and be cheerful in our acceptance. Our motive in so doing is to help Christ in His work of saving souls: "For unto you it is given for Christ, not only to believe in Him, but also to suffer for Him" (Phil. 1: 29).

Christians do not rejoice in suffering just for the sake of suffering. It is wrong to take a morbid delight when we are badly treated. Our religion does not remove from us the power to feel keenly this suffering; but it does show us how the hard things of life may be made spiritually profitable to us. Our faith that God permits the good to suffer, and that we should all mourn for our sins, is not the same thing as stoicism or fatalism. An American priest, Father Stanton, was suffering horribly from cancer but never lost his smile. Someone remarked that he had a lot of courage. "It is not courage," he replied, "it's faith." When troubles come, God "bids us look them in the face, meet them in the light of faith, shape our conduct with regard to them as reason and truth require, and then He promises us not that they shall be taken away, but that they shall be made the sources of joy and consolation" (Maturin).

Do not fret, therefore, or run away from the hard tasks of life. Do not think that God is hard or cruel if He does not give opportunities for greatness or popularity. In all hard things, say: "Thy will be done." When mourning over our own sins, we recall that Christ expects effort to overcome defects and to conquer obstacles.

MATT. 5: 6. Blessed are they that hunger and thirst after justice: for they shall have their fill.

In the process of developing Christlike qualities and of finding thereby happiness in the service of God, the first three beatitudes stress restraint. The striking qualities in Christ, however, were His positive qualities. We must view the Beatitudes as a whole. They emphasize positive acts. The fourth beatitude sends us into the world fired with one ideal — holiness, which is the same as Christlikeness. In Scripture, justice usually means holiness. Holinesss is acquired only by those who seek to serve God by doing good to others. And this implies a zeal for justice as we understand the term today.

Most students want to do good. However, daydreaming, bodily desires, worldly ambitions may gradually drown out desire for holiness. It is natural for a person to have an appetite for food. If there be no appetite, something is wrong. Likewise, we ought to possess a deep desire (appetite, hunger) to know Christ, to become like unto Him. If we dislike hearing about Him, if we dislike going to church, something may be wrong in us.

We acquire holiness by a desire to serve God through service to our neighbor. We develop an appetite for Christlikeness by making acts of faith, hope, love, contrition, by doing little acts of kindness. Christ intends us to be men and women of action — Catholic action. As we grow older we learn to desire justice in the modern meaning of the term. Evil, of course, will always be present in the world. It may appear that we cannot do much to remedy the situation. But God is strong, and we should join hands with those who are fighting for clean movies, adequate wages for working people, sanitary working conditions, respect for law, honesty in public office, a true presentation of God's rights over men and of men's duties to God. There is no joy like aggressive fighting for the right, said Theodore Roosevelt. That point of view omits the supernatural motive, yet it is naturally good. The joy of true holiness will come if, instead of seeking primarily for our own happiness, we aim to bring happiness and justice to others. Hence, in any question of modern justice, be on fire with zeal and moral courage. Our Lord was meek, but study His courage in driving the sellers out of the Temple.

Modern man needs to have explained to him just what holiness is, and what is meant by living a supernatural life here on earth. It is mainly through the sacraments that we are "filled" with holiness. God Himself, who *is* Holiness, comes to make His abode in us when grace comes to us. Hence, keep alive this craving to be worthy of your Guest. Try always to keep your motive unselfish. Let all your work be done for the motive of bringing credit to God. In striving to make justice reign in your city or community or school, do not seek human gratitude as a reward. Do it for God, and then will come the reward from Him.

* *

If your neighbor often buys new things which you are unable to buy will you be unhappy? Two students in a boarding school are unwilling to walk downtown because they have no money to spend. What is wrong in their view? A girl tells her mother that she must have more dresses in order to be happy. Does she understand the secret of happiness? A young man says he had too much religion in school. Granted that the course may have had may defects, is his attitude intelligent?

* *

> MATT. 5: 7. Blessed are the merciful: for they shall obtain mercy.

It is hard to live with some people; the very presence of certain individuals irritates us. We often desire to "get even" with our enemies; we are apt to rejoice in the misfortune of those who have mistreated us. But we cannot claim to be truly Catholic, to love God, so long as we refuse to forgive from our hearts, and to practice mercy.

At first sight there appears to be much mercy in modern life. Laws are broken; offenses against God are condoned, and no one seems to care. But this cheap sentimentality, this indifference to right and wrong is not the mercy that Christ has in mind. We may never make light of sin; it is always wrong. On the other hand, temperament, environment, and training have much to do with the faults or sins of our acquaintances. Christ wills that we be merciful to such persons, that we learn to live with cranky, conceited, selfish, or sometimes hypocritical people, and at the same time stand for the principle that certain things are always wrong. One may be merciful and at the same time firm. A student must stand for right principles, and be firm in cases of injustice or dishonesty. At the same time he can distinguish between wrong in itself and the person who is wrong. Note how Christ acted toward His enemies, toward Judas, toward sinners.

And God grants mercy to us for our faults, if we are kind, forgiving, and patient toward others. This applies to our innermost thoughts, our grudges, our spites. "We always get from God what we give to our neighbor."

Others usually respond to what they see in us. A student who is mean will receive meanness from his associates. We draw out and make cheerful those who see cheerfulness and kindness in us. Superiors and bosses sometimes attempt to crush those under their charge. "Personality has rights, and those rights are sacred, and he who refuses to recognize them, though it be a father with his own children, will surely bear the almost ineffaceable marks of the wrong he has done, branded on his own character" (Maturin). A group of Belgian children were praying at a wayside shrine, shortly after foreign soldiers had passed through and devastated their land. The children hesitated at the words: "As we forgive those who trespass against us." A man behind them noticed the hesitation. He completed the *Our Father* for them. It was King Albert of Belgium, teaching by example the spirit of mercy and forgiveness.

> MATT. 5: 8. Blessed are the clean of heart: for they shall see God.

The sixth beatitude states that an innocent heart, a boy or girl who remains wholesome, who does not shut God out of his or her daily life will develop a capacity for enjoying religion, for obtaining true fun in life and will one day see God face to face. Purity of heart does not refer only to what is usually known as purity. It includes all the thoughts that are permitted to rule our minds. No unworthy ambition of fame, power, or sensual indulgence should be permitted to take root. It is all right to think of business, or sports, or studies; but all such things must be connected with our ideal of doing such things in such a way as to bring honor to God.

You have felt pity for the physically blind who cannot see. Each person has a soul; each one has been given an ability to find God while here on earth; each baptized person has been given, in potentiality, the light of faith. And yet, how pitiable it is to observe persons who hate God, hate religion, who cannot find God in a leaf, in the order of the stars, in the wonders of the radio, and in the terrific laws by which the atom is held together. A few individuals sneer at those who pray; certain ones scoff at students who remain pure.

Something has happened to such people; they are blind. It may be that in their youth they received no instruction and their spiritual faculty of vision has never been developed. Often, impurity, pride, jealousy, love of money, selfishness have taken such a hold that they can no longer see straight. It is often our secret faults that blind us to the goodness in others. Our ambitions, our cravings may blind us because we do not ask God what He thinks of them. Not merely our mind, but, as we say, our heart must be open, frank, humble. Then we obtain real fun out of life; we find God everywhere, except in sin. And we thank Him for giving us our minds and the world in which we live.

The way to acquire this spiritual sight is to look for virtue, for beauty, for God in our daily lives. There is so much of sin and vice, so much attention paid to crime and wealth that we are liable to think that true virtue does not exist. It does. We need, however, ability to see it, to find it. "We need to see the beauty of goodness in order to realize the ugliness of sin. We need the vision of human life as God designed it, that we may be dissatisfied with what man has made it" (Maturin). Hence, observe the best in your companions, in life around you. Follow Christ as He lived His life before the eyes of the apostles; study Mary, or Father William Doyle, or Margaret Sinclair, or Joyce Kilmer. What an attractive person is a clean young man, a chaste girl! There are millions of these people. Sin is so deceptive that it seeks to insinuate that such persons do not exist. Retain your ability to "see" them, to feel the joy of living for God, and of discovering the workings of God in this everyday world of ours.

MATT. 5: 9. Blessed are the peacemakers: for they shall be called the children of God.

In reading the lives of the saints we note frequent references to their ability to settle quarrels. Bitter family feuds were often pacified by these men of God who knew the secret of peace. In your own community a priest or nun, a quiet and sympathetic layman or laywoman has brought peace of mind to numerous individuals or families. Peacemaking is an important part of a true Catholic's life.

The preceding beatitudes, if worked into our character, prepare us for the task of peacemaker. The spirit of poverty develops detachment; meekness brings inner control; mourning enables one to pass through trials; thirst for justice trains one in following God's will; mercy aids one to blend compassion with justice; purity keeps one's heart unsullied from wrong standards. With such a preparation, the peacemaker does not antagonize. He knows that many troubles arise from misunderstandings, or from greed, selfishness, suspicion, and he takes these factors into account. Christ's example has given him an insight into human nature that science cannot give. He establishes a reputation for fairness; he collects facts before he judges. He cannot be moved by money, or improper influences. He prays for guidance. Such people are equipped to do God's work; they are the children of God.

MATT. 5: 10. Blessed are they that suffer persecution for justice' sake: for theirs is the kingdom of heaven.

Fidelity to Christ and to His Church often brings persecution from the worldly-minded. "If I yet pleased men, I should not be the servant of Christ" (Gal. 1: 10). Opposition may not always be in the open; it may be a whispering campaign. Students are apt to accuse their teachers unjustly; teachers sometimes are wrongly suspicious of students. Old people may misjudge the young; the young may think the old are unjust.

However, we must not misunderstand opposition to ourselves. What we consider persecution may be due to our own faults and mistakes which irritate others. Religion does not supply for lack of common sense. Certain natural qualities are necessary for social success. One may be good, and yet not shrewd. Participation in the Mass does not make up for laziness or shiftlessness in business. Our Lord was not slipshod in the carpenter shop. Try to acquire those qualities necessary in your occupation, and then do your work for God's honor. Once you are sure that a certain thing is right and ought to be done, then go ahead, despite opposition. The obstacles may be due to the natural conservatism of older people who think the dreams of the young impractical.

At present the world allures with gilded promises — fame, wealth, pleasure. We may be jeered at, or dropped by certain acquaintances if we do not yield. In old age the temptation is different; the world will try to take from us what it now holds out to us. Old people find themselves alone, and are subject to sourness, suspicion, loss of hope. In both trials, keep your eye on our Lord. We may not always understand hatred or misrepresentation; but God awaits to receive those who pass through the temptations of youth and the trials and burdens of old age.

Such are the Beatitudes — guiding rules for true contentment and explanations of the qualities necessary for entrance into the presence of God. They are all a development of this one important principle: that true service to God is the only source of human happiness, whether rendered directly to Him or indirectly to Him through service to our neighbor. The Person who devised these rules is divine. He knows and understands boys and girls, men and women. He does not have to experiment as does a psychologist or a scientist. We can trust His advice because He is the Creator of our nature. People of today seek for experts. There is only one expert in the question of human happiness — God. The craving for happiness can be ultimately satisfied only by following the rules laid down by our Lord. Cheerfulness is, therefore, the outstanding virtue resulting from a life built on the Beatitudes. Catholic life at its best is full of an inner joy and contentment. Other leaders have drawn virtue from their followers; only Christ can draw a cheerful holiness from people.

Learn if the following people exemplified the beatitude numbered in front of their names: First — St. Francis of Assisi, St. Thomas More; second — Columbus, St. Francis de Sales, the Little Flower, Cardinal Gibbons, General Lee, Marshal Foch; third — The Curé of Ars, St. John of the Cross; fourth — Matt Talbot, John L. Stoddard, William Gaston, St. Gabriel the Passionist; fifth — Frederick Ozanam, Levi Stillman Ives, Thomas Mulry; sixth — St. Aloysius, Cardinal Newman, Margaret Sinclair, Joyce Kilmer; seventh — St. Bernardine of Siena, Bishop Cheverus of Boston, Fr. De Smet, Don Bosco, St. Peter Claver; eighth — St. Ignatius Loyola, St. Philip Neri, Bishop Fisher.

1. Just what is the purpose of the Beatitudes?
2. What is the difference between the Beatitudes and the Commandments?
3. Give two applications to daily life for each of the Beatitudes.
4. A Communist says belief in God is a delusion. Why can he not see the truth?
5. How would you prove that there is true wisdom in the Beatitudes?
6. A high-school boy and girl make a sixty-mile journey Saturday night to attend a dance. Monday morning in school they seek adulation as heroes for having reached a speed of ninety miles an hour on the journey. Discuss their intelligence.

Chapter 26

CHRIST PERFECTED OLD IDEAS OF RIGHT AND WRONG

MATT. 5: 17. Do not think that I am come to destroy the law, or the prophets. I am not come to destroy, but to fulfill. . . . 20. For I tell you, that unless your justice abound more than that of the Scribes and Pharisees, you shall not enter into the kingdom of heaven.

THE Sermon on the Mount was delivered to a large, outdoor audience. This crowd was excited with the hope that Christ would free the Jews from the tyranny of the Romans and that He would establish them in comfort and pleasure. Recall also that the Pharisees were entrenched in authority so far as the religious life of the people was concerned. Consequently, the Sermon on the Mount went directly against popular expectation. Christ did not go into politics. He knew that behind injustice lies sin. He attacked the roots of sin. He did not fill the poor with false hopes. Courageously, He taught religious truth. The whole scheme of regulations revealed by God through Moses was called the Mosaic Law. The moral code, that is, rules of right and wrong, was summed up in the Commandments, which had been in effect nearly fifteen centuries before Christ's appearance. Christ did not abolish the Commandments; He perfected them and stripped them of the man-made regulations added by the Scribes and Pharisees. They had made religion to consist in mere external observance of a number of their own interpretations.

By the word, "fulfill," then, our Lord meant that He was the fulfillment of all that God had promised the Jews. He came to give a more perfect revelation of the nature of God and of the nature of true religion. The Mosaic Code was adapted to the needs of the semi-barbaric Israelites of the fourteenth century B.C., yet it was not a complete moral code. Now was to come through Christ the final and perfect revelation of the nature of God and of the nature of our duties to Him. Christ was the fullness of time (Gal. 3: 16), the completion of the revelation God had begun with Abraham (Rom. 4: 10). The Catholic religion is a revealed religion; it was not built up by a process of human thinking only. "For Moses more than Abraham, the prophets more than Moses, the Apostles more than the Prophets received instruction in the knowledge of almighty God."

The ceremonial part of Mosaic Law, which was but a symbol, a prefiguration of the truths Christ would give us, was due for a change. Christ stood firm, however, for the divine, unchangeable principles of the Old Testament. He clarified, refined them and fulfilled the prefigurations.

We have no right to change God's law. They who speak of modernizing the Commandments regard them as human productions. Christ refined the moral code sufficiently to make it eternally modern. He summed up the Ten Commandments in the two great positive duties of love of God and neighbor. We cannot change these because they are divine. And the truly divine never becomes old.

> MATT. 5: 21. You have heard that it was said to them of old: Thou shalt not kill. And whosoever shall kill, shall be in danger of the judgment. 22. But I say to you, that whosoever is angry with his brother, shall be in danger of the judgment. And whosoever shall say to his brother, Raca, shall be in danger of the council. And whosoever shall say, Thou fool, shall be in danger of hell fire. 23. If therefore thou offer thy gift at the altar, and there thou remember that thy brother hath anything against thee; 24. Leave there thy offering before the altar, and go first to be reconciled to thy brother, and then coming thou shalt offer thy gift. 25. Be at agreement with thy adversary betimes, whilst thou art in the way with him: lest perhaps the adversary deliver thee to the judge, and the judge deliver thee to the officer, and thou be cast into prison. 26. Amen I say to thee, thou shalt not go out from thence till thou repay the last farthing.

Christ now became specific. The Scribes taught that only the external act of killing was sinful. Christ corrected this opinion by showing that the internal thought of killing may be a mortal sin when the individual desires and wills to kill but is prevented by some circumstance. The momentary thought of so doing may not even be a venial sin, because of lack of reflection; but a carefully prepared design would be murder even if the external act did not take place. "Raca" is a term of contempt. "Fool" here means the charge of being something like an atheist or apostate. We must be careful of the thoughts we nourish.

Before participating in the Mass or receiving the sacraments, forgive your enemies. Settle quarrels out of court when you can. There may be here a reference to purgatory. It depends on the meaning given to the word, "till."

> MATT. 5: 27. You have heard that it was said to them of old: Thou shalt not commit adultery. 28. But I say to you, that whosoever shall look on a woman to lust after her, hath already committed adultery with her in his heart. 29. And if thy right eye scandalize thee, pluck it out and cast it from thee: for it is expedient for thee that one of thy members should perish, rather than thy whole body be cast into hell. 30. And if thy right hand scandalize thee, cut it off, and cast it from thee: for it is expedient for thee that one of thy members should perish, rather than that thy whole body go into hell.

Impure thoughts, deliberately meditated upon and desired in action are mortal sins. The world condemns only the external act; God condemns the thought also. Thoughts that come unbidden, that linger against our effort to banish them are not sinful. The best practice is to shift one's attention to some other activity, or to some topic in which one is interested. An aspiration to our Lord is strong aid. It is not so much the word, or the look, but the thought behind them which is sinful. Christ makes it clear, that the basis of purity is to control the thoughts that course through our minds. If wrong thoughts are not allowed to linger, gradually strength of mind is acquired by which temptations can be conquered. Then, we must remove from us the occasions of sin. He does not mean to tell us actually to pluck out our eyes, but He requires that anything that is a continual temptation, though it be as dear to us as an eye or a hand, should be removed. People permit their legs, their arms to be amputated in order to save life. Why should we hesitate to shun occasions of sin which destroy the life of the soul?

MATT. 5: 33. Again you have heard that it was said to them of old: Thou shalt not forswear thyself: but thou shalt perform thy oaths to the Lord. 34. But I say to you not to swear at all, neither by heaven for it is the throne of God: 35. Nor by the earth, for it is his footstool: nor by Jerusalem, for it is the city of the great king: 36. Neither shalt thou swear by thy head, because thou canst not make one hair white or black. 37. But let your speech be yea, yea: no, no: for that which is over and above these, is of evil. 38. You have heard that it hath been said: An eye for an eye, and a tooth for a tooth. 39. But I say to you not to resist evil: but if one strike thee on thy right cheek, turn to him also the other: 40. And if a man will contend with thee in judgment, and take away thy coat, let go thy cloak also unto him. 41. And whosoever will force thee one mile, go with him other two. 42. Give to him that asketh of thee, and from him that would borrow of thee turn not away.

Swearing here means calling God to witness; Christ says we must avoid a careless and frivolous taking of oaths. In courts an oath is lawful. Perjury in a court is a direct insult to God, an asking Him to back up a lie.

Leviticus 24: 20, refers to the authority of the State, in its right to inflict punishment, for an officer of the law must physically resist evildoers. Discretion is necessary in dealing with attacks upon us. Our Lord wishes to impress gentleness, and meekness. An attacker may expect us to fight back or to run. If we do neither we show moral courage; and anger often yields in the presence of calm, quiet, moral courage. Such is the spirit of turning the other cheek. When our Lord was struck at His religious trial He demanded the reason (John 18: 22–23). Slurring remarks, like "fish-eaters," should be passed over. But organized efforts to dispel falsehoods are necessary. Circumstances will dictate when to refuse a fight, or to give aid, or to loan money. Prudence is always necessary. To loan a person money with which to commit sin is certainly wrong.

MATT. 5: 43. You have heard that it hath been said: Thou shalt love thy neighbor, and hate thy enemy. 44. But I say to you:

Love your enemies: do good to them that hate you: and pray for them that persecute and calumniate you: 45. That you may be the children of your Father who is in heaven, who maketh his sun to rise upon the good and bad, and raineth upon the just and the unjust. 46. For if you love them that love you, what reward shall you have? Do not even the publicans this? 47. And if you salute your brethren only, what do you more? do not also the heathens this? 48. Be you therefore perfect, as also your heavenly Father is perfect.

The Old Testament itself does not teach hatred of enemy, but rabbis had so taught that Jews considered it all right to hate others. Hatred and a desire for vengeance were deeply rooted in the Oriental clans and tribes. Everyone outside of the clan was an enemy. Greeting of friends was an elaborate ceremony, but no greeting was given to an enemy. Christ rose above all teachings, whether of Greek or rabbi, and made it obligatory that we love enemies because they have souls destined for God. A true Catholic is one who overcomes all thoughts of hate, one who continues to be kind even to those who are mean or ungrateful. To refuse to speak to one who has injured us shows that we are not true followers of Christ. Actually, love of enemies is a very practical rule, for it gives peace of mind, makes us better tempered and cheerful. Ill health, sourness, uneasiness often follow when one nurses his hate against others. It is not necessary, however, that we cultivate a special affection for every individual.

From verse 45 we conclude that worldly prosperity is no sign of God's blessing; neither is failure, nor absence of talent, indicative of lack of God's love for us. Worldly shrewdness brings worldly success. Religious people who lack good business judgment should not blame God for permitting success to come to the shrewd.

Seeking for perfection means a striving to imitate Christ in the manner in which He prayed, treated His enemies, forgot self, and practiced gentleness. This perfection can be sought for in any state of life in which we find ourselves. We should love God because He is perfect. God is likable and lovable because He possesses in perfection all the qualities which we admire in the best of our friends — kindness, sympathy, mercy, patience, impartiality, power, courage, personality, intelligence. We are told to love God for what He is in Himself. When this is our motive in loving Him, then we have perfect love, supernatural love. The highest motive we can have in being good, or in doing good to others is to be such or do such out of love of God for His own sake.

1. In years to come a classmate who has been mean to you falls into misfortune. Will you call on him or her?
2. A boy finds that a certain companion is a continual occasion of sin for him. Should he break the companionship?
3. An indifferent student tells his friends or parents that he failed a course because the teacher was not fair. What virtue does he lack?
4. A boy is continually threatening to "get even" with another, but never has the opportunity. Has he sinned?
5. Out of spite, a teacher gives a low mark to a student. What should the student do? The teacher?
6. Explain the Mosaic Law and show it is not the outgrowth of social custom.
7. Why are the Commandments never out of date?
8. Why is Christ called the "Fullness of time"?
9. What does St. Paul mean in Rom. 12: 21?
10. How would you answer a person who said impurity is not a sin because it is natural?
11. Why is it that no State, no group of individuals have the right to reject the Commandments and decide what is fundamentally right or wrong?

Chapter 27

HOW TO PRAY, AND HOW TO TRUST GOD

MATT. 6: 1. Take heed that you do not your justice before men, to be seen by them: otherwise you shall not have a reward of your Father who is in heaven. 2. Therefore when thou dost an almsdeed, sound not a trumpet before thee, as the hypocrites do in the synagogues and in the streets, that they may be honored by men. Amen I say to you, they have received their reward. 3. But when thou dost alms, let not thy left hand know what thy right hand doth: 4. That thy alms may be in secret, and thy Father who seeth in secret will repay thee.

IN OUR good deeds, God examines our motives. Motives must be supernatural; that is, deeds should be performed to honor God, not ourselves. The student who does good in order to "show off," to acquire a reputation for generosity, gains little reward from God. The best charity is hidden, not done to obtain publicity in the newspapers. On the other hand Christ expects us to give a good example to others, to let our light shine before them.

MATT. 6: 5. And when ye pray, you shall not be as the hypocrites, that love to stand and pray in the synagogues and corners of the streets, that they may be seen by men. Amen I say to you, they have received their reward. 6. But thou when thou shalt pray, enter into thy chamber, and having shut the door, pray to thy Father in secret: and thy Father who seeth in secret will repay thee. 7. And when you are praying, speak not much, as the heathens. For they think that in their much speaking they may be heard. 8. Be not you therefore like to them, for your Father knoweth what is needful for you, before you ask him.

There was much "showing off" in prayer in our Lord's day. He condemns ostentation, not public prayer that is earnest. Christ

Himself attended public worship, such as the Paschs. Repetition of *Hail Mary's* and *Our Father's* is all right. Our Lord repeated the same prayer in the garden. But the superstition that a certain number of prayers automatically produces results is wrong. Not the quantity but the quality of prayers is important; they must come from the heart. There are no magic formulas in prayer. We should trust God, but not attempt to force Him.

> MATT. 6: 9. Thus therefore shall you pray: Our Father who art in heaven, hallowed be thy name. 10. Thy kingdom come. Thy will be done on earth as it is in heaven. 11. Give us this day our supersubstantial bread. 12. And forgive us our debts, as we also forgive our debtors. 13. And lead us not into temptation. But deliver us from evil. Amen.

The *Our Father* was composed by Jesus in response to a request from His disciples that He teach them how to pray (Luke 11: 1). Today, nineteen centuries after its composition, its use is universal. From tiny chapel and stately cathedral, from bedside and cloister, from lips of children, students, business men, athletes, soldiers, airmen, statesmen; from torrid South and frozen North, from West and East, in every language, this prayer continually rises to the Father of us all. Thus, the *Our Father* is like an international hookup on the radio, bringing many together.

a) The human race is one family. All men, all races are our brothers, for all have souls. It is an impelling duty to think of them when we say: *Our.*

b) One great truth which we must understand is the *Fatherhood of God.* God actually is a Father to each person. Through laws arranged by God, we receive our bodies from our parents. Parents, however, cannot transmit an immortal soul. Sometime before birth, most likely at the first moment of life, God personally creates out of nothing a spiritual (invisible, indivisible) and immortal soul for each human person. This gift of the soul makes us capable of knowing and choosing. God is the Father of each person because He supplies to each individual that which makes him significant and of high worth. No one lacks dignity or value. What a thought that is! Not beauty, not money, not great athletic or scholastic ability make us important, but the fact that we have a soul, and an invitation to prepare ourselves for life with God.

Secondly, through Baptism we are adopted by God, raised to a supernatural plane of living, incorporated with Christ our Head. God becomes our Father at Baptism through grace; we are then His heirs, provided we remain loyal to our Head, Christ. We become members of a vast organism. A man joins a club or becomes a Communist because he thinks thereby he will have status or prestige when the proletariat rules. If he but knew the truth, it is from God he receives dignity and value. And true status or prestige comes from Baptism, which is membership with Christ. Communism blinds a man to his real value when it tells him he is just matter with no immortal principle in him.

Thirdly, God is our Father through His Providence. The world, its resources, its glories, its beauties were prepared by Him for us. Someone designed the human eye. No blind law of evolution could design the origin and function of the eye. Behind every law is a lawgiver, a designer. When Christ used the term *Our Father* He revealed that it was God who provided for what we have in the human body.

The word *Father* speaks of the close, endearing relationship between God and each human person. Anyone can approach this loving Father. If moderns deny this fatherhood of God, they have no reason to use the phrase: brotherhood of man.

c) It is so urgently necessary for each of us to know just why we are living, that Jesus often repeated His own dominant aim in life. This we are supposed always to have in mind, namely, to honor God by our lives—"Hallowed be Thy name." When we realize what a glorious thing it is to be alive, to be baptized (which enables us to believe in Christ), and to be invited to immortal happiness with God, we hasten to reverence His name.

d) The kingdom is belief in Christ as God, and the presence of God through grace in men's souls. The coming of the kingdom means the spreading of the influence of Christ; it means conversions to the Church; it means the gradual deepening of a person's appreciation or realization of what it is to be a Catholic. If we realized what we have in our Faith, we would wish to lead others to the kingdom.

e) We like to have our own way in life; many try to dictate to God rather than to trust Him. God has a plan for each one of us. It is not always easy to see just what that arrangement is. But we have Christ's word that God cares for us, loves us. Many things happen to us, and we do not know why. This we know: God wants us to make the best of whatever we have; He wants us to ask for guidance on what to do with our lives, our opportunities. He wants us to plan, to work, to study, to do all that we humanly can, and then to leave the rest in His hands. When we cannot have our own way, He wants us to say: "Thy will be done." The one who says that is not a quitter. Christ Himself finished what He started, and yet it was Christ who taught us to say: "Thy will be done." Our best energy and prudence must go into everything that we attempt. And then, if we do not succeed in the eyes of the world, we shall have succeeded in the eyes of God by being cheerfully resigned to what is His will. In personal sorrow try to say: "Thy will be done."

How does the first half of the *Our Father* differ from the second half? What conclusion do you draw from Christ's arrangement of the prayer?

f) God is interested in our temporal welfare. He gave the Ten Commandments to protect us in our rights. He will back up those Commandments on the day of judgment. Meanwhile He leaves all men free. It is not God's fault if the greed of some men takes food away from those who have a right to food. Just as in college the professor gives an examination at the end of the semester to test what the student has been doing, so God gives an examination at the end on the Commandments. "Bread" means all the things necessary for the sustenance of human life. God wants us to ask for the necessities, but in the right way. We may pray for success in examinations, for a position; we should pray for the right partner in marriage. We should pray for others as well as for ourselves. Christ said: "Give us," not: "Give me." He was the first to teach the brotherhood of man.

g) Debts are sins, negligences, mean acts, unkind remarks. An accounting for all such must one day be made. We may hope for forgiveness only when we have forgiven others.

h) We ask to be spared those temptations which would conquer us; we ask that God's help be not withdrawn from us. God does not tempt us. In Scripture God is often described as *doing* what in reality He is merely *permitting to be done* to us.

i) We desire God's aid in overcoming evil in general, or in conquering the devil (the evil one).

When we study carefully the *Our Father* we are astonished at all that it contains. It was composed by One who knows what God is like, who knows our relationship with God. The Fatherhood of God and the brotherhood of man are two divinely revealed truths. We are bound to honor God because He is our Father; we must never look down on any person, because he is our brother, and as such, dear to his Father. Knowing these truths, we then learn how to pray — God's honor first, human needs second. Hence, prayer is not mere asking for self; it is well-wishing, and thoughtfulness for God and for our neighbor. The most perfect prayer ever composed is the most unselfish in design.

* *

Show how Christ taught that the motive in our good acts is important. Explain the Fatherhood of God to (*a*) a younger brother or sister, (*b*) a non-Catholic chum in a public high school or college who thinks God a tyrant, (*c*) your own father, (*d*) a group of children dependent on charity because of the neglect of their own father. In the light of the right order in prayer as shown in the *Our Father* analyze the nature of your prayers during the past month. Why may all people call God their Father? What aim of Christ should be our aim?

* *

MATT. 6: 16. And when you fast, be not as the hypocrites, sad. For they disfigure their faces, that they may appear unto men to fast. Amen I say to you, they have received their reward. 17. But thou, when thou fastest, anoint thy head, and wash thy face; 18. That thou appear not to men to fast, but to thy Father who is in secret: and thy Father who seeth in secret, will repay thee. 19. Lay not up to yourselves treasures on earth: where the rust and moth consume, and where thieves break through, and steal. 20. But lay up to yourselves treasures in heaven: where neither the rust nor moth doth consume, and where thieves do not break through, nor steal. 21. For where thy treasure is, there is thy heart also.

Long faces are not Christian faces. Sometimes we like to appear heroic; we like to show how holy we are. This is secret pride. Self-love is a subtle poison. It is dangerous to put on a show of piety just to obtain high marks, to please a teacher, or to win a prize. God sees our secret, hidden motives. Christ wants us to be cheerful and light-hearted in our religious duties.

A dollar in a bank may be lost; a Mass attended, a *Hail Mary* well said, a kind deed done in His name are never lost. If we develop the desire to be real Catholics, then our hearts will be in our religion.

> MATT. 6: 25. Therefore I say to you, be not solicitous for your
> life, what you shall eat, nor for your body, what you shall put
> on. Is not the life more than the meat: and the body more than
> the raiment? 26. Behold the birds of the air, for they neither
> sow, nor do they reap, nor gather into barns: and your heavenly
> Father feedeth them. Are not you of much more value than they?
> 27. And which of you by taking thought can add to his stature
> one cubit? 28. And for raiment why are you solicitous? Con-
> sider the lilies of the field, how they grow: they labor not,
> neither do they spin. 29. But I say to you, that not even
> Solomon in all his glory was arrayed as one of these. 30. And
> if the grass of the field, which is today, and tomorrow is cast into
> the oven, God doth so clothe: how much more you, O ye of little
> faith! 31. Be not solicitous therefore, saying: What shall we
> eat, or what shall we drink, or wherewith shall we be clothed?
> 32. For after all these things do the heathens seek. For your
> Father knoweth that you have need of all these things.

Christ expects us to use prudence and foresight, and to work hard. But this is far from the action of one who is continually worrying about social position, marks, fame, dress, pleasure. Anxiety about these things is wrong. And Christ has taught us that the earth and its resources were provided by God for us. God is a Father to us. Hence, the more we learn about nature through science, the more should we be drawn to love of Him who arranged all of nature's laws. Christ, not science, tells us the purpose of nature as a whole.

> MATT. 6: 33. Seek ye therefore first the kingdom of God, and
> his justice, and all these things shall be added unto you. 34. Be
> not therefore solicitous for tomorrow; for the morrow will be
> solicitous for itself. Sufficient for the day is the evil thereof.

Our foremost aim in all we do is to glorify God, and so to live as to be an honor to Him. To do this we need grace, or God's justice. Many devout Catholics have had worldly success, but they did not make such success their chief aim. William Gaston (of Carolina), Chief Justice Taney, Thomas Mulry, Admiral Benson, Louis Pasteur, Cardinal Gibbons, and Marshal Foch all rose high.

Fulfillment of today's duties is preferable to dreaming about the future. Provision for the future should be such as not to result in a neglect of present duties. Our Lord does not prohibit work but rather foolish anxiety. Each day has sufficient problems without storing up troubles for ourselves. God is good. Christ proved that to us. Therefore we can cheerfully trust God no matter how difficult life may be for us. We show trust by never complaining about hard duties.

1. Does Christ expect us to pray for conversions? Is anything more besides such prayer required?
2. The condition which we should always add to our prayers is ________________.
3. Is appearance always a safe index to character?
4. A Catholic professional man in a city of good Catholic schools sends his daughter to a public high school in order to draw trade. Discuss.
5. What is the meaning of: "Work as if everything depended on yourself; pray as if everything depended on God."
6. Does God expect holy people to practice also good judgment, caution?
7. Does sin destroy forever the effects of previous prayers (cf. art. "Penance," in *Cath. Encyc.*)?
8. Is the best type of Catholic boy or girl outlined in the *Our Father?* If most of your prayers are for yourself, check your habit by examining the *Our Father*. Is the boy or girl who thinks only of the salvation of his or her own soul truly Catholic according to the teaching in the *Our Father?* Is *socialness* or *plural* thinking a good name for the virtue or mental outlook implied in the words *our* and *us?* Note the emphasis Jesus places on these words our and us. How does the *Our Father* teach that the best development of a boy or girl comes, not from thinking about oneself, but from thinking of God's honor and of our neighbor's needs? How does the *Our Father* teach that the best way to obtain happiness is not to seek directly for it but first to develop the habit of "giving" to God before seeking to "get" from Him? Is the aim of seeking to reflect credit on God our Father by loving God and our neighbor taught anywhere in the *Our Father?* Compare the "giving" before "getting" structure of the *Our Father* with the structure of the Mass from the Offertory to the Communion.

Chapter 28

THE WISDOM FOUND IN THE WORDS OF CHRIST

MATT. 7: 1. Judge not, that you may not be judged. 2. For with what judgment you judge, you shall be judged: and with what measure you mete, it shall be measured to you again. 3. And why seest thou the mote that is in thy brother's eye; and seest not the beam that is in thy own eye? 4. Or how sayest thou to thy brother: Let me cast the mote out of thy eye; and behold a beam is in thy own eye! 5. Thou hypocrite, cast out first the beam out of thy own eye, and then shalt thou see to cast out the mote out of thy brother's eye.

GOD alone can judge people; we may judge things or sins when they are public; but we should be very slow about speaking unkindly of others. God will judge us unfavorably if we indulge in rash judgment, which He is here condemning. A mote is a splinter; a beam is a large piece of wood. We should think of our own faults rather than speak of the faults of others. It is so easy to misjudge others, so easy to assign motives to them which they do not have, that it is better to say nothing. It is our duty, of course, to condemn crime and sin when the public good demands such condemnation, yet we should be kind to sinners (Cf. John 8: 11). Likewise it is our duty to expose modern misrepresentations of God and religion.

MATT. 7: 6. Give not that which is holy to dogs; neither cast ye your pearls before swine, lest perhaps they trample them under their feet, and turning upon you, they tear you. . . . 12. All things therefore whatsoever you would that men should do to you, do you also to them. For this is the law and the prophets.

In our efforts to explain Christ to the modern world, we must be prudent. Some groups do not want to hear the truth about the Church; some resent pious conversations. Talk holy things with those who want the truth. Dogs and swine were legally "unclean" animals. A beautiful axiom was called a pearl.

Verse 12 contains the golden rule. Confucius in China and Socrates in Greece had formulated golden rules, but they assigned only natural motives. Confucius did not advise that injury be repaid by kindness as Christ did. There is another golden rule in Scripture (Tob. 4: 16), as old as that of Confucius. The Law and the prophets mean the entire Old Testament. All of Christ's teaching in regard to our treatment of people is summed up in this golden rule, but we must have a supernatural motive, that is, treat people kindly *for God's sake,* out of regard for God's interest in each human person. We forgive our enemies in order that we may thereby lead them to God. When we follow out this very difficult rule, we bring honor to God, because we trust Christ rather than our instinct, or what others might tell us to do. Forgiveness makes a student a friend of Christ (Cf. fifth beatitude).

> MATT. 7: 13. Enter ye in at the narrow gate: for wide is the gate, and broad is the way that leadeth to destruction, and many there are who go in thereat. 14. How narrow is the gate, and strait is the way that leadeth to life: and few there are that find it!

Only God knows how many are saved and how many lost. To remain outside the Church is a grave sin for those who realize the obligation of becoming Catholics. Only God knows the hidden motives of people who refuse to believe. In ancient times the gates of walled cities were very narrow. The narrow gate means a life of self-control, penance, and strong faith; but it leads somewhere — to God's presence. The broad gate is the easy, lazy and indifferent life which leads to loss of God.

> MATT. 7: 15. Beware of false prophets, who come to you in the clothing of sheep, but inwardly they are ravening wolves. 16. By their fruits you shall know them. Do men gather grapes of thorns, or figs of thistles? 17. Even so every good tree bringeth forth good fruit, and the evil tree bringeth forth evil fruit. 18. A good

tree cannot bring forth evil fruit, neither can an evil tree bring forth good fruit. 19. Every tree that bringeth not forth good fruit, shall be cut down, and shall be cast into the fire. 20. Wherefore by their fruits you shall know them. 21. Not every one that saith to me, Lord, Lord, shall enter into the kingdom of heaven, but he that doth the will of my Father who is in heaven, he shall enter into the kingdom of heaven. 22. Many will say to me in that day: Lord, Lord, have not we prophesied in thy name, and cast out devils in thy name, and done many miracles in thy name? 23. And then will I profess unto them: I never knew you: depart from me, you that work iniquity.

A person of high ideals needs prudence and shrewdness in analyzing the remarks thrown out by some modern leaders, teachers, writers. Certain people smile at ideals, at the habit of prayer. Strictly speaking, false prophets are those who assume they have been commissioned by God to start something new, or change some of the doctrines about Christ. There may be nothing to blame in their outward lives, but time tests their opinions by the fruit of heresy and confusion which they produce. Practically, false prophets for us may be gilded promises, made to entice us from the path of virtue, from trust in Christ or the Church. Watch the results among those who yield to the snare: "Everyone is doing it." The fact that thousands justify divorce or drunkenness is no argument that such actions are right or that we should yield to them.

Some who claim to be Catholics will be rejected by Christ on judgment day because they did not live Catholic lives. Real faith in Christ means living up to the example He set. Since religion is not a mere study, not a system of truths merely to be believed, but a *life to be lived,* a Christlike life, we must have such faith in Christ that we practice love of neighbor. "Faith without works is dead."

MATT. 7: 24. Every one therefore that heareth these my words, and doth them, shall be likened to a wise man that built his house upon a rock: 25. And the rain fell, and the floods came, and the winds blew, and they beat upon that house, and it fell not, for it was founded on a rock. 26. And every one that heareth these my words, and doth them not, shall be like a foolish man that built his house upon the sand: 27. And the rain fell, and the floods came, and the winds blew, and they beat upon that house, and it fell, and great was the fall thereof. 28. And it came to pass when Jesus had fully ended these words, the people were in admiration at his doctrine. 29. For he was teaching them as one having power, and not as the Scribes and Pharisees.

Winds always accompany the winter rains in Palestine. Hence, the forcefulness of the comparison, which implies that in the words of Christ we have divine, unchangeable truth. Wisdom consists in following the directions given in His words. Read what the floods of time have done to those who refused to listen to Christ and the Church in matters of doctrine and morals. We cannot build society on science, for science cannot command our conscience. No popular writer, no new scheme of morals or of marriage can replace the divine code given by Christ in the Sermon on the Mount. It is this scheme that the Church, the Rock, brings to us.

Thus ends the Sermon on the Mount. Every truth was proposed in language with which each of the listeners was familiar. It came from His heart, because He knew intimately the life of His audience; it went directly to their hearts because they felt His love for them. Enraptured, they listened for a number of hours. All — the old and young, the poor and the well-established, the strong and the weak — recognized His superiority to anything human.

Long years of reflection are necessary for a full appreciation of this sermon. Whoever wishes to learn just what a Catholic is supposed to be like needs only to read the sermon as a whole.

Of all the people whom we trust in life, only one, the Author of this sermon, is God. He alone can lead us up the hills of a happy immortality. He does not weary by subtle reasonings as does a philosopher; He does not draw out legal distinctions as did the Scribes; He does not have to experiment as does the scientist; He does not employ mere rhetoric as does an orator or a writer. He knows all things; He reads all thoughts. He is God, and He here tells the moderns what qualities or virtues to develop if they wish to be members of the kingdom. He shows in what holiness consists. It is wisdom to make His words part of our daily thinking.

1. What remedy would you suggest for rash judgment?
2. What is meant by the Law and the prophets?
3. Explain the golden rule.
4. Show that neither faith alone, nor a naturally good life alone, is sufficient for salvation.
5. Do you admire a student who tries to find something good to say about a person whom others are condemning?
6. How did Christ advise prudence in conversation?
7. Why is the Sermon on the Mount never out of date?
8. How would you account for Christ's power as a speaker?
9. Why do not more people appreciate Christ's words?
10. Was the audience anxious to leave, after Christ finished speaking? Why?
11. Cf. Exodus 19, 20, and contrast the manner of giving the Ten Commandments to the giving of the Sermon on the Mount.
12. What would be the weakness of a code of morals built only on science, or upon a system proposed by those who desire to be modern?

Chapter 29

KINDNESS TO NON-CATHOLICS

LUKE 7: 1. And when he had finished all his words in the hearing of the people, he entered into Capharnaum. 2. And the servant of a certain centurion, who was dear to him, being sick, was ready to die. 3. And when he had heard of Jesus, he sent unto him the ancients of the Jews, desiring him to come and heal his servant. 4. And when they came to Jesus, they besought him earnestly, saying to him: He is worthy that thou shouldest do this for him. 5. For he loveth our nation; and he hath built us a synagogue. 6. And Jesus went with them. And when he was now not far from the house, the centurion sent his friends to him, saying: Lord, trouble not thyself; for I am not worthy that thou shouldest enter under my roof. 7. For which cause neither did I think myself worthy to come to thee; but say the word, and my servant shall be healed. 8. For I also am a man subject to authority, having under me soldiers: and I say to one: Go, and he goeth; and to another: Come, and he cometh; and to my servant: Do this, and he doth it.

A CENTURION was the captain of a hundred soldiers. This one was evidently a wealthy Gentile, and naturally courteous. His attitude toward Jews was exceptional for Romans of that day. He felt hesitant about approaching Christ personally, just as many non-Catholics hesitate to approach a priest. He realized that Jews incurred a legal defilement if they entered the home of a Gentile.

Christ knew how to be kind. This willingness of Jesus touched the Roman. To courtesy, he united faith — a splendid combination. He said that if he, though not the chief officer, could yet give orders and have them obeyed, then Christ could cure merely by a word, without troubling to come personally. These words have become immortalized, not only in Scripture but in the Mass.

> LUKE 7: 9. Which Jesus hearing, marvelled: and turning about to the multitude that followed him, he said: Amen I say to you, I have not found so great faith, not even in Israel. 10. And they who were sent, being returned to the house, found the servant whole who had been sick.

Jesus admires humble faith wherever He finds it. He compared the centurion to Israel in general, not to individuals such as the apostles. As a race, the Jews rejected Him. Individual non-Catholics sometimes put us to shame by their manly reverence, and deep, sincere spirit of religion, even if they have not the true religion. Christ went out of His way to work a miracle for the centurion because the latter had humble faith. It is our special obligation to recognize sincerity in non-Catholics, and to be willing to go out of our way to be kind to them, especially when they are in trouble. We can always afford to say a kind word. Christ expects it of us.

> LUKE 7: 11. And it came to pass afterwards, that he went into a city that is called Naim; and there went with him his disciples, and a great multitude. 12. And when he came nigh to the gate of the city, behold a dead man was carried out, the only son of his mother; and she was a widow: and a great multitude of the city was with her. 13. Whom when the Lord had seen, being moved with mercy towards her, he said to her: Weep not. 14. And he came near and touched the bier. And they that carried it, stood still. And he said: Young man, I say to thee, arise. 15. And he that was dead, sat up, and began to speak. And he gave him to his mother. 16. And there came a fear on them all: and they glorified God, saying: A great prophet is risen up among us: and God hath visited his people. 17. And this rumor of him went forth throughout all Judea, and throughout all the country round about.

Crowds usually tagged at His heels. Naim was about 25 miles southwest of Capharnaum. There were no coffins. The dead were wrapped in linen and carried in open biers. The plight of a widow was especially bad in Palestine. Christ did not wait to be asked. He understood. He practiced, and also expects of us, intelligent kindness. We must cultivate the habit of foreseeing the needs, of picturing the condition of others.

How calmly He did it all. "He raises the dead as if He were performing the commonest act, He speaks as a Master to those sleeping the eternal sleep, and we are aware that he is the God of the dead as well as of the living, never calmer than when performing the greatest deeds." Genesis, the first book of the Bible, relates how God's mere word created the world and the laws by which the planets roll in their spheres, by which life continues. This same Christ has power to call the dead back to life on the day of general judgment.

St. Luke has given us pictures of the courteous, the understanding Christ. No grief of the lowly or of the poor escapes the attention of God. These miracles were performed in the open, before witnesses, and with the motive of being kind to others, of relieving human suffering. There was no trickery, no desire to show off, or to crush by display of power. Christ's miracles do indeed prove that He is God. Yet He wishes us to believe Him on His word, without asking God to do something astounding. Some count forty miracles that Christ performed; others say thirty-three. Not all of His deeds were recorded. Three times He brought people back to life.

> LUKE 7: 18. And John's disciples told him of all these things. 19. And John called to him two of his disciples, and sent them to Jesus, saying: Art thou he that is to come; or look we for another? 20. And when the men were come unto him, they said: John the Baptist hath sent us to thee, saying: Art thou he that is to come; or look we for another? 21. (And in that same hour, he cured many of their diseases, and hurts, and evil spirits: and to many that were blind he gave sight.) 22. And answering, he said to them: Go and relate to John what you have heard and seen: the blind see, the lame walk, the lepers are made clean, the deaf hear, the dead rise again, to the poor the gospel is preached: 23. And blessed is he whosoever shall not be scandalized in me.

Perhaps a month or more elapsed between the miracle at Naim and this incident. John had been languishing about three months in a dungeon, called Macherus, four or five miles east of the Dead Sea. Strengthened as he had been by the hard but free outdoor life of the desert, and still in the prime of physical and moral manhood, this gloomy, restrained life of inactivity was a martyrdom to him. Evidently, his followers had some access to him, for they brought him news of Christ's ever-growing power, or of the Naim miracle.

Looking at John's life as a whole we see that he understood his task. Therefore in this incident there is no solid reason for thinking that John doubted about Christ. He may have been impatient for the great day of the Judgment. He was delicately trying to soften the jealousy of his followers and to attach them to Christ. He knew the very presence of Christ would be the best means of winning these disciples, as it had John and Andrew. Christ allowed His deeds to speak for Himself. The disciples of the Baptist witnessed miracles. John had worked no miracles. Therefore these disciples should accept Christ instead of being jealous of Him. Isaias had foretold that the Messias would work such miracles (35: 4–6; 61: 1). Christ did not go to the aid of the Baptist because He knew he was rooted in the truth. His praise of John shows this.

Luke 7: 24. And when the messengers of John were departed,
he began to speak to the multitudes concerning John: What went
you out into the desert to see? A reed shaken with the wind?
25. But what went you out to see? A man clothed in soft garments? Behold they that are in costly apparel and live delicately,
are in the houses of kings. 26. But what went you out to see?
A prophet? Yea, I say to you, and more than a prophet. 27.
This is he of whom it is written: Behold I send my angel before
thy face, who shall prepare thy way before thee. 28. For I say
to you: Amongst those that are born of women, there is not a
greater prophet than John the Baptist. But he that is the lesser
in the kingdom of God, is greater than he. 29. And all the people
hearing, and the publicans, justified God, being baptized with
John's baptism. 30. But the Pharisees and the lawyers despised
the counsel of God against themselves, being not baptized by
him. 31. And the Lord said: Whereunto then shall I liken the
men of this generation? And to what are they like? 32. They
are like to children sitting in the marketplace, and speaking one
to another, and saying: We have piped to you, and you have
not danced: we have mourned, and you have not wept. 33. For
John the Baptist came neither eating bread nor drinking wine;
and you say: He hath a devil. 34. The Son of man is come

eating and drinking; and you say: Behold a man that is a glutton and a drinker of wine, a friend of publicans and sinners.

Christ often taught by asking questions. Tall, slender reeds grow along the Jordan and bend in whatever direction the wind blows. He illustrated the virtue of constancy by a living example. The inconstancy, the moral softness of many listening to Jesus were indirectly exposed by His perfect portrayal of the character of John. Here God pays tribute to the holiness of a human being. No hero of the Old Testament had risen so high as John. He towered supreme among the long line of leaders who had told the world of Christ's coming. Christian Baptism, however, confers a greater dignity.

The self-centered leaders had rejected John. Out of that situation Christ drew a lesson, for courtesy and kindness should not hinder one from speaking the truth when necessary. The Pharisees said John was too strict and Christ too lax, which shows they did not want the truth. Some stubborn children do not want to play at anything that their companions propose. Some students, and some childish adults are like that. Nothing in the Church pleases them. They are self-centered. The strictness, the fasting of John, and the sociable, amiable mixing of Christ with all classes of people had the approval of God. The man who rejects the Church because he has concentrated on lax Catholics, may not be looking for truth which exists, notwithstanding bad representatives. He is a Pharisee, but he might be won to see truth by kindness. The Catholic who drops out of the Church because she will not loosen up on divorce, or because it is too hard to go to Mass every Sunday, may be substituting his own views on right and wrong for God's views. The truly wise are those who, desiring a strict life, enter the Church and are not scandalized by lax Catholics, or who, touched by the mercy of the Church for penitent sinners, come to her for divine aid.

1. Show why loyalty to the Church need never prevent you from welcoming goodness or praising it, wherever found?
2. How might a student develop imagination or thoughtfulness in foreseeing the needs of others?
3. Find the words of the centurion in the Mass.
4. What two noble qualities did the centurion possess?

5. Show how there was no vain display of power, no trickery in Christ's miracles.
6. What is meant by strength of character? Would the acquisition of a noble aim help to develop will power?
7. Read *The Crisis* by Churchill and learn how Brice came to be attached to Lincoln. Did John the Baptist use the same method?
8. May one who tries to do right hope to please everybody?
9. Have you found any people who have the same attitude toward the Church as the Pharisees had toward John the Baptist and Christ?
10. How might the quality of constancy or steadiness be acquired? Christ taught that John the Baptist possessed this virtue by asking ———.

Chapter 30

SIN, FORGIVEN AND UNFORGIVEN

LUKE 7: 36. And one of the Pharisees desired him to eat with him. And he went into the house of the Pharisee, and sat down to meat. 37. And behold a woman that was in the city, a sinner, when she knew that he sat at meat in the Pharisee's house, brought an alabaster box of ointment; 38. And standing behind at his feet, she began to wash his feet with tears, and wiped them with the hairs of her head, and kissed his feet, and anointed them with the ointment. 39. And the Pharisee, who had invited him, seeing it, spoke within himself, saying: This man, if he were a prophet, would know surely who and what manner of woman this is that toucheth him, that she is a sinner.

PERSISTENTLY Jesus spoke the truth about the Pharisees, yet they often invited Him to meals despite their hatred of Him (cf. pp. 270, 276). These leaders simply could not ignore Jesus. And so, like many prominent people of our day, Simon thought he should become acquainted with a Man whose name was on everyone's lips. He was curious; he would invite Christ, but would omit those courtesies to guests which are the rule in the East. He would let Him feel that He was not the equal of the social élite. Christ realized the attitude of the host and of the guests toward Him; but He, the unwelcomed, minutely scrutinized Guest, said nothing. Disrespect never ruffled His poise and calm. They treated Him condescendingly and He who is God patiently submitted.

It was customary in the East for anyone to stray into a house and to observe guests at a banquet. There was little privacy in such affairs. So there came a notorious, public sinner. Her action, however, shows her estimate of Christ's character and goodness. Experts do not agree on who this woman was. It is possible that her name was Mary Magdalen. But it is perhaps best to hold that this woman, Mary Magdalen, and Mary the sister of Martha and Lazarus were three distinct persons.

At the table the guests reclined on couches, or on rugs, the left elbow resting on a pillow and the feet over the outside of the couch. The Pharisee knew the reputation of the woman. He imagined that Christ was not shrewd enough to guess her character, and he concluded that Christ could not be a prophet, since He did not reject contact with this sinner. A Pharisee would shun this woman as we shun contact with smallpox.

> LUKE 7: 40. And Jesus answering, said to him: Simon, I have somewhat to say to thee. But he said: Master, say it. 41. A certain creditor had two debtors: The one owed five hundred pence, and the other fifty. 42. And whereas they had not wherewith to pay, he forgave them both. Which therefore of the two loveth him most? 43. Simon answering, said: I suppose that he to whom he forgave most. And he said to him: Thou hast judged rightly. 44. And turning to the woman, he said unto Simon: Dost thou see this woman? I entered into thy house, thou gavest me no water for my feet; but she with tears hath washed my feet, and with her hairs hath wiped them. 45. Thou gavest me no kiss; but she, since she came in, hath not ceased to kiss my feet. 46. My head with oil thou didst not anoint; but she with ointment hath anointed my feet. 47. Wherefore I say to thee: Many sins are forgiven her, because she hath loved much. But to whom less is forgiven, he loveth less.

Christ had read the thoughts of Simon. Thus far the meal had not been thrilling. There had been no sparkle in the conversation. Now the guests were open-eyed with amazement. Christ delicately respected the social amenities by asking permission of the host to speak. A socially prominent host was to be examined by the unwelcomed Guest. As the guests entered a house their sandals were removed and feet washed. During the meal drops of oil were poured on their hair. The woman may have observed the failure to do this to Christ.

Simon was irritated; but he gave the obvious answer. He had misinterpreted her actions. Had he reflected on God's mercy, he might have seen that this woman was repentant of her sins and had either received or was now seeking forgiveness from Him whose mercy had led her to sorrow. Her previous admiration for

Christ now deepened into love as she knelt in His presence. Hers would seem to be a case of perfect contrition. The greatness of God's mercy often moves sinners to deep love of God. Simon was indirectly reprimanded, the woman vindicated, and God's mercy sustained. Her generous action should have shown Simon that he was judging rashly.

Hitherto Christ had not seemed to notice her. Now, while all listened, He spoke of her marks of courtesy to Him, which Simon had purposely omitted. Some people fulfill rigidly the rules of etiquette toward the socially prominent, but are ashamed to pay outward marks of respect to God, to the Church, to priests, to brothers, and nuns, who represent Christ.

> LUKE 7: 48. And he said to her: Thy sins are forgiven thee. 49. And they that sat at meat with him began to say within themselves: Who is this that forgiveth sins also? 50. And he said to the woman: Thy faith hath made thee safe: go in peace.

This puritanical, "better-than-thou" audience gasped. The unwelcomed Guest showed His divine power to forgive sins. The Catholic Church is never ashamed to protect repentant sinners. Despite criticism, she openly defends those who seek pardon for sin. Whoever is tempted to think that he does not belong in church, should remember Christ's public kindness to this sinner; for sin will always be forgiven if the sinner has the courage sorrowfully to go to confession.

> LUKE 8: 1. And it came to pass afterwards, that he travelled through the cities and towns, preaching and evangelizing the kingdom of God, and the twelve with him. 2. And certain women who had been healed of evil spirits and infirmities: Mary who is called Magdalen, out of whom seven devils were gone forth. 3. And Joanna the wife of Chusa, Herod's steward, and Susanna, and many others who ministered unto him of their substance.

Through personal contact with their Leader the twelve were receiving their training. For some weeks or months this journey endured. Since He did not have time to work at a trade, Jesus permitted these probably somewhat wealthy women to accompany the group, and they supplied the expenses. It was not unusual to have women supply some of the expenses of the rabbis. These women had found that noble service for God gives greater joy than a life of sin or of empty court life. In thus allowing them to show their gratitude for the new and higher view of life which He had given them, Jesus sanctioned the religious communities of women who dedicate their talent, their energy to God's work of caring for the sick, protecting the wayward, housing the orphan, instructing young hearts in the way Christ desires them to live. To the modern girl who is generous Christ also says: "Come."

> MARK 3: 20. And they come to a house, and the multitude cometh together again, so that they could not so much as eat bread. 21. And when his friends had heard of it, they went out to lay hold on him. For they said: He is become mad.

In these closely packed words we obtain a picture of the daily pressure of human beings on Jesus. We think of Him so frequently as God that we are prone to forget how thronging crowds jostled Him about. They did not fear to approach Him. He was so sympathetic, so kind that each one could imagine Him a friend, an understanding leader. What a mystery is here, that one whose eye could chase the sellers from the Temple, could also be so inviting as to encourage sinners, or permit multitudes to consider Him on their own plane! They seemed to forget His greatness. So overwhelming was this enthusiasm that His relatives thought He had lost His head. He was going too far, when He would not even take time out to eat. They decided to rescue Him, to calm Him down, to make Him rest and eat.

> MATT. 12: 22. Then was offered to him one possessed with a devil, blind and dumb: and he healed him, so that he spoke and saw. 23. And all the multitudes were amazed, and said: Is not this the Son of David? 24. But the Pharisees hearing it, said: This man casteth not out devils but by Beelzebub, the prince of the devils. 25. And Jesus knowing their thoughts, said to them: Every kingdom divided against itself shall be made desolate: and every city or house divided against itself shall not stand. 26. And if Satan cast out Satan, he is divided against himself: how then shall his kingdom stand? 27. And if I by Beelzebub cast out devils, by whom do your children cast them out? Therefore they shall be your judges. 28. But if I by the Spirit of God cast out devils, then is the kingdom of God come upon you. . . . 31. Therefore I say to you: Every sin and blasphemy shall be forgiven men, but the blasphemy of the Spirit shall not be forgiven. 32. And whosoever shall speak a word against the Son of man,

it shall be forgiven him: but he that shall speak against the Holy Ghost, it shall not be forgiven him neither in this world, nor in the world to come.

The Pharisees made the terrible accusation that this doer of good was in league with the devil. Quickly Christ exposed their slander. How could the devil work against himself? In accusing Him, the Pharisees also accused their own disciples, Jewish exorcists, of doing the devil's work. Christ told the Pharisees that the Holy Ghost, the Spirit of truth, guided Him in His actions, and His miracles were plain proof that He is from God. When a person becomes a slave of sin, the devil sometimes gets such a hold on him that he will fill himself with every form of hate against the Church, against priests, or against purity. What is your opinion of a person who is always seeking for and imputing evil to someone he dislikes? Is it a pharisaical attitude?

Satan wars against Christ. No one can be neutral in this warfare. They who refuse to accept Christ are indirectly aiding Satan. This may often be called indifference. But the Pharisees, and some in our day, were more than indifferent. In accusing Christ of being in league with the devil they committed the greatest of sins which is, attributing to Satan a good work that was divine, the healing of one possessed. This was not done in ignorance, as are many sins; but it was done with malice. It is called the unforgiven sin because people who commit it seldom repent. Pride hardens them and they will not submit to the Church. Christ could stand abuse against Himself but it hurt Him to see the Spirit of truth and of love thus blasphemed. Many attacks of bigots against the Church will be forgiven because they are done in ignorance. But it looks bad for those who are too proud, too conceited to believe, or who, once having believed, have driven the light of the Holy Ghost out of their lives. If grace is withdrawn by God then "the heart becomes incapable of seeing the truth against which it has closed itself" (Geikie). Such was the case of these Pharisees. Christ plainly hints of purgatory here, by implying that some sins can be forgiven in the world to come.

LUKE 8: 19. And his mother and brethren came unto him; and they could not come at him for the crowd. 20. And it was told him: Thy mother and thy brethren stand without, desiring to see thee. 21. Who answering, said to them: My mother and my brethren are they who hear the word of God, and do it.

This scene of Mary's patient waiting on the fringe of the crowd should be connected with earlier efforts of His relatives to withdraw Him from the crowd. We see the anxiety with which she had been following Him. Our Lord understood; but at the same time He wished to establish the principle that a priest, a religious is dedicated to God, and must consider all men his brethren instead of limiting his affection to the family circle. One who becomes a priest, a brother, a nun, must give himself wholly to God and to those who need to be made children of God. In fact, family ties may never be permitted to interfere with duty to God. Christ not only taught this; He practiced it. Likewise we notice here the underlying truth that each human being is valuable in the eyes of God. Anyone can approach God; anyone can become an heir. The only condition is full acceptance of Christ.

1. Compare Simon's treatment of Christ with a Catholic who thinks priests are below his social or intellectual standing and hence refuses to pay them deference; or who is ashamed to ask if he can get to Mass while on a week-end party; or who does not want his associates to know that he is a Catholic.
2. What is wrong with a boy who says that it does not do him any good to go to confession because he commits the same sins over and over?
3. How may one who is afraid to go to confession because of his or her many sins, build up courage to go?
4. Why was the woman of sin forgiven, while the Pharisees seem to have remained unforgiven?
5. Did Christ want religious communities?
6. Is Christ too far above students to be approached by them?
7. Besides mixing with the crowds, what did Christ do in regard to prayer and meditation? Must we do the same?
8. How would you explain the hatred that some fallen-away Catholics have for the Church?
9. What is a sin against the Holy Ghost?
10. Show that a priest, or brother, or nun must possess a spirit of detachment.
11. Why should you be generous in support of the Church if you are wealthy?

Chapter 31

LIVING PICTURES

OUR Lord had now been before the public about a year. Attitudes toward Him were gradually taking permanent shape. While He was still the popular idol, we notice that the leaders, the Pharisees and Scribes, were definitely leagued against Him. Their attributing His work to the devil was a climax in their hatred, jealousy, and blindness.

This situation brought a change into the methods of Christ. Later we shall see how He gradually withdrew from the public and concentrated on the apostles. For the present we remark His shift (not entirely, of course) to the plan of teaching through parables. Many of His thoughts would now be repeated, but under a different form. Fundamentally His teaching remained the same for two and a half years. Doing God's will was His constant aim; love of God and neighbor was His daily practice. But circumstances now dictated that He present the idea of the kingdom under a new light.

A *parable* is a story with a moral. It need not be a true story, but unlike a fable or myth, it never exceeds the laws of nature. A parable is a comparison between something known or possible, and an idea or truth of a higher order. It is an illustration of a supernatural truth.

Christ was observant of every form of life. He saw possible comparisons and analogies between natural things around Him and the supernatural truths which He came to teach. These parables are a true picture of Galilean life as He saw it day by day. He wove these natural scenes into stories, parables which illustrated what He wanted to teach. Hence a parable is a mode of instruction. It is simple, yet deep; it is easy, yet difficult. It can be readily remembered, but it can never be exhausted. It is an invitation to think, to reflect, and to seek for further information.

> LUKE 8: 4. And when a very great multitude was gathered together, and hastened out of the cities unto him, he spoke by a similitude. 5. The sower went out to sow his seed. And as he sowed, some fell by the wayside, and it was trodden down, and the fowls of the air devoured it. 6. And other some fell upon a rock: and as soon as it was sprung up, it withered away, because it had no moisture. 7. And other some fell among thorns, and the thorns growing up with it, choked it. 8. And other some fell upon good ground; and being sprung up, yielded fruit a hundredfold. Saying these things, he cried out: He that hath ears to hear, let him hear.

He may have spoken from a boat along the shore, probably in November. Stretching out before Him were the fields where men planted, perhaps the plain of Gennesaret. In the crowd were both friends and enemies; literate and illiterate, city and country people. Orientals love mysterious sayings. Parables appeal to them; they easily indulge in poetic fancy, in dreamy reverie. And now the motley crowd heard about the sower. The pointed stick of a plow merely tore up the earth, without turning it. Wheat planted in December or January might be harvested in April, so strong is the sun along the lake. There were no fences; trodden pathways across the fields hardened some ground so that seed would not penetrate. Much of the soil was rocky. Cactuslike thistles grew in the fields; thorns were abundant.

Not a word was wasted; the picture was graphic; its telling short. And only the ending startled them. "Ears to hear" means willingness to be taught, openness to grace, desire for the truth.

> LUKE 8: 9. And his disciples asked him what this parable might be. 10. To whom he said: To you it is given to know the mystery of the kingdom of God; but to the rest in parables, that seeing they may not see, and hearing may not understand.

Now we reach the difficulty of trying to determine why Christ taught in parables. The background needs to be explained first.

(*a*) Recall that Christ only gradually revealed the full nature of Himself and of His doctrines. He had to rid minds of prejudices and misconceived ideas. Even the apostles were slow to grasp the meaning of His statements. Constant repetition was necessary. (*b*) Recall the hatred of His enemies, which led them to twist everything He said. Likewise, His disciples eagerly drew rash conclusions from His teachings. Both classes made up His audience. (*c*) A gift implies effort to appreciate on the part of a receiver. Grace, faith, Christ Himself are God's gifts to us. When given, it is our clear duty to develop appreciation, for the truths of revelation are magnificent, startling facts and rich possessions. For instance, no item of information is equal in value to the fact that God became Man.

First, if we bear in mind that some of His hearers wanted more instruction, we may say that Christ used the parables to instruct the willing ones. In using a parable He put the responsibility on the hearers. If interested, they would come for clearer enlightenment, and thus avoid rash conclusions. A parable usually has a double effect. It enlightens, and it puzzles. It tests the hearer, and shows whether He wants the truth or not.

Second, if we bear in mind the antagonistic attitude of the Pharisees, we may say that Christ adopted the parable in order to teach the well-intentioned and at the same time permit the Pharisees to confound themselves. That person alone understands religious truth whose heart is in sympathy with truth. God does not cause spiritual blindness in anyone, but He permits it. That means that He wants everyone to know the truth, but He does not cast pearls before swine; He does not force holy things on those who despise holy things. So, He was really merciful to the Pharisees by giving them truth in a protected form, truth which they could understand if they wished, but which would also confuse them if they attempted to twist it.

A third reason why Christ employed parables may be seen in their effectiveness in bringing out the contrast between life on earth and life in heaven, between qualities found in the world and in the true Christian.

> LUKE 8: 11. Now the parable is this: The seed is the word of God. 12. And they by the wayside are they that hear; then the devil cometh, and taketh the word out of their heart, lest believing they should be saved. 13. Now they upon the rock, are

they who when they hear, receive the word with joy: and these have no roots; for they believe for a while, and in time of temptation, they fall away. 14. And that which fell among thorns, are they who have heard, and going their way, are choked with the cares and riches and pleasures of this life, and yield no fruit. 15. But that on the good ground, are they who in a good and perfect heart, hearing the word, keep it, and bring forth fruit in patience.

The sincere Catholic opens up his soul to Christ, to his confessor and receives illumination as did the disciples.

The seed is grace, or a sermon, a remark, a book. The parable tells of the working of grace.

(*a*) Grace, or supernatural life, has to be planted in us before we can become holy. The full possibilities of a student are developed only when he co-operates with grace. (*b*) Grace has power in itself, but it will not develop without our co-operation. (*c*) Grace can be hindered, by refusal to allow it to enter (the hard soil — the Catholic or non-Catholic who will not listen); by not thinking or meditating on it and making it part of ourselves (no roots — the superficial individual); by filling ourselves with wrong literature, wrong thoughts, wrong persons (thorns). (*d*) One student gets more out of school, or religion, or Mass than another because he co-operates (good soil).

We need to be receptive to the influences for good which surround us. There are two kinds of graces — sanctifying and actual. Sanctifying grace is that which comes ordinarily through the sacraments. It makes us partakers of God's life. It endures permanently in the soul as long as sin does not drive it out. Actual grace is a transient, supernatural help, which God grants for a particular need at a particular time. A sermon, a book, a conversation may be the occasion for actual graces. Resolutions to love God, effort to reflect on the words of Christ are due to actual graces:

Matt. 13: 24. Another parable he proposed to them, saying: The kingdom of heaven is likened to a man that sowed good seed in his field. 25. But while men were asleep, his enemy came and oversowed cockle among the wheat and went his way. 26. And when the blade was sprung up, and had brought forth fruit, then appeared also the cockle. 27. And the servants of the good man

of the house coming said to him: Sir, didst thou not sow good
seed in thy field? Whence then hath it cockle? 28. And he said
to them: An enemy hath done this. And the servants said to him:
Wilt thou that we go and gather it up? 29. And he said: No,
lest perhaps gathering up the cockle, you root up the wheat also
together with it. 30. Suffer both to grow until the harvest, and in
the time of the harvest I will say to the reapers: Gather up first
the cockle, and bind it into bundles to burn, but the wheat gather
ye into my barn.

Christ Himself will later explain this parable. It deals with hindrances to grace that come from outside of the individual. Evil is sown, like grace, only in the germinal state. One small act, one word, one suggestion that we allow to take root may cause our downfall in years to come. From a tiny scratch on the finger may come infection which will cause us to lose an arm or even life. So, while we are negligent (asleep) sin may take root. It is not God's plan to strike lax Catholics or His enemies dead. We must be patient with them as He is.

Matt. 13: 31. Another parable he proposed unto them, saying:
The kingdom of heaven is like to a grain of mustard-seed, which
a man took and sowed in his field. 32. Which is the least indeed
of all seeds; but when it is grown up, it is greater than all herbs,
and becometh a tree, so that the birds of the air come, and dwell
in the branches thereof. 33. Another parable he spoke to them:
The kingdom of heaven is like to leaven, which a woman took
and hid in three measures of meal, until the whole was leavened.

Here again we see the immense power of grace where it is not hindered. In hot countries the mustard stalks become very large. The Church grew rapidly from small beginnings. Imagine the conversions due to the apostles. One student of sterling qualities may influence hundreds, and all this unknown to himself. Our task is to be an influence for good, to be a leavener. Christ relies on us to lead others upward.

Matt. 13: 36. Then having sent away the multitudes, he came
into the house, and his disciples came to him, saying: Expound to
us the parable of the cockle of the field. 37. Who made answer
and said to them: He that soweth the good seed is the Son of
man. 38. And the field is the world. And the good seed are the
children of the kingdom. And the cockle are the children of the

wicked one. 39. And the enemy that sowed them, is the devil.
But the harvest is the end of the world. And the reapers are the
angels. 40. Even as cockle therefore is gathered up, and burnt
with fire, so shall it be at the end of the world. 41. The Son of
man shall send his angels and they shall gather out of his kingdom all scandals, and them that work iniquity: 42. And shall
cast them into the furnace of fire. There shall be weeping and
gnashing of teeth. 43. Then shall the just shine as the sun, in
the kingdom of their Father. He that hath ears to hear, let him
hear.

Here is the correct attitude — the desire to learn more, to advance in grace. The apostles showed their earnestness; they met the test. During the past week have the words of Christ at any time occupied our minds? Or has the world claimed all of our attention? Students who delight in reading works against religion, who delight in thoughts of revenge or impurity, are in reality allowing the devil to sow cockle.

God is patient with sowers of untruth; but there is a time of judgment. "Gnashing of teeth" eloquently portrays the sense of defeat experienced by the haters of Christ. If it should be our duty to pass our lives in circumstances where there is little good example, this parable says to struggle on. "He that hath ears" indicates that we show our character by the attitude we take toward religion, toward the Church, Mass, and Communion. The one who is intellectually honest will welcome a chance to learn more about Christ; the self-centered, conceited person will unconsciously reveal his nature by his views on religion.

MATT. 13: 44. The kingdom of heaven is like unto a treasure
hidden in a field. Which a man having found, hid it, and for joy
thereof goeth, and selleth all that he hath, and buyeth that field.
45. Again the kingdom of heaven is like to a merchant seeking
good pearls. 46. Who when he had found one pearl of great
price, went his way, and sold all that he had, and bought it.
47. Again the kingdom of heaven is like to a net cast into the
sea, and gathering together of all kinds of fishes. 48. Which,
when it was filled, they drew out, and sitting by the shore, they
chose out the good into vessels, but the bad they cast forth.
49. So shall it be at the end of the world. The angels shall go out,
and shall separate the wicked from among the just, 50. And

shall cast them into the furnace of fire: there shall be weeping and gnashing of teeth.

A tragedy, a retreat or some event sometimes wakes us up, and reveals to us what a great treasure we have in the Faith. Then, we must be willing to give up other things in order to appreciate Jesus. The highest joy of our life should be this search, this striving to grasp and realize what a treasure is the Catholic Faith. It must also be protected.

The Church is like a net. It is moved about by waves of persecution; its members, even, try to force it here and there. We are always asking: "Why does not the Church do this or that?" But all the while a strong Hand holds the net. We should thank God often that there is a higher, restraining Hand, holding us from rushing into waters where we would be lost.

1. The advantage of presenting religious truth in the form of parables is ———.
2. Show how Christ could adjust Himself to His hearers.
3. What is the meaning of "ears to hear"?
4. How do you explain the case of a student who lost his Faith after attending a Catholic school?
5. Show that you are a Catholic for others as well as for yourself.
6. What parable teaches the duty of co-operating with grace? Protecting grace? Giving up something for the Faith? Finding our joy in the Faith?
7. Why does not the Church expel all bad members?

Chapter 32

NATURE'S MASTER

MARK 4: 35. And he saith to them that day, when evening was come: Let us pass over to the other side. 36. And sending away the multitude, they take him even as he was in the ship: and there were other ships with him. 37. And there arose a great storm of wind, and the waves beat into the ship, so that the ship was filled. 38. And he was in the hinder part of the ship, sleeping upon a pillow; and they awake him, and say to him: Master, doth it not concern thee that we perish? 39. And rising up he rebuked the wind, and said to the sea: Peace, be still. And the wind ceased: and there was made a great calm. 40. And he said to them: Why are you fearful? Have you not faith yet? And they feared exceedingly: and they said one to another: Who is this (thinkest thou) that both wind and sea obey him?

FROM the strain of that busy life they now sought rest. The apostles were to have Him all to themselves. They were to be the protectors, for they were sailors. Yet they likely did not enjoy His request to cross at evening, for storms arise quickly at night on the Lake of Galilee; and He had no cloak. At this point it was five or six miles across. Lustily they dipped the oars or hoisted a sail. Lights flickering from the shore, and wild animals piercing the night with their cries did not attract them nor break their silence, for Jesus was asleep. They whispered to one another that He was tired. They were in charge of God, and they realized how precious was their Passenger.

The lake is 695 feet below sea level. Behind the steep cliffs on the eastern shore stretch hilly wastes, and east of that the hot desert. The wind, sweeping in and meeting colder currents of air, often rouses the placid lake into angry waves. It was December, the season of storms. In fact fishermen today do not venture far out between afternoon and midnight. So frightful was this storm that these experienced sailors were helpless before its fury. And they thought He was not interested in their plight, just as we often think God is unconcerned about us when we are in trouble. But He is there — ready to help.

Despite the rocking, the creaking of the boat, and the noise of panic, Jesus slept, with the calm of one at peace with God. Human skill being of no avail, these erstwhile protectors turned to the One whom they had thought they would protect. Noise failed to awaken Him but a cry for aid did. Nerve and presence of mind are seen in the awakened Christ. More than that, the divine grandeur of His Person appears as He rises calmly, in the midst of disorder, to speak words of command to the wind and the waters: "Peace!" What a word on the lips of the God-Man! "Nature . . . obeys Him, like a docile and intelligent servant." How majestic, confident He must have appeared in that sudden midnight calm. It awed the apostles. Who would not tremble in the presence of divine power at work!

Jesus wanted from them, as He does from us, not appeal only; He wants faith, confidence in Him. He has taught us that the world is not ruled by blind forces. God's providence means that there is a divine Person above all the calamities, the trials, and the sorrows of life. In the midst of every storm, whether physical, mental, spiritual, political, or social, maintain trust in Him. Christ is with the Catholic Church today; the bark of Peter still bears Him. Are we loyal to Him if we think the bark is sinking?

Luke 8: 26. And they sailed to the country of the Gerasens, which is over against Galilee. 27. And when he was come forth to the land, there met him a certain man who had a devil now a very long time, and he wore no clothes, neither did he abide in a house, but in the sepulchres. 28. And when he saw Jesus, he fell down before him; and crying out with a loud voice, he said: What have I to do with thee, Jesus, Son of the most high God? I beseech thee, do not torment me. 29. For he commanded the unclean spirit to go out of the man. For many times it seized him, and he was bound with chains, and kept in fetters; and breaking the bonds, he was driven by the devil into the deserts. 30. And Jesus asked him, saying: What is thy name? But he said: Legion;

> because many devils were entered into him. 31. And they be-
> sought him that he would not command them to go into the abyss.
> 32. And there was there a herd of many swine feeding on the
> mountain; and they besought him that he would suffer them to
> enter into them. And he suffered them. 33. The devils therefore
> went out of the man, and entered into the swine; and the herd
> ran violently down a steep place into the lake, and were stifled.
> 34. Which when they that fed them saw done, they fled away,
> and told it in the city and in the villages. 35. And they went
> out to see what was done; and they came to Jesus, and found the
> man out of whom the devils were departed, sitting at his feet,
> clothed, and in his right mind; and they were afraid. 36. And
> they also that had seen, told them how he had been healed from
> the legion. 37. And all the multitude of the country of the
> Gerasens besought him to depart from them; for they were taken
> with great fear. And he, going up into the ship, returned back
> again. 38. Now the man, out of whom the devils were departed,
> besought him that he might be with him. But Jesus sent him
> away, saying: 39. Return to thy house, and tell how great things
> God hath done to thee. And he went through the whole city, pub-
> lishing how great things Jesus had done to him.

The next morning they landed. A frightening, repulsive spectacle met them, in the form of a man (there may have been more than one), hardly recognizable as human. No hospitals, no asylums were then in existence to care for maddened individuals. They dwelt in the caves of hills. The most terrible of them now confronted Christ. This was clearly a case of demoniac possession. The devils recognized Christ as God. Would He send them back to hell? The devil used the man's voice in speaking; and he delights to cause men to rave in fury against God. It is true that primitive peoples, in their belief that spirits caused disease, would often call an ordinary case of epilepsy or hysterics a case of possession by the devil. Yet, cases of demoniac possession have been and are real. Missionaries in countries where Christianity has not gained a solid hold meet weird cases of possession. The presence of Christ (sanctity itself) caused torment to these evil spirits. No mere epileptic or lunatic could by his own powers thus discern the nature of Christ. Christ's word was sufficient to make the devils obey, for His power is always superior to that of the devils. There are other cures recorded in the Gospels which have not been referred to in this book.

We do not know why the devils chose this petition. Possibly it was to injure Christ. If so, they were caught in their own trap, for the 2,000 swine perished. Christ permitted, but did not command the destruction of the swine. All life is His, by the supreme right of creation. He permits men to kill one another; He permits earthquakes. As St. Thomas says, "He permitted the demons to inflict harm on the man for the instruction of man." The good of souls is the highest good. If these swine belonged to Jews, the Jewish law was being broken, and they deserved to lose them; if they belonged to Gentiles and were being sold to lax Jews we can have little sympathy with the owners, just as we should condemn the nations that are making money on the dope traffic today. The excited villagers saw a cured, sane man — a human life saved in exchange for the loss. The villagers had known him; he was one of their own. These pagans trembled before the Stranger who had such power. They should have balanced the cure against the loss, but Christ understood their fear. He did not blame them. He was always patient. He would wait.

> LUKE 8: 40. And it came to pass, that when Jesus was returned, the multitude received him: for they were all waiting for him. 41. And behold there came a man whose name was Jairus, and he was a ruler of the synagogue: and he fell down at the feet of Jesus, beseeching him that he would come into his house. 42. For he had an only daughter, almost twelve years old, and she was dying. And it happened as he went, that he was thronged by the multitudes.

Christ was now back on the western shore. Imagine the strain of this continual pressure of the crowds. He was a marked Man everywhere; and Jairus was prominent. The rich and powerful have their troubles as well as the poor.

> LUKE 8: 43. And there was a certain woman having an issue of blood twelve years, who had bestowed all her substance on physicians, and could not be healed by any. 44. She came behind him, and touched the hem of his garment; and immediately the issue of her blood stopped. 45. And Jesus said: Who is it that touched me? And all denying, Peter and they that were with

him said: Master, the multitudes throng and press thee, and dost thou say: Who touched me? 46. And Jesus said: Somebody hath touched me; for I know that virtue is gone out from me. 47. And the woman seeing that she was not hid, came trembling, and fell down before his feet, and declared before all the people for what cause she had touched him, and how she was immediately healed. 48. But he said to her: Daughter, thy faith hath made thee whole; go thy way in peace.

Christ had started to the house of Jairus. The narrow streets were filled by the accompanying throng. The reputation of Jairus would make this a celebrated case. Meanwhile, crouched in one of the doorways was a woman, with an internal malady, a flow of blood. She is an instance of the thousands who secretly longed for aid from Christ. Modesty, or dislike of publicity held her back from coming openly to Him. But her faith was firm. For months, perhaps, she had thought over this scheme and awaited an opportunity. She reasoned that since Christ was a miracle worker His garments also could cure. So she came from behind and touched the tassel, which was hanging over His back (Num. 15: 38).

Despite the crowd, Jesus was aware that the woman was cured. He did not want her faith to be overlooked, nor to lose the opportunity of teaching, nor to permit the woman to believe in magic. He stopped. Jairus, the important man was perhaps, impatient; the apostles more so. Peter thought Christ's question foolish. But Christ wished to emphasize that it was He, His divine power working through the tassel, that had caused the effect. The woman in her modesty thought He would resent her action as stealth. Instead, He wished to comfort her, and to testify to her faith. Not her touching the garment but her faith merited the reward. In that crowd many were touching Him, but she had faith.

The Church approves the veneration of relics of the saints, whose bodies were the temple of the Holy Ghost. That does not mean belief in a "magical virtue, or physical curative efficacy residing in the relic itself" (Cf. art. "Relics" in *Cath. Encyc.*). Christ said: "virtue (healing power) is gone out from Me." It is always the power of God working *through* the saints or relics. The more saintly we become the more does God's grace work *through us* for the good of others. We honor a relic for what the saint was. Touching a relic is a way of showing faith in Christ the Healer.

> LUKE 8: 49. As he was yet speaking, there cometh one to the ruler of the synagogue, saying to him: Thy daughter is dead; trouble him not. 50. And Jesus hearing this word, answered the father of the maid: Fear not; believe only, and she shall be safe. 51. And when he was come to the house, he suffered not any man to go in with him, but Peter and James and John, and the father and mother of the maid. 52. And all wept and mourned for her But he said: Weep not; the maid is not dead, but sleepeth. 53. And they laughed him to scorn, knowing that she was dead. 54. But he taking her by the hand, cried out, saying: Maid, arise. 55. And her spirit returned, and she arose immediately. And he bade them give her to eat. 56. And her parents were astonished, whom he charged to tell no man what was done.

Christ had lingered, apparently careless of the danger which the daughter of Jairus was in. This was a test for the anxious father especially when news of her death was brought to him. Even in death, our faith in Christ's power to call forth the dead on the last day must continue.

Professional mourning was a custom. People were paid for weeping and playing the flute at time of death. The hypocrisy of it all disgusted Jesus. He put the mourners out. Here in Capharnaum, where He had worked so many miracles, where all should have known His power, He was jeered at. Jairus, however, had faith; and Christ acted — acted as God, with no waste of words, no hesitancy, no trickery, but a simple command: "arise." How tender is Christ, how easy to be loved if we but knew Him. Little children were not afraid of Him. "From her mattress she reached up to Him and loved Him." It is not God's fault that the poor children do not have sufficient food. Usually it is due to man's perversity — greed among the strong, human failings sometimes in the parents.

The professional mourners had had the same opportunity as Jairus to believe in Christ but they preferred to sneer, so they were excluded. No person, Catholic or non-Catholic, will ever experience the joy of belief, so long as a sneering, scornful attitude guides him. Jairus seems to have been grateful but speechless. "Such is perfect prayer — believing, loving, trusting, adoring, unable to express itself in words and Jesus understood the silence" (Goodier).

The sincere Catholic has a deep attachment to Jesus. Some people with the boast of being able to measure the divine, prefer to trust a philosopher or a scientist instead of Christ. The Catholic knows that his faith in nature's Master who commanded the winds, the sea, the evil spirits, and death itself is a faith well placed, a faith bringing peace here and hereafter.

1. What is often the motive behind expensive funerals?
2. Why should we wear a scapular medal or carry a small crucifix?
3. Is Christ aware when we are apparently struggling alone with a temptation?
4. Can we always ascertain God's purpose in permitting a physical catastrophe, as the San Francisco earthquake?
5. What is meant by God's supreme domination over all things?
6. We know that the world is not ruled by blind forces because ———.
7. What is the reason for veneration of relics?
8. A Catholic mother refuses to be consoled after the death of her daughter. What does she lack?
9. May a long delay in answer to our prayers be a test of our faith?
10. Should we be silent while carrying Christ, after Communion?
11. If you came home some night tired from work and you were asked to call on a sick person would you go?
12. Would you hesitate to offer the Mass and receive Communion if someone jeered at you for being overpious, or silly?
13. If a person sneered at you for believing in the resurrection of the dead what would you do?
14. The Church permits a priest to anoint a person if he arrives an hour or so after death because ———.

Chapter 33

FRIENDS CONVEY HIS MESSAGE

MARK 6: 1. And going out from thence, he went into his own country; and his disciples followed him. 2. And when the sabbath was come, he began to teach in the synagogue: and many hearing him were in admiration at his doctrine, saying: How came this man by all these things? And what wisdom is this that is given to him, and such mighty works as are wrought by his hands? 3. Is not this the carpenter, the son of Mary, the brother of James, and Joseph, and Jude, and Simon? Are not also his sisters here with us? And they were scandalized in regard of him. 4. And Jesus said to them: A prophet is not without honor, but in his own country, and in his own house, and among his own kindred. 5. And he could not do any miracles there, only that he cured a few that were sick, laying his hands upon them. 6. And he wondered because of their unbelief, and he went through the villages round about teaching.

WE SEE that His second return to His fellow townsmen argues for His love of the spot of His boyhood. Meanwhile the apostles were learning how to meet ingratitude with patience.

It was December. The heavenly beauty of the discourse moved even the antagonistic audience. It is hard to imagine how these people could be so mean. In their eyes Joseph and Mary and the relatives were insignificant, so He had to be insignificant. But they were afraid of Him so they did not maltreat Him. Staring, cold faces met Him everywhere. Their attitude toward Mary and Himself allows us to picture the heroic reserve, the long monotony of the 30 years passed here so unobtrusively by the Holy Family. Suffering, but saying nothing, had been, and continued to be, Mary's part, a woman who did not gossip, did not boast, who willingly remained, in the eyes of the Nazarenes, obscure Mary.

Matt. 9: 35. And Jesus went about all the cities and towns, teaching in their synagogues, and preaching the gospel of the kingdom, and healing every disease and every infirmity. 36. And seeing the multitudes, he had compassion on them: because they were distressed, and lying like sheep that have no shepherd. 37. Then he saith to his disciples: The harvest indeed is great, but the laborers are few. 38. Pray ye therefore the Lord of the harvest that he send forth laborers into his harvest.

Opportunity and grace had come again to Nazareth and had been rejected so Christ moved on to other cities. Failure never disheartened Him; appreciated or neglected, He continued day by day to explain the purpose of life. So, too, when people refuse to hear about the Church we must not give in to discouragement.

What hurt our Lord then, as now, was the absence of true leaders — the laziness, the worldliness of those who would not instruct the people. Then, as now, many people wanted the truth. They were distressed about whom to follow, for false prophets, such as communists, seem to possess energy and zeal in spreading error. Promoters of vice are active always. Pray, therefore, for laborers — priests, brothers, sisters, and an active laity. The obligation is on all of us to show non-believers what the true purpose of life is.

Matt. 10: 5. These twelve Jesus sent: commanding them, saying: Go ye not into the way of the Gentiles, and into the city of the Samaritans enter ye not: 6. But go ye rather to the lost sheep of the house of Israel. 7. And going, preach, saying: The Kingdom of heaven is at hand. 8. Heal the sick, raise the dead, cleanse the lepers, cast out devils: freely have you received, freely give. 9. Do not possess gold, nor silver, nor money in your purses:

He limited the field of activity for the apostles in their first mission. They were not yet ready to go among strangers, although two months or more had elapsed since His second appearance in Nazareth. One theme was to dominate their preaching — the kingdom, the opportunity to be joined to Christ, to become a member of that universal Christian family into which we are adopted through Baptism. Jesus endowed them with divine power, hence they were to be generous with their time, their sympathy, and their resources. Healing the sick certainly implies that Christ expects all of us to work for the social and economic welfare of all the people. He did not want people to be kept out of churches or away from the sacraments because they have no money. Grace, of which the Church is the official dispenser, must always be given freely. Friends of Christ gladly convey His message of startling truths.

Under our economic system the Church needs money. It was somewhat different in Palestine. And yet, essentially, financial resources do not make the Church successful. Neither pope, bishop, priest, nor layman should ever fall into the error of believing that money is fundamental to personal happiness or necessary to obtain the grace of God. Today the missionary has to keep more the spirit than the letter of these original directions. Christ expects all of us to pay what we can toward church expenses. And people are usually generous when they see a self-sacrificing priest. "The teachers should receive their sustenance from the people, their reward from God," says St. John Chrysostom. It is the spirit of detachment from money that Christ requires in those who are His representatives.

> MATT. 10: 11. And into whatsoever city or town you shall enter, inquire who in it is worthy, and there abide till you go thence. 12. And when you come into the house, salute it, saying: Peace be to this house. 13. And if that house be worthy, your peace shall come upon it; but if it be not worthy your peace shall return to you. 14. And whosoever shall not receive you, nor hear your words: going forth out of that house or city shake off the dust from your feet. 15. Amen I say to you, it shall be more tolerable for the land of Sodom and Gomorrha in the day of judgment, than for that city. 16. Behold I send you as sheep in the midst of wolves. Be ye therefore wise as serpents and simple as doves.

While not shielding them from sorrow, yet God does bless those families that receive wholeheartedly the priest, the nun, or the brother. Peace of mind, a spiritual contentment comes to him who receives God's messenger. When the missionary, or the priest who is seeking lapsed Catholics is rejected, salvation becomes difficult. The indifferentist who neglects religion needs to reflect on verses 14 and 15. Fire and brimstone had destroyed Sodom and Gomorrha (Cf. Gen. 19: 24–25).

Our Faith is a gift from God. The world, the flesh, and the devil often combine to destroy this Faith. As St. Jerome says, by being wise as serpents we permit no one to deceive us; by being simple as doves we never attempt to deceive others. The Catholic who relies sincerely on Christ will merit the protection of God's graces. The world cares little if we lose our religion, hence the necessity for prudence, wisdom as well as simplicity. Without prudence the person of simple faith would fall into many traps; without simplicity, that is, frankness, openness or intellectual honesty, and faith, the prudent individual might become crafty in a worldly sense. We are working for Christ when we attempt to save others from wolves, that is, from false teachings which many writers try to instill into the people. Many theories look nice on the surface. Underneath them is the craftiness of Satan, seeking to deceive.

> MATT. 10: 22. And you shall be hated by all men for my name's sake: but he that shall persevere unto the end, he shall be saved. . . . 24. The disciple is not above the master, nor the servant above his lord. . . . 28. And fear ye not them that kill the body, and are not able to kill the soul: but rather fear him that can destroy both soul and body in hell. . . . 32. Every one therefore that shall confess me before men, I will also confess him before my Father who is in heaven. 33. But he that shall deny me before men, I will also deny him before my Father who is in heaven.

If we be true friends of Jesus we must expect hatred against us. We do not fear this hatred, but we should have fear of God. However, love, not fear, is the main quality in the real Catholic. The Catholic religion is not a cold system, nor merely a set of doctrines to be believed; it is loyalty to Christ as shown by loyalty to the Church. Christ does not consider Catholics as hired servants; they are His friends. We are not to be blind, mechanical followers but devoted friends. And who does not stand up for his friend? Loyalty to Mass, Friday abstinence, and to other laws of the Church are in reality acts in which we "confess Christ before men." The majority of students cannot be intellectual leaders; every student can be loyal. And loyalty is a nobler thing than leadership. As a matter of fact, good example to others is the best method of conveying Christ's message. Leadership in holy living is possible to each individual.

> MATT. 10: 37. He that loveth father or mother more than me, is not worthy of me; and he that loveth son or daughter more than me, is not worthy of me. 38. And he that taketh not up his cross, nor followeth me, is not worthy of me. 39. He that findeth his life, shall lose it: and he that shall lose his life for me, shall find it.

At the age of twelve (p. 55) Jesus taught us that God must come first in our lives. No creature may rank higher in our love than He. Christ showed us how to be loyal to God first and also loyal to parents.

From His first mention of the cross we learn that living for Him and working for Him requires courage. "Take up your cross," He says; that is, accept the burdens of being a Catholic. No person has ever yet gone through life without suffering, pain and agony, physical, mental, or spiritual. They who run away from suffering — by lying, cheating, or giving up their religion — are eventually worse off than those who accept. Christ does not want students who quit, who are cowards, who won't fight. He wants people with moral courage, who take up their crosses. One's cross may be lack of beauty, of talent, of popularity; or, ill health, or poverty. What happens if we are courageous enough to attempt these "hard" things in life? We learn to be happy, for Christ gives to the courageous Catholic an inner joy.

It is the subtle poison of self-centeredness that prevents many from enjoying the Faith. Our worst danger lies in selfishness — in seeking fame, riches, pleasure for ourselves. The student who is always selfish is in reality unhappy; the student who is continually complaining about his lack of this or that, his failure to receive a square deal at school, his lack of a chance in life, is secretly selfish and a coward. Christ's command is to "lose" one's life, that is, to forget self and to work for Christ, for parents, for school, for wife and children. They "find" themselves who seek a goal, an aim that is outside of themselves. The girl who does not want to marry because she does not wish to be tied down with children will never find herself. Parents find themselves because they lose this selfish viewpoint.

Acceptance of the cross, or unselfishness, must not be confused with what is called defeatism. A Catholic never says: "What's the use?" Christ wants us to work, to seek to improve ourselves physically, mentally, spiritually — to make the world a little better for having lived in it. He wants us to do our best with what we have and to leave the rest in God's hands. We can overcome a great many disadvantages by effort, and also find happiness by cheerfully accepting what we cannot change through effort.

> Mark 6: 14. And king Herod heard (for his name was made manifest), and he said: John the Baptist is risen again from the dead, and therefore mighty works shew forth themselves in him. 15. And others said: It is Elias, But others said: It is a prophet, as one of the prophets. 16. Which Herod hearing, said: John whom I beheaded, he is risen again from the dead. 17. For Herod himself had sent and apprehended John, and bound him in prison for the sake of Herodias, the wife of Philip his brother, because he had married her. 18. For John said to Herod: It is not lawful for thee to have thy brother's wife. 19. Now Herodias laid snares for him: and was desirous to put him to death, and could not. 20. For Herod feared John, knowing him to be a just and holy man: and kept him, and when he heard him, did many things; and he heard him willingly. 21. And when a convenient day was come, Herod made a supper for his birthday, for the princes, and tribunes, and chief men of Galilee. 22. And when the daughter of the same Herodias had come in, and had danced and pleased Herod and them that were at table with him, the king said to the damsel: Ask of me what thou wilt, and I will give it thee. 23. And he swore to her: Whatsoever thou shalt ask I will give thee, though it be the half of my kingdom. 24. Who when she was gone out, said to her mother: What shall I ask? But she said: The head of John the Baptist. 25. And when she was come in immediately with haste to the king, she asked, saying: I will that forthwith thou give me in a dish the head of John the Baptist. 26. And the king was struck sad. Yet because of his oath, and because of them that were with him at table, he would not displease her: 27. But sending an executioner, he commanded that his head should be brought in a dish. 28. And he beheaded him in the prison, and brought

his head in a dish: and gave it to the damsel, and the damsel gave it to her mother. 29. Which his disciples hearing, came and took his body, and laid it in a tomb.

The horrible, yet glorious, end of one who worked courageously is exemplified in John the Baptist. For almost a year this confessor of Christ, who showed "no dread of human royalty and no compromise with sin" in high places had been in prison. The relentless Herodias could not for a long time induce Herod to kill John, for Herod feared him. In fact, John touched the better part of Herod. But loose living gradually rots the moral fiber of a person, and robs him of manliness. Salome was the dancer; she was the daughter of Herodias, before Herod married Herodias. Her sensuality was now to lead Herod into a trap where he showed his lack of character. A man with any manliness would have said *No!* to the request for John's head. It is a sad insight into the guests that no one had courage to speak out against murder. The cold cruelty of Herodias and the icy heart of her daughter were shown by their craftiness in taking advantage of the opportunity so long desired. The sin of human respect is shown by Herod's fear of being ridiculed by the guests. No promise can bind one to a sinful act. A man of character will take his stand on principles, and be unmoved by fear of what false friends will say.

1. Should we continue to do good, to fight for justice even though no one apparently applauds our efforts?
2. Show how Christ trusted the apostles.
3. There is an obligation to pray for vocations because ———.
4. Show that Christ was never disheartened by failure.
5. Catholic action is participation by the laity in work of the hierarchy. What is that work?
6. On what statement of Christ is the fifth commandment of the Church based?
7. What is necessary in your home when the priest comes on a sick call?
8. How would you explain the opposition so often shown to a vocation to the priesthood and to religious life?
9. Whom do you welcome to your home when you receive a priest?
10. Explain the relative value of prudence and simplicity in acquiring an appreciation of your religion.

11. Financial backing is not the most important consideration in achieving success as a Catholic because ———.
12. What should be your attitude toward a priest who is not a worthy representative of Christ?
13. What is meant by saying that the giving of good example can make every student who gives it a conveyor of Christ's message?

Chapter 34

THE CONCLUSION FROM THE MULTIPLICATION

MARK 6: 30. And the apostles coming together unto Jesus related to him all things that they had done and taught. 31. And he said to them; Come apart into a desert place, and rest a little. For there were many coming and going: and they had not so much as time to eat. 32. And going up into a ship, they went into a desert place apart. 33. And they saw them going away, and many knew: and they ran flocking thither on foot from all the cities, and were there before them. 34. And Jesus going out saw a great multitude; and he had compassion on them, because they were as sheep not having a shepherd, and he began to teach them many things. 35. And when the day was now far spent, his disciples came to him, saying: This is a desert place, and the hour is now past: 36. Send them away, that going into the next villages and towns, they may buy themselves meat to eat.

THEIR first mission tour ended, the apostles returned to tell Christ of their success. Note their frankness with Him, and the hold that He had on their affections. He confided in them; they confided in Him. Peter would be talkative at this meeting; John would not say much; Philip would smile in thanksgiving for the confidence he now felt; Judas would probably relate how he had told his hearers to "beware of men." The priest on his lonely mission, the student home from school, and the lay person on his way back from work can drop into a church and talk over his or her success with Christ.

Christ had sympathy then, and He has it now, for all earnest Catholics. He knew the apostles needed rest. And the crowds were gathering. Just as we enter upon a retreat, so Christ invited the apostles to leave the din of city life, to "come apart." Relaxation from continued activity is a necessity. No one will ever be a real Catholic unless he takes time out now and then to reflect on the meaning of friendship with Jesus. Fear of sinning is not the main motive which brings Catholics to Mass. Religion is love of a Person; it is doing good for that Person.

The public is merciless on a busy leader. The apostles could tell us that companionship with Christ is never without its thrills. He worked hard; He also taught the need of taking time out to pray and to reflect. The crowd saw the boat start eastward across the lake from some spot near Capharnaum and immediately set out on foot along the northern shore of the lake. So happy were the apostles to be with Christ, that, while sailing or rowing leisurely, they were not aware of the growing crowd of people along the eastern shore. A two- or three-hour walk would bring the crowd over to the region of Bethsaida-Julius, northeast of the lake.

As the boat was about to land Christ looked up into the expectant faces of the people. What drawing power He must have had! Far out into the country had they come, away from the towns. His heart was touched. Their official instructors, their regular guides had done little for them. He had sought rest, and lo! here were throngs anxious to be instructed. He passed up among them, healing some, encouraging others, and instructing all in the nature of the kingdom. The hours passed; the day approached night. No one was anxious to leave. The apostles were worried; they suggested that He send the people away before dark.

> John 6: 4. Now the pasch, the festival day of the Jews, was near at hand. 5. When Jesus therefore had lifted up his eyes, and seen that a very great multitude cometh to him, he said to Philip: Whence shall we buy bread, that these may eat? 6. And this he said to try him; for he himself knew what he would do. 7. Philip answered him: Two hundred pennyworth of bread is not sufficient for them, that every one may take a little. 8. One of his disciples, Andrew, the brother of Simon Peter, saith to him: 9. There is a boy here that hath five barley loaves, and two fishes; but what are these among so many?

The large crowd is accounted for by the fact that the annual Pasch was nigh. It was a holiday season; and multitudes were on their way to Jerusalem. But Jesus, the One who spoke with power, was more attractive to them now than was Jerusalem. He glanced over the assemblage. What orator ever had such an audience in the country hills! What leader ever conceived such an idea for his followers!

He turned to Philip, to test him. And He must have had a kindly twinkle in His eye as He did so. These human touches show us how natural and at ease He was before a problem. He expects us to think, and to plan, to have initiative. But more than that, He expects us to trust Him who always showed mastery of a problem. "The enthusiastic regard of the people, which public men find so intoxicating, did not affect His calm; it neither elated nor troubled Him." He knew the faults of the people; but He also knew that many of them were blindly searching for peace of mind.

Philip missed his cue. He forgot he was in the presence of divine power, and he thought that money was necessary. Sometimes we imagine that money, talent, or prestige would enable us to do something for Christ. They might, indeed, but it would be better still if we realized the power of Christ's grace which is near. The apostles heard the question to Philip. Likewise materially minded, they hurt Christ by lack of imagination. He wanted them to say that He could provide out of His divine power. It was His way of training them to make correct decisions. These fishes were small, and, like our sardines, were tasty when merely dried and salted.

> LUKE 9: 14. Now there were about five thousand men. And he said to his disciples: Make them sit down by fifties in a company. 15. And they did so; and made them all sit down. 16. And taking the five loaves and the two fishes, he looked up to heaven, and blessed them; and he broke, and distributed to his disciples, to set before the multitude.
> MARK 6: 42. And they all did eat, and had their fill.

In this scene Jesus shows us how foresight and methodical efficiency can be united to sanctity. Likewise, He teaches us to take a deep interest in the temporal welfare of the people. It was in the springtime, April of 29, and just a year previous to the institution of the Holy Eucharist.

The apostles passed among the crowd to arrange the groups. This arrangement made orderly distribution possible. The crowd was submissive, but no one knew what was coming. The number could now be easily estimated. Jesus must have been on an elevation along the hillside. Silently, expectantly the vast crowd watched. He thanked the Father for food by which we live; He blessed it to remind us to be grateful to God for food. The Jews usually carried baskets and so each apostle took a basket. The small sections given to each apostle by Christ were continually multiplied in the basket so that it was never empty.

> JOHN 6: 12. And when they were filled, he said to his disciples: Gather up the fragments that remain, lest they be lost. 13. They gathered up therefore, and filled twelve baskets with the fragments of the five barley loaves, which remained over and above to them that had eaten.

Skeptical were the apostles at the start; but the marvel increased their trust as they went along. The generosity of divine goodness caused their hands to tremble. Each person received all he wanted. It was real food; it satisfied hunger. The Gospel accounts give us facts; this miracle was a reality. He who gave us the animal and vegetable world for our daily nourishment could easily feed thousands, for Christ is God. It is stupid to argue that miracles cannot take place. Instead of theorizing, the modern world should first get the facts. The fact is, that He is God. No other conclusion is possible from the multiplication.

In the presence of such liberality, the apostles probably felt cheap in gathering up the fragments. But Christ knew that every detail was to be important in this miracle, hence His care. He was generous; He was also practical. Each piece passed out by an apostle was real bread. Each host in a ciborium, each particle placed on your tongue at Communion is the real Body of Christ. Divine power worked through the apostles then; the same divine power works through the priest today.

> MATT. 14: 22. And forthwith Jesus obliged his disciples to go up into the boat, and to go before him over the water, till he dismissed the people.
>
> JOHN 6: 14. Now those men, when they had seen what a miracle Jesus had done, said: This is of a truth the prophet that is to come

into the world. 15. Jesus therefore, when he knew that they would come to take him by force, and make him king, fled again into the mountain himself alone.

Night was approaching. The matter-of-fact way in which the Evangelists describe, with no attempt at flourish or embellishment, this unique marvel in the world's history may cause us to forget the thrill and the emotions that ran through the apostles. Christ understood them; they would easily lose their heads over this event. They would yield to the rising excitement of the crowd. The liberal Christ now changed to the commanding Christ. He did not wish them to be deceived by the enthusiasm of a king-seeking people. He ordered the apostles to cross to the west of the lake. They did not want to go. How the heart of St. Peter sank! But that indefinable something in the face of Christ hushed Peter. Meekly they pushed off in the boat, expecting at each moment to hear shouts from the people.

The people were acquainted with all the Old Testament events — Melchisedech bringing forth bread and wine to Abraham (Gen. 14: 18–19); Moses and the manna in the desert (Exod. 16: 13–15); David describing divine favors under the image of a banquet, a table (Ps. 22: 5) — and they suddenly realized that in Christ was fulfilled all that had been promised to them. He was the expected great prophet and He was to begin for them another period of plenty and of freedom, so they must make Him king. Such was their conclusion. Neither should we forget that the recent murder of the Baptist stirred them up to renewed thoughts of revolt. Christ could have started a revolution in an instant.

One test of greatness is not to be deceived by popularity. He who came to redeem and to keep His will obedient to His Father's wishes was not going to play with the possibility of an earthly kingdom. Hence we here learn to love Jesus all the more for keeping His true purpose, His cross, ever before Him. "Hiding His glory in outward lowliness, and never seeking honor from men He had, throughout, identified His will with that of God, with a self-restraint which showed the grandest force of will" (Geikie). We admire also the firmness with which He handled the whole situation. The crowd did not find Him craving popularity; neither could they resist His orders to disperse, to rest for the night. The apostles heard no shouts from the shore. From the scene of His greatest Galilean triumph He quietly withdrew, for, tired as He was, He had more yet to do on that night.

* *

The main value of a retreat is ———. The origin and meaning of the custom of saying grace before and after meals is ————. How may a young person prevent success or popularity from "going to his head"? Contrast Christ's multiplying of the loaves with His refusal to change a stone into bread at the request of the devil. Why the difference? Was each multiplied loaf really bread? What relation does this miracle have to our belief that Christ is present in each host that we receive at Communion? Give an instance in which Christ may have tested playfully His apostles.

* *

> Mark 6: 46. And when he had dismissed them, he went up to
> the mountain to pray. 47. And when it was late, the ship was in
> the midst of the sea, and himself alone on the land. 48. And
> seeing them laboring in rowing (for the wind was against them),
> and about the fourth watch of the night, he cometh to them
> walking upon the sea, and he would have passed by them. 49.
> But they seeing him walking upon the sea, thought it was an
> apparition, and they cried out. 50. For they all saw him, and
> were troubled. And immediately he spoke with them, and said
> to them: Have a good heart; it is I, fear ye not.

He had given a feast; the banqueters had departed happy. What a contrast to that scene at Herod's banquet of murder! And now He was alone — alone to pray. A leader must often withdraw. Do we do the same after our triumphs? This night He prayed that the apostles would be loyal in the crisis that would arise on the morrow.

He prayed for hours. Meanwhile things were not going well with the apostles. A strong west wind had arisen. Up to about 3:00 a.m., they had covered around three miles (John 6: 19). Little did they realize that He was thinking of them, just as we often imagine that God is not watching when we are in distress. It is a mistake to say that God does not see us. He is near, and waiting to be called. As He came near them, He could see them laboring at the oars. While anxious to help, He pretended to go by them. He wanted them to ask for help, just as He waits till we show our reliance on Him. He first tests us. The apostles did not recognize Him. They were frightened; they thought Him a ghost. And the fact that these fishermen admitted later their doubts, shows us how truthfully the Gospels were written. The Evangelists did not cover up their own faults when composing the Gospels. What a relief it was to them when they heard those reassuring words.

> MATT. 14: 28. And Peter making answer, said: Lord, if it be thou, bid me come to thee upon the waters. 29. And he said: Come. And Peter going down out of the boat, walked upon the water to come to Jesus. 30. But seeing the wind strong, he was afraid: and when he began to sink, he cried out, saying: Lord, save me. 31. And immediately Jesus stretching forth his hand took hold of him, and said to him: O thou of little faith, why didst thou doubt?

Impulsive Peter, willing to ask a great favor, thought he was applying a test to the one standing there. He calculated that if it were Christ he was not asking too much. We admire Peter's courage. None of the others dared ask as much in that wild, heaving scene. Would we have asked?

A thrill shot through Peter when he heard the word: "Come." Christ admires those who attempt hard things in order to reach Him. Peter started; the water held him. He was all right as long as he kept his eye on Christ, but he made one psychological mistake. A big wave loomed up beside him. He took his eye off Christ and looked at the wave and his faith faltered; he lost confidence and began to sink. Had he kept his eye on Christ, instead of watching the wave and thinking about the danger, he would have triumphed. He failed, but we love him for his attempt. He was not ashamed or afraid to try. His very faults show the greatness of his soul. Like many generous natures, Peter became alarmed by his first obstacle. Christ did not blame Peter for his request but merely for his weak faith. His "little faith," which is big in comparison to that which we often show, has taught us that "if, like Peter, we fix our eyes on Jesus, we too may walk triumphantly over the swelling waves of disbelief, and unterrified amid the rising winds of doubt; but if we turn away our eyes from Him in whom we have believed — if, as it is casy to do, and as we are so much tempted to do, we look rather at the power and fury of those terrible and destructive elements than at Him who can help and save — then we too, shall inevitably sink" (Farrar).

It is wrong to keep our gaze always on difficulties, on how hard it may be to study, to be honest and pure, or to write. Look rather on the source of help, Christ, or at the goal you have in mind (law, medicine, priesthood, religious life, a home of your own), and the obstacles will lose their difficulties. Catholic life becomes easier when we keep our eyes on Christ. Do not fume or fret over difficulties. Act. Football players keep an eye on the goal, not merely on obstacles in front of them.

> MATT. 14: 32. And when they were come up into the boat, the wind ceased. 33. And they that were in the boat came and adored him, saying: Indeed thou art the Son of God. 34. And having passed the water, they came into the country of Genesar.

The presence of Christ is peace, calm, and security. At this early morning hour, while men slept and only the moon kept watch over the waters these fishermen grasped an awesome, sublime truth. Their Leader was God. They dropped on their knees. Yesterday their hearts had been blind and they had not realized the significance of the multiplication of the loaves. They had felt that Christ was the Messias promised to the Jews but only now did it begin to dawn on them that this Messias was in reality God. By His actions Christ was gradually leading them to higher things, to stanch faith in His divinity. Each event was strengthening them for the test that would come when He first proposed the doctrine of Holy Communion. Believing Him divine after the multiplication, they would believe His statements about Communion.

1. Select that quality of leadership which you most admire in our Lord.
2. Has Christ the same power today that He had near the lake?
3. Show that our Lord had no worldly ambitions.
4. Show that our lack of faith does not please Christ.
5. Why is St. Peter so lovable a character?
6. Show how an aim, a specific goal is the real secret of will power.
7. Cf. Matt. 15: 29–39 for a multiplication of loaves and fishes on another occasion.

Chapter 35

FOOD FOR OUR LIFE WITH GOD

JOHN 6: 24. When therefore the multitude saw that Jesus was
not there, nor his disciples, they took shipping, and came to
Capharnaum, seeking for Jesus. 25. And when they had found
him on the other side of the sea, they said to him: Rabbi, when
camest thou hither? 26. Jesus answered them, and said: Amen,
amen I say to you, you seek me, not because you have seen
miracles, but because you did eat of the loaves, and were filled.
27. Labor not for the meat which perisheth, but for that which
endureth unto life everlasting, which the Son of man will give
you. For him hath God, the Father, sealed.

MANY had remained all night on the eastern shore. They searched at dawn for Christ. Not finding Him, some walked back along the northern shore and others came by boat over to Capharnaum. They were puzzled as to how He got to Capharnaum.

Our Lord never wasted time on idle questions. He quickly dispelled their hope that He would be their king. His supplying bread miraculously for them was intended as proof that He came from God, armed with truth and grace, two things which we need in order to prepare for everlasting life with God. The fundamental object of all search should be to find the truth about God and man and the world. Christ has something of eternal value to give to us. When we learn the truth about Him we have something that is endurable, something that never grows old. Whoever desires to know the truth about God must listen to Christ.

In verse 27 He shows how the miracle of yesterday is connected with the announcement He is about to make. The sixth chapter of St. John contains the promise of the Eucharist, a promise given one year before its institution at the Last Supper. Verses 28–47 emphasize one dominant thought, the necessity for complete faith in Christ, if one wishes to be able to accept the doctrine of the Eucharist. Verses 48–59 deal with the Holy Eucharist itself.

JOHN 6: 28. They said therefore unto him: What shall we do,
that we may work the works of God? 29. Jesus answered, and
said to them: This is the work of God, that you believe in him
whom he hath sent. 30. They said therefore to him: What sign
therefore dost thou shew, that we may see, and may believe thee?
What dost thou work? 31. Our fathers did eat manna in the
desert, as is written: He gave them bread from heaven to eat.
32. Then Jesus said to them: Amen, amen I say to you; Moses
gave you not bread from heaven, but my Father giveth you the
true bread from heaven. 33. For the bread of God is that which
cometh down from heaven, and giveth life to the world. 34. They
said therefore unto him: Lord, give us always this bread. 35.
And Jesus said to them: I am the bread of life: he that cometh to
me shall not hunger: and he that believeth in me shall never
thirst.

The recollection of yesterday's miracle was still fresh with the crowd. Before telling them about Communion, Christ insisted that their first duty was to accept Him wholeheartedly. Faith in Christ is the only way of pleasing God. "To live by the earth, man must apply to it his energy and activity, for it is only fruitful on these conditions; but to live by God, man has only to open himself to Him and to receive Him; and this opening of the soul is faith. The supreme act of man in his relations with God is faith; faith implies forgetfulness of self, complete submission and full surrender to the word, will and Spirit of God" (Didon). Hence, it makes all the difference in the world whether or not a person believes Christ is divine. Christ strongly condemns all those moderns who say that it does not matter much what one believes just so he is a decent chap. Only by believing Christ can we learn the whole truth about God, for God sent Christ to us. And belief in the divinity of Jesus is the foundation of a true understanding of man. Man is made for a life with God. That life must be prepared for; Christ alone can tell man how to prepare for it. Accept Christ, and most intellectual difficulties in religion vanish.

It was an insult to ask for a sign, after witnessing the miracle that He had performed on the day previous. They began to argue that He was no greater than Moses, who had given the people manna in their starving days in the desert (Exod. 16). But this manna was only for bodily needs; it was a material food. Christ brought from heaven grace and truth. Inasmuch as He is truth, He satisfies our minds; He feeds those who are hungry for truth. The audience failed or refused to grasp His meaning and kept asking for bodily food. Like Nicodemus, like the Samaritan woman they failed to rise from the material to the spiritual meaning of our Lord's words.

This steady unwillingness to catch the spiritual meaning of Christ's remarks illustrates the modern habit of refusing to believe that man has an immortal soul. There is a spiritual side to our nature. People who never give a thought to the soul may become hardened and think religion unnecessary. They rant against dogmas because they want to make God according to their own rules. Since the theory of evolution became popular, less than a century ago, people have eagerly accepted the idea that man is only an animal. They still like to be called men, but they are so materially minded that they cannot see that it is the soul that makes man a man. And there is no evidence for mental evolution. Hence the materialists cannot explain man's thoughts. They miss the point of Christ's teaching and seldom find true happiness. The very restlessness and unhappiness of modern man is an indication that he has not been taught the spiritual truths which satisfy.

> JOHN 6: 36. But I said unto you that you also have seen me,
> and you believe not. 37. All that the Father giveth to me shall
> come to me; and him that cometh to me, I will not cast out.
> 38. Because I came down from heaven, not to do my own will,
> but the will of him that sent me. 39. Now this is the will of the
> Father who sent me: that of all that he hath given me, I should
> lose nothing; but should raise it up again in the last day. 40.
> And this is the will of my Father that sent me: that every one
> who seeth the Son, and believeth in him, may have life everlasting,
> and I will raise him up in the last day. 41. The Jews therefore
> murmured at him, because he had said: I am the living bread
> which came down from heaven. 42. And they said: Is not
> this Jesus the son of Joseph, whose father and mother we know?

How then saith he: I came down from heaven? 43. Jesus therefore answered, and said to them: Murmur not among yourselves.
44. No man can come to me, except the Father, who hath sent me,
draw him; and I will raise him up in the last day. 45. It is
written in the prophets: And they shall all be taught of God.
Every one that hath heard of the Father, and hath learned,
cometh to me. 46. Not that any man hath seen the Father; but
he who is of God, he hath seen the Father. 47. Amen, amen I
say unto you: He that believeth in me, hath everlasting life.

Our faith in Christ did not originate within ourselves; it came as a gift from God. It is not like the faith we have in our friends; it is based on the goodness of God who sent Christ to us. And by doing always what His Father willed Christ has taught us to make the same practice our rule. Note how frequently Jesus repeated that thought.

Here, as afterward in his Gospel, John uses the word "Jews" to designate, not all of the people, but those particular leaders, usually Pharisees, who were His bitter enemies. For the third time these leaders threw in His face His Nazarene background, with a view of discrediting His claim to be from heaven. In each instance they refused to consider the proofs that He offered.

Modern man often acts like the Pharisees. He tries to measure and to size up God by his own puny intellect. When God speaks, it is our duty to believe. Only God has the right to demand this absolute faith from us, because He is truth itself and cannot deceive us. Truth-seeking people in each age find God, and God continues to enlighten them. God is not disturbed by modern ranters against religion. Christ calmly, coolly continued to teach the truth even when they taunted Him with being a common workman, a "son of Joseph."

In some mysterious way God draws those who are deserving of the Faith. Accordingly, "taught of God" means the interior promptings of grace, the desire for holiness. This drawing does not force us. The body is drawn pleasurably toward its satisfactions but does not force the will. An inducement or an invitation to play ball does not force us. So the soul yearns for God, once it has accepted God's enlightening grace. When we learn that two and two make four we consent. In consenting we do not lose our free will. All are given sufficient grace to believe; not all accept the invitation. God leaves us free to accept or reject. But the responsibility for our choice is ours.

Christ continually insisted on the idea of immortality — everlasting life. Our belief in immortality does not rest on what a scientist or a writer may say. Of all the world's leaders, Christ alone could say that He had been with God and therefore knew what He was talking about when He explained God and immortality. They who refuse to believe Christ will always remain muddled, will easily murmur against God.

* *

Christ prepared the people for the announcement of the doctrine of the Eucharist by ———. Prove with a text that divine faith is a gift. Why do moderns object to dogmas in religion? We should say an act of faith each evening because ———. Memorize verse 27. Why is Christ superior to any modern leader in matters of God and the soul?

* *

> JOHN 6: 48. I am the bread of life. 49. Your fathers did eat manna in the desert, and are dead. 50. This is the bread which cometh down from heaven; that if any man eat of it, he may not die. 51. I am the living bread which came down from heaven.

Hitherto Christ had been emphasizing belief, acceptance of Him. He shifted now to the Eucharist.

The idea of receiving Communion first came from the lips of the God-Man. Steadily, fearlessly, in the midst of enemies, Christ had advanced up to this point where He announced the doctrine of the Holy Eucharist. If we have faith in Him as divine, we have little trouble in believing that we receive Christ's Body and Blood at Communion. We are supposed to live a supernatural life on earth; Communion is the nourishment for that life. It is *the* preparative for God's presence, because it is intended to reproduce in us the qualities of our Leader. Communion is said to give an increase of sanctifying grace, which means, that it increases, deepens our capacity to enjoy and appreciate divine truths here and God's presence when we enter eternity. Anyone can see the necessity of preparation for law or medicine. Technical preparation is also necessary for life in heaven. Natural goodness alone does not prepare us. We need a supernatural preparative for a supernatural existence. Holy Communion is that preparative. And just as continual practice in shooting baskets gives us not only skill but appreciation of skill in others, so frequent Communion gives one the capacity to love and appreciate God and His qualities. This appreciation begins while we are here on earth, but the full result of receiving Communion frequently is to be had in heaven. Capacity to understand God there depends on the degree to which we employ here the preparative that Christ gave us.

This is the first mention of *eating* (50). It is something different from "coming" to, or believing in Christ. To live a complete life we must be incorporated with Christ, united to Him, through belief and through eating. What a privilege! "To eat the Man-God is to bring within ourselves that which is in the Man-God Himself." "As earthly bread gives a share in the life of nature, so the bread of heaven gives us a share in the life of God." We partake of divine life when we receive Communion, for, when grace comes, God comes into us, making us "partakers of the divine nature" (2 Pet. 1: 4).

> JOHN 6: 52. If any man eat of this bread, he shall live forever; and the bread that I will give, is my flesh, for the life of the world. 53. The Jews therefore strove among themselves, saying: How can this man give us his flesh to eat? 54. Then Jesus said to them: Amen, amen I say unto you: Except you eat the flesh of the Son of man, and drink his blood, you shall not have life in you.

The answer to those who say that Holy Communion is just a symbol, a remembrance, and not really the Body of Christ is seen in the fact that the Jews took Christ's statements literally. They grasped His meaning as to the reality but they thought only of visible flesh.

Our Lord permitted the literal interpretation to remain. He was looking ahead to the Last Supper, to the Mass and Communion of our day. Not only did He show them that He meant what He said, but He made it an obligation to receive Communion. And by their Mosaic Law the Jews were forbidden to use blood as food (Gen. 9: 4; Lev. 3: 17). So, it is clear that in these verses of St. John, *eating* means much more than believing in Christ. The mouth itself must receive Him. It is to be an eating of the Victim offered on Calvary. It should be unnecessary to add that going to Communion is not cannibalism. We do not use our senses in judging of Communion; we do not seek to taste. It is food in the supernatural order, not in the order of the senses. It is divine, spiritual food, not natural food. And Christ is present, whole and entire, under the form of bread and also whole and entire under the form of wine. Only the appearances of bread and wine remain after transubstantiation. We receive the whole Christ if we receive only the host. Four times in the sixth chapter of St. John, Christ promises eternal life to those "eating," with no reference to drinking.

> JOHN 6: 55. He that eateth my flesh, and drinketh my blood, hath everlasting life: and I will raise him up in the last day.
> 56. For my flesh is meat indeed: and my blood is drink indeed.
> 57. He that eateth my flesh, and drinketh my blood, abideth in
> me, and I in him. 58. As the living Father hath sent me, and
> I live by the Father; so he that eateth me, the same also shall
> live by me. 59. This is the bread that came down from heaven.
> Not as your fathers did eat manna, and are dead. He that eateth
> this bread, shall live forever. 60. These things he said, teaching
> in the synagogue, in Capharnaum.

Holy Communion is also the pledge of our glorious resurrection, provided we do not destroy the effects of Communion by sin. Baptism is, of course, necessary and also ensures everlasting life to infants, for it removes the obstacles in the way of our union with Christ. Baptism presupposes a desire for Communion in which we receive the divine life which joins us with Christ and fits us to rise from the dead ready for life with God, equipped with the means for loving Him.

After the host has dissolved in our bodies, grace is still there. The divinity of Jesus comes with grace, so that we actually abide in Him. God is our companion; He maintains the divine life in us so long as we do not sin gravely. Living in the state of grace actually means companionship with three divine Persons. For where one Person of the Trinity is, there are also the others. A person need never be alone nor lonesome. Moreover, Communion is the bond that keeps all Catholics united with Christ. It should unite us to one another, just as the cells of our body are joined into a unity.

It is through grace, through the dwelling of God in us that we become holy. Holiness, therefore, in its nature is different from natural goodness. "We cannot please God unless we resemble Jesus Christ, and the Blessed Sacrament is instituted for the very object of perfecting in us this likeness" (Leen). True, we cannot be supernaturally good if we fail to practice what some call the natural virtues. A thief who is never repentant could not be supernaturally good, yet the fact remains that we need grace to live a supernatural life. The food which we receive in Communion makes us sharers here in the divine life; and fits us, shapes us, if we co-operate, for eternal life with God.

When we go to Communion we should recall that Christ wants us to trust Him, to believe Him when He tells us what Communion does for us. Only in heaven shall we realize fully why He wants us to go to Communion frequently. It is not necessary to experience an exaltation, to feel devout when we receive; it is only necessary to go in the belief that Christ knows best what prepares us for eternity. We may not even feel that we are advancing, nevertheless we should continue trusting Him. It is not our will we are to follow, it is His. And we are to recall always that the purpose of receiving is to train our wills to follow His will. In so doing we acquire the ability to understand and love the qualities of God when we reach His presence.

> JOHN 6: 61. Many therefore of his disciples, hearing it, said:
> This saying is hard, and who can hear it? 62. But Jesus, know-
> ing in himself, that his disciples murmured at this, said to them:
> Doth this scandalize you? 63. If then you shall see the Son
> of man ascend up where he was before? 64. It is the spirit that
> quickeneth: the flesh profiteth nothing. The words that I have
> spoken to you, are spirit and life. 65. But there are some of
> you that believe not. For Jesus knew from the beginning, who
> they were that did not believe, and who he was, that would be-
> tray him. 66. And he said: Therefore did I say to you, that
> no man can come to me, unless it be given him by my Father.

In the great test of faith the materially minded failed. They could not believe a mere Nazarene! They preferred their own intellect to God's word. (Many today take the same attitude.) But Jesus was patient. He was willing to fail in convincing them, provided that He did His duty in teaching truth. He felt no anger, no indignation. Continual advancement in revealing the whole truth was His aim. And He hinted at another proof, namely, His ascension into heaven. The ascension would show that He is divine, and therefore not the son of Joseph. This removal of His body would also show them that He had not implied the eating of visible flesh.

It is not by a mere act of the mind that one is enabled to understand the doctrine of the Eucharist; grace or divine help is needed. Anyone trusting to his own natural powers of reasoning (flesh) will never accept the Eucharist. Just as our soul keeps the body alive, so, the Holy Ghost (Spirit) gives us the ability to believe in the Eucharist. If we believe the words of Christ, then grace and the Holy Ghost come to us. For, Holy Communion is a spiritual food, not the gross, carnal flesh which these hearers in Capharnaum pictured to themselves (Cf. 1 Cor. 2: 10–15).

> JOHN 6: 67. After this many of his disciples went back; and
> walked no more with him. 68. Then Jesus said to the twelve:
> Will you also go away? 69. And Simon Peter answered him:
> Lord, to whom shall we go? Thou hast the words of eternal life.
> 70. And we have believed and have known, that thou art the
> Christ, the Son of God. 71. Jesus answered them: Have not I
> chosen you twelve? And one of you is a devil.

Saddened as He was, Christ would not retract His statements. And He will not force Himself upon us. He even tests those whom He loves. He asked the apostles if they wished to depart. (Recall Mary's great decision as the angel waited for her answer.) The crowd in the synagogue had turned their backs on Him. The twelve looked at one another; heaven was hushed. The suspense was too much for the great soul of Peter. He could not bear that look of sadness on the face of Christ; so the rugged, manly commander burst forth with an act of faith that each Catholic should burn into his or her heart. He did not understand; but he could trust. What a joy to Christ to find them loyal — all except one. They did not fail in the test. This one was now being warned, in words that should have melted his hardness. Perhaps Judas had thought that Christ would be a powerful, worldly king. His castles had fallen on Thursday and Friday when he perceived Christ's real purpose; hence the warning Christ was now giving him.

At some period in life the crucial test comes. Whom shall we believe — a false scientist, a clever writer, a cynical teacher, a sneering sensualist, or Christ? If we do not understand our religion correctly, if we judge it by prejudiced standards, it may appear "hard," and, like Judas, we shall imagine we have been deceived by it; when, in reality selfishness has captured our heart. Watch the beginnings of attitudes. Many things will puzzle us, but if we have a heart like Peter's — open, honest, manly — we shall realize that in the Church alone are found Christ's "words of eternal life." And not only does Communion aid us to lead good lives now; not only is it a pledge, a means of everlasting life (a thing which everyone desires), but it fits us for that life, develops invisibly in us our ability to enjoy and appreciate our life with God.

Christ said that He came in order that we might have "life." He alone knows what prepares us to "live" in the next world. Life at its highest is knowing and loving. Hence this "life" or grace which we receive in Holy Communion deepens or increases our capacity to know and to love the Trinity when we reach eternity. There is life or activity within the Trinity, and Communion gives us the capacity to participate in that life. Hence the main effects of receiving Communion will not be seen until we enter eternity. Meanwhile we simply take Christ's word and receive in faith.

1. Memorize 54, and 69.
2. Prove that Christ wants us to receive Communion.
3. What is the exact purpose of Communion?
4. What type of student finds religion "hard"?
5. Show how St. John presumes that everyone knew there were 12 apostles, even though he refers only to 5 when telling of their vocation.
6. Should a student change his principles to meet a popular prejudice? Show how Christ acted.
7. Did the Jews realize that Christ claimed to have had a heavenly origin?
8. Should a student remain away from Communion just because he cannot feel any effect from going?
9. What is the best method of getting ready for life with God?
10. Prove that our Lord meant more than belief in Him when He spoke of "eating" the bread He would give.

Chapter 36

BELIEF IN, AND PROFESSION OF THE DIVINITY OF CHRIST

MATT. 16: 1. And there came to him the Pharisees and Sadducees tempting: and they asked him to shew them a sign from heaven. 2. But he answered: . . . 4. A wicked and adulterous generation seeketh after a sign, and a sign shall not be given it, but the sign of Jonas the prophet. And he left them, and went away. 5. And when his disciples were come over the water, they had forgotten to take bread. 6. Who said to them: Take heed and beware of the leaven of the Pharisees and Sadducees. 7. But they thought within themselves, saying: Because we have taken no bread. 8. And Jesus knowing it, said: Why do you think within yourselves, O ye of little faith, for that you have no bread? 9. Do you not yet understand, neither do you remember the five loaves among five thousand men, and how many baskets you took up. 10. Nor the seven loaves, among four thousand men, and how many baskets you took up. 11. Why do you not understand that it was not concerning bread I said to you: Beware of the leaven of the Pharisees and Sadducees? 12. Then they understood that he said not that they should beware of the leaven of bread, but of the doctrine of the Pharisees and Sadducees.

AFTER His sermon in Capharnaum our Lord journeyed westward, curing as He went, and exposing the formalism of the Pharisees. He spent some time up north, near Tyre and Sidon (Mark 7: 24), a pagan country. Then He cut back eastward to the Jordan and down to the lake, where again His enemies met Him.

The Pharisees hated the Sadducees, yet they united in an effort to destroy Christ, which fact indicates the depth of their resentment against Him. Their action illustrates for us how some of those who are continually asking for proofs are, in reality, unwilling to be convinced. Christ gave His enemies a sign, a hint about His resurrection, from the story of Jonas. He left them puzzled, and entered a boat on the lake and headed north along the shore. He was silent; sorrow at the blindness of the leaders filled His heart. Desiring to warn the apostles against the influence of such men, He told them to avoid the leaven (teaching) of these leaders. The apostles missed the point. Just as we often worry about food, or pleasure, or about loss of prestige if we do not go to a certain school or read a certain book, while we think little about the effect of these things on our soul, so these disciples were again too materially minded to understand.

The Pharisees were proud, too attached to their own ideas. The Sadducees were lax and materialistic. Unless we are on our guard, pride may infect us, and then we lose the gift of understanding our religion. Chief Justice Taney was a deeply intellectual Catholic. After Mass one Sunday a companion said: "That was an awful sermon today." Mr. Taney replied: "I have never, in all my life heard a poor sermon." If we are humble, we may learn from the worst sermon. On the other hand, if we are lax and indifferent, we may easily believe the taunts that are flung against decent students, or the ridicule that is often heaped on religious persons. The Communistic campaign against God is based on ridicule and misrepresentation. It calls belief in God and the soul superstition. Materialists hold that matter alone exists. But since this assertion does not explain the facts of life, such as the striving of men for justice, which is abstract and unseen though real, since materialism, which reduces men to things whereas they are persons, falls to pieces when examined by cold reason, the materialists resort to ridicule in their effort to get rid of God.

> MATT. 16: 13. And Jesus came into the vicinity of Caesarea Philippi: and he asked his disciples, saying: Who do men say that the Son of man is? 14. But they said: Some John the Baptist, and other some Elias, and others Jeremias, or one of the prophets. 15. Jesus saith to them: But who do you say that I am? 16. Simon Peter answered and said: *Thou art Christ the Son of the living God.*

It was July of the year 29. The boat was left behind, and they began that walk that led them thirty miles north of the lake.

They followed the course of the Jordan till they passed beyond the border of Palestine, and were in what is now Syria, near a pagan city called Caesarea Philippi, now Baneas. They were in the foothills of the 9,000 feet, snowcapped Hermon. Philip had constructed here a city and named it in honor of the Roman emperor. A magnificent, white marble temple was built there and dedicated to Pan.

What a coincidence! Our Lord, at the moment that His followers were dropping away from Him, brought the apostles up somewhere near this city and its temple. Here where everything spoke of paganism and the universal power of the Roman emperor, Christ confidently announced His plan for an everlasting Church; and He did it just when the prospects of success seemed dark. Opposition or failure never unnerved Him.

Luke (9: 18) tells us that at the start of this trip Christ had prayed. Something was in the air; the apostles felt the tension, but did not know what was coming. He was going to ask them a most significant question; and He prayed for them. In some respects, Christ's sojourn on earth was more a life of prayer than of outward action. He prayed that the apostles would make the right answer. To grasp a divine truth we need light from God. It is this light, called grace, which comes when we pray. And just as He prayed for those who had been entrusted to Him, so we should pray that those under our charge might make the right decisions. After His prayer, and while they were trudging along the road, in the silence of that country district, He suddenly put the question to them. A leading question came first. He was not looking for information; He was teaching them. In public, Christ had not explicitly claimed to be God. Great truths are realized but slowly. Christ, as a wise teacher, had to consider the belief of the Jews in one God (monotheism). Only after acquiring trust in Christ could they learn that there are three equal Persons in this one God. By revising the moral law, by forgiving sins, by working miracles in His own name He was actually offering proofs that He is God. He wanted people to draw the conclusion. When the apostles told Him that the public had only false views, just as multitudes have today, He said nothing, though it hurt Him to see that His own people were rejecting His claims.

"Great souls frequently maintain perfect serenity beneath the hardest strokes of injustice" (Le Camus).

Now came the crucial question. A solemn stillness settled over the twelve. Would they rise superior to national prejudices? Had they finally realized the marvelous truth that God had actually become Man, that in the Son of Man they beheld the Son of God? Were His patience with, and prayer for, these twelve to have their effect? His question showed the desire of His soul; but He wanted their belief to be voluntary. He would put the case up to them, just as He leaves us free.

Simon burst forth in a wholehearted act of faith which expressed His limitless love of our Lord. Faith is a complete giving over of our whole person to Christ because of what He is. Peter's belief is a fine example of what our act of faith should be. He did not ask for a sign, as had the Pharisees. The very character of Christ was proof enough for him. And was it not fitting that the first public acknowledgment, in answer to the direct question: "Who do you say that I am?" should come from one who was to be the first pope. Peter believed and professed, just as we do. The belief in the fact that Christ is both God and Man, two natures in one Person, is the foundation on which is reared every Catholic church and school in this country. What a joy to Christ to see young people of today equipped with Simon's generous faith and love!

> MATT. 16: 17. And Jesus answering, said to him: Blessed art thou, Simon Bar-Jona: because flesh and blood hath not revealed it to thee, but my Father who is in heaven. 18. And I say to thee: That thou art Peter; and *upon this rock I will build my church,* and the gates of hell shall not prevail against it. 19. And I will give to thee the keys of the kingdom of heaven. And whatsoever thou shalt bind upon earth, it shall be bound also in heaven: and whatsoever thou shalt loose on earth, it shall be loosed also in heaven.

Christ accepted Peter's statement as being the truth. Christ is God. The Church did not raise Christ to divinity; He always knew that He is divine. Christ told Peter that grace had aided him in making this declaration. It was not merely human reasoning (flesh and blood) that enabled Peter to make his act of faith; God enlightened him because he was deserving.

God's plans are farseeing. At their first meeting Christ had changed Simon's name to Peter. In the Aramaic dialect, which our Lord used, the word, *Kepha*, "Cephas" means *rock*. So, Cephas, or Peter, is the rock on which the Church was to be built. Christ Himself personally set Peter out from the others, and made him the bedrock support of the whole superstructure. And not only that, but the gates of hell will never close down on this Church, that is, the Church will never die; she will never be conquered by error or the devil. Christ brought to earth precious, divine truth. There will be no more Christs. This revelation which He brought is final. Hence it follows that the Church ought to be infallible in guarding and interpreting this revelation. If the Church were not infallible, then this revelation might be lost, or misinterpreted, and we would not have the truth about God.

The keys are the symbol of supreme power and authority. The figure comes down from the days when cities were walled and gates were locked. Peter was to have supreme legislative and judicial authority. What was prohibited was said to be bound; and what was loosed was said to be lawful. Peter was to have power to prohibit certain things and to declare other things lawful, in other words, supreme power. Peter's authority was not to be merely an honor; it was real, and was to be backed up by heaven.

Since Christ implied that the Church was to continue, we naturally conclude that Peter's power was to pass on to his successors in the papacy. The pope has supreme legislative and judicial authority in the Church because Christ so desires. In more advanced religion courses further explanations will be given of the tremendous implications of our Lord's words to Peter. For the present we stress the fact of the reward that came to Peter for his profession of the divinity of Christ. When we fully accept the truth that Christ is divine, then we have no difficulty in realizing that Peter and the popes should have such power as they possess in order to preserve for us the great truths that Christ brought to earth. For, Christ is still our Leader; He is the invisible Head of the Church. Even though there have been personal faults in some of the two hundred and sixty men who have succeeded Peter in the office of the papacy, yet we know that Christ is behind that office, and that the Holy Ghost directs it in His name. When we are loyal to the Church we are loyal to Christ.

A reference to the idea of indulgences is also contained in this power of loosing and binding. An indulgence does not forgive sin; only in the sacrament of Penance is that ordinarily done. But even after a sin has been forgiven there is a fine, or punishment attached. An indulgence refers to the lessening or remitting of this fine or punishment after the sin has been forgiven. When the pope declares (looses) that merits earned by Christ and all good Catholics and not needed by them are applied to lessen the time of punishment of someone who has not atoned for all of his sins, then God ratifies (looses) this decree. In granting an indulgence the idea is that the strong help the weak, the same principle as in an insurance company.

> MATT. 16: 20. Then he commanded his disciples, that they should tell no one that he was Jesus the Christ. 21. From that time Jesus began to shew to his disciples that he must go to Jerusalem, and suffer many things from the ancients and scribes and chief priests, and be put to death, and the third day rise again. 22. And Peter taking him, began to rebuke him, saying: Lord, be it far from thee, this shall not be unto thee. 23. Who turning said to Peter: Go behind me, Satan, thou art a scandal unto me: because thou savorest not the things that are of God, but the things that are of men.

The thing we most dread is suffering. The apostles were like us; they had to be taught that suffering is part of life, that it is the way to glory. Little could they see that Calvary was to be endured, before heaven was to be opened. And the apostles seem also to have been blind to the meaning of: "third day rise again." Loving Peter could not endure the thought that Christ would have to suffer. He felt strong over his promised promotion. He would protect Christ! In reality, Peter was telling Christ to avoid a task for which He had come into the world. It is never up to us to dictate to God on what is right or wrong. Christ rebuked His chief apostle because the chief apostle was now trying to put human reasoning above the plans of God.

We should take care of our health, should always fight against injustice, but whenever it is necessary to suffer, or to do a hard thing, meditate on the cool courage of Christ. "Thy will be done."

> MATT. 16: 24. Then Jesus said to his disciples: If any man will come after me, let him deny himself, and take up his cross, and follow me. 25. For he that will save his life, shall lose it: and he that shall lose his life for my sake, shall find it. 26. For what doth it profit a man, if he gain the whole world, and suffer the loss of his own soul? Or what shall a man give in exchange for his soul? 27. For the Son of man shall come in the glory of his Father with his angels: and then will he render to every man according to his works.

> MARK 8: 38. For he that shall be ashamed of me and of my words in this adulterous and sinful generation, the Son of man also will be ashamed of him, when he shall come in the glory of his Father with the holy angels.

True Catholic life requires the doing of things considered hard by the world. But it is precisely in doing difficult things, for instance, the practice of purity, that one develops character, strength, and poise. The difficulties of such a life are as nothing compared to the difficulties one encounters when he or she is afraid to do what is right. The misery of one who falls into the habit of stealing, of lying, of drunkenness or impurity is indescribable. He who takes up his cross is saved from all this misery.

Ambition and hard work are good things, but our motive must be unselfish. Become an expert; be an efficient scholar or athlete or professional man, or father or mother, but do it *for the honor of God,* for Christ. We give the honor of our success and our achievements to Him, not to ourselves. When we aim at success just for success, when we seek for happiness just to be happy, we are usually disappointed. On the other hand, when we strive merely to do our duty, or to reflect honor on God, then God gives us contentment. Worldly fame will be worth little, if, in achieving it we give up the Faith, become dishonest, or sell our soul to the devil. God will judge us on our motives and our works, not on worldly reputation.

A glorious challenge is set before the youth of today. It is the task of giving the truth about God and the soul to the unchurched multitudes. Without knowing it, they want God. Their very willingness to worship the State shows their need of God. They do not understand Him. If they meet stronghearted, fearless youths who openly profess allegiance to the divine Christ, they may be brought to the joy of knowing the true and eternal God.

1. Our confidence that the Church will continue till the end of time is based on ———.
2. What may be wrong with a student in a religion class who constantly says: "I can't see why we have to do this or that"?
3. Make a list of the modern leavens to be avoided.
4. Where was Caesarea Philippi?
5. Why did Christ pray for the apostles?
6. Why did our Lord only gradually claim explicitly to be God?
7. What is the scriptural meaning of the word, "keys," of "bind" and "loose"?
8. How are you loyal to Christ when you are loyal to the Church?
9. What is the best view to take toward the problem of suffering?
10. What is necessary before one can come to a complete belief in the divinity of Jesus?
11. Is every Mass that you attend a profession of belief in the divinity of Jesus?
12. Show that Christ predicted that He would arise from the dead.
13. Show that Christ intended the pope to have supreme power in the Church.

Chapter 37

PRIVILEGED TO SEE

MARK 9: 1. And after six days Jesus taketh with him Peter and James and John, and leadeth them up into an high mountain apart by themselves, and was transfigured before them.
LUKE 9: 29. And whilst he prayed, the shape of his countenance was altered, and his raiment became white and glittering.
MARK 9: 2. And his garments became shining and exceeding white as snow, so as no fuller upon earth can make white.

A WEEK after the apostles had asserted their belief in His divinity our Lord went again into seclusion. It is generally held that He was now down in Galilee and that Mt. Tabor was the place of the Transfiguration. It is possible, however, that they were still up near the snowcapped Mt. Hermon.

Christ's divine nature was veiled in a human body. However, three human persons were privileged to behold something of the awesome majesty of divine presence. We love our Lord for His humility. He had held back that which would frighten people into belief. It is not God's plan to crush the modern enemies of the Church, or to kill sinners outright. God is patient; He holds in check, till the day of judgment, that striking divine power which He possesses. The Transfiguration is not so surprising as the manner in which Christ restrained and held in leash His divine power.

It is reserved for those of deep faith to experience the full splendor of divinity. To the real Catholic Christ often grants a realization of how preferable is faith in Him to all the glory that results from worldly renown. It is a glimpse of the joy that will come from God's presence. Yet, human words can never picture what it means to see God. Perhaps you have had an opportunity to see a man under some strong emotion. The soul seems to come to the face — the eye gleams, the countenance brightens, and you are held spellbound by that indefinable majesty. So, on this night, Christ allowed His divine nature to come to the surface. His countenance changed and human eyes caught something of what God is like. If you can, try to imagine white light.

> MARK 9: 3. And there appeared to them Elias with Moses; and they were talking with Jesus. 4. And Peter answering, said to Jesus: Rabbi, it is good for us to be here: and let us make three tabernacles, one for thee, and one for Moses, and one for Elias. 5. For he knew not what he said: for they were struck with fear. 6. And there was a cloud overshadowing them: and a voice came out of the cloud, saying: This is my most beloved Son; hear ye him. 7. And immediately looking about, they saw no man any more, but Jesus only with them.

While Christ was praying, the three had fallen asleep. The brightness of the scene, reflected against the night splendor of the sky, and the sound of voices awakened them. They were thrilled and enraptured, yet frightened. In an instant they recognized the significance of the scene. The unity of God's slowly maturing plans was now evident. Moses represented the ancient Mosaic Law; Elias stood for the prophets. The Law and the prophets had one aim — to point the way to Christ, to prepare the world for His coming. These two leaders were now paying homage to the founder of the New Law, the New Testament. The Old had done its work; the New was to replace it. These messengers from heaven, whose coming on that night shows us that not only is the soul immortal but that it is conscious in the next world, talked with Christ about His approaching Passion and death.

Peter spoke without thinking. His heart told him that he was witnessing the greatest scene of his life. In future years he would look back gratefully to this event (2 Pet. 1: 16–18). Now he wished either to commemorate or to prolong his glimpse of heaven. But it is not our happiness to have heaven always on earth; earth is a place of struggle, of testing whether or not we are willing to be unselfish. God gives glimpses to spur us on, to strengthen us for coming trials, while convincing us that it is a high privilege to be a Catholic, to "see" divinity in Christ. The greatest thrills of life are those moments when we first realize the hidden values of our religion. Such enjoyments come only to those who are Catholic at heart. They come as a reward; they come also to strengthen us against those days when the outlook will be dark, when we shall be discouraged, when the Church appears weak and the world alluring. Humans cannot live always on a Mount of Transfiguration. Catch the vision and then descend to battle, for life has its Calvaries even for the young. Meanwhile, "Hear ye Him."

It may be said that the Transfiguration had a twofold purpose: to show our Lord that the Father was with Him even though the Pharisees rejected Him, and to prove to the apostles that their faith had been rightly placed. The Transfiguration came after their profession of faith in His divinity, and likewise, our glimpse, our realization of all that is hidden in Christ and in our religion comes only after we have made a profession of belief such as Peter had made up north.

> MARK 9: 8. And as they came down from the mountain, he charged them not to tell any man what things they had seen, till the Son of man shall be risen again from the dead. 9. And they kept the word to themselves; questioning together what that should mean, when he shall be risen from the dead.

The week previous Christ had told the apostles to say nothing publicly of Peter's profession (p. 230); now the three were to keep to themselves this great secret. It was all in line with His plan of preparing them for their future work. He placed full confidence in them. He expects us to guard the confidence that is placed in us, never to break our word of honor, to be always men and women of honor; and especially to be honorable and open toward God.

At the end of the scene only Jesus was with them. "Rapidly the old familiarity came back, the old security, the old courage, the old unconscious assumption that so long as He was present all was well. Great men inspire greatness; strong men inspire strength; true men inspire trust and confidence; the closing of this scene is eloquent proof that Jesus inspired all three. And great men are great without arrogance; strong men are gentle in their strength; true men are simple, transparent, guileless, so that others may with ease see through their very souls and not fear. As this group of four joined together, and turned to come down the mountain in the morning light, none was more conspicuous than the other. A stranger might have met them and would never have known that One among them was Jesus Christ, the Son of God, whose glory a few moments before had been so conspicuously revealed. Such is the greatness, the strength, the truth of the greatest, the strongest, the truest Man of men" (Goodier).

* *

What value has the Transfiguration for us? How may we obtain a deeper insight into our religion as we grow older? What is your opinion of a person who is continually seeking to impress on others the fact that he or she has unusual gifts, or wealth, or powerful friends?

* *

MATT. 17: 14. And when he was come to the multitude, there
came to him a man falling down on his knees before him, saying:
Lord, have pity on my son, for he is a lunatic, and suffereth much;
for he falleth often into the fire, and often into the water. 15.
And I brought him to thy disciples, and they could not cure
him. 16. Then Jesus answered and said: O unbelieving and
perverse generation, how long shall I be with you? How long shall
I suffer you? Bring him hither to me. 17. And Jesus rebuked
him, and the devil went out of him, and the child was cured from
that hour. 18. Then came the disciples to Jesus secretly, and
said: Why could not we cast him out? 19. Jesus said to them:
Because of your unbelief. For, amen I say to you, if you have
faith as a grain of mustard-seed, you shall say to this mountain:
Remove from hence hither, and it shall remove: and nothing shall
be impossible to you. 20. But this kind is not cast out but by
prayer and fasting.

No sooner was the return of Christ noticed than the appeals began. He did not condemn the father entirely, nor the disciples, but the unbelieving crowd. We must have strong faith when we ask God for a favor. An unbeliever needs the prayer of this father. God always has power; we are not always deserving. While Christ had been on Tabor the disciples had tried in vain to work a miracle. The crowd had jeered and had ridiculed. Now the healing Physician was on the case. The gift of working miracles is a special grace not granted to everyone. But by prayer and self-denial any special difficulty ("This mountain") can be rooted out.

MARK 9: 29. And departing from thence, they passed through Galilee, and he would not that any man should know it. 30. And he taught his disciples, and said to them: The Son of man shall be betrayed into the hands of men, and they shall kill him; and after he is killed, he shall rise again the third day. 31. But they understood not the word, and they were afraid to ask him. 32. And they came to Capharnaum. And when they were in the house, he asked them: What did you treat of in the way? 33. But they held their peace, for in the way they had disputed among themselves, which of them should be the greatest. 34. And sitting down, he called the twelve, and saith to them: If any man desire to be first, he shall be the last of all, and the minister of all.

Leaving the father and son to rejoice, Jesus slipped quietly away. His time was necessary for His future bishops. He had difficulty in impressing on them the fact that a cross was awaiting Him. They seemed unable to comprehend such a situation, just as we run away from things that look hard. He taught us to look mental and physical suffering in the face.

Christ had preceded the apostles while entering the town. Note the honesty of the Gospels in recording these faults. These men, after all their training were still worldly, and ambitious for fame and desirous of prestige. They had quarreled among themselves as to who was the greatest, just as we often imagine that we are as talented, as deserving as someone else who has been chosen or elected ahead of us. Christ knew of these petty jealousies. He does not want us to quarrel among ourselves. He gave a concrete application of the principles He had often taught. Anyone who wants to be an outstanding leader needs to examine his motives. Let him do kind things to others — work around the home, associate with timid and backward students, help those who need help, and volunteer to do jobs that others shun.

MARK 9: 35. And taking a child, he set him in the midst of them. Whom when he had embraced, he saith to them:
MATT. 18: 3. Amen I say to you, unless you be converted, and

become as little children, you shall not enter into the kingdom of heaven. 4. Whosoever therefore shall humble himself as this little child, he is the greater in the kingdom of heaven. 5. And he that shall receive one such little child in my name, receiveth me. 6. But he that shall scandalize one of these little ones that believe in me, it were better for him that a millstone should be hanged about his neck, and that he should be drowned in the depth of the sea. 7. Woe to the world because of scandals. For it must needs be that scandals come: but nevertheless woe to that man by whom the scandal cometh. . . . 10. See that you despise not one of these little ones: for I say to you, that their angels in heaven always see the face of my Father who is in heaven. . . . 14. Even so it is not the will of your Father, who is in heaven, that one of these little ones should perish.

MATT. 10: 42. And whosoever shall give to drink to one of these little ones a cup of cold water only in the name of a disciple, amen I say to you, he shall not lose his reward.

Hardened self-seekers had wilted and fled before His indignant face in the Temple. Now a little child was not afraid to come to that kindly face. Jesus was to teach these men a virtue, and to do it effectively from a life situation. A child is simple, and trustful. To understand the Catholic religion we must have these qualities of trust and humility. We too easily reach a sense of our own importance. We do not like to be "bossed"; we think people should take more notice of us; sometimes we imagine we know more than the Church. We are hurt if we cannot have our own way. All of this is pride. The truly great people are humble. In worldly affairs it is all right to be shrewd; in our relations with God we trust Christ and the Church. We do not ask to be promoted or recognized. To become great in the eyes of God, one must first become little.

Christ's remarks on the giving of bad example are striking. To non-Catholics we are the Catholic Church. Has our example prevented them from arriving at a true estimate of Catholicism? Have we ever led innocent people into sin? For, sin is to be punished. There is a hell.

The Catholic position on birth control, on the right of a child to know God, on guardian angels, on the unlimited value of one single human individual may be traced back to these words of Christ. The Catholic sees Christ in each child. That is why there are so many orphanages and parochial schools.

MATT. 18: 21. Then came Peter unto him and said: Lord, how often shall my brother offend against me, and I forgive him? Till seven times? 22. Jesus saith to him: I say not to thee, till seven times; but till seventy times seven times. 23. Therefore is the kingdom of heaven likened to a king, who would take an account of his servants. 24. And when he had begun to take the account, one was brought to him, that owed him ten thousand talents. 25. And as he had not wherewith to pay it, his lord commanded that he should be sold, and his wife and children, and all that he had, and payment to be made. 26. But that servant falling down, besought him, saying: Have patience with me, and I will pay thee all. 27. And the lord of that servant, being moved with pity, let him go and forgave him the debt. 28. But when that servant was gone out, he found one of his fellow servants that owed him a hundred pence; and laying hold of him, he throttled him, saying: Pay what thou owest. 29. And his fellow servant falling down, besought him, saying: Have patience with me and I will pay thee all. 30. And he would not: but went and cast him into prison, till he paid the debt. 31. Now his fellow servants seeing what was done, were very much grieved, and they came, and told their lord all that was done. 32. Then his lord called him, and said to him: Thou wicked servant, I forgave thee all the debt, because thou besoughtest me: 33. Shouldst not thou then have had compassion also on thy fellow-servant, even as I had compassion on thee? 34. And his lord being angry, delivered him to the torturers until he paid all the debt. 35. So also shall my heavenly Father do to you, if you forgive not every one his brother from your hearts.

Is it possible to picture more effectively the high value that God places on forgiveness? And the amount that we have to forgive others is so small in comparison to the amount that God forgives us! We must forgive from our hearts. We may not even harbor a wish for revenge, nor take delight in the downfall of an enemy.

MATT. 17: 23. And when they were come to Capharnaum, they that received the didrachmas, came to Peter, and said to him: Doth not your master pay the didrachma? 24. He said: Yes. And when he was come into the house, Jesus prevented him, saying: What is thy opinion, Simon? The kings of earth, of whom do they receive tribute or custom? Of their own children, or of strangers? 25. And he said: Of strangers. Jesus said to him: Then the children are free. 26. But that we may not scandalize them, go to the sea, and cast in a hook: and that fish which shall first come up, take: and when thou hast opened its mouth, thou shalt find a stater: take that, and give it to them for me and thee.

Every male over twenty years of age had to pay an annual tax for the support of the Temple. Peter too readily said Christ would pay it. His too-readiness shows that we must watch for the principles involved in the questions that are put to us. We must withhold consent until we understand the principle implied. Christ put the case up to Peter in a different light. The Temple was God's. Christ was the Son of God, and therefore free from taxation according to the custom in worldly affairs. However, our Lord got Peter out of the predicament. Christ always avoided giving scandal. He expects us to be honest in paying taxes to the State, and in supporting the Church. And whenever possible we should be generous in helping others out of embarrassing situations.

1. How does this lesson show that not only was divinity veiled in Christ, but also that the attractive virtues of prudence, courage, kindness, humility, and mercy were there?
2. What lessons might impulsive students learn from Peter's mistakes?
3. Why are there so many Catholic orphanages?
4. What is the reason for the practice of sending money to far-off missions to "buy a baby"?
5. Show how a student is responsible for the reputation of his school, his Church?
6. What is included in the term "forgiveness"?
7. Describe what companionship with Christ must have meant to the apostles?
8. James is angry because he was not given the leading rôle in a play, or because he did not receive a high mark in class, so he quits the play or ceases to study. What is his real trouble?

Chapter 38

MASTERFUL YET MERCIFUL IN THE MIDST OF HATRED

JOHN 7: 2. Now the Jews' feast of tabernacles was at hand. 3. And his brethren said to him: Pass from hence, and go into Judea; that thy disciples also may see thy works which thou dost. 4. For there is no man that doth any thing in secret, and he himself seeketh to be known openly. If thou do these things manifest thyself to the world. 5. For neither did his brethren believe in him. 6. Then Jesus said to them: My time is not yet come; but your time is always ready. 7. The world cannot hate you; but me it hateth: because I give testimony of it, that the works thereof are evil. 8. Go you up to this festival day, but I go not up to this festival day: because my time is not accomplished. 9. When he had said these things, he himself stayed in Galilee. 10. But after his brethren were gone up, then he also went up to the feast, not openly, but, as it were, in secret.

WE ARE now at the end of September, in the year 29. The countryside was all astir. This feast drew thousands to Jerusalem, where they built temporary tents of boughs (booths), and lived in them for a week, to commemorate the tent life in the wilderness under Moses (Exod. 23: 16). Likewise, it was a harvest feast, for the crops had been gathered. Hence there was a note of rejoicing and thanksgiving.

In their rustic way, many of Christ's relatives knew He was far above them; hence He was wasting His time out in the country. Let Him go up to the big city, and make a name for Himself, just as in our day an athlete wishes to reach the big leagues. Ability does give one the right to go up higher. Yet, self-seeking relatives often spoil the lives of young people. Sometimes one must be prepared for sneers from relatives who do not understand what nobility is. It did not occur to these brethren that Christ always followed the guidance of the Holy Ghost, that He had already been in Jerusalem and He would go again, but not for the worldly reasons that they were proposing to Him. By the "world" our Lord here means the life and outlook of the Scribes and Pharisees. They who think of worldly success are not so unpopular as they who try to follow God's will, as they who stand up for justice. It requires courage to reprove the world for its sins, for its effort to make man the center of life instead of God; Christ did that.

> LUKE 9: 51. And it came to pass, when the days of his assumption were accomplishing, that he steadfastly set his face to go to Jerusalem. 52. And he sent messengers before his face; and going, they entered into a city of the Samaritans, to prepare for him. 53. And they received him not, because his face was of one going to Jerusalem. 54. And when his disciples James and John had seen this, they said; Lord, wilt thou that we command fire to come down from heaven, and consume them? 55. And turning, he rebuked them, saying: You know not of what spirit you are. 56. The Son of man came not to destroy souls, but to save. And they went into another town.

Our Lord was now leaving Galilee, to return no more. Six months only remain. He knew what was coming in Jerusalem. What a picture of moral courage is here: "He steadfastly set His face!" He looked calmly into the hatred of next week, and beyond that into the cross of Good Friday. He had come to enlighten men and He would permit no hatred to deter Him from teaching truth.

When pilgrimages were on their way to Jerusalem the Samaritans were never in a good mood. The anger of hot-tempered James and John was enflamed at this attitude. They were not spineless creatures. They had, however, forgotten all that He had told them about love of enemies. The occasion gave Him another chance to drive home the nature of the Catholic religion. The Church is here to *save* sinners, not to force them to hell. She is not for the select members of society; she is for all. God is patient, and demands patience of us; yet He does not expect us to permit enemies to deceive us.

LUKE 9: 57. And it came to pass, as they walked in the way, that a certain man said to him: I will follow thee whithersoever thou goest. 58. Jesus said to him: The foxes have holes, and the birds of the air nests; but the Son of man hath not where to lay his head. 59. But he said to another: Follow me. And he said: Lord, suffer me first to go, and to bury my father. 60. And Jesus said to him: Let the dead bury their dead: but go thou and preach the kingdom of God. 61. And another said: I will follow thee, Lord; but let me first take my leave of them that are at my house. 62. Jesus said to him: no man putting his hand to the plough, and looking back, is fit for the kingdom of God.

Christ was honest with the first prospective follower. He no longer had so much as a home. He who told us not to attach our heart to any worldly possessions actually lived in poverty. The hesitation of the second man brought out the remark that God's law must come first in life. It is our duty to take care of parents as Christ did of Mary; but concern for relatives may never be permitted to cause us to neglect a duty to God. In the third case Christ showed that a priest, or brother, or nun who looks longingly back at the world is not worthy of a vocation. And a Catholic who wishes he were not a Catholic so that he might join a certain society, or marry a divorced person, or obtain social prestige lacks constancy, and is disloyal to Christ.

JOHN 7: 11. The Jews therefore sought him on the festival day, and said: Where is he? 12. And there was much murmuring among the multitude concerning him. For some said: He is a good man. And others said: No, but he seduceth the people. 13. Yet no man spoke openly of him, for fear of the Jews. 14. Now about the midst of the feast, Jesus went up into the temple, and taught. 15. And the Jews wondered, saying: How doth this man know letters, having never learned? 16. And Jesus answered them, and said: My doctrine is not mine, but his that sent me. 17. If any man will do the will of him; he shall know of the doctrine, whether it be of God, or whether I speak of myself. 18. He that speaketh of himself, seeketh his own glory: but he that seeketh the glory of him that sent him, he is true, and there is no injustice in him. 19. Did not Moses give you the law, and yet none of you keepeth the law?

The remark of His relatives: "manifest thyself," contrasts strangely with the prominence of His name. (The word *Jews* means the leaders in Jerusalem.) Honest people of today recognize that He has been the world's greatest Man. Jesus is "always living, always loved, always hated." No one can be neutral in regard to Him. They who say: "religion is the opium of the people" are using the same type of argument as that employed in Jerusalem. In your own community observe whether or not social pressure is used to prevent some from becoming Catholics.

Unannounced, unafraid Christ appeared in the Temple; and His very words showed the mastery of His thoughts. Notice His plan. He was now in a center of learning, where knowledge was considered power. He met His enemies in their own special field. The brilliance of His thoughts staggered those who were filled with erudition. The leaders made the same mistake that is often made today, namely, imagining that only in certain schools can one become learned. Schools are necessary, but there is a wisdom that cannot be learned from books. There is the wisdom acquired through native intelligence. There is also a wisdom acquired by meditating on God's word. God can directly enlighten good people. No school can impart the wisdom that God gives to His faithful souls.

The wisdom of Christ, however, was above all human wisdom because He is God. He wished it to be distinctly understood that He came from God and was sent by God. Anyone who believes this fact will receive a wisdom that is beyond the learning of schools. No scientist, no writer can give the truths that Christ gave. But a certain attitude, a certain type of humility is required before one can grasp these divine truths. Pascal said: "If in order to love human things we must know them, in order to know divine things we must begin by loving them, and we reach the truth only by way of charity."

> John 7: 20. Why seek you to kill me? The multitude answered,
> and said: Thou hast a devil; who seeketh to kill thee? . . . 25.
> Some therefore of Jerusalem said: is not this he whom they seek
> to kill? 26. And behold, he speaketh openly, and they say
> nothing to him. Have the rulers known for a truth, that this is
> the Christ? 27. But we know this man, whence he is: but when
> the Christ cometh, no man knoweth whence he is.

They who had come from outside of Jerusalem were not aware of the plots in the city. Dwellers of the city were more alive to the hatred against Christ. They were astonished at His courage. He was always one step ahead of His enemies; He brought their plot out into the open.

JOHN 7: 28. Jesus therefore cried out in the temple, teaching,
and saying: You both know me, and you know whence I am:
and I am not come of myself; but he that sent me, is true, whom
you know not. 29. I know him, because I am from him, and
he hath sent me. 30. They sought therefore to apprehend him:
and no man laid hands on him, because his hour was not yet come.
31. But of the people many believed in him, and said: When the
Christ cometh, shall he do more miracles, than these which this
man doth? . . . 45. The ministers therefore came to the chief
priests and the Pharisees. And they said to them: Why have you
not brought Him? 46. The ministers answered: Never did
man speak like this man. 47. The Pharisees therefore answered
them: Are you also seduced? 48. Hath any one of the rulers
believed in him, or of the Pharisees? 49. But this multitude,
that knoweth not the law, are accursed. 50. Nicodemus said to
them (he that came to him by night, who was one of them):
51. Doth our law judge any man, unless it first hear him, and
know what he doth? 52. They answered, and said to him: Art
thou also a Galilean? Search the scriptures, and see, that out of
Galilee, a prophet riseth not. 53. And every man returned to
his own house.

The evidence for Christ's divine origin was clear to anyone who was not prejudiced. Then, as now, there were many who thought that their own ideas of God were more reliable than the teachings of Christ. Such people are infuriated at others who accept Christ wholeheartedly. Christ alone knows what God is like, hence the wisdom of trusting Him.

The police were powerless to lay a hand on Him. We have here a picture of the moral majesty of the God-Man. The cowardly Pharisees were themselves afraid to do anything. The police had more honesty than these leaders who sneeringly referred to the crowd as not being intellectual. It stung the Pharisees to the quick to hear some of their own henchmen pay tribute to Christ. If you should ever hear a teacher or writer sneeringly refer to those who accept Christ, or who pray, as "simple," as "credulous," as not being able to think, you will understand that, like the ancient Pharisees, they are attempting to cover up their own confusion. There are unbelievers who are honest, but they seldom sneer; they never use the arguments that the Pharisees employed. One does not need to be a product of schools to see truth. Today many of the highest of the truly intellectual accept the Faith, just as Nicodemus the intellectual, the ruler gave the lie to the Pharisee statement that no ruler accepted Christ; and five years later Paul, the Pharisee, finally came to see the light. Christ, the Master continues to rule, to enlighten all who wish to see the light. And He conquers despite the lies and misrepresentations of those who hate God. The Pharisees lied in saying that no prophet had come from Galilee, for Jonas the prophet was from Galilee (4 Kings 14: 25); and now a greater Galilean Prophet was before them, and towered majestically, calmly, and victoriously over them.

> JOHN 8: 1. And Jesus went unto Mount Olivet. 2. And early in the morning he came again into the temple, and all the people came to him, and sitting down he taught them. 3. And the scribes and Pharisees bring unto him a woman taken in adultery: and they set her in the midst, 4. And said to him: Master, this woman was even now taken in adultery. 5. Now Moses in the law commanded us to stone such a one. But what sayest thou? 6. And this they said tempting him, that they might accuse him. But Jesus bowing himself down, wrote with his finger on the ground. 7. When therefore they continued asking him, he lifted up himself, and said to them: He that is without sin among you, let him first cast a stone at her. 8. And again stooping down, he wrote on the ground. 9. But they hearing this, went out one by one, beginning at the eldest. And Jesus alone remained, and the woman standing in the midst. 10. Then Jesus lifting up himself, said to her: Woman, where are they that accused thee? Hath no man condemned thee? 11. Who said: No man, Lord. And Jesus said: Neither will I condemn thee. Go, and now sin no more.

Jesus had spent the night on Mt. Olivet. Vigorous and healthy, He loved the open air. Meanwhile there had been revelry in the city on the last night of the feast. The Pharisees, men who covered up their own sins, saw a chance to entrap Christ. It was known that He was merciful. If He declared against the ruling of the Mosaic Law they would have a legal case against Him. If He declared for stoning, He would be held for defying the Romans who perhaps had taken away from the Jews the right to impose capital punishment.

There was hypocrisy in their use of the title: "Master." But the Master was not going to be caught. The eyes of all in the crowd were centered on Him. We do not know what He wrote on the ground. It must have been a hint to the accusers, to give them a chance to escape. He may have written classical Hebrew, while the crowd could only understand Aramaic, the dialect of Hebrew. The Law said that the witnesses of the sin should cast the first stone at the sinner. When He straightened up, something in those eyes told the accusers that He knew their secret sins. They suddenly became aware that the eyes of the crowd had shifted to them. Exposure of their secret sins was the last thing that they had thought of. They had unwittingly made a trap for themselves. Blushing, confused, and defeated they sneaked away from the wilting force of a divinely innocent gaze. The woman then looked at Jesus: "Degraded misery was set before the bar of perfect Mercy." In her case the gaze meant forgiveness.

It is Christ who looks into our souls when we go to confession. When others lead us into sin and then throw us over, there is One who can save and forgive. He will always reprove sin; but He will pardon the penitent sinner. From the lips of the God-Man we learn that sin is always wrong. They who say there is nothing wrong in impurity will one day have to meet this Judge — a merciful Judge, yes, but also a masterful one who is never deceived.

1. On p. 176 Christ taught constancy by a comparison. How does He teach it in this chapter?
2. What method does Pascal advise for arriving at an appreciation of divine truth?
3. Which was worse: the attitude of the Pharisees or the sin of the woman?
4. If a student possessed talent and loved Christ would he study

religion and also science so as to be able to meet, in their own field, false scientists?

5. Prove with an incident in Samaria that Christ does not permit a spirit of revenge.
6. What is the fault with those who assert that sin is an outworn, outmoded idea?
7. A student may acquire moral courage by ———.
8. Some of the intelligentsia assert that only cowards go to church. Judge this assertion in the light of Christ's own life.

Chapter 39

THE LIGHT THAT IS A GUIDE TO US

JOHN 8: 12. Again therefore, Jesus spoke to them, saying: I am the light of the world: he that followeth me, walketh not in darkness, but shall have the light of life. . . . 20. These words Jesus spoke in the treasury, teaching in the temple: and no man laid hands on him, because his hour was not yet come.

IN THEIR escape from Egypt the Jews had been guided by a pillar of fire. Later they learned from Isaias (9: 2–6) that the Messias would be a light to them. Hence a custom arose of recalling at their feasts these prefigured qualities of the Messias. Two or four huge candlesticks (perhaps about eighty feet high) were lighted on some evenings of the feast and a torchlight procession was held around these lights. Apparently, Jesus now directed His steps toward that portion of the grounds where the procession was taking place. With a loud voice He as much as announced Himself to be the Messias. The Pharisees caught the point and said that He was giving testimony of Himself. But a light is its own proof; it is self-evident. Christ's very character and His deeds were proof of His claim.

Under various comparisons Christ had taught the same truths. He called Himself the living water, the bread of life, the truth, and life itself. We need truth for our minds; we need grace for the supernatural life we are to lead here on earth. Christ is both truth and grace. In this lesson we are regarding Him as the truth, as the light that guides us. Millions of Americans belong to no Church; they look not to Christ for guidance. They are often unaware of the fact that they are in darkness. They are not using their lives intelligently. Christ enlightens us on the really important truths — truths of which science can tell us nothing.

Search for scientific truth is good and necessary, but the modern man often makes the mistake of thinking we have yet to discover the truth about the purpose of life. We have that truth already. It has been revealed to us.

JOHN 8: 23. And he said to them: You are from beneath, I am from above. You are of this world, I am not of this world. 24. Therefore I said to you, that you shall die in your sins. For if you believe not that I am he, you shall die in your sin. 25. They said therefore to him: Who art thou? Jesus said to them: The beginning, who also speak unto you. 26. Many things I have to speak and to judge of you. But he that sent me, is true; and the things I have heard of him, these same I speak in the world. 27. And they understood not that he called God his Father. 28. Jesus therefore said to them: When you shall have lifted up the Son of man, then shall you know that I am he, and that I do nothing of myself, but as the Father hath taught me, these things I speak. 29. And he that sent me, is with me, and he hath not left me alone: for I do always the things that please him.

Deliberate rejection of Christ bars a person from the presence of God. To refuse to believe Christ is a great sin. Hence there is an obligation on every American to investigate the claims of Jesus. He was not merely a superman. He came from above, from the presence of God. He has faithfully told us all that we need to know about God. The crucifixion, the resurrection would be final proofs of His claims.

How frequently Christ repeated His life aim — "I do always the things that please Him!" That is the supreme rule for every Catholic — to act, to live, and to pray so that God will be pleased. In the acceptance of that rule lies happiness.

JOHN 8: 30. When he spoke these things, many believed in him. 31. Then Jesus said to those Jews, who believed him: If you continue in my word, you shall be my disciples indeed. 32. And you shall know the truth, and the truth shall make you free. 33. They answered him: We are the seed of Abraham, and we have never been slaves to any man: how sayest thou: You shall be free? 34. Jesus answered them: Amen, amen I say unto you: that whosoever committeth sin, is the servant of sin. 35. Now the servant abideth not in the house for ever; but the son abideth for ever. 36. If therefore the son shall make you free, you shall be free indeed. 37. I know that you are the children of Abraham: but you seek to kill me, because my word hath no place in you. 38. I speak that which I have seen with my Father: and you do the things that you have seen with your father. 39. They answered, and said to him: Abraham is our father. Jesus saith to them: If you be the children of Abraham, do the works of Abraham. 40. But now you seek to kill me, a man who has spoken the truth to you, which I have heard of God. This Abraham did not.

Our Lord told those who believed in Him that by accepting Him they would be preserved from all the errors and excesses which you may observe in the man-made religions of our day. In the eyes of those who rejected Christ the mere fact of being descendants of Abraham was enough to insure salvation for them. However, Abraham had won renown for believing God when He asked him to do a hard thing, just to test him (to sacrifice his son Isaac). Had this group possessed the faith of Abraham they would have accepted Jesus, who was greater far than Abraham. Pride of family ancestry is a good thing up to a certain degree, but it sometimes blinds one to facts.

JOHN 8: 46. Which of you shall convince me of sin? If I say the truth to you, why do you not believe me? 47. He that is of God, heareth the words of God. Therefore you hear them not, because you are not of God. 48. The Jews therefore answered, and said to him: Do not we say well that thou art a Samaritan, and hast a devil? 49. Jesus answered: I have not a devil: but I honor my Father, and you have dishonored me. 50. But I seek not my own glory: there is one that seeketh and judgeth. 51. Amen, amen I say to you: If any man keep my word, he shall not see death for ever.

Only once in history did a man in His right senses calmly dare His enemies to prove that He had ever committed a sin. Only God could speak with such assurance. Some may hate Christ and the Church because they are ignorant. But generally, one's character or intellectual honesty is shown by the attitude he takes toward the Nazarene. If he really wants the truth he does not have much trouble in believing, for God gives him grace.

JOHN 8: 52. The Jews therefore said: Now we know that thou hast a devil. Abraham is dead, and the prophets, and thou sayest:

If any man keep my word, he shall not taste death for ever. 53.
Art thou greater than our father Abraham, who is dead? And the
prophets are dead. Whom dost thou make thyself? 54. Jesus
answered: If I glorify myself, my glory is nothing. It is my
Father that glorifieth me, of whom you say that he is your God.
55. And you have not known him, but I know him. And if I
shall say that I know him not, I shall be like to you, a liar.
But I do know him, and do keep his word. 56. Abraham your
father rejoiced that he might see my day: he saw it, and was
glad. 57. The Jews therefore said to him: Thou are not yet
fifty years old, and hast thou seen Abraham? 58. Jesus said to
them: Amen, amen I say to you, before Abraham was made, I
am. 59. They took up stones therefore to cast at him. But Jesus
hid himself, and went out of the temple.

Blind, national pride prevented these leaders from regarding Christ as more than mortal man, as greater than Abraham. It was useless for Jesus to argue that God the Father was approving His statements by the miracles which He performed. Man's view of God will never be right unless it is based on what Christ has told us about God. Christ's divine nature had existed long before the day of Abraham. Therefore He is divine, and is eternal. And at the same time Christ in His human nature was a descendant of Abraham. His claim to be eternal was the climax of the dispute. He passed from among them; and they remained in blindness. It will be our own fault if we lose the Faith, if Christ hides Himself from us.

We adore Him whom the Pharisees tried to kill. For us He is the light that guides us to eternity — our home. And our Light, Christ, is truly God. That truth must be implanted firmly in our hearts. At the Chicago Eucharistic Congress in 1926, 150,000 men held lighted candles in their hands in the stadium as the silver moon shone from a June sky. The light of the candle signified belief in the divinity of Christ. "The light of faith and the fire of the love of God." For claiming to be eternal, the Pharisees sought to stone Him. Nineteen centuries later, 150,000 candles testified to the fact that He is the Light Eternal. What a joy to have that light!

JOHN 9: 1. And Jesus passing by, saw a man who was blind from
his birth: 2. And his disciples asked him: Rabbi, who hath

sinned, this man or his parents, that he should be born blind?
3. Jesus answered. Neither hath this man sinned, nor his parents;
but that the works of God should be made manifest in him. 4.
I must work the works of him that sent me, whilst it is day:
the night cometh, when no man can work. 5. As long as I am in
the world, I am the light of the world.

Quietly, deftly the work of God goes on in the world despite opposition from some men. God can keep His promises. He is what He says He is because He is truth. In each of His trips to Jerusalem Christ had found an unwillingness to believe. His usual method there was to meet the intellectual leaders on their own ground — argument, exposition, verbal proof. This time He was to add a miracle, a clinching proof of His statements. This man, who was physically blind through no fault of his own, was to learn that Christ is a light to us. Suffering often comes to good people. By their acceptance of it they show their trust in God.

JOHN 9: 6. When he had said these things, he spat on the ground,
and made clay of the spittle, and spread the clay on his eyes.
7. And said to him: Go, wash in the pool of Siloe, which is
interpreted, Sent. He went therefore, and washed, and he came
seeing. 8. The neighbors therefore, and they who had seen him
before that he was a beggar, said: Is not this he that sat and
begged? Some said: This is he. 9. But others said: No, but he
is like him. But he said: I am he. 10. They said therefore to
him: How were thy eyes opened? 11. He answered: That man
that is called Jesus made clay, and anointed my eyes, and said to
me: Go to the pool of Siloe, and wash. And I went, I washed,
and I see. 12. And they said to him: Where is he? He saith: I
know not. 13. They bring him that had been blind to the
Pharisees. 14. Now it was the Sabbath, when Jesus made the
clay, and opened his eyes. 15. Again therefore the Pharisees
asked him, how he had received his sight: But he said to them:
He put clay upon my eyes, and I washed, and I see. 16. Some
therefore of the Pharisees said: This man is not of God, who
keepeth not the Sabbath. But others said: How can a man that is
a sinner do such miracles? And there was a division among them.
17. They say therefore to the blind man again: What sayest thou
of him that hath opened thy eyes? And he said: He is a prophet.

It was forbidden to apply spittle to the eyes on the Sabbath. Saliva was commonly thought to be a remedy for affliction of the eyes. We do not know why our Lord used the spittle. Perhaps it was to help the man in his faith; perhaps He foresaw that the Pharisees would attack Him for thus breaking a Sabbath and thus He would have a chance to correct the wrong teaching that one could not aid another on the Sabbath. It may have been His intention to show us that He would make material things the means of bringing life or grace to the soul, for this is the idea behind the sacraments. The cure sent a thrill through all the neighborhood, for Jerusalem had not seen many miracles.

JOHN 9: 18. The Jews then did not believe concerning him, that he had been blind, and had received his sight, until they called the parents of him that had received his sight, 19. And asked them, saying: Is this your son, who you say was born blind? How then doth he now see? 20. His parents answered them, and said: We know that this is our son, and that he was born blind: 21. But how he now seeth, we know not; or who hath opened his eyes, we know not: ask himself: he is of age, let him speak for himself. 22. These things his parents said, because they feared the Jews: for the Jews had already agreed among themselves, that if any man should confess him to be Christ he should be put out of the synagogue. 23. Therefore did his parents say: He is of age, ask himself.

The parents feared these mighty Pharisees, who looked so menacingly at them. We cannot blame them too much for being afraid of excommunication. Fear of social ostracism keeps many from becoming Catholics. Fear of criticism, however, should not deter one from doing what he knows to be right and proper.

JOHN 9: 24. They therefore called the man again that had been blind, and said to him: Give glory to God. We know that this man is a sinner. 25. He said therefore to them: If he be a sinner, I know not: one thing I know, that whereas I was blind, now I see. 26. They said then to him: What did he to thee? How did he open thy eyes? 27. He answered them: I have told you already, and you have heard: why would you hear it again? Will you also become his disciples?

The Pharisees remembered how Christ had walked away from them; they realized also that this miracle was a proof that He is the light of the world. To prevent their own prestige from being lost, they did all in their power to induce this man to condemn Christ for breaking the Sabbath. They tried to intimidate him. The man tripped them up at each step. He stood his ground and used good logic. "The conscience of the people, spontaneous and sincere, is ever ready to support a fact and treat with contempt the learning which denies it" (Didon). Like the moderns who deny miracles, the Pharisees did not want to study facts. This man even dared to twit his judges. He had a sense of humor. His irony cut them deeply.

JOHN 9: 28. They reviled him therefore, and said. Be thou his disciple; but we are the disciples of Moses. 29. We know that God spoke to Moses: but as to this man, we know not from whence he is. 30. The man answered, and said to them: Why, herein is a wonderful thing, that you know not from whence he is, and he hath opened my eyes. 31. Now we know that God doth not hear sinners: but if a man be a server of God, and doth his will, him he heareth. 32. From the beginning of the world it hath not been heard, that any man hath opened the eyes of one born blind. 33. Unless this man were of God, he could not do anything. 34. They answered, and said to him: Thou wast wholly born in sins and dost thou teach us? And they cast him out.

The man stuck to facts and their correct interpretation, while the judges became abusive. A miracle is always a *good deed.* God, who is goodness itself, lends approval only to good deeds. Instead of meeting this argument the Pharisees became personal and mean and guilty of calumny. It was a hard blow for them to be taught by an illiterate person how to interpret facts. This poor man had to stand personal abuse in order to defend Jesus. Christ has been good to us; courage in defense of Christ and of His Church is our duty, especially against the intelligentsia who refuse to see facts.

JOHN 9: 35. Jesus heard that they had cast him out: and when he had found him, he said to him: Dost thou believe in the Son of God? 36. He answered, and said: Who is he, Lord, that I may believe in him? 37. And Jesus said to him: Thou hast both seen him; and it is he that talketh with thee. 38. And he said; I believe, Lord. And falling down, he adored him. 39. And Jesus said: For judgment I am come into this world; that they who see not, may see; and they who see, may become blind. 40. And some of the Pharisees, who were with him, heard: and they said unto him: Are we also blind? 41. Jesus said to them: If you were blind, you should not have sin: but now you say: We see. Your sin remaineth.

The loyalty and gratitude of the man pleased Christ. How clearly our Lord made known to him just who He is. Many people would believe in the Church if they but knew the truth about the Church. One who seeks to make this truth known, who is never ashamed of his religion, but openly professes his belief in Christ will gain new favors from Jesus who will seek him out to encourage him (Cf. Acts 18: 9–10; 23: 11). The blind man rejoiced in his newly found privilege of seeing the Light of the world. Christ was now clearly defined in his mind. Likewise we must acquire a clear, accurate knowledge of Christ and then we shall love Him. "Nascent faith, without a well-defined object to which it may attach itself, soon feels its glow become dim; it recoils upon itself and dies" (Le Camus).

The result of Christ's coming into the world is that men are split into two camps. They who imagine that their learning, or their wealth enable them to get along without Christ actually blind themselves to the light. They remain in their sin because they lack humility. They talk of "seeing straight," of taking a "reasonable view," when, indeed, they fail to see facts, just as the Pharisees failed. They reject the only light that can guide them, that can enable them to see truly.

1. How many occasions can you recall on which Christ repeated the supreme rule that guided His life while here on earth?
2. Show that there is an obligation on each person to study Christ.
3. Why may atheistic Communism be termed darkness?
4. When a person says that he does not believe in the possibility of miracles, may he be called unscientific?
5. In the catacombs, candles served a practical purpose. What is their function now?
6. Scientific knowledge is also a light; but in what questions is it incapable of giving us accurate or true light?
7. Show by a text from Scripture that Christ claimed to be eternal.

8. Show how they are in darkness who assert that the Catholic religion is a survival from primitive myths.
9. Show how grace and truth are two fundamental advantages for a Catholic.
10. What types of people today resemble the Pharisees? The blind man?
11. Loss of belief in the divinity of Christ leaves a person in darkness because ———.
12. Belief in the divinity of Christ keeps us free from what errors or superstitions?
13. Do you think that Christ rewards interiorly those who remain loyal to Him?

Chapter 40

A SHEPHERD AND HIS WORK

John 10: 1. Amen, amen I say to you: He that entereth not by the door into the sheepfold, but climbeth up another way, the same is a thief and a robber. 2. But he that entereth in by the door is the shepherd of the sheep. 3. To him the porter openeth; and the sheep hear his voice: and he calleth his own sheep by name, and leadeth them out. 4. And when he hath let out his own sheep, he goeth before them: and the sheep follow him, because they know his voice. 5. But a stranger they follow not, but fly from him, because they know not the voice of strangers. 6. This proverb Jesus spoke to them. But they understood not what he spoke to them.

OUR Lord here drew pictures of shepherd life in Palestine. Sheep and shepherds are as familiar a sight in that country as cornfields in our Middle West. Several shepherds left their sheep in a common enclosure during the night. The gatekeeper was the night watchman. Each sheep had a name. So intimate was the daily association between sheep and shepherd that the animals came to recognize the voice of their owner. In those days sheep were more often led than driven. It is likely that Jesus spoke this parable on a hillside near Jerusalem and not far from a sheep enclosure. The Pharisees, who heard Him, considered themselves to be the shepherds of the people. However, our Lord entered the fold legitimately because God sent Him to the people. They who are willing to obey God easily recognize Christ.

John 10: 7. Jesus therefore said to them again: Amen, amen I say to you, I am the door of the sheep. 8. All others, as many as have come, are thieves and robbers: and the sheep heard them not. 9. I am the door. By me, if any man enter in, he shall be saved: and he shall go in, and go out, and shall find pastures. 10. The thief cometh not, but for to steal, and to kill, and to destroy. I am come that they may have life, and may have it more abundantly.

Our Lord now changed the analogy to a door, showing that they who enter through Him are safe. The Pharisees were not legitimate rulers because they thought always of their own interests rather than of the good of the sheep, the people. They were attempting to steal the sheep (people) from Christ. The same principle applies to those who start new religions. They have not entered by the door, which is Christ; they have not been commissioned by Christ. Loyal friends of Jesus sense the danger of following self-commissioned leaders. They do not recognize the voice of Christ in much of the modern literature, or in many of the fads of the day. They are not deceived by a pleasant style or dressed-up sin. In the presence of allurements to a life of sin they realize that the life (grace, supernatural life) which Christ brought to earth is far more precious.

JOHN 10: 11. I am the good shepherd. The good shepherd giveth his life for his sheep. 12. But the hireling, and he that is not the shepherd, whose own the sheep are not, seeth the wolf coming, and leaveth the sheep, and flieth: and the wolf catcheth, and scattereth the sheep.

Sheep are very helpless animals. They often fell while climbing the stony hills of Judea. And wild animals were numerous. The good shepherd was compassionate, and led his sheep along safe paths. He would risk his life to save even a young lamb. His life was lonely, yet full of unselfishness.

We often miss the full effect of Christ's words because we are unfamiliar with shepherd conditions. Yet, the comparison holds true for our day. A good priest, or a good teacher works unselfishly for the people and for students. The example of Christ laying down His life on Calvary is ever before us. A hireling, that is, one not deeply devoted to Christ, will think of his own comfort before providing for the welfare of others. The "wolf" that draws young people away from Christ may be a clever writer, a scoffer, a subtly poisoned book, or a bad companion. In warning us against corrupting influences the Church, or a priest, does not intend to hold us down, or to cramp our development. Christ has obliged priests to warn us of wolves that come in the clothing of sheep. Sin is often so attractive that we are not aware of its hidden danger.

> JOHN 10: 14. I am the good shepherd; and I know mine, and
> mine know me. 15. As the Father knoweth me, and I know the
> Father: and I lay down my life for my sheep. 16. And other
> sheep I have, that are not of this fold: them also I must bring,
> and they shall hear my voice, and there shall be one fold and
> one shepherd. 17. Therefore doth the Father love me: because
> I lay down my life, that I may take it again. 18. No man taketh
> it away from me: but I lay it down of myself, and I have power
> to lay it down; and I have power to take it up again. This commandment have I received of my Father.

Jesus knows the problems of each person; He is aware of all the efforts of people to remain loyal to Him. God knows us individually. On the other hand, do we really *know* Christ? In some mysterious way the true-hearted Catholic goes straight to the heart of Christ; he does not have much trouble in keeping the Faith. Because of his honesty of heart God gives him secret graces by which he reaches an appreciation of what it means to have Christ as a friend. Meditation on the personal qualities of the Good Shepherd draws one closer to Him. Likewise, it seems that some people outside the Church are drawn to Christ and readily become Catholics. It is the desire of our Lord that all Christians be united under one head, and in one fold. He expects that we make an effort to bring all into the fold, that we pray for the reunion of all Christians. We know that there are many noble people in other religions. Christ died for them; and He is standing at the door of the fold, waiting for them to enter. The giving of His life was voluntary on His part. This love of His was in direct contrast to the selfishness of the Pharisees.

> LUKE 10: 1. And after these things the Lord appointed also other seventy-two: and he sent them two and two before his face into every city and place whither he himself was to come. . . . 3.
> MATT. 10: 40. He that receiveth you, receiveth me: and he that receiveth me, receiveth him that sent me.
> Go: behold I send you as lambs among wolves.

Previously Christ had sent out the twelve to do mission work. However, His followers were not limited to twelve. Dangerous as it was for anyone to support Him, yet these disciples seem to have been attached to Him for some time. These seventy-two may have crossed over the Jordan into Perea. A representative of Christ is not always welcomed. Nevertheless the work must go on. Christ shows clearly that religion is necessary. To turn down Christ is to turn down God the Father. These seventy-two may be considered as the forerunners of the laity who participate today in the work of spreading a knowledge of Christ the Leader (Cf. 1 Pet. 1: 8 and 2: 9).

LUKE 10: 17. And the seventy-two returned with joy, saying: Lord, the devils also are subject to us in thy name. 18. And he said to them: I saw Satan like lightning falling from heaven. 19. Behold, I have given you power to tread upon serpents and scorpions, and upon all the power of the enemy: and nothing shall hurt you. 20. But yet rejoice not in this, that spirits are subject unto you; but rejoice in this, that your names are written in heaven. 21. In that same hour, he rejoiced in the Holy Ghost, and said: I confess to thee, O Father, Lord of heaven and earth, because thou hast hidden these things from the wise and prudent, and hast revealed them to little ones. Yea, Father, for so it hath seemed good in thy sight. 22. All things are delivered to me by my Father; and no one knoweth who the Son is, but the Father; and who the Father is, but the Son, and to whom the Son will reveal him.

Christ had given unusual power to these disciples. Through His aid the hold of Satan on mankind was being broken. It was more necessary that miracles be plentiful in the early days of Christianity so that the true religion might make progress in a world that was sunk in superstition. Superstition and the influence of the devil seem to increase whenever people lose hold on true religion.

Just as Christ followed the work of the disciples, so He follows our efforts to spread His influence in the modern world. If we should be successful in working for Him, we should not take credit to ourselves. We should rejoice in this, that we have the truth about God. Some men reject the Catholic Faith because it does not agree with what they think God ought to be.

Only Christ knows God the Father perfectly. To know God perfectly means to be equal to God. Only those who accept Christ will learn the true nature of God.

> MATT. 11: 28. Come to me, all you that labor, and are burdened, and I will refresh you. 29. Take up my yoke upon you, and learn of me, because I am meek, and humble of heart: and you shall find rest to your souls. 30. For my yoke is sweet and my burden light.

Ponder this invitation. He is easy to approach. No theorist or Communist will ever make a heaven of earth. Labor and burdens will always be the part of the majority. Religion does put burdens on us; but actually Christ makes these burdens seem light because He knows how to fill with joy those hearts who accept Him. The yokes which He made for oxen were well-fitting and smooth and did not irritate the shoulders of the cattle; so likewise is His religion easy to bear for those who are working for Him. The world needs to learn that we find joy in our religion.

1. Christ expects us to make an effort to know Him because He said ———.
2. Show how our Lord possesses the qualities of a good shepherd.
3. If we seek an expert in the care of teeth, or for an operation, can it be said that they who go to an expert (Christ or a priest) are weak thinkers in matters of religion or in questions that concern the soul?
4. Do those scoffers who sneer at a student for accepting the guidance of the Church object to being considered as guides themselves?
5. Show from the practice of Christ that He intended the Church to be visible.
6. Does God really know us? What reason have you to think that Christ is today personally conscious of our own individual problems and dangers?
7. Self-denial does not make a true Catholic gloomy. Why?
8. In an investigation, 400 Catholic high-school students claimed that they were attached to their teachers because the teachers spent hours in an unselfish work for the welfare of the students. Is that the ideal in the parable of the Good Shepherd?
9. Luke 10: 22 is one of the best texts for showing the divinity of Christ because ———.

Chapter 41

LOVE OF GOD REQUIRES LOVE OF NEIGHBOR

LUKE 10: 25. And behold a certain lawyer stood up, tempting
him, and saying: Master, what must I do to possess eternal life?
26. But he said to him: What is written in the law? How readest
thou? 27. He answering, said: *Thou shalt love the Lord thy
God with thy whole heart, and with thy whole soul, and with
all thy strength, and with all thy mind: and thy neighbor as thyself.* 28. And he said to him: Thou hast answered right: this do,
and thou shalt live.

OUR LORD Himself summed up the Commandments in the same manner in which this lawyer spoke. The first part of the answer was as familiar to every Jew as the *Our Father* is to us (Cf. Deut. 6: 5). Morning and evening it was repeated. The second part is from Lev. 19: 18, and was not so well known. This book of the Old Testament teaches that one should love one's friends; but in practice one's friends meant only one's countrymen, not strangers. In practice, the Jews had laid emphasis on: "eye for eye; tooth for tooth." We can scarcely conceive how new in our Lord's day was this emphasis that He placed on love of neighbor. And nearly all peoples feared their gods; even the Jews were more moved by fear than by love. Christ is unique in revealing that God is love.

LUKE 10: 29. But he willing to justify himself, said to Jesus:
And who is my neighbor? 30. And Jesus answering, said: A
certain man went down from Jerusalem to Jericho, and fell
among robbers, who also stripped him, and having wounded him
went away, leaving him half dead. 31. And it chanced, that a
certain priest went down the same way: and seeing him, passed
by. 32. In like manner also a Levite, when he was near the
place and saw him, passed by. 33. But a certain Samaritan

being on his journey, came near him; and seeing him was moved with compassion, 34. And going up to him, bound up his wounds, pouring in oil and wine: and setting him upon his own beast, brought him to an inn, and took care of him. 35. And the next day he took out two pence, and gave to the host, and said: Take care of him; and whatsoever thou shalt spend over and above, I, at my return, will repay thee. 36. Which of these three, in thy opinion, was neighbor to him that fell among the robbers? 37. But he said: He that shewed mercy to him. And Jesus said to him: Go, and do thou in like manner.

This parable of the Good Samaritan is one of the most effective of the world's short stories. Observe the number of words used, the setting, and the action. Jesus was a master of language. Not a word was wasted, yet each phrase enlivens the picture. And we never forget the story, having once heard it. No better way for a teacher to answer a question could be imagined. In traversing the sixteen miles between Jerusalem and Jericho one descends three thousand feet. It is a winding, desolate, and dangerous road. And it is likely that Christ told the story along that very road. He could make a present occasion supply the theme for His lesson.

The priest should have been compassionate, for he lived on tithes given by the people. A levite was one who had special functions in the Temple services. They both had frigid hearts and lacked imagination. But the Samaritan, traveling in the country of the Jews and knowing that the Jews despised the Samaritans, was touched by the misery of the stranger in front of him. He did not ask: Is he one of my countrymen? Would we have overcome the prejudice against us, as did the Samaritan, who saw, felt, and acted? It was a noble thing to do. Religion means kindness, not only to friends but to strangers, to enemies, and to the poor. There should be no distinction of persons in our charity, granted that we must be prudent. In practice, we may claim to love God only when we are kind and noble in our actions. Our neighbor, therefore, is anyone in need, even an enemy, or one who despises us. Interest in our neighbor's welfare is an obligation, a requirement. This is the principle taught by the perfect story.

LUKE 10: 38. Now it came to pass as they went, that he entered into a certain town: and a certain woman named Martha received him into her house. 39. And she had a sister called Mary, who sitting even at the Lord's feet, heard his word. 40. But Martha was busy about much serving. Who stood and said: Lord, hast thou no care that my sister hath left me alone to serve? Speak to her therefore, that she help me. 41. And the Lord answering, said to her: Martha, Martha, thou art careful, and art troubled about many things. 42. But one thing is necessary. Mary hath chosen the better part, which shall not be taken away from her.

This village was Bethania, just east of Mt. Olivet. We shall hear of Lazarus, their brother, later. The frankness of these sisters permits us to conclude that Christ knew them well. It must have been a home of refinement.

Hospitality to guests is important in the East. Martha, evidently the older, was responsible for the fulfillment of this custom. She was practical and steady, but lacked imagination. Martha thought that the way to show respect for Christ was to serve a good meal, and to make His stay comfortable. Mary was different; she possessed imagination. As soon as Christ arrived she was all eyes and ears for the words which fell from His lips. She knew how to place the most important things in life first. She realized that to listen to Him was a rare opportunity, and one not to be lost. Martha, on the other hand, thought that Mary was shirking in that which counted most. It was unkind of her to ask our Lord to reprimand Mary. Jesus defended Mary. He did not condemn Martha; but He condemned her anxiety, her appeal for a humiliation of Mary. He taught the principle that seeking the kingdom of God, seeking to know God is the most important affair in this life and must not be neglected because of business duties or social duties. The one thing that is necessary is to reach God's presence. That alone is success.

They who say: "Why waste time in church?" "What is the use of prayer?" do not understand that the most practical thing in life is to learn what life itself is for. Work is good; hospitality is good. But what Christ condemns is worry, anxiety about material things, and neglect of spiritual duties. Continual thought about making money, about social or athletic success takes our mind off the daily duty of listening to and meditating on what Christ has told us. Our occupation in heaven will be the finding of delight in God. We must practice that occupation here and now as Mary was doing. Then we shall not be fretful, uneasy, or nervous as was Martha. Religion is peace, poise, and contentment. Through meditation on the words of Christ, His wisdom becomes part of our very being. If we show signs of ill temper, envy, and restlessness, the reason probably is that we have not listened sufficiently to Christ. "To work for Him is good; to love Him is better." In true love of neighbor there is no envy.

Luke 11: 1. And it came to pass, that as he was in a certain
place praying, when he ceased, one of his disciples said to him:
Lord, teach us to pray, as John also taught his disciples. . . .
5. And he said to them: Which of you shall have a friend, and
shall go to him at midnight, and shall say to him: Friend, lend
me three loaves, 6. Because a friend of mine is come off his
journey to me, and I have not what to set before him. 7. And
he from within should answer, and say: Trouble me not; the
door is now shut, and my children are with me in bed; I cannot
rise and give thee. 8. Yet if he shall continue knocking, I say
to you, although he will not rise and give him, because he is
his friend, yet, because of his importunity, he will rise, and give
him as many as he needeth. 9. And I say to you: Ask, and it
shall be given you: seek, and you shall find: knock, and it shall
be opened to you. 10. For every one that asketh, receiveth; and
he that seeketh, findeth; and to him that knocketh, it shall be
opened. 11. And which of you, if he ask his father bread,
will he give him a stone? Or a fish, will he for a fish give him a
serpent? 12. Or if he shall ask an egg, will he reach him a
scorpion? 13. If you then, being evil, know how to give good
gifts to your children, how much more will your Father from
heaven give the good Spirit to them that ask him!

The *Our Father*, which was explained in Chapter 27, was probably composed on this occasion. The fervor, and the attention of the strong Son of God impressed the disciples. This worker of miracles, this matchless speaker was praying in order to give us an example, and to give the lie to those who say that only weak persons pray. Strong men pray because no human is independent. God is not harsh or unkind, but our prayers are often of too selfish a nature. He does not grant those petitions which would be to our spiritual harm; but He expects us to be alert, sincere, and persistent in prayer, even though He appear not to answer. When our prayers are for the welfare of our neighbor, God is pleased with that unselfishness, for He showed that we are all children of the same Father.

> LUKE 11: 27. And it came to pass, as he spoke these things, a
> certain woman from the crowd, lifting up her voice, said to him:
> Blessed is the womb that bore thee, and the paps that gave thee
> suck. 28. But he said: Yea rather, blessed are they who hear the
> word of God, and keep it.

Just previous to this declaration of the woman, the Pharisees had been hurling calumnies at Christ. He was goodness itself. And goodness is attractive except to those who are extremely self-centered. This woman thought that Christ must have had a wonderful mother. "Happy mother to have such a Son." When we praise a mother for the achievements of a son, it is praise given to the son also. When we honor Mary we honor Christ at the same time. Yet, here, our Lord saw an opportunity to repeat that important truth, namely, that real credit and honor are due to any person who strives to live in a Christlike manner, whether he or she be business man, professional man, workingman, cleric, office girl, or mother. Christ did not deny that Mary had a right to honor. He knew that Mary was keeping God's word; but there were around Him many who needed to be told the necessity of obeying God. We keep God's word when we take literally His command to love our neighbor.

1. May we honestly say that we love God if we refuse to speak to an acquaintance?
2. How did Jesus teach us to persevere in prayer?
3. Who is your neighbor?
4. Write out five reasons why you should love God.
5. One student says that religion is a belief or a study. What is lacking?
6. A person says that he is too busy to pray or to go to church. What is wrong?
7. One student merely tries to keep from doing wrong; another seeks to fill his life with good deeds, with prayer for others. Which one has the better plan?

8. How may a person avoid becoming restless, nervous, envious, or dissatisfied?
9. What made the story of the Good Samaritan so effective?
10. The extremely selfish person cannot claim to be a true Catholic because ———.
11. A girl secretly thinks that being "catty" or a gossiper is the best bid for popularity. Discuss.

Chapter 42

COURAGE TO SPEAK THE TRUTH AND FOLLOW THE TRUTH

Matt. 5: 14. You are the light of the world. A city seated on a mountain cannot be hid. 15. Neither do men light a candle and put it under a bushel, but upon a candlestick, that it may shine to all that are in the house. 16. So let your light shine before men, that they may see your good works, and glorify your Father who is in heaven.

Luke 11: 34. The light of thy body is thy eye. If thy eye be single, thy whole body will be lightsome: but if it be evil, thy body also will be darksome. 35. Take heed therefore, that the light which is in thee, be not darkness. 36. If then thy whole body be lightsome, having no part of darkness, the whole shall be lightsome; and as a bright lamp, shall enlighten thee.

AN HONEST, firm Catholic is a light to many in doubt. Jesus wants the clean living, and the holiness of students as a group to be known. He was speaking on this occasion to a crowd. Men will be edified when they can say that a Catholic cannot be bribed or seduced. We are not Catholics for ourselves only, or for our family, but we are to assist others to come to Christ. Our responsibility is to demonstrate to them the advantage of being a Catholic. Christ insists that religion is not merely something to be learned or believed; it is to be lived and exemplified in daily life. In practicing the leadership of good example, our motive must be unselfish, that is, we must aim to bring honor on God.

A healthy eye enables one to see well. Likewise an unprejudiced heart and an unbiased mind help one to accept Christ, to see the truth in Him. The mind is made to see truth. Acquired prejudice often prevents a person from seeing a truth which is very apparent to others. If Christ notes that we are unworthy of our religion, if He sees the spirit of the Pharisees in us, then He may withdraw grace (a light) from us, and we would be in total darkness so far as understanding the true religion is concerned.

LUKE 11: 37. And as he was speaking, a certain Pharisee prayed him, that he would dine with him. And he going in, sat down to eat. 38. And the Pharisee began to say, thinking within himself, why he was not washed before dinner. 39. And the Lord said to him: Now you Pharisees make clean the outside of the cup and of the platter; but your inside is full of rapine and iniquity. 40. Ye fools, did not he that made that which is without, make also that which is within? 41. But yet that which is within, give as alms; and behold, all things are clean unto you. 42. But woe to you, Pharisees, because you tithe mint and rue and every herb; and pass over judgment, and the charity of God. Now these things you ought to have done, and not have left the other undone. 43. Woe to you, Pharisees, because you love the uppermost seats in the synagogues, and salutations in the market place. 44. Woe to you, because you are as sepulchers that appear not, and men that walk over are not aware.

Whatever was the motive of this man in inviting Jesus to dine, whether to trick Him in some statement or to learn more about Him, we are astonished at Christ's courage in speaking the truth about the inner lives of the Pharisees. They were high in social standing. However, our Lord could not approve social sham. If He had not exposed the hypocrisy of the Pharisees, they would later have said that He approved their practices. They were very scrupulous about paying taxes on such small herbs as mint and rue; but they had little regard for true love of God or neighbor or for the larger points of justice. Their desire for the best seats showed their egotism. People were deceived by this exterior of the Pharisees, and thus fell under the influence of their hidden corruption. Today men who steal fortunes often parade as prominent citizens, while the petty thief is hailed as a great criminal.

LUKE 11: 45. And one of the lawyers answering, saith to him: Master, in saying these things, thou reproachest us also. 46. But he said: Woe to you lawyers also, because you load men with burdens which they cannot bear, and you yourselves touch not the packs with one of your fingers. . . . 52. Woe to you lawyers, for you have taken away the key of knowledge: you yourselves have not entered in, and those that were entering in, you have hindered. 53. And as he was saying these things to them, the Pharisees and the lawyers began violently to urge him, and to oppress his mouth about many things.

The lawyers were known as Scribes. They interpreted the law. They had so increased the legal regulations that the burden on the people was almost insupportable. Meanwhile, the lawyers did not themselves observe these regulations. More people would have accepted Christ had not these leaders misinterpreted (taken away the key) the Old Testament. The vice of these men in not being honest with the people brought upon the leaders then, as it will today, the terrible punishments of God.

Just as it is dangerous for an honest man today to expose vice in high places, so by thus incurring the hatred of the leaders Christ was marked for death. Every word He uttered was examined, to find some point on which to accuse Him. We admire His calmness and poise while surrounded with this undying hate. He who meekly went about doing good had also the courage to speak the truth in the very midst of corrupt leaders. "Love of truth is the basis of character." Had Karl Marx made an honest study of Jesus and curbed his own arrogance, he could never have said that religion is the opium of the people.

LUKE 12: 13. And one of the multitude said to him: Master, speak to my brother that he divide the inheritance with me. 14. But he said to him: Man, who hath appointed me judge, or divider, over you? 15. And he said to them: Take heed, and beware of all covetousness; for a man's life doth not consist in the abundance of things which he possesseth.

Christ taught religion; He refused to be drawn into petty quarrels. To condemn injustice is a duty; to seek to manage secular affairs is another thing. He does not want priests to indulge in secular affairs to the extent that they forget their main duty, to be expert in the things of God. What Americans need to be taught is that the purpose of life is so to live as to bring credit on God, and thus to prepare for life with Him. Mixing in business often develops a craving for power, for money, and shuts out the thought of God. Covetousness often leads people to object to their relatives leaving money to the Church or for charity or education.

> LUKE 12: 16. And he spoke a similitude to them, saying: The land of a certain man brought forth plenty of fruits. 17. And he thought within himself, saying: What shall I do, because I have no room where to bestow my fruits? 18. And he said: This will I do: I will pull down my barns, and will build greater; and into them will I gather all things that are grown to me, and my goods. 19. And I will say to my soul: Soul, thou hast much goods laid up for many years, take thy rest; eat, drink, make good cheer. 20. But God said to him: Thou fool, this night do they require thy soul of thee: and whose shall those things be which thou hast provided? 21. So is he that layeth up treasure for himself, and is not rich towards God.

Our Lord went directly to the heart of the problem of what is most desirable in life. In our day it is well to provide some financial security for old age; but such an action must not be governed by the pernicious principle that the making of money is the main purpose of life. Neither must we be deceived into believing that economic security is the sole means of contentment. The object of life is to honor God by the way we live. Hence, if we possess wealth we should use as much of it as possible for the welfare of others instead of hoarding it for selfish purposes. A bachelor once accumulated $75,000. He refused to give anything for some needed repairs on the church. Two years later, he had lost all his money. He could find no peace of mind. Had he given some for education or for charity or for the support of the Church, and given it willingly for Christ's sake, he would have had an imperishable fund on which to rely when death arrived. Likewise, he would have had happier memories in this life. Deposits in the bank of eternity are not lost in a panic or depression.

> LUKE 12: 49. I am come to cast fire on the earth: and what will I, but that it be kindled? 50. And I have a baptism wherewith I am to be baptized: and how am I straitened until it be accomplished! 51. Think ye, that I am come to give peace on earth? I tell you, no; but separation. 52. For there shall be from henceforth five in one house divided: three against two, and two against three. 53. The father shall be divided against the son,

and the son against his father, the mother against the daughter, and the daughter against the mother, the mother-in-law against her daughter-in-law, and the daughter-in-law against her mother-in-law.

Malachias (3: 2) had predicted that the Messias would be a "refining fire." Christ was to cleanse men of sin, and to be persecuted for so doing. Christ's baptism of blood was the death on Calvary, which was now not far away. This death was to result in the coming of the Holy Ghost to complete the work of Christ.

The presence of Christ in a person's life gives interior peace; but outwardly the result is often division. The world seems to resent attachment to Jesus. Worldly members of a family become bitter against those members who are loyal to our Lord. Christ came for all, but resentment is often shown to Him and to those who stand for truth and for justice. The apostles must have been deeply impressed by those flashes of indignation through which Christ spoke the truth against the Pharisees. Then He warned His friends. He gave us an example of a life built upon truth. We need His aid, not only for courage to speak the truth, but to live it, and to follow it even when others resent it and try to make life miserable for us.

1. Show how prejudice may blind one to the good qualities of another person.
2. What pleases God: the fact that you have talent and fame, or the fact that you co-operate with grace?
3. Must a student sometimes hurt the feelings of others in order to expose sham or hypocrisy?
4. One student is afraid of ridicule from other students; another has "fear of the Lord." Which is better?
5. What do you think is the real reason why some Catholics lose the Faith?
6. What reason have we to believe that bad companionship causes the downfall of many people?
7. What impression does the courage of Christ make on you?
8. What would our Lord think of a student who spends freely on shows or dances, but who never has anything for the offertory collection on Sundays?
9. What is meant by the leadership of good example?

Chapter 43

NO EYES TO SEE

JOHN 10: 22. And it was the feast of the dedication at Jerusalem: and it was winter. 23. And Jesus walked in the temple,
in Solomon's porch. 24. The Jews therefore came round about
him, and said to him: How long dost thou hold our souls in
suspense? If thou be the Christ, tell us plainly. 25. Jesus
answered them: I speak to you, and you believe not: the works
that I do in the name of my Father, they give testimony of me.
26. But you do not believe, because you are not of my sheep.
27. My sheep hear my voice: and I know them, and they follow me. 28. And I give them life everlasting; and they shall
not perish for ever, and no man shall pluck them out of my
hand. 29. That which my Father hath given me, is greater than
all: and no one can snatch them out of the hand of my Father.
30. I and the Father are one.

DREARY, rainy winter was at hand; dreary discouragement lay upon the apostles. Christ alone remained constant, and even dared to return to Jerusalem about the middle of December for the commemoration of the time that the Temple had been rededicated under Judas Machabaeus (1 Mac. 4: 36–59). Solomon's Porch was the covered colonnade running along the east side of the Temple grounds. (Later the Christians met in this spot. Cf. Acts 3: 11; 5: 12.)

Only two months previous to this, Christ had given a clear statement. He had definitely shown that He considered Himself to be God. He showed that there is a distinction of Persons in the Trinity but a oneness of nature. He always refused, however, to describe Himself in terms of a national liberator such as they desired. In Jerusalem He had always to deal with unscrupulous officials, with men capable of twisting a statement into sedition against Rome or against what they thought was the Mosaic Law. Repeatedly He had to correct false notions of His purpose on earth. Of course the Jews were accustomed to think of only one Person in God; hence the difficulty of realizing that Christ and the Father are equal and one. But the works which Christ accomplished should have convinced them of His claims. Because He did not fit into the picture of what they thought He ought to be, they rejected Him, much as the moderns do, who think that God ought to be thus and so, acccording to the way they want Him to be.

> JOHN 10: 31. The Jews then took up stones to stone him. 32.
> Jesus answered them: Many good works I have shewed you from
> my Father. For which of those works do you stone me? 33. The
> Jews answered him: For a good work we stone thee not, but for
> blasphemy; and because that thou, being a man, makest thyself
> God. . . . 37. If I do not the works of my Father, believe
> me not. 38. But if I do, though you will not believe me, believe
> the works: that you may know and believe that the Father is in
> me, and I in the Father. 39. They sought therefore to take him;
> and he escaped out of their hands. 40. And he went again be-
> yond the Jordan, into that place where John was baptizing first;
> and there he abode.

In their response they not only show that they understood what He was claiming, but they also refute those moderns who say that Christ never claimed to be God. Prejudices of people constantly prevent them from seeing facts. He accepted the accusation that He made Himself God, for it is true. He had looked straight at them as they picked up the stones. "The rage of men ever found Him in that calm condition of mind which is conferred by holiness and truth." Not a hand was raised as He majestically passed from view.

The hush of imminent catastrophe brooded over Jerusalem. Nothing is sadder than the case of a man or woman who has rejected God. The light has gone out of such a life. Jerusalem ceased to be a city of joy when Christ was rejected; and now there remains but the sad symbol of the wailing wall. A blight seems to come into the lives of those who, once having known truth, reject it.

Luke 14: 1. And it came to pass, when Jesus went into the house of one of the chiefs of the Pharisees, on the sabbath day, to eat bread, that they watched him. . . . 7. And he spoke a parable also to them that were invited, marking how they chose the first seats at the table, saying to them: 8. When thou art invited to a wedding, sit not down in the first place, lest perhaps one more honorable than thou be invited by him: 9. And he that invited thee and him, come and say to thee: Give this man place: and then thou begin with shame to take the lowest place. 10. But when thou art invited, go, sit down in the lowest place; that when he who invited thee, cometh, he may say to thee: Friend, go up higher. Then shalt thou have glory before them that sit at table with thee. 11. Because every one that exalteth himself, shall be humbled; and he that humbleth himself, shall be exalted.

Our Lord crossed over the Jordan again into Perea. Here also the Pharisees were considered social leaders. They were to receive a much-needed lesson in etiquette and fundamental virtue. There is often more true refinement in a humble, religious soul than in social leaders. The true friend of Christ is courteous, thoughtful of others, gentle, and poised. The foundation of such virtues is humility. It is a steppingstone to God's graces. Humility means that one does not take credit to himself for achievements, or talents; he gives the credit to God. If he possesses real character and ability, others will ordinarily push him to the front; he need not push himself. A sense of true humility does not lessen one's energy or stunt development or initiative. And if no one seems to acknowledge his achievements, there is One who will exalt him. The ultimate test of worth is not the place one occupies in this world. It is, instead, the place he will be called to take at the table of the great King.

Luke 14: 12. And he said to him also that had invited him: When thou makest a dinner or a supper, call not thy friends, nor thy brethren, nor thy kinsmen, nor thy neighbors who are rich; lest perhaps they also invite thee again, and a recompense be made to thee. 13. But when thou makest a feast, call the poor, the maimed, the lame, and the blind; 14. And thou shalt be blessed, because they have not wherewith to make thee recompense: for recompense shall be made thee at the resurrection of the just.

A true Catholic does not seek to be "in" with the important people of the world, but with the poor and the defeated. He aids the poor by being kind to them, by joining the St. Vincent de Paul Society, by taking on his own shoulders some of their problems. He makes his life to be the sunshine of those who live in hovels and city alleys.

> LUKE 13: 31. The same day, there came some of the Pharisees,
> saying to him: Depart, and get thee hence, for Herod hath a
> mind to kill thee. 32. And he said to them: Go and tell that
> fox: Behold, I cast out devils, and do cures today and tomorrow,
> and the third day I am consummated. 33. Nevertheless I must
> walk today and tomorrow, and the day following, because it can-
> not be that a prophet perish, out of Jerusalem. 34. Jerusalem,
> Jerusalem, that killest the prophets, and stonest them that are
> sent to thee, how often would I have gathered thy children as
> the bird doth her brood under her wings, and thou wouldest not!
> 35. Behold your house shall be left to you desolate. And I say
> to you, that you shall not see me till the time come, when you
> shall say: Blessed is he that cometh in the name of the Lord.

Either Herod had told the Pharisees to scare Jesus out of Perea, or the Pharisees were trying again to entrap Him into a seditious statement. Fearlessly and coolly Christ threw His challenge back at them. Let them carry it to Herod, if they wish! Herod had been false to his nation, his friends, and his wife; and so he deserved the biting remark of our Lord. Herod would vainly try to change the actions of Christ until the day for the crucifixion arrived.

God had been patient with Jerusalem, just as He is with a selfish student, a lax Catholic, or even with an enemy of the Church. Yet, just as divine protection was withdrawn from Jerusalem, so the Faith may be withdrawn from those who reject the call of God to better their lives. When there is no effort to appreciate the Faith, then begin that desolateness of heart and sadness without hope which are the lot of those who turn down God too often. Without the light of divine leadership moderns have no eyes to see. A convert once wrote: "The few persons I have met who have definitely abandoned the Faith show no pride in the fact, and are certainly in no mood of thanksgiving. I have never met one who could be described as happy. Whereas, in those of us who have been given the grace to travel in the opposite direction the language of praise wells up spontaneously." Do you agree with this observation?

1. Would fear of ridicule prevent you from doing good?
2. What is blasphemy?
3. How do you account for the rejection of Christ in Jerusalem?
4. What is the value in humility when it is rightly understood?
5. May a humble person be a very strong character, and also a real doer of deeds?
6. What is the difference between the sorrow felt by such people as Mary Magdalen or Peter and the sadness of those who have abandoned the Faith?
7. May a person's actions now have an influence on his later loss of the Faith?
8. Prove with a text that Christ taught that He is divine.
9. Should a Catholic give evidence of poise and calmness under attack? Did Christ?
10. They who speak of modernizing the idea of God make the mistake of ———.

Chapter 44

GOD IS MERCIFUL, BUT HE DEMANDS THAT WE ACT WISELY

LUKE 15: 1. Now the publicans and sinners drew near unto him to hear him. 2. And the Pharisees and the scribes murmured, saying: This man receiveth sinners, and eateth with them. 3. And he spoke to them this parable, saying: 4. What man of you that hath a hundred sheep: and if he shall lose one of them, doth he not leave the ninety-nine in the desert, and go after that which was lost, until he find it? 5. And when he hath found it, lay it upon his shoulders, rejoicing: 6. And coming home, call together his friends and neighbors, saying to them: Rejoice with me, because I have found my sheep that was lost? 7. I say to you, that even so there shall be joy in heaven upon one sinner that doth penance, more than upon ninety-nine just who need not penance.

FAILURE never soured Jesus. It is more than a coincidence that these parables of mercy come after the attempt to stone Him. In this and the two following parables it is the Son of God who is drawing for us a very human picture of that great quality in God — mercy.

The frequency of this murmuring against Christ is due to the fact that He met the same attitude in many places. Class distinctions have always more or less separated people. The poor and the outcasts have always been looked upon with scorn by people who considered themselves better than others. Smug respectability, as exemplified in the Pharisees, has often resented any attempt to give respectability to those who have repented of their sins. On this occasion our Lord was the champion of the latter class. Each human is dear to God. Christ here represents God as actually seeking the sinner. God draws sinners by grace, by sermons, by books, and by the good example of other people. A person is of more value than a sheep. How mean, then, for the well-fed people to object to a priest's visiting the outcasts and begging help for them. Sheep easily become lost for they have little sense of direction. Just as the shepherd carefully carries home the sheep, so God is not harsh or cruel with sinners. God does not, however, neglect the just, for Christ's statement is an Oriental way of saying that the return of a sinner is pleasing to God.

> LUKE 15: 8. Or what woman having ten groats, if she lose one
> groat, doth not light a candle, and sweep the house, and seek
> diligently until she find it? 9. And when she hath found it,
> call together her friends and neighbors, saying: Rejoice with me,
> because I have found the groat which I had lost? 10. So I say
> to you, there shall be joy before the angels of God upon one
> sinner doing penance.

The woman lost one tenth of her wealth. She was anxious to recover it, just as a woman seeks for a coin that she has dropped in a street car. God is thus represented as searching for sinners. God does not need sinners; they can add nothing to Him. But the parable interprets His mercy and His love. The coin was stamped with an image, but was lost and was serving no purpose. Man's intelligence and free will were stamped on him to lead him to God. Unless man employs these faculties for the purpose that God has in mind, his life is futile. God is the One who has decided what the purpose of life is. Man's duty is to learn from God how to use his life.

> LUKE 15: 11. And he said: A certain man had two sons: 12.
> And the younger of them said to his father: Father, give me the
> portion of substance that falleth to me. And he divided unto them
> his substance. 13. And not many days after, the younger son,
> gathering all together, went abroad into a far country; and there
> wasted his substance, living riotously. 14. And after he had
> spent all, there came a mighty famine in that country: and he
> began to be in want. 15. And he went and cleaved to one of
> the citizens of that country. And he sent him into his farm to
> feed swine. 16. And he would fain have filled his belly with the
> husks the swine did eat; and no man gave unto him. 17. And
> returning to himself, he said: How many hired servants in my

father's house abound with bread, and I here perish with hunger! 18. I will arise, and will go to my father, and say to him: Father, I have sinned against heaven, and before thee: 19. I am not worthy to be called thy son: make me as one of thy hired servants.

Every detail of these stories was familiar to the people of Judea. This parable is perhaps the most touching of all. Study the perfection and skill of the picture, either as an insight into God's nature or as a story of life. The younger son was restless, hot-blooded, and thoughtless. He imagined that home life was dry and drab. He wanted freedom; he resented restraint. His father could foresee the results of his foolishness, but he gave him his share. God gives us free will; He will not force us to remain Catholics.

It is sad to see an individual waste the endowments God has bestowed. It is sad to see a student yield to that lie, that one must be able to boast of a nonvirtuous past. Losing one's virtue or losing one's Faith usually brings an interior famine. Just as nothing was more repulsive to a Jew of that day than swine, so the world, the tempter, that promises so much to a young person who will give up the Faith or accept a bribe or compromise on virtue, usually rewards him with misery, disgrace, or disease. The effort necessary to become a true Catholic or to remain virtuous is not difficult when compared to the misery of the suffering which sinners experience.

Fortunately, some fallen-away Catholics wake up to their loss. The emptiness of fast living, of social prestige, or popularity sometimes sends them back to the sacrament of Penance. They have lost much and gained nothing. The worldly goods which they sometimes obtain are like the swine husks, when compared to grace and truth found at home in the Church. We have admiration for those who are willing openly to admit that they made a mistake, who do not hesitate to do penance, to go promptly to confession.

LUKE 15: 20. And rising up he came to his father. And when he was yet a great way off, his father saw him, and was moved with compassion, and running to him fell upon his neck, and kissed him. 21. And the son said to him: Father, I have sinned against heaven, and before thee: I am not now worthy to be called thy son. 22. And the father said to his servants: Bring forth quickly the first robe, and put it on him, and put a ring on his hand, and shoes on his feet: 23. And bring hither the fatted calf, and kill it, and let us eat and make merry: 24. Because this my son was dead, and is come to life again: was lost, and is found. And they began to be merry.

God is compassionate. He, more than anyone else, understands a person's heart. As soon as He sees true contrition, He robes us in sanctifying grace; He rejoices at every true confession; He admits us to Communion. As long as we are in sin we are dead to God. They who mistrust God are unfair to Him. God sees His own property in each human being.

LUKE 15: 25. Now his elder son was in the field, and when he came and drew nigh to the house, he heard music and dancing: 26. And he called one of the servants, and asked what these things meant. 27. And he said to him: Thy brother is come, and thy father hath killed the fatted calf, because he hath received him safe. 28. And he was angry, and would not go in. His father therefore coming out began to entreat him. 29. And he answering, said to his father: Behold, for so many years do I serve thee, and I have never transgressed thy commandment, and yet thou hast never given me a kid to make merry with my friends: 30. But as soon as this thy son is come, who hath devoured his substance with harlots, thou hast killed for him the fatted calf. 31. But he said to him: Son, thou art always with me, and all I have is thine. 32. But it was fit that we should make merry and be glad, for this thy brother was dead, and is come to life again; he was lost, and is found.

People who are apparently good may be selfish, or they may be hypocritical and subservient for a hidden motive, like Uriah Heep in *David Copperfield*. They may be calculating people, like Judas. In this case, the older brother represents the Pharisees — who were concerned about self, who had no love for their fellow Jews, who did not know the meaning of pardon. His actions show that there was a meanness in his attitude. Goodness is seldom genuine when it is mean, hard, and unforgiving. He had served his father, yes, but he had not loved him nor his brother.

The father was wealthy, and hence there was plenty for the older son. The father did not love the younger son more than the older. The latter was always with the father while the other had been "dead." If a sinner receives the sacraments just before death why should we be jealous? Should we not rejoice at the recovery of a person from the devil's influence? The elder son should have felt glad at the joy that had come to the father.

These three parables teach one thing — the mercy of God, and that sinful man can return to God, where he belongs. Their immediate purpose was to show the Pharisees how little there was of true religion in their hearts. By application to our life these stories shed light on various problems: (*a*) The sheep is the type of ignorant sinner, straying blindly from the fold. (*b*) The coin is the type of modern who leads a useless life because he is not in the hands of his owner, God. (*c*) The prodigal represents the deliberate sinner.

God will search for the first two; the latter must first repent of his ways. However, all three imply that God's grace precedes the return. The sinner must correspond with this grace. The stupidity of many who are ignorant of religion, the restlessness of youth, the unhappiness of conscious sinners can be removed only through a learning of the wisdom of God. Christ shows us that true contentment is found only in working for God. Persons who have never sinned seriously or deliberately should always think of the joy and happiness of God the Father when a sinner is converted, rather than make comparisons. A sinner, despite his sins, is our brother.

> LUKE 16: 1. And he said also to his disciples: There was a certain
> rich man who had a steward: and the same was accused unto him,
> that he had wasted his goods. 2. And he called him, and said
> to him: How is it that I hear this of thee? Give an account of
> thy stewardship: for now thou canst be steward no longer. 3.
> And the steward said within himself: What shall I do, because
> my lord taketh away from me the stewardship? To dig I am not
> able; to beg I am ashamed. 4. I know what I will do, that when
> I shall be removed from the stewardship, they may receive me
> into their houses. 5. Therefore calling together every one of his
> lord's debtors, he said to the first: How much dost thou owe my
> lord? 6. But he said: A hundred barrels of oil. And he said

> to him: Take thy bill and sit down quickly, and write fifty. 7.
> Then he said to another: And how much dost thou owe? Who
> said: A hundred quarters of wheat. He said to him: Take thy
> bill, and write eighty. 8. And the lord commended the unjust
> steward, forasmuch as he had done wisely: for the children of
> this world are wiser in their generation than the children of light.
> 9. And I say to you: Make unto you friends of the mammon of
> iniquity; that when you shall fail, they may receive you into
> everlasting dwellings. 10. He that is faithful in that which is
> least, is faithful also in that which is greater: and he that is un-
> just in that which is little, is unjust also in that which is greater.
> 11. If then you have not been faithful in the unjust mammon,
> who will trust you with that which is the true? 12. And if you
> have not been faithful in that which is another's, who will
> give you that which is your own? 13. No servant can serve two
> masters: for either he will hate the one, and love the other; or
> he will hold to the one, and despise the other. You cannot serve
> God and mammon.

Confidence in the mercy of God does not imply that God fails to check up on accounts. There must be an atoning for all personal sins.

The steward was general manager of the large olive and grain estates of the rich man. The latter lived most of the year in cities. Meanwhile, the manager wasted or spent on himself much of the return from the land. The owner resolved to dismiss him. The steward had led a soft life and knew that he could not stand the hard toil of laborers in the field. Moreover, he was too proud to go about begging. Various men to whom he had rented out large sections of the estate were supposed to pay their rent in shares, that is, in so much wheat or olive oil. He called them in and made a crooked deal with them. They rewrote the original contract. The oil was cut down, let us say, from $600 to $300; a fifth part of the wheat value, or $120, was cut off. He knew that these men would not dare say anything to the owner, and so he hoped that they would take care of him when he lost his job. It was an unjust but a shrewd move. The owner recognized later that the steward had been shrewd.

Christ did not examine the morality of the act of the steward. He referred to him as one of the children of the world, therefore as unscrupulous. He did not approve the injustice; He merely praised the idea of foresight. In interpreting a parable the rule is to keep in mind the ***point*** of comparison. If there is a worldly prudence, is there not also a spiritual prudence? He advises us, not indeed to imitate the criminal cleverness of the steward, but to use practical wisdom and prudence in preparing for life in the next world. The day will come when we shall have to die and to render to God an account of our use of our talent, money, education, friends, family, and graces. We are but the stewards of these possessions. Knowing that that day will come, it is wisdom to give some of our money for charity and for education; to give our time to the poor, the lonely, and the outcast; to offer our Masses for the poor souls, for unbelievers, and sinners. These deeds win for us the friendship of the saints, the angels, and Christ, and they will help us after death. Likewise, Christ expects us to use foresight and prudence in the business world. Efficiency should be joined to holiness.

LUKE 16: 14. Now the Pharisees, who were covetous, heard all these things: and they derided him. 15. And he said to them: You are they who justify yourselves before men, but God knoweth your hearts; for that which is high to men, is an abomination before God.

The Pharisees sneered because our Lord's remarks hit true. Just as He condemned them, so shall the unjust rich receive condemnation from God. Christ never bowed down before the rich or the powerful. He uncovered the injustice of those who paraded as prominent citizens.

LUKE 16: 19. There was a certain rich man, who was clothed in purple and fine linen; and feasted sumptuously every day. 20. And there was a certain beggar, named Lazarus, who lay at his gate, full of sores, 21. Desiring to be filled with the crumbs that fell from the rich man's table, and no one did give him; moreover the dogs came, and licked his sores. 22. And it came to pass that the beggar died, and was carried by the angels into Abraham's bosom. And the rich man also died: and he was buried in hell. 23. And lifting up his eyes when he was in torments, he saw Abraham afar off, and Lazarus in his bosom: 24. And he cried, and said: Father Abraham, have mercy on me, and send Lazarus, that he may dip the tip of his finger in water, to cool my tongue: for I am tormented in this flame. 25. And Abraham said to him: Son, remember that thou didst receive good things in thy lifetime, and likewise Lazarus evil things, but now he is comforted, and thou art tormented. 26. And besides all this, between us and you, there is fixed a great chaos: so that they who would pass from hence to you, cannot, nor from thence come hither. 27. And he said: Then, father, I beseech thee, that thou wouldst send him to my father's house, for I have five brethren, 28. That he may testify unto them, lest they also come into this place of torments. 29. And Abraham said to him: They have Moses and the prophets; let them hear them. 30. But he said: No, father Abraham: but if one went to them from the dead, they will do penance. 31. And he said to him: If they hear not Moses and the prophets, neither will they believe, if one rise again from the dead.

What effect will circumstances have on us, whether wealth or poverty, health or sickness, popularity or unpopularity, success or failure? Will we be hardened or made generous; will we complain or be patient; will we blame God or trust in God; will we strive to be rich before men or rich before God? There are those who live well and eat well. But they give little for charity; they pay starvation wages; they claim that the poor are poor because they deserve to be. They see no reason why they should be concerned about their neighbor. However, the divine Supreme Court reverses many of the judgments of the powerful of this world. The inequalities of life must somewhere be rectified. Wealth had hardened this rich man; but Lazarus represents the type of patient sufferer. God is just. He cannot permit the hardened, the cynical, the proud to be in the same place as those who relied on His wisdom.

Conditions are unchangeable if one is in hell. Help cannot be given to one who is there. Neither is there a way out for him; he cannot send warnings to anyone on earth. Hence the claim of spiritualism or spiritism as a religion that one can get in touch with the dead is futile. God decides that question, not man. People who reject God now would not willingly change their views even if someone returned from the dead to warn them. God does not work miracles to scare us into believing. The authority of God, of Christ, and of the Church is of far greater importance to us than would be the testimony of anyone returning from the grave.

No one has given us a better insight into the mercy of God than has Christ. Yet, Christ has also assured us that God is just. There is a sanction behind His Law just as truly as there are examinations at the end of the semester. Note how balanced is Christ's explanation of the nature of God. Hence, we must beware of one-sided views of Him, presuming that He will forgive us without penance on our part, or presuming that He is not interested in the poor.

1. Does a student understand Christ if he or she is afraid to go to confession?
2. Read *The Hound of Heaven* by Francis Thompson for a picture of God seeking a sinner.
3. What three conditions are necessary for a mortal sin?
4. What is often the reason for jealousy, or the feeling that others have undeservedly received more than ourselves?
5. A person says that he will not believe in the soul unless he can see one. Would he believe if he did see one? Did he ever see an idea?
6. Pick out two good traits in the prodigal son after he saw his mistake.
7. What would be Christ's view of a person who thought that his wealth or talents placed him above others?
8. Can you recall an incident, an event, or a sentence which in your past life turned out to be God's protecting hand held out to save you?
9. Why is the doctrine of hell reasonable?
10. What is the meaning of wisdom? of spiritual prudence?
11. What great truth underlies the parables of the lost sheep, lost coin, and the prodigal son?

Chapter 45

WHAT HE DID TO OTHERS HE CAN DO TO US

JOHN 11: 1. Now there was a certain man sick, named Lazarus, of Bethania, of the town of Mary and of Martha her sister. 2. (And Mary was she that anointed the Lord with ointment, and wiped his feet with her hair: whose brother Lazarus was sick.) 3. His sisters therefore sent to him, saying: Lord, behold, he whom thou lovest is sick. 4. And Jesus hearing it, said to them: This sickness is not unto death, but for the glory of God: that the Son of God may be glorified by it. 5. Now Jesus loved Martha, and her sister Mary, and Lazarus. 6. When he had heard therefore that he was sick, he still remained in the same place two days. 7. Then after that, he said to his disciples: Let us go into Judea again.

JESUS was in Perea, east of the Jordan, perhaps thirty miles from Bethania. The fact that this family kept in touch with Christ and were able to send a messenger to Him shows how close they felt to Him. In a former lesson (Chap. 41) we saw how Christ visited at the home of Lazarus, for the village was only two miles east of Jerusalem. He loved its peace and quiet; its religious spirit was different from the superficiality of Jerusalem. This home bears a resemblance to a good Catholic home today — a place where Christ would be welcomed. He is just as interested in the young of today and their efforts to build a religious family life as He was in these sisters and brother. He knows how to be a companion to the young. We are told very little of Lazarus, except that Christ loved him, and that is a volume in itself. The sisters did not ask for anything, they simply told Christ that one whom He loved was sick. Their remark, showing His friendship with them, also indicates that the Gospels do not give all the details of the impression made by Jesus on the noble people of Palestine.

St. John the apostle, who is the only Evangelist to tell us of the raising of Lazarus, was loved by Christ. He wrote his Gospel when he was old. A hint of his honesty, his freedom from jealousy is found in his statement that Christ loved Lazarus. No true Catholic is ever jealous when God gives favors to another. There is room for all in the house of God's love. The anointment to which John refers is the one yet to come. The manner in which John relates details proves that he was an eye witness. This story could not have been invented. For instance, the characters fit in so well with the description given by Luke in Chapter 41 that the event could not have been merely imagined. The other Evangelists may have omitted all reference to Lazarus in order to shield him from the hatred of the Pharisees, which endured years after the triumph of Christ. John, writing about A.D. 90, after the destruction of Jerusalem (A.D. 70), could give details about this greatest miracle that we have thus far studied.

God's ways are not man's ways. Mary and Martha wondered why Christ did not come. When God does not comply with our wishes He often has a reason which we cannot fathom. Our Lord's delay was for a purpose. He is never in a hurry because He is always sure of Himself.

> JOHN 11: 8. The disciples say to him: Rabbi, the Jews but now sought to stone thee: and goest thou thither again? 9. Jesus answered: Are there not twelve hours of the day? If a man walk in the day, he stumbleth not, because he seeth the light of this world: 10. But if he walk in the night, he stumbleth, because the light is not in him. 11. These things he said; and after that he said to them: Lazarus our friend sleepeth; but I go that I may awake him out of sleep. 12. His disciples therefore said: Lord, if he sleep, he shall do well. 13. But Jesus spoke of his death; and they thought that he spoke of the repose of sleep. 14. Then therefore Jesus said to them plainly: Lazarus is dead. 15. And I am glad, for your sakes, that I was not there, that you may believe: but let us go to him. 16. Thomas therefore, who is called Didymus, said to his fellow-disciples: Let us also go, that we may die with him.

Christ led a dangerous life but that did not ruffle His interior and exterior calm. He is our Light; we will never stumble if we maintain our faith in Him.

The apostles were very literal-minded. They little knew what was coming and they were afraid. Dangers seemed to surround them and their beloved Master at every step. And in a sense their fears were reasonable, for in this March, of the year 30, the storm was gathering swiftly which would end in the death of our Lord. But we admire their loyalty, even if they were slow to realize that in faith we never question Christ's power. Thomas was a man of few words, but weighty ones, which reveal the attachment that these men had to Jesus. It is touching to see willingness to suffer death in order to remain loyal to Him.

> JOHN 11: 17. Jesus therefore came, and found that he had been
> four days already in the grave. 18. (Now Bethania was near
> Jerusalem, about fifteen furlongs off.) 19. And many of the
> Jews were come to Martha and Mary, to comfort them concern-
> ing their brother. 20. Martha therefore, as soon as she heard
> that Jesus was come, went to meet him: but Mary sat at home.
> 21. Martha therefore said to Jesus: Lord, if thou hadst been here,
> my brother had not died. 22. But now also I know that what-
> soever thou wilt ask of God, God will give it thee. 23. Jesus
> saith to her: Thy brother shall rise again. 24. Martha saith to
> him: I know that he shall rise again, in the resurrection at the
> last day. 25. Jesus said to her: I am the resurrection and the
> life: he that believeth in me, although he be dead, shall live:
> 26. And every one that liveth, and believeth in me, shall not die
> for ever. Believest thou this? 27. She saith to him: Yea Lord,
> I have believed that thou art Christ the Son of the living God,
> who art come into this world.

Lazarus must have died the same day the messengers went to tell Christ of his sickness. The prominence of the family brought many from Jerusalem. Practical Martha had faith, but she, too, little guessed Christ's intentions. Christ tried out Martha. Belief in the resurrection of the dead was quite general. But He opened up a new vista to her. He has life in Himself. The life that He imparts guarantees a glorious resurrection and immortality. Anyone believing firmly in Him and living as He desires will never lose the supernatural life (grace) which He bestows.

Martha did not, perhaps, fully understand all of this, but she did believe that Christ was divine. Every time you attend a funeral this dialogue between Christ and Martha is repeated in the Gospel of the Mass. The spirit of hope and joy of the Catholic outlook on life there shines brightly in contrast to the dreary outlook of moderns who deny immortality.

Many of those who advocate cremation do so as a sign that there is no soul in man. Because of this attitude the Church does not permit cremation, except where sanitation requires it. The body is worthy of decent burial because it has been the temple of the Holy Ghost; God inhabited it. We believe in the resurrection of the body because Christ has taught it.

John 11: 28. And when she had said these things, she went, and
called her sister Mary secretly, saying: The master is come, and
calleth for thee. 29. She, as soon as she heard this, riseth quickly, and cometh to him. 30. For Jesus was not yet come into the
town: but he was still in that place where Martha had met him.
31. The Jews therefore, who were with her in the house, and comforted her, when they saw Mary that she rose up speedily and
went out, followed her, saying: She goeth to the grave to weep
there. 32. When Mary therefore was come where Jesus was,
seeing him, she fell down at his feet, and saith to him: Lord, if
thou hadst been here, my brother had not died. 33. Jesus, therefore, when he saw her weeping, and the Jews that were come with
her, weeping, groaned in the spirit, and troubled himself. 34. And
said: Where have you laid him? They say to him: Lord, come
and see. 35. And Jesus wept. 36. The Jews therefore said:
Behold how he loved him. 37. But some of them said: Could
not he that opened the eyes of the man born blind, have caused
that this man should not die? 38. Jesus therefore again groaning
in himself, cometh to the sepulcher. Now it was a cave; and a
stone was laid over it.

Mary's grief was deep. She appeared listless, but the mention of one name aroused her. It is an instance of the effect of Christ's personality on people of deep emotion and strong views. Neither Mary nor Martha asked Christ why He had not come sooner.

Was Christ human; did He have human feelings as the rest of men? The answer is here. He groaned, perhaps, because He foresaw that His deed of kindness for a friend would result in hatred and in His own death verdict. Certainly He had that lovely trait of *sympathy*. He understands us. Sympathy means the gift of suffering with others, of entering into their feelings. Christ knew well how Mary felt. The fact that He wept shows how sensitive He is to whatever brings grief to us. Some might think that a person of strong, virile character would be above such things as weeping, but actually sensitiveness to suffering in others is one of the noblest traits of noble men and women. God is not indifferent to human suffering. Jesus wept because He loved with a divine love.

In his Gospel St. John's primary aim was to show us the divine nature of Jesus, yet he seems to have taken delight also in showing us how human Christ is. He has two natures in one Person. Christ was not cold as marble, nor so majestic as to repel the young, nor entirely spiritual like angels. Human traits that we so admire — courage, gentleness, consistency, mercy, justice, tenderness, loyalty, unselfishness, understanding, and lightning-like intelligence — were not smothered by His divinity but, rather, raised to the highest perfection ever found in human flesh. And He desires to enter into our joys and sorrows, to become part of our daily life, in order thereby to keep our thoughts and actions supernatural in motive. The crowd assembled there was convinced that Christ thought a great deal of Lazarus. Likewise, each person is dear to Him.

The best of men have enemies. The cynics soon began to blame Christ for not having prevented the death of Lazarus. Poor cynics!

JOHN 11: 39. Jesus said: Take away the stone. Martha, the sister of him that was dead, saith to him: Lord, by this time he stinketh, for he is now of four days. 40. Jesus said to her: Did not I say to thee, that if thou believe, thou shalt see the glory of God? 41. They took therefore the stone away. And Jesus lifting up his eyes said: Father, I give thee thanks that thou hast heard me. 42. And I knew that thou hearest me always; but because of the people who stand about have I said it, that they may believe that thou hast sent me. 43. When he had said these things, he cried with a loud voice: Lazarus, come forth. 44. And presently he that had been dead came forth, bound feet and hands with winding bands; and his face was bound about with a napkin. Jesus said to them: Loose him, and let him go.

In Palestine burial took place on the same day as death. Coffins were not used. Martha thought of the practical difficulties instead of the divine power of God. Only they of deep faith are privileged to see the glory of God. Christ had a reason for waiting four days. There was a current belief that the soul hovered about the body for two days or more after death. Since decay had now set in, no one could deny that the return to life was a miracle — beyond the power of chance or of nature, and also excluding a state of coma. Martha's very objection serves to show that Lazarus was actually dead and that the miracle was real. We are told nothing of the happy reunion because the Evangelist wished to keep his central Figure before our eyes.

JOHN 11: 45. Many therefore of the Jews, who were come to
Mary and Martha, and had seen the things that Jesus did, believed in him. 46. But some of them went to the Pharisees, and
told them the things that Jesus had done. 47. The chief priests
therefore, and the Pharisees, gathered a council, and said: What
do we, for this man doth many miracles? 48. If we let him alone
so, all will believe in him; and the Romans will come, and take
away our place and nation. 49. But one of them, named
Caiphas, being the high priest that year, said to them: You know
nothing. 50. Neither do you consider that it is expedient for
you that one man should die for the people, and that the whole
nation perish not. 51. And this he spoke not of himself: but
being the high priest of that year, he prophesied that Jesus should
die for the nation. 52. And not only for the nation, but to
gather together in one the children of God that were dispersed.
53. From that day therefore they devised to put him to death.
54. Wherefore Jesus walked no more openly among the Jews;
but he went into a country near the desert, unto a city that is
called Ephrem, and there he abode with his disciples.

Bethania was, so to say, a suburb of Jerusalem. The news spread rapidly. A miracle had occurred under the very noses of His enemies. Some converts were won by the event, but the deed itself became the immediate occasion of His death sentence. Jealous leaders seldom see good in any act of their rival. Christ was, indeed, no rival. He had refused to allow the people to consider Him as king after the multiplication of the loaves and fishes. The leaders had not the slightest reason to accuse Him of inciting an insurrection against Rome. And yet, so deep was their hatred that the suggestion of killing Him came from the high priest. Unconsciously the high priest fulfilled God's plan that His Son should offer His life for us. Wicked men in designing to kill Christ brought about good where they intended evil. Jesus, knowing the danger, withdrew for the present into a desert-like section northeast of Jerusalem, near the border of Samaria. We, six to ten thousand miles away from that scene, have been gathered together in God. There are others whom He wants gathered.

> LUKE 17: 11. And it came to pass, as he was going to Jerusalem,
> he passed through the midst of Samaria and Galilee. 12. And as
> he entered into a certain town, there met him ten men that were
> lepers, who stood afar off; 13. And lifted up their voice, saying:
> Jesus, master, have mercy on us. 14. Whom when he saw, he
> said: Go, shew yourselves to the priests. And it came to pass, as
> they went, they were made clean. 15. And one of them, when
> he saw that he was made clean, went back, with a loud voice
> glorifying God. 16. And he fell on his face before his feet,
> giving thanks: and this was a Samaritan. 17. And Jesus answer-
> ing, said: Were not ten made clean? And where are the nine?
> 18. There is no one found to return and give glory to God, but
> this stranger. 19. And he said to him: Arise, go thy way; for
> thy faith hath made thee whole.

A few weeks had elapsed since the raising of Lazarus. Jesus was only gradually and indirectly journeying back to Jerusalem. He was up between Samaria and Galilee and moving from east to west.

The poor and the afflicted always sought out Christ. In that hardened land He was the one Man of pity, whose heart went out to suffering humanity. But He is not always appreciated. It were sad if our gratitude were limited to one out of ten! Samaritans were despised by the Jews, yet the only grateful one here was a Samaritan. It might be that some non-Catholics have more gratitude than some of us.

Christ brought Lazarus back to life; He also cured the lepers. He can raise us up on the last day; He can cleanse us from our sins; He can fulfill all the promises that He has made to us, if we continue to trust Him, to be grateful and loyal to Him. What He did to others He can do to us.

1. Show that Christ was interested in young people.
2. Show from specific deeds and words of Christ that He may have a purpose in not answering our petitions immediately.
3. What do you like about the statement of Thomas?
4. What are the words of the Gospel at a funeral Mass?
5. What is the meaning of the words: *Vita mutatur non tollitur* in the preface of a funeral Mass?
6. What is the meaning of sympathy? Show that Jesus had this quality.
7. Need you be surprised if your enemies misinterpret a good deed that you do?
8. Show how people who intend evil are sometimes indirectly occasions of good.
9. There is a story about a homecoming that the virtues had in heaven and it was found that generosity and gratitude had never met. Illustrate this idea from Christ's life. What lesson does the illustration suggest?

Chapter 46

GOD SETS THE STANDARD, NOT MAN

LUKE 18: 9. And to some who trusted in themselves as just, and despised others, he spoke also this parable: 10. Two men went up into the temple to pray: the one a Pharisee, and the other a publican. 11. The Pharisee standing, prayed thus with himself: O God, I give thee thanks that I am not as the rest of men, extortioners, unjust, adulterers, as also is this publican. 12. I fast twice in a week: I give tithes of all that I possess. 13. And the publican, standing afar off, would not so much as lift up his eyes towards heaven; but struck his breast, saying: O God, be merciful to me a sinner. 14. I say to you, this man went down into his house justified rather than the other: because every one that exalteth himself, shall be humbled: and he that humbleth himself, shall be exalted.

A VIEW often expressed by those who do not go to church is that they are honest and fair, while churchgoers are frequently hypocrites. Likewise, a student may remark that he keeps away from Communion because he does not see any improvement in those who go. These too-prevalent attitudes are not, indeed, based always on facts. Even if it were so, is the modern "decent," "better-than-thou" man justified in his view? Study our Lord's answer. The Pharisee had a good opinion of himself; in fact, he did more than the Law required; he was legally guiltless. But to take pride in being guiltless is itself a sin; to despise others is a sin. Christ continually condemned self-justification, or self-righteousness. God alone is perfect; He sets the standard of what a man should do. The Pharisee was comparing himself favorably with God; the Publican admitted his defects. The latter is an example of the attitude that we all should have when we go to church and when we pray. He who exalts himself before God will never reach God.

The modern man who compares himself favorably with those who go to church is, like the Pharisee, telling God how good he is. He sets up his own standards. He presumes that he does not need God's help, that he can choose his own way, regardless of what God wants. He expects God to accept him on his own terms. He is like the man who wished to go to the South Pole with an explorer but refused to accept the advice of the explorer on what equipment was necessary for the expedition. He had never been there himself but he thought himself capable of choosing the equipment necessary. To be honest, fair, and decent is good and necessary; but that alone will not get us to heaven. We must be humble enough to ask God what equipment is necessary. People go to church to obtain the equipment.

Some churchgoers may be hypocrites; many of them are sinners. God alone can see the heart; and He will handle the cases of the hypocrites. However, neither hypocrisy nor sin in others excuses anyone from the duty of paying public worship and honor to God or from humbling himself before the holiness of God. G. K. Chesterton, the brilliant writer, was asked why he became a Catholic; "To get rid of my sins," he replied. The point is, not how we compare with others, but how we rank in what Christ expects from us. And it may be easy for those who are born into wealth, or who have a protected life, to remain honest and decent. They do not have the burdens to bear that are the lot of the poor and of the socially disadvantaged.

> MATT. 19: 3. And there came to him the Pharisees tempting him, saying: Is it lawful for a man to put away his wife for every cause? 4. Who answering, said to them: Have ye not read, that he who made man from the beginning, made them male and female? and he said: 5. For this cause shall a man leave father and mother, and shall cleave to his wife, and they two shall be in one flesh. 6. Therefore now they are not two, but one flesh. What therefore God hath joined together, let no man put asunder. 7. They say to him: Why then did Moses command to give a bill of divorce, and to put away? 8. He saith to them: Because Moses by reason of the hardness of your heart permitted you to put away your wives: but from the beginning it was not

so. 9. And I say to you, that whosoever shall put away his wife, except it be for fornication, and shall marry another, committeth adultery; and he that shall marry her that is put away, committeth adultery.

MATT. 5: 32. But I say to you, that whosoever shall put away his wife, excepting the cause of fornication, maketh her to commit adultery: and he that shall marry her that is put away, committeth adultery.

MATT. 19: 10. His disciples say unto him: If the case of a man with his wife be so, it is not expedient to marry. 11. Who said to them: All men take not this word, but they to whom it is given. 12. For there are eunuchs, who were born so from their mother's womb: and there are eunuchs, who were made so by men: and there are eunuchs, who have made themselves eunuchs for the kingdom of heaven. He that can take, let him take it.

Then, as now, there was much effort to tamper with God's unchangeable law. Jesus recalled to their minds God's original command — inseparable union of two in one. Moses, in certain cases, had permitted divorce. But Christ is a divine legislator; He placed marriage on the plane where God originally wanted it and wants it today — a union formed by God. The real meaning of Christ's reference to impurity is that, although the husband and wife might separate, yet neither can marry again because the bond made by God remains. The sense is that even if a man should separate from his wife, he cannot remarry.

Marriage is a contract between two individuals; yet it is more than that because it is a sacrament. It is a compact between two individuals and God for the purpose God intends. Christian marriage seems hard to the moderns because they have too often substituted their own selfish purposes for God's ennobling purpose. It is a holy career because its primary aim is the procreation of children for God's honor. Its secondary aim is to make the couple holy and happy. The married couple are under obligation to follow the standards laid down by God. To marry with the intention of not having children is a defiance of God's standard. The majority of divorces are among couples not having children, which is an indication that selfish purposes do not bring happiness.

The disciples thought Christ too strict, but they did not yet realize that each sacrament gives a grace proportionate to the needs of the person receiving it. Matrimony gives grace appropriate and necessary for that state. And, on the other hand, if God calls one to the state of virginity, as in the priesthood or sisterhood or brotherhood, He gives the individual sufficient grace.

MATT. 19: 13. Then were little children presented to him, that he should impose hands upon them and pray. And the disciples rebuked them. 14. But Jesus said to them: Suffer the little children, and forbid them not to come to me: for the kingdom of heaven is for such. 15. And when he had imposed hands upon them, he departed from thence.

The mothers understood what a blessing it would be to have Jesus smile on their children, ragged and dirty as they might be. He took the occasion, not only to show His affection for them, but to teach us that whenever God's word or God's will is made known to us, our duty is to have the same simple, unquestioning trust in it that children have in their protectors. It is all right to be wary, to be slow to trust in worldly affairs, but toward God our attitude must be that of children. We must trust Him wholly, sincerely, and instantaneously. The millions of modern children who know nothing about Christ are being cheated of their rights, for they have a right to learn about Jesus, about Baptism, about divine adoption.

MATT. 19: 16. And behold one came and said to him: Good master, what good shall I do that I may have life everlasting? 17. Who said to him: Why askest thou me concerning good? One is good, God. But if thou wilt enter into life, keep the commandments. 18. He said to him: Which? And Jesus said: Thou shalt do no murder, Thou shalt not commit adultery, Thou shalt not steal, Thou shalt not bear false witness. 19. Honor thy father and thy mother: and, Thou shalt love thy neighbor as thyself. 20. The young man saith to him: All these have I kept from my youth, what is yet wanting to me? 21. Jesus saith to him: If thou wilt be perfect, go sell what thou hast, and give to the poor, and thou shalt have treasure in heaven: and come, follow me. 22. And when the young man had heard this word, he went away sad: for he had great possessions.

The young man had been impressed by Christ's mention of eternal life, just as any of us is interested in the thought of a joy or happiness that will endure forever. Perhaps the youth regarded Christ as only a man; Jesus wished him to realize that perfect goodness is in God alone and that He, Jesus, is God. Jesus loved the young man for as much as he had done well (Mark 10: 21); but the youth offered to do more. All right! Jesus now opened up to him a higher standard — the life of the evangelical counsels of poverty, chastity, and obedience, such as is found in religious orders. Everyone is obliged to keep the Commandments, but in Catholic life some are called to a higher state. The idea of giving up everything that he owned cooled the ardor of the youth. The desire for possessions is strong in all of us. Attachment to such possessions prevents us from giving our whole heart to God. Once we reach that condition of being attached to no creature, then our heart can climb to God. The standard set by God is detachment from all possessions, but He asks a more perfect detachment among those in the higher state.

> MATT. 19: 23. Then Jesus said to his disciples: Amen I say to you, that a rich man shall hardly enter into the kingdom of heaven. 24. And again I say to you: It is easier for a camel to pass through the eye of a needle, than for a rich man to enter into the kingdom of heaven. 25. And when they had heard this, the disciples wondered very much, saying: Who then can be saved? 26. And Jesus beholding said to them: With men this is impossible: but with God all things are possible.

There are great possibilities for good in the young, but to achieve true greatness they must be willing to practice self-denial. Jesus wants self-sacrificing young men and women; He wants priests, brothers, and nuns who are willing to give up ease, comforts, popularity, and position in order to follow Him and to live His life.

Christ's reply to the rich youth is an apt answer to modern man who asserts that he can set up his own standard of religion. The danger of money, talent, and position is that they often lead the possessors to think that God cannot get along without them; they imagine they can dictate the terms; they make the mistake of trusting in their wealth. On the other hand, some imagine that their wealth is a sign that God approves their manner of living. Temporal prosperity is no proof of God's blessing. The object of living is not to make money, or to acquire fame. Christ did not set any such standard as that. The rich and the powerful can indeed enter heaven, but only through God's aid, only when they conquer the temptation to rely solely on money and power. We do not need money or high talent to reach heaven; we do need that which Christ earned for us — grace. With His grace both rich and poor can be saved.

> MATT. 19: 27. Then Peter answering, said to him: Behold we have left all things and have followed thee: what therefore shall we have? 28. And Jesus said to them: Amen, I say to you, that you, who have followed me, in the regeneration, when the Son of man shall sit on the seat of his majesty, you also shall sit on twelve seats judging the twelve tribes of Israel. 29. And every one that hath left house, or brethren, or sisters, or father, or mother, or wife, or children, or lands for my name's sake, shall receive a hundredfold, and shall possess life everlasting. 30. And many that are first, shall be last: and the last shall be first.

They who accept the standard set by God — a spirit of detachment from self, from persons, places, and things will be rewarded by God with the joy of His presence. Even on earth they gain an interior contentment. Names not found in the world's "Who's Who" are registered in the book of eternal life.

> MATT. 20: 1. The kingdom of heaven is like to a householder, who went out early in the morning to hire laborers into his vineyard. 2. And having agreed with the laborers for a penny a day, he sent them into his vineyard. 3. And going out about the third hour, he saw others standing in the market-place idle. 4. And he said to them: Go you also into my vineyard, and I will give you what shall be just. 5. And they went their way. And again he went out about the sixth and the ninth hour, and did in like manner. 6. But about the eleventh hour he went out and found others standing, and he saith to them: Why stand you here all the day idle? 7. They say to him: Because no man hath hired us. He saith to them: Go ye also into my vineyard, 8. And when evening was come, the lord of the vineyard saith to his steward: Call the laborers and pay them their hire, beginning from the last even to the first. 9. When therefore they were come, that came about the eleventh hour, they received every

> man a penny. 10. But when the first also came, they thought that they should receive more: and they also received every man a penny. 11. And receiving it they murmured against the master of the house, 12. Saying: These last have worked but one hour, and thou hast made them equal to us, that have borne the burden of the day and the heats. 13. But he answering said to one of them: Friend, I do thee no wrong: didst thou not agree with me for a penny? 14. Take what is thine, and go thy way: I will also give to this last even as to thee. 15. Or, is it not lawful for me to do what I will? Is thy eye evil, because I am good? 16. So shall the last be first, and the first last. For many are called, but few chosen.

This parable is not intended as a discussion of the theory of wages. A fixed contract was made only with the first group hired. The others had no definite arrangement. The first group stands for the Jews with whom God had made a covenant. But God is master of His graces. If He chose to call the Gentiles later, or at the last moment, sinners, there should be no jealousy. He is good and just to all without distinction. They who are just and have served Him long should not complain of His goodness.

Another application is that it is wrong to work only for wages. The call to work is a vocation. It is Baptism. If we realize that we are working for a Person, the monotonous tasks of life become easier. It will be a case of working for love; and we should rejoice if at the end of their lives others who never knew God accept the call to work for the Master. If we work for Him rather than for a reward (wages) we shall be glad when others come to know Him.

1. What attitude did Jesus often condemn?
2. What is wrong with the view of a person who says that he does not go to church because there are too many hypocrites in church?
3. What wrong principle is followed by the person who says: "I am as good a Catholic as he or she is"?
4. God expects us all to be "decent." But does decency by itself enable us to reach heaven? What else is essential?
5. Why must a couple consider God's rights when they marry?
6. Why is it that they who try to do their duty are usually more contented than they who run away from duty and seek only selfish pleasure?

7. Give two incidents showing that our Lord was approachable.
8. What are the evangelical counsels and for whom are they intended?
9. What quality did the rich young man lack?
10. How may one avoid the dangers connected with wealth or talent or position?
11. What motive does our Lord expect you to have in all your actions?
12. Cite some examples of modern life showing how certain people are aiming to set up man-made standards for marriage: for religion.
13. Which parable shows what Christ thinks of those who boast of being better than others?

Chapter 47

CONTRASTS IN THE EFFECTS OF BEING CLOSE TO CHRIST

MARK 10: 32. And they were in the way going up to Jerusalem: and Jesus went before them, and they were astonished, and following were afraid. And taking again the twelve, he began to tell them the things that should befall him.

LUKE 18: 31. . . . Behold, we go up to Jerusalem, and all things shall be accomplished which were written by the prophets concerning the Son of man. 32. For he shall be delivered to the Gentiles, and shall be mocked, and scourged, and spit upon: 33. And after they have scourged him, they will put him to death; and the third day he shall rise again. 34. And they understood none of these things, and this word was hid from them, and they understood not the things that were said.

THIS fear of the apostles is eloquent testimony of the official hatred against our Lord. In his description of the scene Mark reflects the impression that had been made at the time on St. Peter — an impression of His courageous leadership. Christ walking ahead alone! Our God-Man Leader started to mount to His martyrdom. He and the apostles were over near the Jordan coming from the North.

Christ's mind went back through the Old Testament history. Isaias had described the Passion in detail, 750 years before the event. And this present prediction of Christ is the third that He had given them. How clearly the details stood out in His own mind! He knew the feeling of the apostles. They failed utterly to grasp the fact that only through suffering was Christ to enter into glory. "The more they believed in His divinity, the less could they believe that He was to die." And, moreover, He alone was calm. A leader must often encourage the fainthearted. He wanted us to know that, while suffering may frequently visit us during life, the final word for all faithful believers is not suffering but joy — the joy of triumphing with Christ. Christ had no doubt about His own resurrection; we need have no doubt about ours if we suffer for Him. The joy of Easter follows the penance of Lent. But we shall never know true Easter joy until we learn how to keep Lent. Firm trust in Him enables us to understand and accept suffering, to face the realities of life.

MATT. 20: 20. Then came to him the mother of the sons of Zebedee with her sons, adoring and asking something of him. 21. Who said to her: What wilt thou? She saith to him: Say that these my two sons may sit, the one on thy right hand and the other on thy left, in thy kingdom. 22. And Jesus answering, said: You know not what you ask. Can you drink the chalice that I shall drink? They say to him: We can. 23. He saith to them: My chalice indeed you shall drink: but to sit on my right or left hand is not mine to give to you, but to them for whom it is prepared by my Father. 24. And the ten hearing it, were moved with indignation against the two brethren. 25. But Jesus called them to him, and said: You know that the princes of the Gentiles lord it over them: and they that are the greater, exercise power upon them. 26. It shall not be so among you, but whosoever will be the greater among you let him be your minister: 27. And he that will be first among you, shall be your servant. 28. Even as the Son of man is not come to be ministered unto, but to minister, and to give his life a redemption for many.

Some indication of why the prophecy of the Passion failed to grip the apostles is given to us by this incident of an ambitious mother. The apostles had difficulty in ridding their minds of the notion that Christ's kingdom was to be a political state. Just a week or so previous to this event He had spoken of their sitting on twelve thrones. Instead of taking His words in their spiritual meaning, they injected their own wishes into His statements. Man prefers to dream of glory rather than of suffering.

John and James were strong-hearted, ambitious men. Christ had once called them the "sons of thunder." Salome was a "vigorous mother of very vigorous sons." She may have been one of those who helped support Christ and the apostles by their charity. She was proud of her sons; and she had right to be. If Christ was to be the liberator of the Jews she wanted her sons to have prominent positions in the new kingdom. They were, indeed, to be prominent. James was to be martyred, and John was to be cast in boiling oil in Rome, but miraculously saved, so that he might later write his Gospel (A.D. 90–95), his three Epistles, and the Apocalypse. But at this moment both mother and sons were far from understanding why Christ had come upon earth.

The two must have accompanied their mother. Jesus knew they would suffer willingly for Him, but He told them that reward in heaven is based on co-operation with grace, on what the individual does, not upon partiality or influence with the Leader. It was a most inopportune time to ask such a favor. Christ was patient, but not so the other apostles. The ten were indignant. At heart the apostles were good and willing to learn. But closeness to Christ had not eliminated their faults, just as we often keep our faults despite confession, Mass, and Communion. But God is patient if He sees that we are actually trying and are willing to trust Him always.

Masterful teacher that He was, Christ seized the opportunity to impress just what kind of ambition a priest or a Catholic student should have. He should be ambitious to serve rather than to dominate. By His example, Christ has outlined the policy of every Catholic superior. Competition is often ruthless in the business, political, or athletic world. The strong seek to rule the weak. Ambitious men strive for power. Yet He who is God came to us in the form of a servant. What humility! He sought no life of ease or social prestige. He shouldered our sins; He assumed our debts to God, and, by offering His life, paid to God that honor which men by indifference and by deliberate sin refuse to give.

The one answer to all those who say there is no such thing as original sin, that sin is an outworn notion, and that the human race could be made perfect by education, is found in this statement of the God-Man that He came to give His life as a redemption, an atonement, which implies that human nature is in debt to someone. In other words, something is wrong in man. He has been wounded. He is suffering from the original refusal to follow

God's rules. Modern theories of education go to pieces because they reject this primary insight into human nature which was given to us by a divine Leader. Modern theories fail because they refuse the remedy offered by the God-Man. True progress will come when we unite what we learn from science with what the divine educator taught.

> LUKE 18: 35. Now it came to pass, when he drew nigh to Jericho, that a certain blind man sat by the way side, begging. 36. And when he heard the multitude passing by, he asked what this meant. 37. And they told him that Jesus of Nazareth was passing by. 38. And he cried out, saying: Jesus, son of David, have mercy on me. 39. And they that went before, rebuked him, that he should hold his peace: but he cried out much more: Son of David, have mercy on me. 40. And Jesus standing, commanded him to be brought unto him. And when he was come near, he asked him, 41. Saying: What wilt thou that I do to thee? But he said: Lord, that I may see. 42. And Jesus said to him: Receive thy sight: thy faith hath made thee whole. 43. And immediately he saw, and followed him, glorifying God. And all the people, when they saw it, gave praise to God.

Even today blindness is widely prevalent in Palestine. Heat, dust, and disease unite in robbing people of vision. Hence, we need not be surprised at the number of times Christ cured the blind; at least six occasions are recorded. Every time He gave sight to the blind it was meant also to be symbolic of His power to give light to men who wander about in spiritual darkness. Bartimaeus came close to Christ, had faith in Christ, and, as a result, gained vision. Come closer to Christ and you will see your religion differently.

Just as the crowd tried to keep the blind man from our Lord, so do many leaders and many events conspire to keep people away from the divine Light. In the United States multitudes are spiritually blind. They hear Christ spoken of, they see Catholics going to Mass, but misrepresentations and inherited prejudices block them. If they would only cry out, or ask Catholics about the God-Man, Christ would give them the light of faith to believe in Him. They would then thank God all their lives for that power of vision.

LUKE 19: 1. And entering in, he walked through Jericho. 2. And behold there was a man named Zacheus, who was the chief of the publicans, and he was rich. 3. And he sought to see Jesus who he was, and he could not for the crowd, because he was low of stature. 4. And running before, he climbed up into a sycamore tree, that he might see him; for he was to pass that way. 5. And when Jesus was come to the place, looking up, he saw him, and said to him: Zacheus, make haste and come down; for this day I must abide in thy house. 6. And he made haste and came down; and received him with joy. 7. And when all saw it, they murmured, saying that he was gone to be a guest with a man that was a sinner. 8. But Zacheus standing, said to the Lord: Behold, Lord, the half of my goods I give to the poor; and if I have wronged any man of anything, I restore him fourfold. 9. Jesus said to him: This day is salvation come to this house, because thou also art a son of Abraham. 10. For the Son of man is come to seek and to save that which was lost.

Jericho was more than 600 feet below sea level, although but a distance of some sixteen miles northeast of Jerusalem. Springs were abundant. It was a winter resort and was truly an oasis in a desert, with its gardens and wealthy homes. Its balm was famous in all markets, and hence tax gatherers were there to obtain government money from the merchant princes.

Zacheus was a Jew, but was detested by Jews for his dealings in taxes with the Gentiles. He had heard of Jesus, and of His sympathy for the outcast Publicans. The large crowd surrounding Jesus prevented diminutive Zacheus from obtaining sight of the Master. But he possessed ingenuity; and the tree, perhaps, near his home, would serve him well. No one noticed him, except the One who sees all things. Jesus called him by name. Was there not a smile on the lips of the Master? For it was a ludicrous situation — a rich man so anxious to see a poor Man that he climbed up and hid himself in the limbs of a sycamore? At first the crowd enjoyed the situation, seeing that Zacheus was caught. But how the heart of the Publican leaped at the news that Christ wished to abide with him. He may have been a grafter; but there was good in him, and to find himself noticed by One who is Goodness itself won his heart.

The hardness of class distinctions of those days, the merciless coldness with which strict Jews regarded fallen members of society is reflected in the willingness of the crowd to be scandalized at the Man whom they had just previously praised. But Jesus cared little for public opinion, for He had come to open the fountains of grace to sinners. Latent goodness responds to kindness. Zacheus realized the danger that Christ ran in thus noticing him. "As all that was base in him would have been driven into defiance by contempt and hatred, so all that was noble was evoked by a considerate tenderness" (Farrar). Human nobility rose to meet divine mercy. Yet it was something more than that. It was a case of a sinner co-operating with grace. He would show the crowd that closeness to Christ brings out goodness from willing hearts. He gave up that which he most prized — money. He reminds the modern world that restitution is an obligation.

This scene brought joy to the heart of the Master. Manly men are ever thus, when they have made an effort to "see" Christ. And it were well if we who have been close to our Lord would have a word of kindness for outcasts, would appeal to the better side of their nature rather than hold them in contempt.

> LUKE 19: 11. As they were hearing these things, he added and spoke a parable, because he was nigh to Jerusalem, and because they thought that the kingdom of God should immediately be manifested. 12. He said therefore: A certain nobleman went into a far country, to receive for himself a kingdom, and to return. 13. And calling his ten servants, he gave them ten pounds, and said to them: Trade till I come. 14. But his citizens hated him: and they sent an embassage after him, saying: We will not have this man to reign over us. 15. And it came to pass that he returned, having received the kingdom: and he commanded his servants to be called, to whom he had given the money, that he might know how much every man had gained by trading. 16. And the first came, saying: Lord, thy pound hath gained ten pounds. 17. And he said to him: Well done, thou good servant, because thou hast been faithful in a little, thou shalt have power over ten cities. 18. And the second came, saying: Lord, thy pound hath gained five pounds. 19. And he said to him: Be thou also over five cities. 20. And another came, saying: Lord, behold here is thy pound, which I have kept laid up in a napkin; 21. For I feared thee, because thou art an austere man: thou takest up what thou didst not lay down and thou reapest that

which thou didst not sow. 22. He saith to him: Out of thy own
mouth I judge thee, thou wicked servant. Thou knewest that I
was an austere man, taking up what I laid not down, and reaping that which I did not sow: 23. And why then didst thou not
give my money into the bank, that at my coming, I might have
exacted it with usury? 24. And he said to them that stood by:
Take the pound away from him, and give it to him that hath ten
pounds. 25. And they said to him: Lord, he hath ten pounds.
26. But I say to you, that to every one that hath shall be given,
and he shall abound: and from him that hath not, even that which
he hath shall be taken from him. 27. But as for those my
enemies, who would not have me reign over them, bring them
hither, and kill them before me. 28. And having said these
things, he went before, going up to Jerusalem.

To show the disciples that His final triumph was not to come until the end of the world, our Lord related this parable of the pounds, which is similar to the better known parable of the talents. The going into the far country refers to His ascension. He will return at the end of the world to judge. Meanwhile the Church will find that many people do not want to submit to Christ. "Religion is the opium of the people," shouts the Communist. "We will not be tied down with medieval dogmas," say others. "Religion is a survival of primitive fear and myths," harp the liberals.

The second part of the parable refers to those gifts, both natural and supernatural, which God bestows upon us, that we might employ them for His glory. Our Lord knew the business practices that prevailed in His day. The application is that we are God's servants, molding a Catholic character that will be a credit to Him. He does not give everyone the same gifts or opportunities. We should not be envious of others. More or less may be demanded from them. We are personally, and individually responsible for our own character, for the development of our soul. We shall be judged on how we have developed what was given to us. It is an obligation to think of developing or deepening our faith and love rather than to plan only to remain good or to keep from sin. God did not merely give us our souls and then expect them back. He commands us to "trade," that is, to develop, to be active, and to do good to others, to acquire step by step, as far as is possible, the qualities which our Lord possessed. The degree of glory which we shall merit in heaven will depend on how we used the talents (pounds) that were given to us. Talent, education, health, and wealth are responsibilities.

We must avoid the mistake of imagining that we have nothing to develop. Each one has something. If one pound only was given to us, then we are to use that as best we may. If we lose the Faith it will be because we did not seek to develop it. God does not excuse laziness. The only thing that matters is whether or not we shall hear from the lips of Christ the Judge: "Well done." We need not look for gratitude on earth. Rather, it is a beautiful thought to realize that we are working for God, and seeking always to please Him. Giving good example, praying for the spread of the Faith, being cheerful always, doing kind deeds to others, and atoning for the sins of others — all this is "trading," and can be done even by those who have the one pound.

John 12: 1. Jesus therefore, six days before the pasch, came to
Bethania, where Lazarus had been dead, whom Jesus raised to
life. 2. And they made him a supper there: and Martha served:
but Lazarus was one of them that were at table with him.
3. Mary therefore took a pound of ointment of right spikenard,
of great price, and anointed the feet of Jesus, and wiped his feet
with her hair; and the house was filled with the odor of the
ointment. 4. Then one of his disciples, Judas Iscariot, he that
was about to betray him, said: 5. Why was not this ointment
sold for three hundred pence, and given to the poor? 6. Now
he said this, not because he cared for the poor; but because
he was a thief, and having the purse, carried the things that were
put therein. 7. Jesus therefore said: Let her alone, that she may
keep it against the day of my burial. 8. For the poor you have
always with you; but me you have not always. 9. A great
multitude therefore of the Jews knew that he was there; and
they came, not for Jesus's sake only, but that they might see
Lazarus, whom he had raised from the dead. 10. But the chief
priests thought to kill Lazarus also: 11. Because many of the
Jews, by reason of him, went away, and believed in Jesus.

This nard was worth around fifty dollars. There was nothing mean or small in Mary. Her closeness to Christ had developed a love that was truly generous.

When it was a question of belief in Christ, Peter was usually the spokesman. In a matter of denying something to Christ, we are not surprised that Judas took the initiative. Alone of the twelve he had been disappointed in Christ. He must have joined up with our Lord for what he could *get* out of Him. He had administrative talents, and hence he was made the treasurer of the group. While the faults of the other apostles came to the surface so that they could be corrected, Judas was secretive and hid his designs. His case would seem to exemplify the effect on our character of the continual craving for money. He had failed to correct the beginnings of that voracious vice of avarice. When he saw fifty dollars slip away from his fingers his indignation rose. But he was shrewd: he covered up his real motive by mentioning the poor. He knew, far more than the others, that Christ's cause was now hopeless. He wanted to get what he could while he could.

Judas "knew the nearness of betrayal and hated the more; Mary knew the nearness of His death and loved the more" (Edersheim). Jesus came to her defense. Her deed was really symbolic, that is, by anticipation she was preparing Christ's body for burial. His visible presence would soon be removed from them, and then they could give to the poor. We should aid the poor; but is it fitting to provide only a shabby church for Christ? Does not God deserve the best? Our character is disclosed by the attitude we take toward giving to Christ.

A fault that is not now corrected, may later become a vice, and then lead us on to do things which now we despise. We should never hide things from our Lord; He sees into our hearts. Our duty is to be open and frank with Him, as was Peter and then we shall never betray Him. Nearness to Christ drew nobility out of Mary and Zacheus and also from the blind man. Nearness to Christ ruined Judas. Catholic homes, Catholic education, and the Catholic religion bring us very close to Christ. What will the outcome be? Only God knows the real reason why this closeness seems to ruin some persons.

1. Locate Jericho on the map. Trace its Old Testament history. Cf. Josue 6.
2. Describe a specific instance of Christ's courage.
3. Why did Christ find it hard to convince the apostles that He was to suffer?
4. Show how unwillingness to bear suffering or loneliness may be weakness.
5. If one wishes to learn the true joy of Easter he must ———.
6. Must a person be perfect in order to be near our Lord?
7. What is implied in the statement of our Lord that He came to "give His life a redemption"?
8. Show that it is possible to be in a Catholic home or school and yet far from it as regards appreciation of its meaning.
9. Kindness is usually better than harshness because ———.
10. Name some excuses offered by those of our day who do not want Christ.
11. Explain the principles involved in the parable of the pounds.
12. One possible explanation for the action of Judas is ———.
13. Should closeness to Christ assist us in acquiring His aim? Compare John 8:34 on p. 112 with the last words in John 8:29 on p. 250 and then with John 17:4 on p. 377. Note how the aim of Christ was always consistent, always unselfish. Does not this show us that the aim of life, the purpose of life is outside of ourselves, that it is simply to reflect external honor or credit on God by our manner of living?

Chapter 48

PALM SUNDAY, A POPULAR TRIUMPH

JOHN 11: 55. And the pasch of the Jews was at hand; and many from the country went up to Jerusalem before the pasch to purify themselves. 56. They sought therefore for Jesus; and they discoursed one with another, standing in the temple: What think you that he is not come to the festival day? And the chief priests and Pharisees had given a commandment, that if any man knew where he was he should tell, that they might apprehend him.

IT WAS April of the year 30. This was the second, and the immortal occasion, on which our Lord appeared at the annual Passover, when the city swelled its numbers from around 200,000 to perhaps 1,000,000. He had been hounded and hunted before; now His time was fulfilled.

LUKE 19: 29. And it came to pass, when he was come nigh to Bethphage and Bethania, unto the mount called Olivet, he sent two of his disciples, 30. Saying: Go into the town which is over against you, at your entering into which you shall find the colt of an ass tied, on which no man ever hath sitten: loose him, and bring him hither. 31. And if any man shall ask you: Why do you loose him? you shall say thus unto him: Because the Lord hath need of his service. 32. And they that were sent, went their way, and found the colt standing, as he had said unto them. 33. And as they were loosing the colt, the owners thereof said to them: Why loose you the colt? 34. But they said: Because the Lord hath need of him. 35. And they brought him to Jesus. And casting their garments on the colt, they set Jesus thereon. 36. And as he went, they spread their clothes underneath in the way.

Throughout His life Jesus had refused all public ovations. However, it was God's plan that a popular tribute to His Messiasship should come to Christ just before He was to go down in apparent defeat. For a short period, then, we see Him act as a king, accept the honors of a king. Perhaps the owners of the animal were friends of our Lord, and willingly gave the colt to serve the King. (The Pharisees would have no trouble in discovering where He was. He was not one to run away from the appointed hour.) The apostles became excited. Was the victory of Christ at hand? Christ, on this occasion, kept His own counsel. But the love and esteem in which His friends held Him were soon evident. They thought only of one thing — to give their Master a triumphal entry into the crowded city, before all the multitude. In the spirit of the prophecy, it was a religious procession, a mixture of glory and humility.

> JOHN 12: 12. . . . A great multitude that was come to the festival day, when they had heard that Jesus was coming to Jerusalem, 13. Took branches of palm trees, and went forth to meet him, and cried: Hosanna, blessed is he that cometh in the name of the Lord, the king of Israel.
>
> MATT. 21: 4. Now all this was done that it might be fulfilled which was spoken by the prophet, saying: 5. Tell ye the daughter of Sion: Behold thy king cometh to thee, meek, and sitting upon an ass, and a colt the foal of her that is used to the yoke.

The news spread rapidly among those excitable Orientals. Included in the crowd were the northern Galileans and others who had heard of the resurrection of Lazarus. As they left the city to greet Christ, they broke branches from the palm trees. Palm symbolized joy (Lev. 23: 40). It was their way of welcoming their King. Undoubtedly they still hoped He would become a worldly, conquering king. So long had He held back that now they were overjoyed that He was evidently consenting to their wishes. He came from the east, either over the top of Olivet or around its southern slope, and then crossed the brook Cedron and up into the city.

St. Matthew takes pains to show us that this triumph had been predicted (Zach. 9: 9), and was thus part of God's plan. But how few people on that day realized that Christ came as a king of souls, of a spiritual kingdom and not of a worldly power. He had no warlike intentions, for He is the Prince of Peace (Isa. 9: 6). He is the Messias predicted, but He is meek. At the time of this prophecy kings rode donkeys in processions, for the horse was not at that time used by the Jews. The Palestinian donkey was a statelier, livelier animal than our mule. This beast was also a symbol of peace. It was fitting, then, that Christ should ride such an animal.

The present feast of the Kingship of Christ (last Sunday in October) has nothing to do with worldly governments. The Church does not seek temporal power. But all men have only one lawful and rightful ruler of their souls and consciences — the meek Christ. We celebrate this feast, then, to show that Christ is our recognized spiritual Ruler, because He alone opened the way to heaven, and earned the right to be the head of those who have immortal souls. We honor Christ for His achievements; we rely on Him as the invisible Head of the Church; we recognize that through Him alone may we enter heaven. If we honor the heads of secular governments, why not pay public honor to the Head of the entire human race?

> JOHN 12: 16. These things his disciples did not know at the first; but when Jesus was glorified, then they remembered that these things were written of him, and that they had done these things to him. 17. The multitude therefore gave testimony, which was with him, when he called Lazarus out of the grave, and raised him from the dead. 18. For which reason also the people came to meet him, because they heard that he had done this miracle.

The full significance of this day of triumph for Christ was realized by the apostles only later. In all the excitement few could think. The crowd increased as the procession moved along. From high stone walls, from flat-roofed houses in the city the procession could be seen coming along the base of Olivet.

> JOHN 12: 19. The Pharisees therefore said among themselves: Do you see that we prevail nothing? Behold, the whole world is gone after him.
> LUKE 19: 37. And when he was now coming near the descent of Mount Olivet, the whole multitude of his disciples began with joy to praise God with a loud voice, for all the mighty works they had seen, 38. Saying: Blessed be the king who cometh in the name of the Lord, peace in heaven, and glory on high! 39. And some

of the Pharisees, from amongst the multitude, said to him: Master, rebuke thy disciples. 40. To whom he said: I say to you, that if these shall hold their peace, the stones will cry out. 41. And when he drew near, seeing the city, he wept over it, saying: 42. If thou also hadst known, and that in this thy day, the things that are to thy peace; but now they are hidden from thy eyes. 43. For the days shall come upon thee: and thy enemies shall cast a trench about thee, and compass thee round, and straiten thee on every side, 44. And beat thee flat to the ground, and thy children who are in thee: and they shall not leave in thee a stone upon a stone: because thou hast not known the time of thy visitation.

Only the leaders were pained. They saw a superior personality win the crowd away from them. They had lost prestige. And, as often occurs when a bully sees his popularity dwindling, they fell into a state of fear. Lacking manhood, they could only plot in secret for the revenge which they had meditated from the first day He had set foot in Jerusalem. How bitter was this hour to those hardened, self-centered criminals!

Perhaps these Pharisees thought the Roman garrison would suspect a riot and kill some of the people. They should have recognized the peaceful, religious nature of the triumph; but so hard were their hearts that they had not even the sensitiveness of stones. Jesus was a prophet (teacher from God), He was likewise a priest who was to offer Himself a sacrifice to God; but He was also king of souls. And so deep is that threefold office of His, so firmly did God desire this public assertion of His Messiasship, that had not recognition come at least from the well-intentioned, then the very stones themselves would have burst forth in praise of Him, to whom all men, living and dead, are indebted. There are some men, like the Pharisees, who begrudge the least bit of honor shown to God; their one ambition is to prevent people from going to church and from honoring Christ. Some teachers speak of the crowd as having a "herd" mind. The popular mind does indeed have its faults and prejudices, but there are moments when it senses a truth that so-called learned people cannot see because of their conceit. The enemies of Christ could never in the future assert that He had not publicly claimed national recognition as the Messias. Hence the reason for this entry. Common sense should teach men that we owe praise and recognition to God.

Only one Man could look forty years into the future and foresee the horrible catastrophe in store for the city. Tears of sympathy for such a punishment rolled down the cheeks of Christ. He was not afraid of what would happen to Him on the coming Friday, but His heart melted at the thought of the hundreds of thousands who would die in the year A.D. 70, when Titus, the Roman general, drew His legions around Jerusalem. More horrible scenes took place during that siege than were ever recorded in ancient warfare.

> MATT. 21: 10. And when he was come into Jerusalem, the whole city was moved, saying: Who is this? 11. And the people said: This is Jesus the prophet, from Nazareth of Galilee.
>
> MARK 11: 11. And he entered into Jerusalem, into the temple: and having viewed all things round about, when now the eventide was come, he went out to Bethania with the twelve.

Through the narrow streets sped the news, as the shouts reechoed along the way. The One who had been despised by the leaders, because He was from Nazareth, who had never been to the schools of Jerusalem, was now master of the city. There were no captives of war, no spoils, but boundless hope in the hearts of the people that soon Israel would be free. The hope was probably strongest in those thousands who came from outside the city.

A particular meaning is attached to this entrance into the Temple. It was the day after the Sabbath. According to an ancient prescription (Exod. 12: 3–6), on this day each head of a family had to choose the lamb which would be sacrificed the following Friday for the Pasch. Christ knew He was the Lamb chosen to redeem the world. The Gospels do not tell us what thoughts were His as He wandered about the Temple. The old, burned offerings were to pass away; He was to inaugurate a new, spiritual, and divine offering. To no one did He reveal all that He was to suffer. No one could understand His predictions of the Passion. Eyes were turned toward Him as He walked from place to place in the Temple; but His secrets were His own as

He silently dedicated Himself as the Lamb of God—*Agnus Dei.* While the twelve thought of the marvelous demonstration, He heard rather the "Crucify Him" of the following Friday.

1. Why did Jesus permit the demonstration of Palm Sunday?
2. In what way is Christ a king?
3. What was the triple office of the Messias?
4. On what days is the Passion read during Holy Week, and where can you find each of the accounts?
5. Why do we hold palm in our hands on Palm Sunday?
6. Had Palm Sunday been predicted?
7. Christ wept over Jerusalem because ———.
8. What Jewish ceremony took place a few days before the Pasch?
9. The occasions which show that Jesus was never deceived by popularity are ———.
10. What did Christ most likely do in the Temple on Palm Sunday?
11. Inability to believe in Christ is caused by ———.
12. We give banquets or organize parades in order to show honor to human beings. Could you explain to a non-Catholic the principle behind religious processions?

Chapter 49

A FINAL APPEAL TO SEE THE LIGHT

MARK 11: 12. And the next day when they came out from Bethania, he was hungry. 13. And when he had seen afar off a fig tree having leaves, he came if perhaps he might find anything on it. And when he was come to it, he found nothing but leaves. For it was not the time for figs. 14. And answering, he said to it: May no man hereafter eat fruit of thee any more for ever! And his disciples heard it.

AFTER spending the night on a hillside, Jesus was hungry as He led the apostles into the city on Monday. Fig trees were numerous along the road. In Palestine the fig tree is unusual in that the fruit appears before the leaves. Having leaves, therefore, the tree should have had fruit. It had the appearance without the reality; it deceived observers. Our Lord condemned it for its sterility. To understand the incident, we must recall that a fig tree was sometimes used as a symbol for the Jewish nation (Jer. 24). Jesus had previously (Luke 13: 6–9) related a parable about the barren fig tree in reference to the leaders. Now He gave a parable in things instead of in words. It was His manner of showing that the external piety (leaves) of Jerusalem was barren, and hypocritical because it had the appearance only and not the reality of religion. The implication is that He has a divine power to judge and condemn those who appear to be religious but in reality are hypocrites. On the morrow the apostles would see what He had in mind.

MATT. 21: 14. And there came to him the blind, and the lame in the temple; and he healed them. 15. And the chief priests and scribes, seeing the wonderful things that he did, and the children crying in the temple, and saying: Hosanna to the Son of

David; were moved with indignation. 16. And said to him: Hearest thou what these say? And Jesus said to them: Yea, have you never read: Out of the mouth of infants and of sucklings thou hast perfected praise.

The little children, remembering the triumph of yesterday, and recognizing in Christ the kind of a person about whom their mothers had told them stories, spontaneously shouted their childlike trust and praise. Children see through to the heart; their love of God is real, honest, and unspoiled. But just as worldly minded people are shocked or sneer at any manifestation of simple and trustful piety on the part of devout believers, so the Pharisees were resentful. There is something mean and unnatural in those people who object to praise of God.

JOHN 12: 20. Now there were certain Gentiles among them, who came up to adore on the festival day. 21. These therefore came to Philip, who was of Bethsaida of Galilee, and desired him, saying: Sir, we would see Jesus. 22. Philip cometh, and telleth Andrew. Again Andrew and Philip told Jesus. 23. But Jesus answered them, saying: The hour is come, that the Son of man should be glorified. 24. Amen, amen I say to you, unless the grain of wheat falling into the ground die, 25. Itself remaineth alone. But if it die, it bringeth forth much fruit. He that loveth his life shall lose it; and he that hateth his life in this world, keepeth it unto life eternal. 26. If any man minister to me, let him follow me; and where I am, there also shall my minister be. If any man minister to me, him will my Father honor.

We do not know whether or not these Gentiles were successful in seeing Jesus. Their question seems to have prompted Christ's reference to His death which was to bring salvation to the Gentiles. Through His sufferings and death He was to enter upon eternal glory. For us, the secret of all true Christian success is to die to self, to root out selfishness; and whoever does this will develop into a glorious type of Catholic. Sin is selfishness; and no sin can enter heaven. They who have the courage to become Christlike are assured that God will raise them to high honor. Self-centered people never discover the joy that may be had, even on this earth, when strong desire to do the will of God replaces love of self.

JOHN 12: 27. Now is my soul troubled. And what shall I say?
Father, save me from this hour. But for this cause I came unto
this hour. 28. Father, glorify thy name. A voice therefore came
from heaven: I have both glorified it, and will glorify it again.
29. The multitude therefore that stood and heard, said that it
thundered. Others said: An angel spoke to him. 30. Jesus answered, and said: This voice came not because of me, but for
your sakes. 31. Now is the judgment of the world: now shall
the prince of this world be cast out. 32. And I, if I be lifted
up from the earth, will draw all things to myself. 33. (Now this
he said, signifying what death he should die.) 34. The multitude
answered him: We have heard out of the law, that Christ abideth
for ever; and how sayest thou: The Son of man must be lifted
up? Who is this Son of man?

A foretaste of the agony in the garden now came to our Lord. He was always conscious of what He would have to pass through for us. The human nature in Him recoiled at the awful prospect; yet He was determined to finish what He had begun. As at the baptism and the Transfiguration, so now, for the third time in His public career, heaven opened its doors and communicated aloud with the Hero who alone was carrying out God's plan. The one test of successful living is whether the individual has tried to bring glory to God instead of to self. Publicly, God the Father comforted Christ. The crowd was amazed, stunned. It was a warning given to them, a final appeal to see the Light. No one had entered heaven after Adam's fall, and Satan was thus said to have a hold on the world. The raising up of Christ on the Cross atoned for all human sins and opened heaven to souls. The Cross was to become the symbol that would draw men to Christ in gratitude. Christ has overcome the world not by the sword, but by the wood, says St. Augustine. Not by mighty armies or airplane raids does He seek conquests, but through the drawing power of the Cross. Multitudes today would rather die than deny Him. Are we among that number? Millions of others still need to be taught who this Son of Man is.

JOHN 12: 35. Jesus therefore said to them: Yet a little while, the
light is among you. Walk whilst you have the light, that the
darkness overtake you not. And he that walketh in darkness,
knoweth not whither he goeth. 36. Whilst you have the light,

believe in the light, that you may be the children of light. These things Jesus spoke; and he went away, and hid himself from them.

Night was now advancing. Darkness falls suddenly in Palestine. For more than two years these self-centered leaders of the city had preferred their own views to Christ's words. They judged Him before examining His claims. Every time that He cured a blind person it was a proof that He is the Light of the world. His is a beautiful title. And nothing is finer than the sight of Catholic young people resolutely following this Light, despite the efforts made by writers, demagogues, and propagandists to win them over to programs of supernationalism, atheism, animalism, effete intellectualism, and other extremes. The foundation for a solution of world problems is built by adherence to a divine Person. No theory, no economic plan will give the light of hope to young people unless it is based on the teachings of the divine Light. Communism is darkness because it denies the existence of God and of the soul. Marx held that only matter exists. This belief is called materialism. Every self-constituted leader has his own solution. The soundness of his theory is tested by the attitude He takes toward learning from the Light.

John 12: 37. And whereas he had done so many miracles before
them, they believed not in him: 38. That the saying of Isaias
the prophet might be fulfilled, which he said: Lord, who hath
believed our hearing? And to whom hath the arm of the Lord been
revealed? 39. Therefore they could not believe, because Isaias
said again: 40. He hath blinded their eyes, and hardened their
heart, that they should not see with their eyes, nor understand
with their heart, and be converted, and I should heal them. 41.
These things said Isaias, when he saw his glory, and spoke of him.
42. However, many of the chief men also believed in him; but
because of the Pharisees they did not confess him, that they
might not be cast out of the synagogue.
Mark 11: 18. Which when the chief priests and the scribes had
heard, they sought how they might destroy him. For they feared
him, because the whole multitude was in admiration at his doctrine. 19. And when the evening had come, he went forth out of
the city.

John the apostle was a witness when the Pharisees rejected Jesus. He looked back as he wrote this Gospel and saw how the words of the prophet Isaias were fulfilled. God gives sufficient grace to all men to see the truth. However, when men show a continual unwillingness to believe, God often leaves them in darkness, hides Himself from them because they are too filled with a sense of their own importance, too attached to their own ideas to be taught. Even today miracles would not convert many of the unbelievers. However, there are multitudes who have good will. Fear of losing their positions or their friends keeps them from joining the Church. Granting that they love the glory of men, we should not too readily condemn them. It is very difficult for us to realize how old traditions and old attachments hinder them from following the truth. We need to be kind and helpful to them. The point for us to remember is that the light of divine truth may pass from us if we love fame, popularity, and social prestige too much.

Thus ended Monday of Holy Week. The bold statements of our Lord held the crowd in admiration. Tyrants fear a popular man; they dare not attack him while he holds the esteem of the people. Christ was safe enough in the daytime. As on the previous evening, He sought the solitude of the hills outside the city. Judas was forming his plans; Peter was probably downcast. On the morrow the strife would continue.

1. Our Lord could feel hunger because ———.
2. Has God a right to expect spiritual fruit from us during our school days?
3. What is the danger in acting piously when a superior is watching?
4. Need an honest student pay much attention to others who enviously accuse him of trying to win the favor of the teacher?
5. How many occasions can you mention on which Christ showed moral courage?
6. What can children teach us?
7. What is the secret for obtaining joy out of our religion?
8. What do we mean by saying that Christ was victorious over the devil?
9. What is it that draws people to Christ?
10. Can the motto: *Deus lux mea,* be followed in modern life?
11. Look up the ceremonies of Holy Saturday and learn what is meant by the words: *Lumen Christi.*

Chapter 50

THE SUPREME QUESTION: ACCEPTANCE OR REJECTION OF JESUS

MARK 11: 20. And when they passed by in the morning they saw the fig tree dried up from the roots. 21. And Peter remembering, said to him: Rabbi, behold the fig tree which thou didst curse, is withered away. 22. And Jesus answering, saith to them: Have the faith of God. 23. Amen I say to you, that whosoever shall say to this mountain, Be thou removed and be cast into the sea, and shall not stagger in his heart, but believe, that whatsoever he saith shall be done; it shall be done unto him. 24. Therefore I say unto you, all things, whatsoever you ask when ye pray, believe that you shall receive; and they shall come unto you.

ON TUESDAY morning the apostles were following Jesus into the city. He could now convince them that faith is a powerful factor in life. Peter had not been talkative of late but he was observing events and thinking. The withered fig tree showed them: (*a*) the danger of hypocrisy, for God sees the barrenness of those who appear before the public to be good Catholics, but are inwardly cheats or self-centered egotists; (*b*) Catholic faith, such as the saints possess, must be wholehearted. When you ask a favor of God do not half doubt. Believe entirely that God can do what appears to be impossible. It must be an unselfish faith, a petition that is for one's spiritual good. On the day of his first Mass, St. Philip Neri asked God for the conversion of three Jews, and it was granted.

MATT. 21: 23. And when he was come into the temple, there came to him, as he was teaching, the chief priests and ancients of the people, saying: By what authority dost thou these things? And who hath given thee this authority? 24. Jesus answering,

said to them: I also will ask you one word, which if you shall tell
me, I will also tell you by what authority I do these things. 25.
The baptism of John, whence was it? from heaven, or from men?
But they thought within themselves, saying. 26. If we shall say,
from heaven, he will say to us: Why then did you not believe
him? But if we shall say, from men, we are afraid of the multitude: for all held John as a prophet. 27. And answering Jesus,
they said: we know not. He also said to them: Neither do I tell
you by what authority I do these things.

The battle was on. This and the two following chapters will deal with the stirring speeches and thoughts that were packed into that tremendous day — the last day of the public teaching of the God-Man. So toweringly does He stand out on this day that we are likely to forget the listening apostles, the surging, motley crowds that thronged the Temple courts. His Father's house was the scene of His first public utterance and also of His final effort to win the leaders. The Gospel writers use words sparingly, and we must fill in the background of each cryptic sentence. At the end of the Civil War, the North was so absorbed in rejoicing that no one could imagine Booth's plan to kill Lincoln. Likewise, the city-wide ovation that had been given to Jesus on Sunday, the admiration in which He was held by the people on Monday distracted His friends from the plot of the Temple leaders. But hatred is never turned aside from its quest of revenge. These seemingly honest questions that were put to Him had been carefully thought out (Matt. 22: 15). Every move of the Pharisees and rabbis was a shrewd one.

Civil and religious power among the Jews themselves was vested in the body called Sanhedrin, of seventy-one members. No one could officially teach the people without the authorization of these leaders. And the people had deep respect for these men who claimed that they were preserving the traditions of Moses. Tradition was sacred; and they were its interpreters. They represented "all that was venerable in age, eminent in wisdom, or imposing in authority in the great Council of the nation." On the other hand, Jesus was, humanly speaking, a sort of free lance. He had never been taught by these leaders, nor commissioned by them to teach. Hence, knowing the respect of the people for constituted authority, their design now was to undermine the popularity of Christ by showing that He had no authority to teach.

The people had made way for these pompous officials as they approached Christ. Peter's heart sank; Judas leered; Matthew imprinted every detail on his memory. The meek, lonely Galilean maintained His calm of sanctity and His serenity of a divine mind. Strength, dignity, and majesty radiated from His countenance. He who has taught us to permit no man to lay snares for us, was not now going to be entrapped. He would answer them by asking a question which implied what they were seeking for and at the same time exposed the cowardice and trickery of their plot. Of all the debates of intellectual giants, no scenes comparable to Christ's Temple victories have ever been recorded.

Jesus, however, was not seeking merely to win; He wished to enlighten. Since the people venerated John as one sent by God, it was but logical that whoever John recommended should be considered as being from God. John had introduced Christ as the promised Messias; Christ's miracles proved He was from God. And these leaders were supposed to accept whatever came from God. So, intending to confuse Christ, the astute leaders now found themselves in a dilemma. The eyes of the people shifted to them. Our Lord's answer to their question had been too quick for them. They stumbled and hesitated. They, who boasted of being the intellectual judges of the nation, were unable to answer the Man they were attempting to undermine. They confessed ignorance where ignorance was inexcusable. Peter must have felt like shouting. They had rejected the Baptist, and now, in the eyes of the people, they were culpable for rejecting Jesus.

* *

What qualities must our faith in God possess? What was the Sanhedrin? What was the source of Christ's authority? How does a bishop, a priest receive authority? Why did the ancients bring up the question of authority?

* *

MATT. 21: 28. But what think you? A certain man had two sons; and coming to the first, he said: Son, go work today in my vineyard. 29. And he answering, said: I will not. But afterwards, being moved with repentance, he went. 30. And coming to the other, he said in like manner. And he answering, said: I go, Sir; and he went not. 31. Which of the two did the father's will? They say to him: The first. Jesus saith to them: Amen I say to you, that the publicans and the harlots shall go into the kingdom of God before you. 32. For John came to you in the way of justice, and you did not believe him. But the publicans and the harlots believed him: but you, seeing it, did not even afterwards repent, that you might believe him.

This parable was addressed to the high priests and the ancients; they dared not run away as our Lord assumed the offensive. The first son stands for repentant sinners, who admit they make mistakes. The second son stands for those elders, who claiming to observe God's law, were actually rejecting His wishes. There is talk about Catholics who "go to Mass out of fear," who "go to church but are not 'decent' or 'cultured.'" Catholics do, indeed have their faults, but, like the first son, they at least try to work for God. The great crime is to consider oneself too superior to listen to the Church.

MATT. 21: 33. Hear ye another parable. There was a man an householder, who planted a vineyard, and made a hedge round about it, and dug in it a press, and built a tower, and let it out to husbandmen; and went into a strange country. 34. And when the time of the fruits drew nigh, he sent his servants to the husbandmen that they might receive the fruits thereof. 35. And the husbandmen laying hands on his servants, beat one, and killed another, and stoned another. 36. Again he sent other servants more than the former; and they did to them in like manner. 37. And last of all he sent to them his son, saying: They will reverence my son. 38. But the husbandmen seeing the son, said among themselves: This is the heir: come, let us kill him, and we shall have his inheritance. 39. And taking him, they cast him forth out of the vineyard, and killed him. 40. When therefore the lord of the vineyard shall come, what will he do to those husbandmen? 41. They say to him: He will bring those evil men to an evil end; and will let out his vineyard to other husbandmen, that shall render him the fruit in due season.

"The vineyard of the Lord of hosts is the house of Israel" (Isa. 5: 7).

The servants in this parable were the prophets sent by God. The husbandmen were the chief priests and ancients — the past and present false leaders. Each of our Lord's hearers was acquainted with the raising of grapes, and with the common custom of renting out vineyards. Hence the parable had tremendous force for them. Note how effectively our Lord revealed their plot to kill Him. The Gentiles were, in the main, to build up the Church of Christ.

The supreme question for us, and for all Americans is: "Shall we accept or reject the Son of God who was sent to us?" If we Catholics figuratively "kill" Jesus in us by our sinful lives, by our rejection of the sacrament of Penance, by our reading of things which destroy the Faith, then the Faith may be taken from us and given to those more worthy of it.

MATT. 21: 42. Jesus saith to them: Have you never read in the Scriptures: The stone which the builders rejected, the same is become the head of the corner? By the Lord this has been done; and it is wonderful in our eyes. 43. Therefore I say to you, that the kingdom of God shall be taken from you, and shall be given to a nation yielding the fruits thereof. 44. And whosoever shall fall on this stone, shall be broken: but on whomsoever it shall fall, it shall grind him to powder. 45. And when the chief priests and Pharisees had heard his parables, they knew that he spoke of them. 46. And seeking to lay hands on him, they feared the multitudes: because they held him as a prophet.

What terrible consequences for those who reject this cornerstone. The Jews, in spurning Him, were attempting to kill what was indestructible. For Christ was to build a Church that would last till the end of time. At judgment day Christ will condemn those who now reject Him. When someone tells you that belief in the divinity of Christ is not essential, that one may follow his own interpretation of Christ, recall such scenes as these to his mind. Belief in Jesus is one of the fruits that God expects of all men.

Impotent rage flashed again over the faces of the leaders. It galled them to realize that Christ's safety now lay in the fact that the people were for the most part backing Him.

MATT. 22: 1. And Jesus answering, spoke again in parables to them, saying: 2. The kingdom of heaven is likened to a king, who made a marriage for his son. 3. And he sent his servants, to call them that were invited to the marriage; and they would not come. 4. Again he sent other servants, saying: Tell them that were invited, Behold, I have prepared my dinner; my beeves and fatlings are killed, and all things are ready: come ye to the marriage. 5. But they neglected, and went their ways, one to his farm, and another to his merchandise. 6. And the rest laid hands on his servants, and having treated them contumeliously, put them to death. 7. But when the king had heard of it, he was angry, and sending his armies, he destroyed those murderers, and burnt their cities.

Like successive flashes of lightning these parables of Christ came quickly and piercingly across the Temple courts. The chief priests received more answers than they had anticipated. In the marriage feast the Jews were the first guests invited. They had been the chosen people of God. But they neglected the invitation to the feast, which was the Incarnation, the appearance of God among men. It is worldliness, preoccupation with pleasures, or business that causes people to put off the question of going to church, of attempting to find the true religion.

MATT. 22: 8. Then he saith to his servants: The marriage indeed is ready; but they that were invited were not worthy. 9. Go ye therefore into the highways; and as many as you shall find, call to the marriage. 10. And his servants going forth into the ways, gathered together all that they found, both bad and good: and the marriage was filled with guests. 11. And the king went in to see the guests: and he saw there a man who had not on a wedding garment. 12. And he saith to him: Friend, how camest thou in hither not having on a wedding garment? But he was silent. 13. Then the king said to the waiters: Bind his hands and feet, and cast him into the exterior darkness: there shall be weeping and gnashing of teeth. 14. For many are called, but few are chosen.

These verses refer to the call of the Gentiles, the conversion of the Roman Empire to Christianity (Acts 13: 46). Our Lord laid stress on the invitation being given to all classes of people because the Pharisees thought that the Jews alone were dear to God. God, of course, knows the state of conscience of all those who become Catholics, but the story is related in a human way. The wedding garment is the state of grace, or holiness. Hence even Gentiles had to observe the rules of the early Church. There could be no excuse for not having the equipment, for there is reason to believe that ceremonial garments were provided by the hosts at such feasts (Gen. 45: 22; 4 Kings 5: 22); and in the Church, means of grace (garments) are always at hand. This parable is a very effective answer to those who say they do not need churchgoing, or the sacraments, that they do not need to accept dogmas in order to live the right kind of life. Grace is an essential. In the final thought, Christ was not referring to the comparative number of lost and saved. He was giving a proverb. It may refer to the fact that of all the Jews who were invited to accept Christ few would become Catholics. Furthermore, as in the previous parable, this story teaches that the mere fact of being Catholic will not guarantee our salvation. We cannot take salvation for granted; we must co-operate with grace, and do our share in the kingdom. Every religious duty is an invitation to learn more about God.

Perhaps many others would have become better Catholics than ourselves had they been given the Faith. Since we have been invited (baptized), ours is the obligation of preparing, which is an individual responsibility. No matter whether our parents are good Catholics or not, no matter whether we have had many years of study of religion or not, God, on judgment day, will pick us out individually and determine how well we have prepared for life eternal with Him. No excuses will be accepted, because the opportunity is ours of obtaining the wedding garment by living a holy life, by accepting Jesus wholeheartedly.

1. Show how Christ was a master in debate.
2. Explain the parables of the vineyard, and of the wedding feast.
3. Can you see the reason why the Church cannot limit her membership to so-called "decent" people?
4. How do you account for Catholics who lose the Faith?
5. Show how salvation is a personal, individual responsibility.
6. If a Catholic believes strongly in the Church but leads a bad life, is his salvation assured?
7. There is an obligation on all people to accept Christ because ———.

Chapter 51

FREEDOM OF CONSCIENCE

MARK 12: 13. And they sent to him some of the Pharisees and of the Herodians, that they should catch him in his words. 14. Who coming, say to him: Master, we know that thou art a true speaker, and carest not for any man; for thou regardest not the person of men, but teachest the way of God in truth. Is it lawful to give tribute to Caesar; or shall we not give it? 15. Who knowing their wiliness, saith to them: Why tempt you me? Bring me a penny that I may see it. 16. And they brought it him. And he saith to them: Whose is this image and inscription? They say to him: Caesar's. 17. And Jesus answering, said to them: Render therefore to Caesar the things that are Caesar's, and to God the things that are God's. And they marvelled at him.

THE day was advancing. Like the steady drive of a powerful backfield in football, came these loaded questions hurled at Jesus. Alone, He foiled attack after attack. His enemies now planned to catch Him by a touchy political question. National independence is always a burning and dangerous problem in a subject nation. The Pharisees, extreme nationalists, hated Rome. The other party, court followers of Herod, were friendly to the Romans. Only hatred of Him could unite these two parties who now tried flattery.

"Smooth dissimulation, taught to grace
A devil's purpose with an angel's face."

If he advised paying tribute to Caesar He would lose standing with the people; if He objected to paying it, the Romans could be aroused against Him. Rome was tolerant enough of religious practices but very sensitive about payment of taxes. It was another of those delicate situations in which Christ was between two fires. He had no money, so the burden of producing a coin was upon them. The recognition of the head of the Roman Emperor Tiberius on the penny came from them. It was not Jewish or Temple money they brought to Him. Thus far He skillfully did not commit Himself. Instead, He went to the root of the matter. He uttered the principle governing relations between Church and State, civil allegiance and spiritual allegiance in the Christian world. They were using a Roman coin and in so doing silently admitted the lawfulness of paying tribute to Rome. Let them continue to pay this tribute; He would not advise a revolution against that which was their practice. But at the same time let them fulfill their religious duties to God. His answer was not God or Caesar, but both. It was a new and a world-changing principle. In Rome the political ruler was also the religious ruler. The crowd must have laughed at the discomfiture of the erstwhile flatterers.

There are two spheres of authority, the temporal and the spiritual, civil and religious, State and Church. Each is supreme in its own sphere. The Church is concerned with the souls of men; to the State, God has entrusted the temporal welfare of men. In each case authority proceeds from God. We owe civil allegiance to the State; but the State has no authority over our duties to God. The State cannot legitimately interfere with the right of freedom of conscience. Christ it is, who gave us the religious liberty we enjoy in America. The individual must have freedom of conscience because each person has individual worth and value. Christ taught this latter principle and thus laid the foundation for democracy, which holds that each person has value, for the "child is not a mere creature of the State." Christian leaders have not always been Christian at heart. Nevertheless, the modern attack on God and on religion is but a concealed plot to make people worship the State, or to adore the ideas for which certain leaders stand.

MATT. 22: 23. That day there came to him the Sadducees, who say there is no resurrecton: and asked him. 24. Saying: Master, Moses said: If a man die having no son, his brother shall marry his wife, and raise up issue to his brother. 25. Now there were with us seven brethren: and the first having married a wife, died; and not having issue, left his wife to his brother. 26. In like

> manner the second, and the third, and so on to the seventh. 27.
> And last of all the woman died also. 28. At the resurrection
> therefore whose wife of the seven shall she be? For they all had
> her. 29. And Jesus answering, said to them: You err, not know-
> ing the Scriptures, nor the power of God. 30. For in the resur-
> rection they shall neither marry nor be married; but shall be as
> the angels of God in heaven.

Christ remained on the field of battle, a victor. But immediately the Sadducees, the materialists of that day, or like the animalists of our day, approached, thinking they could make the doctrine of immortality appear ridiculous. The marriage custom to which they referred is called levirate. Outwardly, the question seems innocent. In reality, it represents the same attitude as that behind the modern question: "Show me the soul," which is an attempt to laugh religion out of court.

As often happens, these Sadducees did not really know the exact nature of the religious doctrine at which they sneered. Christ confuted them, using the very part of the Old Testament with which they were supposed to be familiar. Their imagined difficulty did not in reality exist. There is no procreation after death. There is no marriage in heaven; heaven is spiritual not material. There are no material or bodily desires there. God will change the qualities of bodies at the resurrection. Hence they who teach that man is merely a higher animal are robbing the young of a right to know that man has a soul, and an obligation to prepare himself for the next life.

> Luke 20: 37. Now that the dead rise again, Moses also shewed,
> at the bush, when he called the Lord, The God of Abraham, and
> the God of Isaac, and the God of Jacob; 38. For he is not the
> God of the dead, but of the living: for all live to him. 39. And
> some of the scribes answering, said to him: Master, thou hast
> said well. 40. And after that they durst not ask him any more
> questions.

Christ's explanation of the text: "God of Abraham," etc., shows that we need an infallible interpreter of the Bible. The Sadducees, professing to be intellectual, had often read this text but did not realize that it meant that Abraham was still living in the next world. Immortality follows from the fact that God is the God of those living in eternity. Moses had uttered those words five or six hundred years after the bodily death of Abraham.

Some of those keen Scribes had sufficient manhood to admit the mastery of the divine Master. No human intelligence ever could equal the instantaneous, decisive answers of Jesus. He alone could speak with first-hand information on the next world. Never once was He lost for an answer; never did He lose ground or make a slip, though in this Temple there were men who had hawkeyes to detect the slightest deviation from the sacred books. What must the presence of God be like, since such scintillating thoughts leaped from the mind of the God-Man.

> MARK 12: 28. And there came one of the scribes that had heard
> them reasoning together, and seeing that he had answered them
> well, asked him which was the first commandment of all. 29.
> And Jesus answered him: The first commandment of all is: Hear,
> O Israel: the Lord thy God is one God. 30. And thou shalt love
> the Lord thy God with thy whole heart, and with thy whole soul,
> and with thy whole mind, and with thy whole strength. This is the
> first commandment. 31. And the second is like to it: Thou
> shalt love thy neighbor as thyself. There is no other command-
> ment greater than these. 32. And the scribe said to him: Well,
> Master, thou hast said in truth, that there is one God and there
> is no other besides him. 33. And that he should be loved with
> the whole heart, and with the whole understanding and with
> the whole soul, and with the whole strength, and that one's neigh-
> bor should be loved as oneself, is a greater thing than all holo-
> causts and sacrifices. 34. And Jesus seeing that he had answered
> wisely, said to him: Thou are not far from the kingdom of God.
> And no man after that durst ask him any questions.

This Scribe was evidently one of those half won over by the brilliance of our Lord. We thank him for his question which drew from our Lord an answer which sets an eternal, unchangeable standard for the Catholic. All religion is summed up in that double commandment. It contains the essence of Catholic life. Faith is the foundation; love is the goal. We attain to that standard when we acquire in our hearts abiding love of God and love of our neighbor for God's sake. We pray, we study religion, and we go to church in order to develop a personal love for God. This is a duty because He first loved us, sent His Son to us in order that we might walk in light and in love. Religion is intended to fill us with a deep and personal attachment to our Father, who gave us a soul with power to know and to will. We are to love our neighbor, and treat him as a brother in Christ, because God wants him in heaven with us. It is not necessary that we feel an affection for our neighbor, such as we have for our parents. It is necessary that we do good to him, treat him as Christ would treat him, and seek to aid him as is outlined in the spiritual and corporal works of mercy. That is Christlike Catholicism.

The holocausts and sacrifices of which the Scribe spoke were bloody sacrifices of the Old Testament, not the Mass. The leaders had taught that ritualistic acts and ceremonies were the essence of religion. Jesus showed that true religion is interior.

The Galilean had silenced the intellectual and religious leaders of the capital of the nation. No argument, no trick that they could devise could deceive Him. In the Temple, where truth should reign, He had stood for the truth, and won. Peter, John, all the twelve watched the opponents of their Master retreat. It was good to hear Him, to be on His side.

> MATT. 23: 1. Then Jesus spoke to the multitudes and to his disciples, 2. Saying: The scribes and the Pharisees have sitten on the chair of Moses. 3. All things therefore whatsoever they shall say to you, observe and do: but according to their works do ye not; for they say, and do not. . . . 9. And call none your father upon earth; for one is your father, who is in heaven. 10. Neither be ye called masters; for one is your master, Christ. 11. He that is the greatest among you shall be your servant. 12. And whosoever shall exalt himself, shall be humbled: and he that shall humble himself shall be exalted.

Our Lord loved justice and hated hypocrisy. Hence, to warn us against wrong influences, He exposed the secret motives of the Pharisees (Cf. Chap. 43). However, He upheld the principle of authority in religion. Dislike of a priest, scandal on the part of a priest never excuses a Catholic from fulfilling the duties of a Catholic. Our obligations remain, no matter how many give us bad example.

All the external ceremonies in religion are means to an end. The end is love, not the mere performance of a ceremony. We must love our parents in God, not allow them to separate us from God. We must never place any human teachings or theories above that which has been taught to us by God. The best citizen of a state is one who accepts Christ as a leader. (In the original Greek the word "master" also means "leader.") Our divine Leader, Christ, has taught us the value of freedom of conscience, and has done more for us than any human hero. In being loyal to Christ we are loyal to the best interests of our country. And we work for our country, not with any thought of a human reward or fame, but we leave the question of reward to our Leader. We work for Him by doing good to all men and women.

> LUKE 21: 1. And looking on, he saw the rich men cast their gifts into the treasury. 2. And he saw also a poor widow casting in two brass mites. 3. And he said: Verily I say to you, that this poor widow hath cast in more than they all: 4. For all these have of their abundance cast into the offerings of God: but she of her want, hath cast in all the living that she had.

Certainly God is one day to fill up the souls of those who live in poverty, and yet are generous. Our Lord is quick to notice the acts of students who quietly and sincerely deny themselves some comfort, some pleasure of the senses, in order to give to the missions or to the poor.

1. The catch in the question put to Jesus about paying tribute to Caesar was ———.
2. What does Christ command in regard to paying taxes to the government?
3. Would you resist if the State began to dictate to you in purely religious matters?
4. In what project for honest civil government, or for decent wages for workers would Christ expect you to interest yourself in your city or state?
5. What mistake does a man make who says he never saw a soul?
6. We know that the soul is immortal because ———.
7. Is an individual able to interpret everything in the Bible, or do we need an infallible interpreter?
8. How would you answer a teacher of a biology class who asserted that man is merely a higher animal?
9. What is meant by freedom of conscience and in what countries is it not permitted?
10. Is a person excused from fulfilling his religious duties if his superiors lead scandalous lives?
11. God has a right to be loved because ———.

Chapter 52

SO LIVING AS TO BE READY FOR THE END

MARK 13: 1. And as he was going out of the temple, one of his disciples said to him: Master, behold what manner of stones, and what buildings are here. 2. And Jesus answering, said to him: Seest thou all these great buildings? There shall not be left a stone upon a stone, that shall not be thrown down.

THE God of the Temple was passing forever from the Temple of God. It was sad, just as it is sad to see the Light of life depart from the temple of the heart of a person who rejects Christ. Our Lord felt sorrowful. Humanly speaking, He appeared to be a failure as a teacher, and as a leader. Rejection of Him by Jerusalem resembles the case of a person rejecting the last sacraments even on his deathbed. The responsibility however is the individual's, not God's.

Throughout that terrifying Tuesday the apostles had listened to those disputes in which He silenced all opponents. And now His prediction that those beautiful buildings of white stone, especially the sanctuary with its marble and gold, would all be ruined, dumbfounded them. In the year 70, Titus wanted to save the sanctuary because of its beauty, but the madness of the besieged made such an act impossible. It is difficult now to realize the awe and pride with which a country Jew would regard that Temple, since it symbolized God's presence among them as the chosen people.

MARK 13: 3. And as he sat on the Mount of Olivet over against the temple, Peter and James and John and Andrew asked him apart: 4. Tell us, when shall these things be? And what shall be the sign when all these things shall begin to be fulfilled? 5. And Jesus answering began to say to them: Take heed lest any man deceive you. 6. For many shall come in my name, saying:

I am he; and they shall deceive many. 7. And when you shall hear of wars and rumors of wars, fear ye not. For such things must needs be, but the end is not yet. 8. For nation shall rise against nation, and kingdom against kingdom, and there shall be earthquakes in divers places, and famines. These things are the beginning of sorrows. 9. But look to yourselves. For they shall deliver you up to councils, and in the synagogues you shall be beaten, and you shall stand before governors and kings for my sake, for a testimony unto them. 10. And unto all nations the gospel must first be preached. 11. And when they shall lead you and deliver you up, be not thoughtful beforehand what you shall speak; but whatsoever shall be given you in that hour, that speak ye. For it is not you that speak, but the Holy Ghost. 12. And the brother shall betray his brother unto death, and the father his son; and children shall rise up against the parents, and shall work their death. 13. And you shall be hated by all men for my name's sake. But he that shall endure unto the end, he shall be saved.

Mt. Olivet is higher than the hill on which was the Temple. As our Lord looked west the sun was sinking into the Mediterranean, suggesting the spiritual darkness that had come over the country.

Our Lord did not give a definite reply to their "when?" He would not answer any curious speculation, for God does not ordinarily tell us when we are going to die. He mingled the events which would precede the destruction of Jerusalem with those calamities which will come at the end of the world. All nations must have a chance to become Christian before the final judgment. The events which were to precede the destruction of Jerusalem are a type, an indication of what will happen at the end.

It was in the dusk of evening that four men listened to the God-Man, in His rôle of prophet, unfold the future. Below the five, over west in the city, the Pharisees were plotting His end, while He was predicting the close of their reign. Apparently, they were to win; the Church is always apparently failing, yet she triumphs. He was being judged then by His enemies; yet He confidently spoke of judging all men. But the main rôle of prophet is not to predict; it is to warn, and to bring people to repentance. And so, Christ warned the apostles, as He warns us. Many would claim to represent Him. Many today boast that science will solve all the problems of the future. "Man may set up in business as a creator on his own account." False Christs, false theories, or an omnipotent State draw people away from Christ. The unwary, the worldly minded are caught by these fake promises. Be not deceived. "Christ having come, there is no longer any Master to be looked for, any Savior to be expected, any new revealer" (Didon).

Fear was in the air from the time of the death of Christ to the end of the Temple in the year 70. Disaster brooded over all the land. But the Christians persevered. Peter was placed in prison but miraculously released. Paul spoke before governors and kings. The Holy Ghost showered special gifts upon the early Christians. They were not afraid, just as we should not fear the hate of men.

> LUKE 21: 24. And they shall fall by the edge of the sword: and shall be led away captives into all nations: and Jerusalem shall be trodden down by the Gentiles; till the times of the nations be fulfilled.
>
> MARK 13: 20. And unless the Lord had shortened the days, no flesh should be saved: but for the sake of the elect which he hath chosen, he hath shortened the days. 21. And then if any man shall say to you: Lo, here is Christ; lo, he is there: do not believe. 22. For there will rise up false Christs and false prophets, and they shall shew signs and wonders, to seduce (if it were possible) even the elect. 23. Take you heed therefore; behold I have foretold you all things. 24. But in those days, after that tribulation, the sun shall be darkened, and the moon shall not give her light.

The siege of Jerusalem lasted five months. The Providence of God intervened to prevent the destruction of all the inhabitants. Most likely some of the survivors became converts. The "elect" may have been these converts and other Christians, or the "elect" may refer to the condition of some at the end of the world.

Tacitus, a Roman historian, says that 600,000 persons perished in the siege; and thousands were carried into captivity. A second fearful destruction took place in Jerusalem in the year 135, under the Roman Emperor Hadrian. A false prophet, Bar Kochba, brought on the attack. Now, in our own day the Jews are beginning to return to Palestine, under the Zionist movement and the protecting arm of England. It is not a religious movement, but who knows what the Providence of God may bring out of it. Our Lord hints here that the day of the Gentiles is to cease; and then Israel may turn to God.

LUKE 21: 25. And there shall be signs in the sun, and in the moon, and in the stars; and upon the earth distress of nations, by reason of the confusion of the roaring of the sea and of the waves; 26. Men withering away for fear, and expectation of what shall come upon the whole world. For the powers of heaven shall be moved; 27. And then they shall see the Son of man coming in a cloud, with great power and majesty. 28. But when these things begin to come to pass, look up, and lift up your heads, because your redemption is at hand. . . . 31. So you also, when you shall see these things come to pass, know that the kingdom of God is at hand. 32. Amen, I say to you, this generation shall not pass away, till all things be fulfilled.

Verses 25–27 seem to refer to the catastrophes which will precede the second coming of Christ at the end of the world. We only know that men will be "withering away for fear." The Jewish race ("this generation") would seem destined to last till the end of time (Cf. Rom. 11, 25). It is thought that toward the end of the world Jews will return to Christ in large numbers.

MATT. 24: 27. For as lightning cometh out of the east, and appeareth even into the west, so shall also the coming of the Son of man be. . . . 36. But of that day and hour no one knoweth, not the angels of heaven, but the Father alone. 37. And as in the days of Noe, so shall also the coming of the Son of man be. 38. For as in the days before the flood, they were eating and drinking, marrying and giving in marriage, even till that day in which Noe entered into the ark, 39. And they knew not till the flood came, and took them all away; so also shall the coming of the Son of man be. . . . 42. Watch ye therefore, because ye know not what hour your Lord will come. . . . 44. Wherefore be you also ready, because at what hour you know not the Son of man will come.

Verse 27 may not refer to the end of the world, but to the rapid movement of His kingdom from east to west. As lightning is manifest, so would be the Church. The end of the world will be sudden. The haters of religion will be caught unawares.

"Watch." Death does not often warn us in advance. There is only one Catholic idea about death — be ready for it. Christ does not want good Catholics to worry, to be anxious. A Catholic should have no fear of death. How calm He was as His death drew near. He does want us to be watchful, alert to the dangers which would destroy the supernatural life in us. Christ's wish is that each one simply "be ready." We may trust His mercy if we have been loyal to Him.

* *

The main function of prophets is ———. To argue about when the end of the world is due is foolish because ———. What is wrong with a Catholic who says he is afraid of death? What persons or forces may deceive Catholics today?

* *

MATT. 25: 1. Then shall the kingdom of heaven be like to ten virgins, who taking their lamps went out to meet the bridegroom and the bride. 2. And five of them were foolish, and five wise. 3. But the five foolish, having taken their lamps, did not take oil with them: 4. But the wise took oil in their vessels with the lamps. 5. And the bridegroom tarrying, they all slumbered and slept. 6. And at midnight there was a cry made: Behold the bridegroom cometh, go ye forth to meet him. 7. Then all those virgins arose and trimmed their lamps. 8. And the foolish said to the wise: Give us of your oil, for our lamps are gone out. 9. The wise answered, saying: Lest perhaps there be not enough for us and for you, go ye rather to them that sell, and buy for yourselves. 10. Now whilst they went to buy, the bridegroom came: and they that were ready went in with him to the marriage, and the door was shut. 11. But at last come also the other virgins, saying: Lord, Lord, open to us. 12. But he answering said: Amen I say to you, I know you not. 13. Watch ye therefore, because you know not the day nor the hour.

Galilean marriage customs supplied the background for this parable. It helps us to understand Matthew's reference to the second part of Joseph's and Mary's marriage. The espousals (equivalent to engagement with us but legal marriage with them) took place about a year before the ceremony here described. On the night the groom was to come to take his spouse, the bridesmaids took lamps and waited for him. When word came that he was on his way, the bride sent the virgins forth to meet him and conduct him and his friends to her home. "Foolish" here means thoughtless; and "wise" means prudent. The application may be twofold. First, be ready for death and the coming of Christ; second, the virgins stand for the contemplative life, the quiet, patient, and steady life of prayer, meditation, and work. Such a life becomes monotonous unless nourished by an inner fire of devotion to Christ. The oil may stand for virtue, or grace. Neither virtue nor grace can be borrowed, when death comes. The responsibility is personal and individual. It is a personal duty to acquire grace, to develop virtue.

The parable of the pounds represents an active life, the life of one who is before the public. The parable of the virgins portrays those who lead quiet lives, removed from the public — mothers at home, working men and women who never receive any publicity or worldly recognition. They too must be fired by an ideal, devoted to some person. Loneliness is taken out of their lives by the ideal of working for, and waiting for Christ. For them, meditation keeps the inner life alive, keeps the flame of love for Christ burning. The mind is fed with reading and meditation; Mass and Communion nourish and strengthen grace in the soul. Patience, perseverance, and fidelity are required, for the average person must wait long before Christ comes to call him. In the rush and excitement at the end, one cannot then borrow or purchase that which he should have already procured.

MATT. 25: 31. And when the Son of man shall come in his
majesty, and all the angels with him, then shall he sit upon the
seat of his majesty: 32. And all nations shall be gathered together before him, and he shall separate them one from another,
as the shepherd separateth the sheep from the goats: 33. And
he shall set the sheep on his right hand, but the goats on his left.
34. Then shall the king say to them that shall be on his right
hand: Come, ye blessed of my Father, possess you the kingdom
prepared for you from the foundation of the world. 35. For I was
hungry, and you gave me to eat; I was thirsty, and you gave
me to drink; I was a stranger, and you took me in; 36. Naked,
and you covered me; sick, and you visited me; I was in prison,
and you came to me. 37. Then shall the just answer him, saying: Lord, when did we see thee hungry, and fed thee; thirsty,

and gave thee drink? 38. And when did we see thee a stranger, and took thee in? Or naked, and covered thee? 39. Or when did we see thee sick or in prison, and came to thee? 40. And the king answering, shall say to them: Amen, I say to you, as long as you did it to one of these my least brethren, you did it to me. 41. Then he shall say to them also that shall be on his left hand: Depart from me, you cursed, into everlasting fire which was prepared for the devil and his angels. 42. For I was hungry, and you gave me not to eat; I was thirsty, and you gave me not to drink. 43. I was a stranger, and you took me not in; naked, and you covered me not; sick and in prison, and you did not visit me. 44. Then they also shall answer him, saying: Lord, when did we see thee hungry, or thirsty, or a stranger, or naked, or sick, or in prison, and did not minister to thee? 45. Then he shall answer them, saying: Amen I say to you, as long as you did it not to one of these least, neither did you do it to me. 46. And these shall go into everlasting punishment: but the just, into life everlasting.

The theme of the Last Judgment now recurs. Christ has designated love of God and neighbor as the essence of Catholic life. Each action of our life should be directed toward God, that is, performed out of a supernatural motive — love of God or desire to bring honor upon Him. We must take time to give direct worship to God, such as that rendered to Him through offering the Mass. However, we prove at all times whether or not we actually love God by the manner in which we render service to our fellow citizens, our acquaintances, and those at home. Christ prayed; He also went about doing good. St. John the apostle says: "He that loveth not his brother whom he seeth, how can he love God, whom he seeth not" (1 John 4: 20). The Catholic religion demands that its members strive for social justice and true social progress. The person who thinks only of his own salvation, of saving only his own soul, may be selfish; he may be placed on the left hand. The selfish, the lazy, the indifferent do not belong in heaven.

What a startling thing it is to hear Christ say that kindness to others is kindness done to Him personally. Through the Incarnation Christ became our Brother. Baptism joins us with Christ, gives us status, and significance. All those accepting Christ become one group, called the mystical body of Christ, or the Church. Life then becomes a joyous partnership in His work. What we do to other people, we do to Christ; kindness to them is our way of showing what we think of Jesus. And if the world seems to treat us badly, after we have been kind to others, we know that Christ never forgets a kind deed done in His name. So, the way to prepare for the Last Judgment, the manner of living which prepares one for the final end is the doing of good for Christ. The seriousness of this obligation is seen in the stern statement of Jesus that there is a hell. Many moderns do not like that word; yet the existence of a hell is based on the word of the God-Man. Modern arguments against hell arise from the desire to dictate to God; they come from people who seek to eliminate God from the universe that He designed.

1. In what state of mind should a Catholic meet death?
2. What is the meaning of the parable of the virgins?
3. What standards of judgment will God use on the last day?
4. What is the meaning of the phrase, "In His name"?
5. Religion is not a mere study, or belief merely but ———.
6. What would Christ think of a student who said: "I have studied a lot of religion; I don't need any more of it"?
7. Explain to a non-Catholic just how and why a Catholic is interested in the betterment of society.

Chapter 53

A TRAITOR IN THEIR MIDST

MATT. 26: 1. And it came to pass, when Jesus had ended all these words, he said to his disciples: 2. You know that after two days shall be the pasch, and the Son of man shall be delivered up to be crucified. 3. Then were gathered together the chief priests and ancients of the people into the court of the high priest, who was called Caiphas: 4. And they consulted together, that by subtilty they might apprehend Jesus, and put him to death. 5. But they said: Not on the festival day, lest perhaps there should be a tumult among the people.

IT WAS Tuesday evening when Jesus sat on Olivet and foretold the end of Jerusalem's Temple. It was now Wednesday. Wednesday and Thursday were passed quietly, perhaps at Bethania, behind Olivet. Two days of rest, and of time with His own. Even the silence of the Evangelists on the interval is eloquent. Certainly, much of the time was given to prayer, to conversation with His Father. Meanwhile, thousands were thronging the streets of Jerusalem and the Temple courts. While He was silently preparing to offer Himself for our sins (an act of love), bitter, relentless officials were plotting His death (an act of hate). What a contrast between God and man!

LUKE 22: 3. And satan entered into Judas, who was surnamed Iscariot, one of the twelve. 4. And he went, and discussed with the chief priests and the magistrates, how he might betray him to them.

MATT. 26: 15. And said to them: What will you give me, and I will deliver him unto you? But they appointed him thirty pieces of silver.

LUKE 22: 5. And they were glad, and covenanted to give him

money. 6. And he promised. And he sought opportunity to betray him in the absence of the multitude.

On Wednesday an unbelievable thing happened. Into the palace of the plotters came a man, an intimate associate of the Galilean. Judas had slipped away from Bethania. St. Luke gives a terrible description of the reason for the action of Judas. It shows what a person will do when he yields to Satan. Judas was a cool-eyed calculator. Moreover, he was a thief. He saw that Christ was doomed, that a crisis was at hand. His love for money had stifled any love for Christ; and maybe he thought he would get what he could before the end. He would betray Christ for money.

The shrewd priests and police realized that Judas was after money. They knew also that only a coward would betray; and so they offered him the paltry sum of eighteen dollars. The devil, of course, rejoiced as Judas walked back to Bethania. And yet, even the devil, thinking to work evil, was actually helping to bring about the occasion which opened up heaven to us. God can draw good out of evil.

LUKE 22: 7. And the day of the unleavened bread came, on which it was necessary that the pasch should be killed. 8. And he sent Peter and John, saying: Go, and prepare for us the pasch, that we may eat. 9. But they said: Where wilt thou that we prepare? 10. And he said to them: Behold, as you go into the city, there shall meet you a man carrying a pitcher of water: follow him into the house where he entereth in. 11. And you shall say to the goodman of the house: The master saith to thee: Where is the guest chamber, where I may eat the pasch with my disciples. 12. And he will shew you a large dining room, furnished; and there prepare. 13. And they going, found as he said to them, and made ready the pasch. 14. And when the hour was come, he sat down, and the twelve apostles with him. 15. And he said to them: With desire I have desired to eat this pasch with you, before I suffer.

It was Thursday evening. It may have been dark, and thus they were able to escape notice on their way into the city. With deep emotion, Jesus showed how He yearned for the occasion to institute the Eucharist, the sacrament of love and union. He was anxious for the time to come in which He would give us the

Mass and Communion, and the priesthood. The meal, to which St. Luke here refers, took place before the institution of the Eucharist. A lamb that had been slain in the Temple was consumed wherever people lodged. Judas was there, as was silent, contemplating John, manly Matthew, timid Philip, stern James, and lovable Peter, eyes animated.

LUKE 22: 24. And there was also a strife amongst them, which of them should seem to be the greater. 25. And he said to them: The kings of the Gentiles lord it over them; and they that have power over them, are called beneficent. 26. But you not so: but he that is the greater among you, let him become as the younger; and he that is the leader, as he that serveth. 27. For which is greater, he that sitteth at table, or he that serveth? Is not he that sitteth at table? But I am in the midst of you, as he that serveth: 28. And you are they who have continued with me in my temptations: 29. And I dispose to you, as my Father hath disposed to me, a kingdom.

So trusting, so unsuspecting were the eleven that they grew confident of Christ's approaching triumph. They thought again of victory, and of who should occupy the most prominent positions (Cf. p. 237). Judas thought the eleven were easily duped if they imagined that Christ could triumph and thus reward them with positions. The eleven did have their faults. However, while always careful to point out these faults, Christ was patient with them because they loved Him, which Judas did not. Our Lord says that popes, bishops, priests are not to care for honor, or to seek for fame. They are to think only of serving God through service to the people. And to anyone who remains loyal to Christ throughout all the trials of life there is that reward, that unending fame — heaven, God's presence.

JOHN 13: 1. Before the festival day of the pasch Jesus knowing that his hour was come, that he should pass out of this world to the Father: having loved his own who were in the world, he loved them unto the end. 2. And when supper was done (the devil having now put into the heart of Judas Iscariot, the son of Simon, to betray him), 3. Knowing that the Father had given all things into his hands, and that he came from God, and goeth to God; 4. He riseth from supper, and layeth aside his garments, and having taken a towel, girded himself. 5. After that, he putteth water into a basin, and began to wash the feet of the disciples, and to wipe them with the towel wherewith he was girded. 6. He cometh therefore to Simon Peter. And Peter said to him: Lord dost thou wash my feet? 7. Jesus answered, and said to him: What I do thou knowest not now; but thou shalt know hereafter. 8. Peter saith to him: Thou shalt never wash my feet. Jesus answered him: If I wash thee not, thou shalt have no part with me. 9. Simon Peter saith to him: Lord, not only my feet, but also my hands and my head.

Years later, when John was writing this account there stood out in his mind the unforgettable love that Jesus had lavished on the apostles, a love that did not balk at humiliation. He bears the same love toward us, unto the end. This Jesus, who came from God and is now with God, performed the task of a servant. He taught, as always, by example. When we are near Him we should not be occupied with selfish designs. And, following Him, we should not hesitate to do humiliating acts for others in order to draw them to Him.

Peter knew he was only human and full of faults. To see a divine Person thus humble Himself before a mere human was too much for Peter. But Jesus knew how to handle the chief apostle. The one thing that Peter could not stand was to be separated from Jesus. To be with Jesus, he would submit to any kind of washing, just as we should submit willingly to the cleansing grace of the sacrament of Penance in order to regain or to retain companionship with our Lord.

JOHN 13: 10. Jesus saith to him: He that is washed, needeth not but to wash his feet, but is clean wholly. And you are clean, but not all. 11. For he knew who he was that would betray him; therefore he said: You are not all clean. 12. Then after he had washed their feet, and taken his garments, being sat down again, he said to them: Know you what I have done to you? 13. You call me Master, and Lord; and you say well, for so I am. 14. If then I, being your Lord and Master, have washed your feet, you also ought to wash one another's feet. 15. For I have given you an example, that as I have done to you, so you do also. 16. Amen, amen I say to you: The servant is not greater than his lord; neither is the apostle greater than he that sent him. 17. If you know these things, you shall be blessed if you do them. 18. I speak not of you all: I know whom I have chosen. But that the scripture may be fulfilled: He, that eateth bread with me, shall lift up his heel against me. 19. At present I tell you, before it come to pass: that when it shall come to pass, you may believe that I am he.

In those days roads were dusty. The guest who had bathed before going on his visit, needed only to have his feet washed when he arrived. Perhaps our Lord had meant this whole scene of the washing to be symbolical to the apostles of the necessary cleansing of their faults before they were to receive Communion. A subtle hint to Judas seems to run through the scene also. Jesus referred to him more than once. The thought of a traitor in their midst cut Him deeply. Certainly He intended to teach us humility and the advantage of a clean heart. Not only should we seek to be free from faults when approaching Communion, but also a boy who intends to be a priest or religious, a girl who wishes to be a nun, a person who hopes to enter the married state — all should aim to have a clean record when they come to that vocation.

Not all were clean. Did Judas recoil at the washing? Evidently not. What majestic poise and self-control in Christ to wash those feet that had trod the dirty path of betrayal to the palace of the high priest. In the East, to eat bread with another is a guarantee of security. An Arab will never harm a man while he is his guest. Judas had eaten with Christ, and concealed his purpose. He was brazen. But the eleven would not forget. They would later serve the lowliest of mankind — the leper, the slave, the street waif, the orphan, and the fallen ones. And young American missionaries are doing the same today in China, while at home the hospital nuns, the nuns of the orphanages and of the homes for the poor carry on the work.

Matt. 26: 21. And whilst they were eating, he said: Amen I say to you, that one of you is about to betray me. 22. And they being very much troubled, began every one to say: Is it I, Lord? 23. But he answering said: He that dippeth his hand with me in the dish, he shall betray me. 24. The Son of man indeed goeth, as it is written of him: but woe to that man, by whom the Son of man shall be betrayed: it were better for him, if that man had not been born. 25. And Judas that betrayed him, answering, said: Is it I, Rabbi? He saith to him: Thou hast said it.

A thunderbolt suddenly hit the group as they reclined on couches or on mats around the table; consternation reigned. It was no longer a hint, which only the guilty one could catch. The betrayal weighed on the heart of Christ! Probably our Lord answered Judas in a low voice. The eye of innocence looked into the eye of guilt. It was the sentence of an infinite Judge. No thought can be hid from God. And Judas must have realized that his soul was being searched. It seems to be implied that Judas never repented. While the thought of disloyalty hurt the others, he remained brazen.

> JOHN 13: 21. When Jesus had said these things, he was troubled in spirit; and he testified, and said: Amen, amen I say to you, one of you shall betray me. 22. The disciples therefore looked one upon another, doubting of whom he spoke. 23. Now there was leaning on Jesus' bosom one of his disciples, whom Jesus loved. 24. Simon Peter therefore beckoned to him, and said to him: Who is it of whom he speaketh? 25. He therefore, leaning on the breast of Jesus, saith to him: Lord, who is it? 26. Jesus answered: He it is to whom I shall reach bread dipped. And when he had dipped the bread, he gave it to Judas Iscariot, the son of Simon. 27. And after the morsel, Satan entered into him. And Jesus said to him: That which thou dost, do quickly. 28. Now no man at the table knew to what purpose he said this unto him. 29. For some thought, because Judas had the purse, that Jesus had said to him: Buy those things which we have need of for the festival day: or that he should give something to the poor. 30. He therefore having received the morsel, went out immediately. And it was night.

The details given by St. John complete the picture of Judas. At table the Jews did not sit on chairs as we do. They reclined on their left arm on couches or mats. John was near Jesus. His whole-souled, silent devotion had won the affection of our Lord. He saw deeper than some of the others. He, being near Jesus, could lean back and quietly inquire and relate the information to Peter. Judas became more than nervous. He looked for an opportunity to depart. The unsuspicious nature of the other apostles prevented them from realizing the hellish plot. And again, note the supreme self-control in Jesus. Judas may have thought that Jesus would miraculously escape from the plot. But a cold shiver must have run down his spine when he realized that all was known to Jesus. We are not sure, but it seems probable that Judas left before the institution of the Eucharist.

To depart from Christ is to go into darkness — black, dreary, dreadful, howling night. How eloquently St. John portrays the conscience of Judas as well as the time of his departure. It is sad to see one give up the Faith. Night remains in the souls of those who reject Him.

1. Show how Jesus was calm and fearless in the presence of the traitor.
2. How do you account for the act of Judas in betraying Christ?
3. Is it God's fault when a Catholic loses the Faith?
4. What is your opinion of a man or woman who is too proud to do manual labor?
5. Should a person in a high position be willing to be a servant of others?
6. If you did a kind deed to others and they were ungrateful would you continue to be kind?
7. What do you like about St. Peter? St. John the apostle?
8. Find out what work was done by Father Damien, Brother Joseph Dutton, Mother Alfonsa Hawthorne. Read, *A Saint in the Slave Trade,* by Arnold Lunn.
9. What advantage has a person who decides that he will always keep his conscience clean and clear, and likewise his record of dealings with others?
10. A person is quite sure that he has committed no mortal sins, but he has many faults. Should he remain away from Communion?

Chapter 54

THE MASS, COMMUNION, AND THE PRIESTHOOD

MATT. 26: 26. And whilst they were at supper, Jesus took bread, and blessed, and broke: and gave to his disciples, and said: Take ye, and eat: This is my body. 27. And taking the chalice, he gave thanks, and gave to them, saying: Drink ye all of this. 28. For this is my blood of the new testament, which shall be shed for many unto remission of sins.

LUKE 22: 19. And taking bread he gave thanks, and broke; and gave to them, saying: This is my body, which is given for you. Do this for a commemoration of me.

THE Gospels abound in short statements of tremendous significance. The words spoken in the upper room by the God-Man are packed with surprises for us. They deal with mysteries, of course, and as such will always remain beyond complete human understanding. Yet, if we study them in their setting, if we place ourselves in that upper room and from there look back on how God had sought to prepare the world for the coming of Christ, and if we try to look forward from that room to the Cross, then we shall be able to grasp the meaning of our Lord's words as He instituted then and there two of the sacraments. Finally, if we rid ourselves of the modern impression that people go to church merely to say some prayers and to hear a sermon, and if we try, instead, to see that by going to church we offer, we present something to God, then we shall realize that the Mass, which is a sacrifice, is an essential thing in church service and that it is both modern and natural.

a) *Looking backward from that night*. With the exception of the Jews (who had been instructed by God), the nations of antiquity were unable to arrive at a clear notion of the nature of

God. But the pagans of antiquity had a custom which kept them in touch with their gods, and which they regarded as a means of showing publicly their dependence on their gods. This custom was called a sacrifice: a setting aside, a dedicating of some of their possessions to their gods (*sacrum facere*). The word as used by the Jews should be understood as a public offering of some material object to God through a priest to show God what man thought of Him. It was an offering and a transfer of a gift to God.

God took this common custom, stripped it of its superstitions and errors, and through Moses showed the Jews how to offer sacrifice. Gradually the Jewish religion became centered around the idea of sacrifice. Hence the importance of the Jerusalem Temple, the one place where sacrifice could be offered. Hence the respect for, and the power of the priests. Yet, all of that was but a temporary arrangement, adjusted to the type of civilization that the Jews then had. This offering of lambs in sacrifice was a suggestion, a hint of the divine Lamb who was to offer Himself on Good Friday. In fact, there had been a prediction of a perfect, an immaculate sacrifice that was to come (Mal. 1: 10, 11). So, behind the apostles on that night were centuries of tradition of the offering of sacrifices to God. The apostles came from a sacrificially minded people; and now it was gradually dawning on them that Christ was here instituting a new form of sacrifice.

God had taught the Jews that the idea of sacrifice is basic in religion. The sacrifices of the Old Testament were, indeed, crude, and imperfect; and they had often degenerated into mere external forms. In condemning the empty ceremonies of His day, in exposing abuses Christ did not intend to destroy the idea of sacrifice. His own main object in coming to earth was to be the divine Lamb, to offer Himself as a sacrifice to God. So, in that upper room, by the words He uttered He was arranging for the new way to replace the old way. Just as He had perfected the ideas in the moral code, so now He was to perfect the way of offering sacrifice to God. Bloody, material offerings were to cease; a spiritual, and divine offering was to begin and continue till the end of time.

b) *Looking forward from that night.* (Cf. p. 417). Why was Christ on earth? We have seen that He is our Leader and teacher of the truth about God and about the purpose of life, and that He is the source of grace, or divine life for us. Now we are to consider Him as Priest and Victim in a sacrifice. He Himself had said: "The Son of Man is not come to be ministered unto but to minister, and to *give His life* a redemption for many" (Matt. 20: 28). And the apostles now heard Him say: "This is My body which *is given* for you," and "This is My blood of the New Testament, which *shall be shed* for many unto the remission of sins." He was both Priest and Victim in the act. The word *priest* means one who offers sacrifice. Likewise, in every sacrifice there is a victim or object offered. And the words *ransom* and *redemption* mean a buying back. The sin of Adam and all other sins had offended our heavenly Father and closed heaven to men; and hence the human race was under the power of Satan. Christ was on earth to atone to God, to do something that mere man was incapable of doing, namely, to offer to an infinite Being a worthy apology for human insults to that Being. That is why we call Christ a Priest and a Victim, a divine Lamb.

By becoming Man, the Son of God became the head and representative of the entire human race. He came to offer to God the Father the honor, the obedience which men refused. His offering of His life on Good Friday was to give more honor to God than sin had taken from God. Being divine, His every act had infinite value in the sight of the Father. His giving up of His life was, therefore, a sacrifice, a ransom, which atoned for Adam's sin and ours. The scales were more than balanced. He ransomed the human race from the power of Satan. His act was effective for all the past and all the future. God accepted the sacrifice and entered into a new agreement (covenant, testament) with the human race. Christ shed His blood and thus earned for all men a new right to enter God's presence. He was acting as our representative.

Christ was looking ahead as He spoke the words in the cenacle. His one act would not only give infinite honor to God and atone for sin, it would also merit the graces or supernatural life we need. He knew that the merits which He earned would have to be applied to each individual; He deposited, as it were, graces for us in the divine bank, but we must go there ourselves to draw them out. Likewise, He realized that we are in need of some means of keeping in touch with our Father, some way of showing Him what we think of Him, some gift or sacrifice which will be acceptable to Him. Christ knew also that men often forget what has been done for them. So, on that night — and here is the sublime mystery — He arranged for the offering of the next day to be renewed, to be continued in a spiritual way before our eyes. He gave us a means of recalling Calvary and of making our own the Victim which was to go to God on Good Friday. The perfect sacrifice was to be continued, extended in time, not in the same manner that it was offered on Friday, but by a reoffering of the same Victim that was offered on Friday and in the manner that He originated at the last supper — through changing bread and wine into His Body and Blood. Calvary was to be remembered and renewed through the Mass.

There is a union between the words used by Christ in the Upper Room and His death on the Cross. Christ died once and of course does not die again in the Mass. He suffers no more. The sacrifice of the Cross and the sacrifice of the Mass differ in the manner of offering. By giving the apostles and priests power to change bread and wine into His Body and Blood, He arranged on that night that He would be reoffered to God in each Mass and for the same purposes that He was to offer Himself on the Cross. Thus we can make our own the Victim that was offered for us on Good Friday, and what was there earned for us is now applied to us. We can thus keep Calvary and His Passion fresh in our minds. We can honor God as Christ wishes us to honor Him. So, each Mass depends on Calvary and is connected with Calvary.

It is not an offering that we can see or feel with our senses; it is a spiritual offering. The bread and wine were actually changed when He first uttered those words in the Upper Room, yet the change was not visible; so at Mass the change is not visible. We cannot understand completely how it is done; but we can believe the words of the God-Man. And He had promised, a year previous to that night, to give us His Flesh and Blood. Such was the institution of the sacrament of the Holy Eucharist, which is both sacrifice and sacrament — sacrifice because a victim is offered, sacrament because it contains and confers grace, under the appearances of bread and wine. As the Code of Canon Law says: In the Holy Eucharist, "Christ Himself THE LORD is contained, offered and received" (canon 801).

c) *The sacrament of Holy Orders.* The question of how the offering on the Cross was to be renewed throughout the centuries leads us to a consideration of the second sacrament which Christ instituted in the upper room. The words: "Do this for a commemoration of Me," were a command. What were the apostles to *do?* To change bread and wine into His Body and Blood. He thus made the apostles priests; He put divine power in their hands. He told them to do what He had just done. Since the essential function of a priest is to offer sacrifice; and since Christ used the words "is given," and "shall be shed," the apostles understood that the changing of bread and wine was to be sacrifice and sacrament. A new kind of priesthood was thus instituted, a type commissioned to offer a divine gift to God the Father. Through the power given to the priests, Christ comes again on the altar to be reoffered to God. The Mass is Christ going to God for us and with us. Through the priest, Calvary lives on through the ages.

d) *A natural approach to an understanding of the Mass.* Thus far in this chapter we have looked at the Mass and the priesthood in their scriptural setting. Perhaps it will help in understanding the Mass and the idea of sacrifice if we try to see how the principles involved are used by people in their everyday life.

Why do you send letters home, or give gifts to others, or send flowers? What do parents think of children who never write home? If we greet our friends daily is it too much to offer the Mass daily?

God is a spirit; but He is also Person. He has intelligence and free will; He is not a mere force. In Himself, He contains all the qualities or perfections which we call good. He is eternal, all-powerful, and all-knowing. He alone is independent and unlimited. He is everywhere, yet distinct from each created thing or person. Moreover, He is our Father. If we but knew Him as He really is, we should realize that He is lovable, likable, and attractive. Everything that is good in any creature is in Him to an infinite degree.

We naturally praise a good athlete, scientist, business executive, writer, or artist. Is it not natural that we should praise the Creator who has made all these human perfections possible? In fact, we are obligated to praise God for we are dependent creatures and He has been good to us. He creates the soul of each human person; it does not come from parents. That means that our ability to reason and to choose comes from Him. He adopted us at Baptism, raised us to the supernatural plane of living and destined us to a life with Him. Our ability to believe in Christ and the Church comes from God. Finally, God is provider for us. What a marvelous gift it is to be able to see, to hear, and to speak. He gave man the power to invent the radio, and the airplane. He arranged the laws by which the leaf grows, and by which the atom is held together. In a threefold sense, therefore, He is our Father. Our *first* and fundamental duty is to *praise* Him, to give Him the credit for our achievements, to *adore* Him, to love Him.

Sometimes selfishness grips us and we fail to obey God's commands; we neglect to put Him first in life and to serve Him through kindness to our neighbor. Should we not make amends or apologize? Do we not owe Him expiation for the dishonor we bring on Him by sin by neglecting Him or failing to be grateful? Our *second* duty is to beg His pardon, to make *atonement*, or propitiation for our sins.

When we start working for an employer we first ask him what he wants us to do and how he wants it done. For each of us life is a new job. God has given each of us a task of becoming Christlike. Is it not natural that we should ask Him how He desires it to be done? No student, no adult is independent — be he rich or poor, talented or untalented. Only the conceited, the spiritually blind are unwilling to pray, for we need help and directions on how to live, and grace for the supernatural life. Prayer as *petition* is our *third* duty.

People who have imagination, who think deeply and unselfishly are usually grateful for favors given to them. Life itself is a glorious gift. The rose, the sunset, the trees, water, food, the radio, the auto, and electricity are all gifts. The soul, Baptism, health, talent, success, Christ, and the Church were all given to us. To whom should we be grateful? To parents, friends, or teachers? Yes. But God made it all possible. In reality, all things, all creatures and we ourselves belong to Him. Everything in life was loaned to us to see if we would use it for His honor. Our *fourth* duty is gratitude, *thanksgiving.*

Now the point arises: How are we to fulfill this fourfold duty to God? One way is to live a good and unselfish life, and to believe what God has told us. But is that sufficient? In ordinary life people give public honor to their heroes, and to their friends. Parents insist not only that their children obey them in private but that they honor and recognize them in public. Friends demand that we greet them in public. The country requires that we salute the flag openly and publicly. Americans buy trophies and present them to friends or heroes whom they wish to honor or praise. The principle behind all of this is that what is felt in the heart must be expressed outwardly and publicly. There must be outward evidence of the inward feeling. A gift, a "good morning," a letter sent home, is an expression of what is felt inwardly. The gift, the present speaks eloquently for the giver.

Should not the same principle be employed in our actions toward our heavenly Father? To pray at home is good and necessary. To be charitable, just, and kind is an obligation. But should we not also express publicly and outwardly by some gift or present what we feel we owe God? Does not God deserve public tribute? If a gift is used to honor some human person, or to express what we think of that person, why is it not natural to use a gift to show God what we think of Him? But what could we human beings give to God? The answer to that problem comes from our Leader. Christ gave us the Mass, which is an offering, a sacrifice, which we may use to fulfill any one or all of the fourfold duties to our Father. The Mass is a means of paying public and collective honor to God.

In Palestine of that day, and in Europe today bread and wine are widely used as food and drink. They are common elements, available even to the poor. Food is God's gift to man. What is more natural than that Christ would employ these common elements as symbols for a higher purpose. In giving the apostles and priests power to change these elements into His Body and Blood, Christ was showing us how we are to offer sacrifice to our Father, how we may fittingly adore Him, apologize to Him for sin, ask Him for favors and thank Him. In the early days of the Church each Catholic brought some bread and wine with him to church. The material for the sacrifice was thus supplied by each one participating. Later the stipend for the Mass was intended to supply the material for the sacrifice, when the custom of bringing bread and wine ceased. The marvelous, the divine fact of the Mass is this, that the human, the material gift is changed into a divine and spiritual gift of infinite value. Each one at Mass is enabled to present Christ to God in his own name and as a member of the group offering.

The Mass, then, is not a mere form of words. It is an action, a recalling of a past event and a transferring of a divine Victim, a divine Gift to God. We do not go to church primarily to hear a sermon, or to pray privately or even to *hear* Mass. We go to *offer* something to God, to participate in the transfer of a gift which represents the giving of our whole selves to God. Fundamentally we must always keep in mind this idea of *giving*. The gift speaks for the giver's heart. And it is a public and a collective action. It is not the priest alone who offers the Mass; it is priest and people together. Each one present is privileged to participate in that offering, that transfer.

This public honoring, adoring, atoning is called worship of God. It is thus that we fulfill the third Commandment of keeping Sunday holy. No greater honor can be conferred on God than this offering to Him of His own Son. We must learn to use the Mass — use it to fulfill any one or all four of our main duties to our Father. The Mass is Christ going to God with us and for us. He is the invisible Priest and Victim at Mass. He is our Head; He it is who presents our hearts, our wishes, our atonements, our petitions, our thanks to our Father.

In the previous chapter we saw that a meal accompanied the Passover sacrifice. The idea behind the meal was a uniting in a common bond of all those participating, and a union with God. In the Mass, Holy Communion is the sacrificial repast. We have studied the purpose of Holy Communion in Chapter 35. Here it needs to be emphasized that Holy Communion is God's return gift to us after we have offered Him the Mass. It is a pledge that the gift was acceptable. Moreover, there should be an intimate union with their Head of all those baptized in Christ. The

Church is a spiritual organism. Christ is the Head; we are the members. Holy Communion, therefore, is also intended to deepen and strengthen the bond between Christ and the members of His mystical body, the Church. It should also strengthen the union between the members themselves, draw them close to one another.

The Mass is offered to God; Holy Communion is received back from God. We should not ordinarily seek to receive Communion before Mass. It belongs in the Mass. We should *give* to God before seeking to *receive* from God. And we cannot offer our Communions for others. The grace of the sacrament is only for the person receiving it. The additional prayers which are said before or after the reception of Communion may be offered for others; but the grace of the sacrament itself is God's return gift to the individual. Such gifts are personal and cannot be given away. For besides being a bond of union, Communion is the necessary technical preparation for our life with God. It develops and increases our capacity to understand, appreciate, and enjoy the presence of God. This is the same as saying that Communion increases our love of God, especially when we receive in order to show complete trust in Christ.

1. Just what is a sacrifice?
2. Show from the daily actions of people that the idea of sacrifice is not out of date.
3. What is the fundamental idea to keep in mind when participating in the Mass?
4. Explain the reason for each of our fourfold duties to God.
5. What is the purpose of Holy Communion?
6. Why should someone always volunteer to serve the priest at Mass if no server appears?
7. Besides offering in spirit the bread and wine at Mass what else should you offer?
8. How far would you walk in order to be able to participate in the Sunday Mass?
9. How would you explain to a non-Catholic what Catholics do at Mass?
10. Historically speaking, what is the primary function of a priest?
11. Show how the apostles would interpret our Lord's words in the Upper Room.

12. What is wrong with the person who says he prays at home but refuses to go to church?
13. Why should each one have a missal at Mass?
14. Compare the *Our Father* with the Mass in regard to structure and the principles involved.
15. When Chief Justice White was a young man he was invited into the country one Saturday night with a group of non-Catholics. President Cleveland overheard him asking how he could get to Mass on Sunday. Mr. Cleveland had not known him but remarked that a man like that could be relied on to do always the right thing. Later Mr. Cleveland made him a justice of the Supreme Court. Comment.
16. Look up Deut. 16: 16–17 and apply it to what you do at Mass, and then compare it with what girls do when they have a "shower" for one of their girl friends.

Chapter 55

LOVE OF NEIGHBOR FOR CHRIST BRINGS THE GUIDANCE OF THE HOLY GHOST

JOHN 13: 33. Little children, yet a little while I am with you. You shall seek me; and as I said to the Jews: Whither I go you cannot come; so I say to you now. 34. A new commandment I give unto you: that you love one another, as I have loved you, that you also love one another. 35. By this shall all men know that you are my disciples, if you have love one for another.

IT WAS still Thursday evening. Christ now began His farewell discourse, which is recorded by St. John and will be treated here and in the following chapter.

There is a sacredness about the last words of a dying friend or relative. The two and a half years of companionship with the apostles were drawing to a close. This farewell, heart-to-heart talk is significant, because He intended it to apply to us as well as to the apostles (Cf. John 17 : 20). He spoke confidently because He was sure of victory. The glory of other heroes passes; the fame of Jesus increases throughout the centuries. Nineteen centuries after His departure, American young men and women live their lives for Him and treasure His final words of friendship for them.

God is love; and the essence of the Catholic religion is summed up in one word — *love.* The word must be understood in the sense in which Christ used it. Parents naturally love their children; some people naturally like one another. But, since Baptism has made us members of Christ, we take His viewpoint toward people. We see in each person a soul that God loves and an individual that has been invited to happiness in God's presence. We want to draw that person to Christ, to God; and so, whether we feel naturally attracted to the person or not, we are asked, commanded in fact, by Christ to be kind to him or her. We are obligated to aid him or her in any way possible — physically, mentally, socially, spiritually. We take an interest not only in individuals but in groups — in civic or national enterprises that promote the well-being of the whole group.

Our first duty is to love God; but we possess true love of God only when we act in a Christlike manner toward our neighbor. A selfish Catholic is a bar to those who might otherwise reach heaven. If people see that we are honest, just, and pure and that it is personal love of Jesus that makes us such, then they will recognize us as followers of the God-Man. This willingness to be unselfish, to forget revenge, to be impartial, and to be sympathetic toward all classes, all races is based, not on any hope of a reward from them or even on a natural liking for them, but on the fact that Christ died for them and that it is our duty to instruct or lead them by good example to belief in Christ. The manner in which Christ loved the apostles is the model for our deeds of kindness. "The life of Jesus, by its holiness, its charity, its sacrifice was but one perpetual song of praise sent up to the Father" (Le Camus). And any Catholic can do likewise. Such a life motive was new in the world then.

JOHN 13: 36. Simon Peter saith to him: Lord, whither goest thou? Jesus answered: Whither I go, thou canst not follow me now; but thou shalt follow hereafter. 37. Peter saith to him: Why cannot I follow thee now? I will lay down my life for thee. 38. Jesus answered him: Wilt thou lay down thy life for me? Amen, amen, I say to thee, the cock shall not crow, till thou deny me thrice.

MARK 14: 27. And Jesus saith to them: You will all be scandalized in my regard this night; for it is written: I will strike the shepherd, and the sheep shall be dispersed. 28. But after I shall be risen again, I will go before you into Galilee. 29. But Peter saith to him: Although all shall be scandalized in thee, yet not I. 30. And Jesus saith to him: Amen I say to thee, today, even in this night, before the cock crow twice, thou shalt deny me thrice. 31. But he spoke the more vehemently: Although I should die together with thee, I will not deny thee. And in like manner also said they all.

The announcing of the new commandment made no impression on Peter because He had heard Christ mention something about being with them for only a "little while" longer. The prospect of such a separation crushed Peter. His ardent soul wanted to be with Christ always. We love Peter for his loyal heart. But Peter still had much to learn. He was too self-confident, as were the others. They had to learn that, besides will power, something else is necessary if one is to remain a Catholic. Grace, God's help, is essential. More than human courage is required. Most young Catholics desire to remain loyal; but some of them do not realize that it is only through prayer and the sacraments that we gain that strength and prudence necessary to defeat the views and habits which may gradually creep upon us and ultimately lead us to deny Christ. He mentioned His resurrection again in order to encourage them in their momentary failure and discouragement at His death. His reference to the cock was occasioned by the belief that roosters crowed at midnight and just before dawn.

LUKE 22: 31. And the Lord said: Simon, Simon, behold Satan hath desire to have you, that he may sift you as wheat: 32. But I have prayed for thee, that thy faith fail not: and thou, being once converted, confirm thy brethren.

The world of spirits, invisible to us, was ever open to the mind of Christ. The devil seems personally to concentrate on those especially close to God — the saints. Because Peter was important, he was to be subjected to a terrible attack from the devil. If Satan could have conquered the first pope, what a victory that would have been for the powers of evil! And not only Peter but the entire eleven were to feel the fangs of Satan. For, in the original Greek, the first "you" (after "to have") is in the plural. Peter and the others were to be miserable failures on that night. They needed to learn the difference between self-confidence and trust in God. Peter's fall would show him the necessity of grace, for, and this is important, Christ Himself prayed for Peter ("thee" is singular); and Peter would thus become a source of strength for the others.

The stability of Peter and the papacy strengthens all the Church. Some popes have failed in moral qualities; but no pope has ever spread false doctrines or failed in faith. Peter and the Church have preserved for us Christ's truths. They can teach us infallibly because Christ prayed for Peter and promised to send the Holy Ghost to guide the Church lest she teach us error. Yes, Christ wanted the primacy and the infallibility of the pope; Christ Himself arranged for one man to be the visible head of the Church. When we learn what a difficult thing it is to keep the truth, and to prevent it from being twisted, we come to admire the papacy that has continued to be strong while nations fell and bitter heresies rose and faded and Satan's agents spread their hate.

> JOHN 14: 1. Let not your heart be troubled. You believe in God, believe also in me. 2. In my Father's house there are many mansions. If not, I would have told you: because I go to prepare a place for you. 3. And if I shall go, and prepare a place for you, I will come again, and will take you to myself; that where I am, you also may be.

On the morrow the mob would be shouting at a crucified Victim, apparently defeated. All of that was clear to Christ. Yet, we find Him here calmly instilling peace of mind. The first thing that God wants from us is depth of faith. We believe implicitly whatever Christ has told us because He is divine. Gradually love of Him comes, after we have shown faith in Him. Trials, and discouragements should only deepen this faith.

Silence, tenseness hung over the eleven human beings as they listened to the God-Man tell them that the soul of man is immortal. There are various arguments for immortality, but for the average person these words of Jesus: "I go to prepare a place for you," are proof sufficient that man is much more than an animal, and that there is a purpose in living. Heaven is a place, yet more essentially it is the presence of God, which is known as the Beatific Vision. There is activity in heaven. Continual delight in contemplating and praising the qualities of God will be our reward. What a thought it is, then, to ponder on that statement of Christ: "I will take you to Myself, that where I am you also may be." It was thrilling to be with Christ when He was visibly on earth. And if we take delight in listening to people of high intelligence or rejoice when in the presence of someone we love, then who can measure the thrill of being in the presence of divine intelligence and divine love. That thought lends zest and purpose to life — preparing to be with Christ. When people lose religion they see no purpose in life. That is why so many young people are restless, why they speak of the futility of life. They are ignorant of the shining hope that Christ puts into the lives of the young.

At the end of the world Christ will come again, visibly, for the general judgment, when His victory will be complete, when we shall all see the wisdom of God's plan. But even before that time, Christ will welcome us personally at death, if we show true love of neighbor while waiting to be taken to Him.

> JOHN 14: 4. And whither I go you know, and the way you know.
> 5. Thomas saith to him: Lord, we know not whither thou goest;
> and how can we know the way? 6. Jesus saith to him: I am the
> way, and the truth, and the life. No man cometh to the Father,
> but by me. 7. If you had known me, you would without doubt
> have known my Father also: and from henceforth you shall know
> him, and you have seen him. 8. Philip saith to him: Lord, shew
> us the Father, and it is enough for us. 9. Jesus saith to him:
> Have I been so long a time with you; and have you not known
> me? Philip, he that seeth me seeth the Father also. How sayest
> thou: Shew us the Father? 10. Do you not believe that I am
> in the Father, and the Father in me? The words that I speak to
> you, I speak not of myself. But the Father who abideth in me,
> he doth the works. 11. Believe you not that I am in the Father,
> and the Father in me? 12. Otherwise believe for the very works'
> sake. Amen, amen I say to you, he that believeth in me, the works
> that I do, he also shall do; and greater than these shall he do.
> 13. Because I go to the Father: and whatsoever you shall ask
> the Father in my name, that will I do: that the Father may be
> glorified in the Son. 14. If you shall ask me anything in my
> name, that I will do.

Thomas felt abandoned; he had been deeply attached to Jesus. It did not occur to him that Christ had come to redeem us and to show us how to live, and that He had soon to return to God to be glorified by the Father. Christ is the "way" in that He is the mediator between God and man. He is the way because He opened up the path to God. Since He came from God and is divine, He is the truth; that is, He told us the truth about

God and ourselves. Because He is divine He possesses divine life, which He communicates to us (grace). When we learn all we can about Christ, we then know what God is like, because the Father and the Son are one. Whoever is anxious to know what God is like has simply to look at Christ. No person who rejects the divinity of Christ can ever tell us how to live. Only through Christ can we learn correct religious truth; only through Him can we reach heaven. That is why the prayers of the Church end with the phrase: *per Dominum nostrum Jesum Christum,* "through our Lord Jesus Christ."

In our day we are accustomed to think of three equal Persons in one God. It is a mystery, but our faith in the word of Christ makes it easy to believe that the Father is in the Son and the Son in the Father, and that to see the Son is to see the Father. In the day of Philip the mystery seemed strange; it was new. And the minds of the apostles were slow to grasp the full meaning of what Christ said.

In His divine nature Christ is equal to the Father. As Man, Christ is head of the human race and intercedes for us with the Father. And since this Person, Christ, is also divine, there is an infinite value to His intercession. So, we should praise, plead, atone, and thank in His name — *per Dominum nostrum.* We should do this especially at Mass, when the divine Victim goes to God the Father in our name. Our Lord wishes us to ask through His merits.

> JOHN 14: 15. If you love me, keep my commandments. 16. And I will ask the Father, and he shall give you another Paraclete, that he may abide with you forever, 17. The Spirit of truth, whom the world cannot receive, because it seeth him not, nor knoweth him: but you shall know him; because he shall abide with you, and shall be in you. 18. I will not leave you orphans, I will come to you.

The commands of Christ were to love God and to love our neighbor. We have, indeed, duties to self, but to counterbalance the natural selfishness in us Christ laid this emphasis on unselfishness. The more we curb selfishness, the better Catholics we shall be. And whoever is unselfish from a supernatural motive will receive the special guidance of the Holy Ghost. We see here that the Holy Ghost is a distinct Person in the Trinity. The visible presence of Christ was from now on to be replaced by the invisible guidance of the third Person of the Trinity. The apostles thought they were to be left alone. No. From now on Christ was to act on the Church and on individuals through the Holy Ghost.

We should pay more attention to devotion to the Holy Ghost because He is God and because He is our Comforter; that is, He supplies for the strengthening effect of Christ's visible presence. Christ was not to desert the apostles or us. He was to ascend to heaven in order that He might send the Holy Ghost to keep us in the truth. Christ brought divine truth to earth. The guidance of the Spirit of Truth keeps that truth intact in the Church. This guidance is invisible but it is real. Ordinarily we say that a certain person has kept the Faith. Actually that means that the unseen hand of God has protected the individual. Whenever any Catholic tries to work for Christ, the Holy Ghost acts invisibly on that Catholic, guiding him, protecting him. Marshal Foch recited the prayer to the Holy Ghost daily.

> JOHN 14: 22. Judas saith to him, not the Iscariot: Lord, how is it that thou wilt manifest thyself to us, and not to the world? 23. Jesus answered, and said to him: If any one love me, he will keep my word, and my Father will love him, and we will come to him, and will make our abode with him. 24. He that loveth me not, keepeth not my words. And the word which you have heard, is not mine; but the Father's who sent me.

We are grateful for all these questions asked by the apostles because we thereby learn how God acts toward us. The secret views and efforts of an individual determine the amount of interior grace that he receives. Some people never "see" anything in religion, in Christ, or in the Church because in some manner they have blocked the grace which enables them to believe and to love. Hence Christ never fully manifests Himself to them or sends the Holy Ghost to them. But to those who are well-disposed, who co-operate with grace, there comes not only the Holy Ghost, but all three Persons of the Trinity. Whenever the Holy Ghost comes to us, then it may be said that God makes His abode in us. Where one Person, is, there are the others.

When sanctifying grace is in us, we are then the Temple of the Holy Ghost. What a privilege that is! The Trinity is, however, never separated. It is actually true that the Trinity indwells in us, although we commonly say that the grace which we receive comes from the Holy Ghost, because whatever is concerned with holiness or sanctification is attributed to this third Person of the Trinity, who is the Holiness of God.

> JOHN 14: 25. These things have I spoken to you, abiding with you. 26. But the Paraclete, the Holy Ghost, whom the Father will send in my name, he will teach you all things, and bring all things to your mind, whatsoever I shall have said to you. 27. Peace I leave with you, my peace I give unto you: not as the world giveth, do I give unto you. Let not your heart be troubled, nor let it be afraid. 28. You have heard that I said to you: I go away, and I come unto you. If you loved me, you would indeed be glad, because I go to the Father: for the Father is greater than I. 29. And now I have told you before it come to pass: that when it shall come to pass, you may believe. 30. I will not now speak many things with you. For the prince of this world cometh, and in me he hath not anything. 31. But that the world may know, that I love the Father: and as the Father hath given me commandment, so do I. Arise, let us go hence.

Since the young, and, in fact, all men, need the truth which Christ revealed and the grace which He earned, we would naturally expect that Christ would provide some means for protecting that truth so that people of today might be sure that they have the real thing. Thousands have set themselves up as interpreters of Christ. Since they contradict one another they cannot have the whole truth. Likewise, many individuals have thought that the Holy Ghost was guiding them when they founded new religions. But the Holy Ghost cannot contradict Himself. A close study of the Catholic religion should convince an honest inquirer that there is an unseen Hand guiding the Church. It is the influence of the Holy Ghost. And, moreover, Christ sent the Holy Ghost as a pledge, a proof that this grace, this divine life is in the Church, ready to be distributed to her members. Pentecost, then, was the completion of the life of Christ and the beginning of the guidance of the Holy Ghost in the Church and in her members.

The true Catholic feels fundamentally happy and contented in his religion, because friendship with Christ means peace and inner joy. Trial and sorrow may come, but they do not remove that interior calmness which Christ imparts to His friends. The human nature in Christ is alone not equal to the Father, but God the Father has glorified the humanity of Christ because Christ sought always to please His Father.

Christ now led the apostles forth from the Upper Room. He started along the path of sorrow and pain. A terrible attack from Satan was also awaiting Him. But the end of that awful journey was not defeat, but triumph, victory, and eternal glory.

1. How do we know that God will reward and honor those who remain loyal to Jesus?
2. Is the love we have toward our neighbor a matter of feeling or sentiment?
3. A successful doctor refuses to take money from the poor. Has he love of God?
4. A boy says that he will never lose the Faith. His resolution is good, provided he ———.
5. Why does God permit us to be tempted?
6. What is meant by immortality and why do we believe in it?
7. When does God abide in us?
8. What relation has the Holy Ghost to your own individual life? to the Church?
9. A man says that God is cruel, or indifferent to human suffering. Answer him.
10. What is wrong with those who say that life has no purpose?
11. What is the proof that one is a true friend of Christ?
12. A person naturally shares his knowledge and joy with others. Does this help us to understand the inner life of the Trinity, where there is eternal communication of knowledge from the Father to the Son and of love from both to the Holy Ghost?

Chapter 56

IN UNION WITH THE VINE THERE IS STRENGTH

JOHN 15: 1. I am the true vine; and my Father is the husbandman. 2. Every branch in me that beareth not fruit, he will take
away: and every one that beareth fruit, he will purge it, that it
may bring forth more fruit. 3. Now you are clean by reason
of the word which I have spoken to you. 4. Abide in me, and
I in you. As the branch cannot bear fruit of itself, unless it
abide in the vine, so neither can you, unless you abide in me.
5. I am the vine; you the branches: he that abideth in me, and
I in him, the same beareth much fruit: for without me you can
do nothing. 6. If any one abide not in me, he shall be cast
forth as a branch, and shall wither, and they shall gather him
up, and cast him into the fire, and he burneth. 7. If you abide
in me, and my words abide in you, you shall ask whatever you
will, and it shall be done unto you. 8. In this is my Father
glorified; that you bring forth very much fruit, and become my
disciples. 9. As the Father hath loved me, I also have loved
you. Abide in my love. 10. If you keep my commandments,
you shall abide in my love; as I also have kept my Father's
commandments, and do abide in his love.

IT IS possible that they were still in the Cenacle or else outside the southern wall or crossing the brook Cedron that lies between the eastern wall and Mt. Olivet. They were going eastward to Gethsemani, a garden that stretched up the slope of Olivet. There must have been grapevines along the way. Jesus seized the occasion to teach us that, by remaining close to Him, a hidden force, called grace, comes to us. The need of grace is clear only to those who realize that God intends that we should lead a supernatural life on earth. Just as food is necessary to the body, so grace is necessary to retain the supernatural life in us. They who are baptized in Christ are joined to Him, engrafted onto a divine vine. There is more than an external union between Catholics themselves and their invisible Head, Christ. The Church is called an organism, with one principle circulating through it and keeping it alive. By the action of grace, Christ truly lives in those joined to Him. When on earth, Christ acted through His human body; now He acts through His mystical body, the Church.

The husbandman (God) plants a vine and hopes for fruit from the branches (ourselves). Prayerful lives, honesty in all dealings, kindness to friend and foe are the results expected from this union with Jesus. And just as a husbandman prunes his trees, cutting off useless, dead branches, so God may send trials to honest people just to draw them closer to Him; or He may withdraw grace from those Catholics who make no effort to remain united to Jesus. Judas was externally with Jesus; but he lacked union of mind and heart. Hence, being Catholic in name does not prove that we are interiorly united with Jesus. Our speech, our views should show that we have reflected long and lovingly on the sentences of the Gospels.

Natural goodness is good. However, it is not sufficient. The divine life which we, the branches, receive from Christ, prepares us for the presence of God. Sin of any serious nature breaks this union. Then we wither spiritually; and, although we might be a success in the world, that interior, divine sap is lacking. And where it is lacking there is no admission to heaven. So, people who profess no religion need to ponder these statements. Christ alone knows the equipment that will prepare us for life in the next world.

> JOHN 15: 11. These things I have spoken to you, that my joy may be in you, and your joy may be filled. 12. This is my commandment, that you love one another, as I have loved you. 13. Greater love than this no man hath, that a man lay down his life for his friends. 14. You are my friends, if you do the things that I command you. 15. I will not now call you servants: for the servant knoweth not what his lord doth. But I have called you friends: because all things whatsoever I have heard of my Father, I have made known to you. 16. You have not chosen me: but I have chosen you, and have appointed you, that you should go, and should bring forth fruit, and your fruit

should remain, that whatsoever you shall ask of the Father in my name, he may give it you.

Neither the Pharisees nor Judas could have had true joy in their hearts on that night. What a contrast to hear the God-Man speak of "My joy." Sorrow for sin would soon afflict Him. But sorrow or despair is never the final word in the life of one who is close to Jesus. There is a contentment, a peace about a truly Catholic life which the world cannot understand. It is an inner grace that Jesus gives to His friends.

It is a thrilling and a human thought to hear Him say: "You are My friends." To know that someone loves us, believes in us, trusts us and expects good of us is bracing and strengthening. But what human friend ever would go to the length that Jesus went to prove His love for us? He laid down His life for us. He chose us to be Catholics. He picked us up and adopted us; made something out of us. Hence He has a right to expect fruit of us, namely that we so live as to be an honor to God. He has made known to us truths of which many Americans know nothing. In gratitude, we try to be a credit to Him. "In following the will of another we model our life on his life, we take as our rule the very thought that governs him; in a word we unite our soul with his soul, and consequently prove to him, in a most eloquent way, our whole affection" (Le Camus).

John 15: 18. If the world hate you, know ye, that it hath hated
me before you. 19. If you had been of the world, the world
would love its own: but because you are not of the world, but I
have chosen you out of the world, therefore the world hateth
you. 20. Remember my word that I said to you: The servant
is not greater than his master. If they have persecuted me, they
will also persecute you; if they have kept my word, they will
keep yours also. 21. But all these things they will do to you
for my name's sake: because they know not him that sent me.
22. If I had not come, and spoken to them, they would not have
sin; but now they have no excuse for their sin. 23. He that
hateth me, hateth my Father also. 24. If I had not done
among them the works that no other man hath done, they would
not have sin; but now they have both seen and hated both me
and my Father. 25. But that the word may be fulfilled which
is written in their law: They hated me without cause. 26. But
when the Paraclete cometh, whom I will send you from the Father,

the Spirit of truth, who proceedeth from the Father, he shall give testimony of me: 27. And you shall give testimony, because you are with me from the beginning.

The fact is obvious that there was hatred of Christ then, and there is hatred of the Church today. Communism claims that religion takes men's minds away from the task of making a heaven here on earth. Often the talk against the Church, against allegiance to a foreigner (the pope), is just a smoke screen thrown out to cover up the effort of some groups to control the conscience and the soul of the people. Be clever enough to expose the real motive behind such arguments. Even people who have no religion see the danger of permitting the State to be a nurse, a doctor, a priest, and even a god. These people may be won by your fearless living as witnesses for Christ. They who are seeking to make a religion out of loyalty to the State are in reality trying to make men live like animals. There is no excuse for saying that we do not know whether or not there is a soul, or a life after the grave. The miracles, the doctrines, and the character of Christ settled all those questions for such people as really wish to know the truth.

JOHN 16: 5. But I told you not these things from the beginning, because I was with you. And now I go to him that sent me, and none of you asketh me: Whither goest thou? 6. But because I have spoken these things to you, sorrow hath filled your heart. 7. But I tell you the truth: it is expedient to you that I go: for if I go not, the Paraclete will not come to you; but if I go, I will send him to you. 8. And when he is come, he will convince the world of sin, and of justice, and of judgment. 9. Of sin: because they believed not in me. 10. And of justice: because I go to the Father; and you shall see me no longer. 11. And of judgment: because the prince of this world is already judged. 12. I have yet many things to say to you: but you cannot bear them now. 13. But when he, the Spirit of truth, is come, he will teach you all truth. For he shall not speak of himself; but what things soever he shall hear, he shall speak; and the things that are to come, he shall shew you.

By repetition our Lord was showing that the strength of His visible presence among the apostles was to be replaced by the invisible guidance of the Holy Ghost in the Church, and in Christ's friends. His death on the cross was to merit this protecting hand of the third Person of the Trinity. Just as Christ could not be deceived, so this unseen Spirit of Truth prevents the Catholic Church from teaching error. That is why we believe that the pope and the body of bishops assembled under the pope are infallible. Under the influence of the Holy Ghost the Church sees more clearly now the meaning of truths taught by Christ. There is a development in Catholic doctrines; but neither the pope nor the bishops teach new doctrines. The remarkable change that took place in the apostles on Pentecost was due to this coming of the Spirit in fulfillment of the promise of Christ. The strength that the Church shows in clinging to the truths taught by Christ, while the sects of Christianity yield to the pressure of those who say: "modernize your doctrines," is evidence that the Holy Ghost has guided the Church to the "whole truth."

Unbelief is a sin because Jesus was just; and moderns will be judged if they refuse to consider the claims of the Church to have God as her founder and guide. The guidance of the Holy Ghost is the same as the strength of Christ circulating through His members. It is all the work of God; but just as we attribute redemption to the Son, so we attribute the distribution of graces earned by the Son to the Holy Ghost. Ask daily for this guidance of the Holy Ghost in detecting the errors in what you read, in what you hear, and in what surrounds you. It is an entrancing story to read how the Holy Ghost has kept the truth intact in the Church for nineteen centuries. A merely human organization could not do this, for the pressure to modernize and to change is strong in each generation. The divine needs no modernization because it is always good news, always new, ever true.

> John 16: 22. So also you now indeed have sorrow; but I will see you again, and your heart shall rejoice; and your joy no man shall take from you. . . . 24. Hitherto you have not asked anything in my name. Ask, and you shall receive; that your joy may be full. . . . 27. For the Father himself loveth you, because you have loved me, and have believed that I came out from God. 28. I came forth from the Father, and am come into the world: again I leave the world, and I go to the Father. 29. His disciples say to him: Behold, now thou speakest plainly, and speakest no proverb. 30. Now we know that thou knowest all things and thou needest not that any man should ask thee. By

this we believe that thou camest forth from God. 31. Jesus
answered them: Do you now believe? 32. Behold, the hour
cometh, and it is now come, that you shall be scattered every
man to his own, and shall leave me alone; and yet I am not alone,
because the Father is with me. 33. These things I have spoken
to you, that in me you may have peace. In the world you shall
have distress: but have confidence I have overcome the world.

Many rejoice when they see the Church being persecuted. Sometimes this punishment is due to our own failures to lead Christlike lives. But aside from this failure, the devil often seems to win. The Church is always apparently defeated; yet she is always living and strong. This has been going on for nineteen centuries, a long time. The strength of Christ enables those in sorrow to persevere. On the other hand, despair is seen in those lives that have not relied on the strong Christ. In Catholic life Jesus turns pain accepted for Him into joy — joy that remains, that is higher and better than any pleasure of the senses. We have the clear statement of Christ that the loyalty of any young person to Him pleases God. Keep that thought always in mind in bearing the burdens of Catholic life. Many there are who become sour and disillusioned. Not so the friend of Jesus, for our Leader came from God; and just as He overcame temptation, sorrow, and the horrors of the Passion, so if we remain united to Him we shall overcome the trials, and disappointments of life.

* *

The "fruit" which God expects from a Catholic is ——. What relation has the Holy Ghost to us? What is admirable in Catholics who have kept the Faith through long years of sorrow? If we did not practice honesty and purity would churchgoing save us? How would you go about the task of developing friendship with Jesus? How would you explain to a lonesome and discouraged individual the idea behind Christ's reference to the vine?

* *

John 17: 1. These things Jesus spoke, and lifting up his eyes
to heaven, he said: Father, the hour is come, glorify thy Son,
that thy Son may glorify thee. 2. As thou hast given him power
over all flesh, that he may give eternal life to all whom thou hast
given him. 3. Now this is eternal life: That they may know
thee, the only true God, and Jesus Christ, whom thou hast sent.
4. I have glorified thee on the earth; I have finished the work

> which thou gavest me to do: 5. And now glorify thou me, O Father, with thyself, with the glory which I had, before the world was, with thee. 6. I have manifested thy name to the men whom thou hast given me out of the world. Thine they were, and to me thou gavest them: and they have kept thy word. 7. Now they have known that all things which thou hast given me, are from thee.

This seventeenth chapter of St. John is called Christ's prayer for Himself (1–5), for the apostles (6–19), for the Church (20–26). It is prayer; yet it is also a conversation with His Father. What a soul-stirring evening this had been since they had entered the upper room; and now, under the starry dome of the night the eleven were silent as this unique Person of history prayed as Man and yet acted as God. As God He could make His prayer effective.

Sufficient grace is given to all to believe (1 Tim. 2: 4), but all do not accept. Thus our faith in what Christ said gives us precious and priceless knowledge. Faith in this case *is* knowledge of the highest value.

Redemption through suffering on the cross was the work the Father had given Christ to do. It was not an easy task. His perseverance teaches us to accomplish the work which God gave us to do: to study, to play, and to work in such a way as to bring honor on our Father. As God, Christ was eternal, had no beginning; but as Man, He lived in Palestine a life of such beauty, power, unselfishness, and steady calmness that He earned for His Humanity immortal glory. His death would be His eternal glorification. That which would be apparently defeat would in reality be victory over death, over Satan, over the world. And it would all glorify the Father.

> John 17: 9. I pray for them: I pray not for the world, but for them whom thou has given me: because they are thine, 10. And all my things are thine and thine are mine, and I am glorified in them. 11. And now I am not in the world, and these are in the world, and I come to thee. Holy Father, keep them in thy name whom thou hast given me; that they may be one, as we also are. 12. While I was with them, I kept them in thy name. Those whom thou gavest me have I kept; and none of them is lost, but the son of perdition, that the scripture may be fulfilled. 13. And now I come to thee; and these things I speak in the world, that

they may have my joy filled in themselves. 14. I have given them thy word, and the world hath hated them, because they are not of the world; as I also am not of the world. 15. I pray not that thou shouldst take them out of the world, but that thou shouldst keep them from evil. 16. They are not of the world, as I also am not of the world. 17. Sanctify them in truth. Thy word is truth. 18. As thou hast sent me into the world, I also have sent them into the world. 19. And for them do I sanctify myself, that they also may be sanctified in truth.

This had been a beautiful friendship between the God-Man and the fishermen whom God had drawn toward His Son. How constant, thoughtful, and patient He had been with them. And now He was praying that they would continue to be faithful in making God's love for men known to the world. Christ submitted His life to the guidance of the Holy Spirit of truth; and He wished the apostles to do the same. He wants priests to sanctify themselves for the sake of their parishioners, parents for the sake of their children, students for the sake of unbelievers who will be led to Christ by good example. It would seem from the words used by our Lord that Judas is lost. He had not given his heart to Christ.

JOHN 17: 20. And not for them only do I pray, but for them also who through their word shall believe in me; 21. That they all may be one, as thou, Father, in me, and I in thee; that they also may be one in us; that the world may believe that thou hast sent me. 22. And the glory which thou hast given me, I have given to them; that they may be one, as we also are one: 23. I in them, and thou in me; that they may be made perfect in one: and the world may know that thou hast sent me, and hast loved them, as thou hast also loved me. 24. Father, I will that where I am, they also whom thou hast given me may be with me; that they may see my glory which thou hast given me, because thou hast loved me before the creation of the world. 25. Just Father, the world hath not known thee; but I have known thee; and these have known that thou hast sent me. 26. And I have made known thy name to them, and will make it known; that the love wherewith thou hast loved me, may be in them, and I in them.

The third part of Christ's prayer was for us. Notice what He desires of us — unity. The harmony in the Trinity is the model for the spirit of friendliness and helpfulness that should exist among us. Since we have been made "partakers of the divine nature" (2 Pet. 1: 4), the world should be forced to admit a more than natural bond among Catholics. Clergy, religious, and laity are all one in Christ.

To be with Jesus forever! Such is the reward granted to faithful friends of Christ. Fascinating, delightful companions may journey with us along the paths of life; tempting, alluring schemes may unfold before us; or black, sour discouragement may seek to eat into our very souls. But whatever be our future, we know that this strong Son of God has prayed for us, the twentieth-century spiritual descendants of those first eleven friends of the Master. His strength awaits us in the Church, in the sacraments, and in meditation on His words. From Christ we have learned what God is like. The Communist and others think that there is no God because they were taught the wrong idea about God. A man's entire outlook on life changes once he knows the truth about God. Not the Communist, not the atheist, not the capitalist, not the self-styled clever professor or columnist can tell us the real truth about our just Father. Only Christ can do that. Do we prize the legacy that has been transmitted to us from the apostles?

The discourse was over, but it was never forgotten by the eleven. Heaven itself now became tense with interest. In the city Judas was getting ready. The devil was waiting to begin his final assaults.

1. Will money, or fame, or even honesty and generosity by themselves get us into heaven?
2. What verse has most appeal for you in Christ's last discourse of Thursday night?
3. How do you know that Christ is interested in each one individually?
4. What is the aim of Catholic education?
5. Did Christ have joy or sadness in His heart most of the time?
6. Is a grouchy person a true Catholic?
7. Why should a young Catholic couple sanctify themselves for the sake of their children?
8. What harm is done by a Catholic who sows dissension among others?
9. Show that Christ has prayed for present-day Catholics.

Chapter 57

IS SIN A SMALL MATTER?

MATT. 26: 36. Then Jesus came with them into a country place which is called Gethsemani; and he said to his disciples: Sit you here, till I go yonder and pray. 37. And taking with him Peter and the two sons of Zebedee, he began to grow sorrowful and to be sad.
MARK 14: 33. And he taketh Peter and James and John with him; and he began to fear and to be heavy.
MATT. 26: 38. Then he saith to them: My soul is sorrowful even unto death: stay you here, and watch with me. 39. And going a little further, he fell upon his face, praying, and saying: My Father, if it be possible, let this chalice pass from me. Nevertheless not as I will, but as thou wilt.

GETHSEMANI was not far up the slope of Olivet. It was an enclosed garden, filled with short, stubby olive trees. Out here, east of the city, the moon silhouetted those silently moving figures against the hillside. It may have been about nine o'clock. The three who had witnessed the glory of the Transfiguration were now to see Him in His agony. The Passion (from the Latin, *patior*, to suffer) generally means all the sufferings, physical and mental, which Christ endured from the beginning of the Last Supper to His death on the cross. Here we consider only the agony in the garden, which was pressing this strong Son of God down to the ground. Hitherto we have seen only strength, courage, and poise in this Man whose masterliness has stood out in every crisis of His life. Suddenly a change came over Him. Fear attacked Him; a loathing filled His soul; sorrow gnawed at Him.

Why? A small word, but a terrible word supplies the answer — sin. It is sometimes hard for us to feel any horror at sin.

The world thinks lightly of it. But the world will not try to understand it. Unbelievers try to tell us that morality, that is, a standard of right and wrong, is either something built up to scare people into being good, or that it is a standard set up by the leaders of society, and which can be changed when people decide to change it. In other words, there is no universal, divinely revealed code of right and wrong. It is, of course, often useless to argue with such people because they do not wish to submit to God. They run away from facts.

The facts are these. Having designed human nature, God alone can decide on what is basically good or bad for human nature. Certain customs are, indeed, man-made. They may be changed; but we refer here to fundamental principles. God has laid down revealed rules of right and wrong. He has a right to decide because He made men for His presence. Ultimate happiness for man is to be found only in the presence of God; and happiness here and now is had only through obedience to these basic, moral principles. Some think that if one does not get caught, that if one can "get away" with a breaking of the Commandments, no harm is done. But God sees the act. He sees the refusal to follow His directions on how to prepare for eternity. And when we wish to discuss sin we do not listen to a professor, to opinions expressed at a bridge party, or to conclusions argued at a meeting of social experts. Only by listening to God's representatives, only by going to the Bible, which is God's revealed word, only by meditating on the Passion can we learn what sin is. All theorizing about changing the moral code, all slurs that sin is an outworn, out-of-date hang-over from the days when men lived in fear, all arguments that hell is unreasonable crumble and die of pride before this terrible historical fact that Christ, the strong Christ, felt fear in the face of the task that He had undertaken in atoning for men's insults to God.

God is holiness and perfection. Nothing tainted can exist in His presence. To reach Him we must acquire holiness. Sin is the opposite of holiness. It is the refusal to obey the rules which God has established for holiness. Sin is the greatest evil in the world because it makes the sinner unfit for the presence of God. It is siding with the devil against God. It is an insult to a loving Father.

It was precisely to render the deserved justice and obedience to God that Christ came to earth. Being divine, His every act gave more honor to God than sin removes from God. We cannot entirely atone for our own sins because the Person whom we dishonor by sin is infinitely greater than we are. We can do great harm because we have free will, because God trusted us. But our little atonements do not pay much tribute to the majesty of the Creator. Only God can fittingly honor God. Therefore, God became Man, in order that, acting as Man, in the place of man, He might render due atonement to God for the sins of men. For no human person could enter heaven until the sins of Adam and of all men were atoned for. That sin is a reality, a horrible and devastating reality, is the only conclusion possible from a consideration of the Passion.

Let us observe Christ in His two or three hours of agony. His petition to "let this chalice pass from Me" gives the impression that to all appearances it was as if the divine nature were not in Him and He were a mere man. We cannot understand how the divine in Him would seem to let the human struggle alone, for the two natures in Christ were inseparably united (the hypostatic union). This Person was God; but He had also a human will, and the human will in Him was tempted not to accept this horrible burden of taking all the guilt of the guilty. We know how hard it often is to keep a good resolution; we look for excuses; we delay. Christ was sad, seemingly afraid, and spoke with the voice of a broken man because He had more to bear than we could bear.

We must try to realize that:

a) By nature Christ had full knowledge of the effects of sin; by nature He was holy; sin was repugnant to Him. He could feel keenly pain, insult, and blasphemy. The real horror of sin was perfectly clear to Him. This clear perception which He possessed made His suffering all the more intense. We know how some people with delicate consciences feel keenly an insult, or shudder at evil. We do not always shudder at sin because our consciences are hardened, blunted. But the all-holy Christ was infinitely delicate of conscience.

b) Christ had a torturing foreknowledge of the flight of the apostles, of the scourging, of His hanging on the cross and of our own ingratitude. Such scenes cut Him to the quick. All the future lay bare before Him. He knew that much of His suffering would be in vain. We often say to ourselves: What is the use of being honest and pure, of standing up for a principle when others are sinning and breaking principles?

c) He consented to take upon Himself a sense of guilt for sin. We know something of the feeling of disgust with ourselves after we have done a wrong thing, or hurt a dear friend. He experienced this sense of guilt not for one sin only but for all the horrible crimes that have been committed in the world. Our uneasy consciences are as nothing compared to the pangs of regret that He felt. "In His astonished soul thundered, as it were, the voices of impiety and blasphemy, the abominable outcries of humanity so long in rebellion, and now suddenly taking refuge in Him to make Him responsible for its scandalous excesses — a thick atmosphere of evil surrounded Him, was overwhelming Him" (Le Camus). Voluntarily He had accepted this load of guilt.

d) The devil was there, insinuating that it was no use thus to suffer, that His efforts would not be appreciated, that they would, in fact, be futile. The foul fiend threw every deception possible against the imagination of the innocent Christ.

e) Since He was human and strong and healthy, the will to live that is in all healthy men was also in Christ. Little wonder that the human nature in Him revolted at the prospect of a horrible death on the cross with all its physical pains.

Is sin a small matter, an outworn idea? Would Christ, who loves us, who even longed for some consoling help from the three, have undertaken the task of atoning, had not He known the need of atonement? He has taught us that not only is sin wrong, but that satisfaction has to be made to God for every sin. Our sins were before Him on that night; and He decided to atone for them so that we might gain heaven.

Christ did not ask absolutely to be relieved of this suffering. His prayer was that He might be spared if sparing was consistent with the purposes of God. Recall the second part of the prayer: "Not as I will, but as Thou wilt." There is true heroism;

there is the rule for us to follow in our sufferings. The test of loyalty is in a period of doubt and of discouragement. It is easy to be a Catholic on Easter; it takes some heroism to pass through a real Lent.

* *

The Passion of Christ means ———. The purpose of Passion Sunday is ———. Sin is loathsome in God's sight because ———. Give five reasons why Christ was so dismayed in the Passion. Why would a merely human code of morals fail to exact obedience from the people? What is the real reason why moderns want to change the Commandments?

* *

LUKE 22: 43. And there appeared to him an angel from heaven, strengthening him. And being in an agony, he prayed the longer. 44. And his sweat became as drops of blood, trickling down upon the ground.

As in the desert, at the beginning of His public career, heaven was watching His choice, so now heaven sent its messenger, since human aid from the apostles was nil. And in the supreme test He did not forget to pray, thus showing us what to do when sorely tempted. Some men take to drink when discouraged. Remember, rather, what Christ did. He clung to His resolution. He was tempted: but the point is that He did not yield. The effort that this struggle cost Him is seen in those drops that oozed through the pores of His skin. Cases of sweating blood have been recorded in history. It is Luke the physician who tells us of this case.

MATT. 26: 40. And he cometh to his disciples, and findeth them asleep, and he saith to Peter: What? Could ye not watch one hour with me? 41. Watch ye, and pray that ye enter not into temptation. The spirit indeed is willing, but the flesh is weak. 42. Again the second time, he went and prayed, saying: My Father, if this chalice may not pass away, but I must drink it, thy will be done. 43. And he cometh again, and findeth them sleeping: for their eyes were heavy. 44. And leaving them, he went again: and he prayed the third time, saying the self-same word. 45. Then he cometh to his disciples, and saith to them: Sleep ye now and take your rest; behold the hour is at hand, and the Son of man shall be betrayed into the hands of sinners. 46. Rise, let us go; behold he is at hand that will betray me.

The first period of struggle must have endured an hour. They who were supposed to be faithful watchers had fallen asleep. He had to struggle alone. And just as we are brokenhearted when a friend fails us, so this lack of sympathy hurt Him. Yet we should not blame them too much. Their own sorrow and the night air brought on a tired feeling. He was gentle each time that He came to them.

The inner struggle continued after the first hour; but His will held resolute in its steadfast purpose of resignation to His Father's will. When hell let loose all its fury against Him, He followed the same course that He had always pursued.

Note the change in Him when He came for the third time to the apostles. The spiritual Athlete was now master of Himself and serene. He had been victorious over the devil and over fear. He drank His cup of sorrow. It was in a garden that the devil had first deceived man; it was in a garden that the devil sought to break the human will of the new Adam. In heaven, perhaps, we shall learn more of that terrible inner conflict in which Christ rejected every effort of him who sows evil in men's hearts, who suggests to us that there is no obligation to remain pure, to be honest, to pray, to offer the Mass, or that there is no harm in reading certain books. The decisions that make or break a young person take place interiorly, in the will. In the secrecy of our hearts we decide whether or not to take God's will as our supreme rule. If we firmly decide to abide by His will, then we gradually acquire strength of character. Note the tone of command, of resolution in Christ as He uttered that word: "Rise." Strength is acquired by prayer.

JOHN 18: 2. And Judas also, who betrayed him, knew the place; because Jesus had often resorted thither together with his disciples. 3. Judas therefore having received a band of soldiers and servants from the chief priests and the Pharisees, cometh thither with lanterns and torches and weapons.

MATT. 26: 48. And he that betrayed him, gave them a sign saying: Whomsoever I shall kiss, that is he; hold him fast. 49. And forthwith coming to Jesus, he said: Hail, Rabbi. And he kissed him. 50. And Jesus said to him: Friend, whereto art thou come? Then they came up, and laid hands on Jesus, and held him.

LUKE 22: 48. And Jesus said to him: Judas, dost thou betray the Son of man with a kiss?

Mischief had been afoot in the quiet of the city's night. There the devil was successful. Men with murder in their hearts were approaching this battleground of the garden where a greater victory than theirs had already been won by the moral force of a resolute will. Did Judas expect to deceive Jesus with a show of affection that was not at all natural to him? Let us hope that he thought Jesus might miraculously escape. Christ called him *friend*. What gentleness, self-control, appeal! No pain on the cross could equal the shaft of sorrow that shot through the heart of the noblest of men as He submitted to deceitful betrayal by one of His own. A kiss is a sacred thing that can be debased to very low uses. Never did it descend lower than here.

JOHN 18: 4. Jesus therefore, knowing all things that should come upon him, went forth, and said to them: Whom seek ye? 5. They answered him: Jesus of Nazareth. Jesus saith to them: I am he. And Judas also, who betrayed him, stood with them. 6. As soon therefore as he had said to them: I am he; they went backward, and fell to the ground. 7. Again therefore he asked them: Whom seek ye? And they said: Jesus of Nazareth. 8. Jesus answered: I have told you that I am he. If therefore you seek me, let these go their way.

The ruffians must have remained at the gate. Having pointed out Jesus, Judas returned to them. But they were to experience the awful majesty of the God-Man. He wanted it known that He freely submitted Himself to them. Swords and soldiers were powerless against His person until He permitted them to use their apparent physical advantage. He walked right up to them. Power went out from Him, as it had so often done before. Having a taste of His power, the mob knew that He meant what He said in regard to the apostles. Not a hand was laid on them. He knows how to protect His own; He is the good shepherd. He follows with watchful eye His own among the modern youth, protecting them while they are not aware, even saving them in their rashness.

LUKE 22: 49. And they that were about him, seeing what would follow, said to him: Lord, shall we strike with the sword? 50.

And one of them struck the servant of the high priest, and cut off his right ear. 51. But Jesus answering, said: Suffer ye thus far. And when he had touched his ear, he healed him.
MATT. 26: 52. Then Jesus saith to him: Put up again thy sword into its place: for all that take the sword shall perish with the sword. 53. Thinkest thou that I cannot ask my Father, and he will give me presently more than twelve legions of angels? 54. How then shall the scriptures be fulfilled, that so it must be done? 55. In that same hour Jesus said to the multitudes: You are come out as it were to a robber with swords and clubs to apprehend me. I sat daily with you, teaching in the temple, and you laid not hands on me. 56. Now all this was done, that the scriptures of the prophets might be fulfilled. Then the disciples all leaving him, fled.

The apostles had never permitted themselves to think that Jesus could be taken. Peter meant to be courageous (John 18: 10), but his action was rash. Christ gave a perfect example of His principle: "Love your enemies, do good to them that persecute and calumniate you." Having healed the ear, He showed them that religion is not to be spread by force, by the sword, but by love, patience, and kindness. We are not to return evil for evil, calumny for calumny. Defense of your person, your home, or a church from a mob is legitimate. Likewise, unjust accusations against the Church must be refuted in writing; but avoid rashness and imprudence. In danger do not permit your resolutions to melt away, as did the apostles. They left Him alone.

He was now a prisoner; and yet He was the only free Man in that mob. He had freely submitted to be taken by the representatives of His own nation. Never did He seek to crush by a full display of power. Only God could have such self-restraint. While He found the cup of suffering bitter, yet He drank it because it was His Father's will. He has thus taught us to bear up manfully under suffering and misrepresentation. Even when emotions and the body seek to bend the will, as they did in the Passion, yet the resolution to keep one's trust in God gives strength to the will to conquer. Whatever be our failings, we must seek always to avoid deliberate sin, for sin shuts us off from God. If we lose God, all is lost. God, not man, can tell us what sin really is.

1. In what sense does deliberate sin aim at the overthrow of God?
2. What was the most difficult thought for Christ to bear?
3. Why cannot man sufficiently atone for his own sins?
4. How would you answer a person who says that there is nothing fundamentally wrong in breaking the sixth Commandment?
5. Would Christ approve of your forcing anyone to be a Catholic?
6. God is merciful. Show, however, that sin is never a small matter in His sight.

Chapter 58

THE RELIGIOUS TRIAL

JOHN 18: 12. Then the band and the tribune, and the servants of the Jews, took Jesus, and bound him: 13. And they led him away to Annas first, for he was father-in-law to Caiphas, who was the high priest of that year. 14. Now Caiphas was he who had given the counsel to the Jews, that it was expedient that one man should die for the people. . . . 24. And Annas sent him bound to Caiphas the high priest.

MARK 14: 53. And they brought Jesus to the high priest; and all the priests and the scribes and the ancients assembled together.

ANNAS was the power behind the throne. He had once been high priest; and five of his sons had in succession held the office. Now his son-in-law, Caiphas, was the nominal religious leader of the Jews. The very fact that Christ was first brought to Annas shows his influence. It was a gesture to gain his support. Perhaps he questioned Christ; but since his son-in-law was the technical judge in any religious trial, he passed the responsibility on to him.

It was now well past midnight. Word of the capture had been spread. The religious officials came, greedy for revenge. The elders were laymen. The priests and elders, who were of the upper classes, were mainly Sadducees. The Pharisees were also represented in this governing council, called the Sanhedrin. It is probable that not all members were present at this night session.

JOHN 18: 15. And Simon Peter followed Jesus, and so did another disciple. And that disciple was known to the high priest, and went in with Jesus into the court of the high priest. 16. But Peter stood at the door without. The other disciple therefore, who was known to the high priest, went out, and spoke to the portress,

and brought in Peter. 17. The maid therefore that was portress, saith to Peter: Art not thou also one of this man's disciples? He saith: I am not. 18. Now the servants and ministers stood at a fire of coals, because it was cold, and warmed themselves. And with them was Peter also, standing, and warming himself.
MATT. 26: 71. And as he went out of the gate, another maid saw him, and she saith to them that were there: This man also was with Jesus of Nazareth. 72. And again he denied with an oath: I know not the man.
LUKE 22: 59. And after the space, as it were of one hour, another certain man affirmed, saying: Of a truth, this man was also with him; for he is also a Galilean.
MATT. 26: 73. And after a little while they came that stood by, and said to Peter: Surely thou also art one of them; for even thy speech doth discover thee. 74. Then he began to curse and to swear that he knew not the man. And immediately the cock crew.
JOHN 18: 26. One of the servants of the high priest (a kinsman to him whose ear Peter cut off) saith to him: Did I not see thee in the garden with him?

Torn between love and fear, Peter had followed the crowd to the palace of Caiphas. John was better known in the city than was Peter. Evidently John did not attempt to hide his connection with Christ. But Peter's furtive look would excite suspicion. Yes, Peter was "terribly alone" there by the fire. He was without his Master's strengthening presence. Where were all his sturdy resolutions? A mere servant maid put him to rout. It is likely that he denied more than once on each of the three occasions, for he had lost all presence of mind. When too many looked at him, he wanted to run. He made for an exit. But no! He would be brazen; he simply could not tear himself away from Jesus. He may have become bolder after the first hour, since his dialect was recognized. A crowd had gathered around him. What a picture he made, for his cursing and swearing were loud! Brave Peter! He was learning the lesson that we all need, namely, that without prayer and reliance on God our resolutions easily melt when face to face with a temptation.

LUKE 22: 61. And the Lord turning looked on Peter. And Peter remembered the word of the Lord, as he had said: Before the cock crow, thou shalt deny me thrice. 62. And Peter going out wept bitterly.

It may be that Jesus was being led from one side of the courtyard to another, or, he was not far from Peter. He was aware of Peter's denials. Their eyes met — those eyes that had so often pierced through to the soul and secret thoughts of His hearers. Peter had denied Christ; but Christ would not deny Peter. He would throw a grace of one more loving glance at His chief apostle. And that shaft of grace hit its mark. Ignoble Peter was really noble of soul; but he had been too boastful. He needed a humiliating lesson; he got it. Christ had looked steadily at Judas; later He would eye Caiphas and Pilate. These men were, however, too self-centered to permit grace to find room in their souls.

Peter's faults were on the surface; they were faults of an unsuspecting, generous, and unselfish temperament. The manly thing about him is that he was not ashamed to admit that he had sinned. There is always hope for a person who is not ashamed to go to confession and to take full blame for his sins. Peter is a noble picture in his tears of penance. We all have faults; but if Jesus sees that there is an unselfish love of Him in the sinner, He will grant the grace of repentance. Keep in mind that picture of a Prisoner turning His eyes on one whom He loved; He wishes to catch our eye before we deny Him by deliberate sin.

> John 18: 19. The high priest therefore asked Jesus of his disciples, and of his doctrine. 20. Jesus answered him: I have spoken openly to the world: I have always taught in the synagogue, and in the temple, whither all the Jews resort; and in secret I have spoken nothing. 21. Why askest thou me? Ask them who have heard what I have spoken unto them: behold they know what things I have said. 22. And when he had said these things, one of the servants standing by, gave Jesus a blow, saying: Answerest thou the high priest so? 23. Jesus answered him: If I have spoken evil, give testimony of the evil; but if well, why strikest thou me?

We are not sure of the right sequence of events during the night and the early morning. There must have been two religious trials, one at night, which was illegal according to their law and at which all the members of the Sanhedrin were not present, and the other in the morning, just before they turned Him over to Pilate for the civil trial. This scene here pictured by John was probably a preliminary hearing before Caiphas, while they were waiting for the judges to assemble. Caiphas hoped to draw out Christ and to catch Him in some treasonable or heretical statement, just as in England in 1534–35 official murderers tried to entrap St. Thomas More in a treasonable statement. They had arrested Jesus; they were supposed to have evidence for so doing; why should they now seek evidence from Him? The Catholic religion is open; it has no secret designs. Anyone who really wants to learn about it can easily obtain the teachings of the Church.

But persecutors seldom want the truth. Our Lord's case was decided beforehand. Hence, He kept His dignity; He was not in the least afraid. In fact, He was judging Caiphas. This is the first time that a man dared to strike God. And what self-possession, what calm dignity in the reply of the meek Christ who was now showing that meekness is not weakness! Always we admire a person who stands for the truth, who will take an unpopular side if truth be on that side. Jesus expects us calmly to stand for the truth, and never to be intimidated by threats or blows. The movie *San Francisco* shows that for years the priest in the picture was able to outbox the hero. Later the hero strikes the priest in a restaurant. But the priest makes no effort to strike back. It is a beautiful example of strong meekness and the priest's self-control touches the hero, who yields. Christ's manly stand is reflected in the priest's self-control.

> LUKE 22: 63. And the men that held him, mocked him, and struck him.
> MATT. 26: 67. Then did they spit in his face, and buffeted him: and others struck his face with the palms of their hands,
> LUKE 22: 64. And they blindfolded him, and smote his face. And they asked him, saying: Prophesy, who is it that struck thee? 65. And blaspheming, many other things they said against him.

Jesus had saved Peter; in fact His life had been one of doing good to others. Now there was not one to take His part. The pent-up hatred of jealousy was let loose. The servants went farther than their masters. No one protested. Low men who have obtained power are capable of diabolical fury. In Mexico, Russia, and Spain priests and the laity have met the same treatment as that here vented on their Leader. He bore it all because He loves us. These insults took place at various intervals while they were waiting for the morning to come.

> LUKE 22: 66. And as soon as it was day, the ancients of the people, and the chief priests and scribes, came together; and they brought him into their council, saying: If thou be the Christ, tell us.
> MATT. 26: 59. And the chief priests and the whole council sought false witness against Jesus, that they might put him to death: 60. And they found not, whereas many false witnesses had come in. And last of all there came two false witnesses;
> MARK 14: 56. For many bore false witness against him, and their evidences were not agreeing.
> MATT. 26: 61. And they said: This man said: I am able to destroy the temple of God, and after three days to rebuild it. 62. And the high priest rising up, said to him: Answerest thou nothing to the things which these witness against thee? 63. But Jesus held his peace. And the high priest said to him: I adjure thee by the living God, that thou tell us if thou be the Christ, the Son of God. 64. Jesus saith to him: Thou hast said it. Nevertheless I say to you, hereafter you shall see the Son of man sitting on the right hand of the power of God, and coming in the clouds of heaven. 65. Then the high priest rent his garments, saying: He hath blasphemed; what further need have we of witnesses? Behold now you have heard the blasphemy: 66. What think you? But they answering, said: He is guilty of death.

This was the official trial, held very early in the morning. The fixed witnesses whom they brought in could offer nothing but contradictions. Even the twisted statement (Cf. p. 95) about His predicted resurrection did not perturb Him. His majestic silence and calm dignity infuriated the judges. Caiphas, however, was shrewd. At the proper moment he placed Jesus under oath to answer the crucial question. They could not condemn Him for merely claiming to be the promised Messias. But if this Messias claimed to be equal to God, one with God, divine in origin, that would be a different matter. He had been careful in making explicit statements on His divinity. He wished to have His character, words, and deeds slowly convince the people that He is actually God, because the Jews had a high regard for the unity of God. Therefore, it was now a solemn, tense moment when Christ openly, publicly, before the religious authorities of the nation made the statement which would make Him a martyr. He had paid no attention to false accusations. He wanted it understood, however, that He was being condemned for claiming to be divine and equal to God, which they would say was blasphemy.

It was the declaration that Caiphas wanted. He was supposed to be a judge presiding at a trial. Not one bit of evidence which would prove Christ's claim was admitted into the trial; no one was allowed to speak for Him. The very rules of the Sanhedrin required that in such trials all evidence in favor of the accused be first studied. But no! In their hearts these men were jealous. Christ had exposed their hypocrisy, their placing of their own views above God's law, their permission of abuses in the Temple. The families of Annas and Caiphas had been made wealthy by the extortions in the Temple. Consequently, the jury that condemned Christ was filled with hate. The judge became the chief accuser. When Easterners rend their garments it means that they are terribly horrified. In this case the horror at blasphemy was not the real reason for their action. But since their law declared death for the blasphemer (Lev. 24: 16), they saw a chance to condemn Christ on that charge.

MATT. 27: 3. Then Judas, who betrayed him, seeing that he
was condemned, repenting himself, brought back the thirty pieces
of silver to the chief priests and ancients, 4. Saying: I have
sinned in betraying innocent blood. But they said: What is that
to us? Look thou to it. 5. And casting down the pieces of silver
in the temple, he departed; and went and hanged himself with
a halter. 6. But the chief priests having taken the pieces of
silver, said: It is not lawful to put them into the corbona, because it is the price of blood. 7. And after they had consulted
together, they bought with them the potter's field, to be a burying place for strangers. 8. For this cause that field was called
Haceldama, that is, The field of blood, even to this day.

The case of Judas is an illustration of how selfish love of money destroys trust in God. Remorse for such a life leads to despair, not to tears of penance. Matthew's account leads us to believe that Judas in some manner had access to the priests before they delivered Christ to Pilate. What a contrast between their apparent horror at Christ's claiming to be God and their utter indifference to the sin of Judas. Murder did not bother them; but they were very scrupulous about accepting back the wages they had paid Judas. Testimony of Christ's innocence did not interest men bent on murder. The end of Judas shows that the devil does not treat any too well those who consent to do his work.

1. What was Peter's fault? How did he differ from Judas?
2. What precaution must one take if he wish to avoid denying Christ or His religion?
3. What would you do if you discovered that you had the habit of condemning others without having the facts or true evidence for so doing?
4. What was the official religious excuse for putting Christ to death?
5. Why do we suspect the so-called righteous indignation of those who have secretly made themselves wealthy while in positions of power?
6. Show from Christ's life that meekness or self-control does not imply weakness.
7. Show that Christ publicly claimed to be God.
8. How may one acquire the strength to stand up for the truth?
9. What may we learn from Peter's tears?
10. Why was the religious trial unjust?

Chapter 59

THE CIVIL TRIAL

LUKE 23: 1. And the whole multitude of them rising up, led him to Pilate.

JOHN 18: 28. Then they led Jesus from Caiphas to the governor's hall. And it was morning; and they went not into the hall, that they might not be defiled, but that they might eat the pasch. 29. Pilate therefore went out to them, and said: What accusation bring you against this man? 30. They answered, and said to him: If he were not a malefactor, we would not have delivered him up to thee. 31. Pilate therefore said to them: Take him you, and judge him according to your law. The Jews therefore said to him: It is not lawful for us to put any man to death.

THEIR purpose in taking Christ to Pilate will become evident as we proceed. Pilate was the Roman governor for Palestine, a position as difficult then as is that of the British High Commissioner there today. He had come to Jerusalem for the Pasch as there was always danger of disturbances at such times. It is likely that Pilate lodged in the fortress Antonia, which was at the northwest corner of the Temple grounds. The fortress had an outer court, paved with large, flat stones and on the same level as the street. Pilate either came into this outer court, or talked down to the people on the street from a wall surrounding the court. The priests did not worry about killing an innocent man; but they would not enter a pagan house for fear of breaking the rule against touching leavened bread (Cf. Exod. 12: 15). The time was possibly between six and seven on Good Friday morning.

Pilate beheld a wild, shouting group of priests, and a bound, unkempt, meek-looking Man. He must have known of the arrest; but possibly he had never seen our Lord. At first the plight of the prisoner made no impression on this haughty Roman. He was not interested in Jewish religious quarrels. Consequently the priests realized that they would have to present some complaint that would concern sedition against Rome. They did not mention anything about blasphemy. He who had done good deeds was now called a criminal. Pilate saw immediately that there was no specific charge, and in a bantering tone he told them to judge Christ. Rome may have taken away from the Jews the right to inflict capital punishment, but just a few years later we see the same people stoning Stephen to death. Evidently, then, there was some hidden reason for their effort to have Pilate decree the death penalty. We recall that Jesus had predicted that He would be turned over to the Gentiles.

> LUKE 23: 2. And they began to accuse him, saying: We have found this man perverting our nation, and forbidding to give tribute to Caesar, and saying that he is Christ the king.
> MATT. 27: 11. And Jesus stood before the governor, and the governor asked him, saying: Art thou the king of the Jews? Jesus saith to him: Thou sayest it.
> JOHN 18: 33. Pilate therefore went into the hall again and called Jesus, and said to him: Art thou the king of the Jews? 34. Jesus answered: Sayest thou this thing of thyself, or have others told it thee of me? 35. Pilate answered: Am I a Jew? Thy own nation, and the chief priests, have delivered thee up to me: what hast thou done? 36. Jesus answered: My kingdom is not of this world. If my kingdom were of this world, my servants would certainly strive that I should not be delivered to the Jews: but now my kingdom is not from hence.

There is an ancient stock argument that Catholics owe allegiance to a foreign power and therefore are not loyal to their country. The argument is always used by those who wish to hide some plot of their own, or who wish to arouse hatred against the true religion. The priests knew that Pilate would be interested if he thought Christ was fomenting sedition against Rome. The accusation was false, of course, for Christ had deliberately refused to be drawn into politics. He had said: "Render to Caesar the things that are Caesar's." However, the mention of the word "king" caught Pilate's ear.

Pilate may have been sitting in his judgment chair, while Christ was standing. Christ had been through the horrors of the Passion, had been beaten and spit upon, had gone through the night without sleep. The charge that such an unkempt and haggard person claimed to be a king may have at first suggested to Pilate that the Jews had handed a fool over to him. He began the first of three examinations that he was to give Jesus.

Pilate knew men. Something in the manner, the voice of Christ touched the Roman. Our Lord answered his questions openly, briefly, and with respect. Rome, the mistress of the political world and the nation of practical men, was, in the person of Pilate, having its first official contact with the God-Man. Anyone with a shred of manhood in him would of necessity feel a surge of his heart in the presence of such a Man. Pilate sensed that those discolored clothes covered something unusual. He brought Christ inside, away from the mob. In all earnestness he asked the same question. Here was a new kind of king. Suddenly, however, Christ became the judge; He asked a question. And the question unsettled Pilate. He was not accustomed to hear a prisoner speak thus. His deep-seated hatred of the Jews came to the surface. Christ did not deny that He is a king; but He began to explain that there is another world besides the world which we see, namely, the world of spiritual beings — God, the angels, human souls. And Christ is King, Ruler, Leader in that world. In fact all things belong to Him; but Christ's kingdom deals mainly with souls and their relation to God. Man is allowed to rule the world of politics, government, business. The Church is spiritual, not political.

> JOHN 18: 37. Pilate therefore said to him: Art thou a king then? Jesus answered: Thou sayest, that I am a king. For this was I born, and for this came I into the world; that I should give testimony to the truth. Every one that is of the truth, heareth my voice. 38. Pilate saith to him: What is truth? . . .

Christ was being kind to Pilate. A great grace was being offered to him; truth was being taught to him. But, just as many Americans never think of the soul or religion; just as they talk about accepting only what is practical or what can be proved to the senses, so Pilate found it hard to think of a king whose kingdom is not of this world. Christ gently but firmly stood for the fact that He is Lord of all creation, that since we have souls we are subjects of this King.

This is not a nature-made world. All things come from God; the world was made for man and man is for God. Americans will continue to be muddled, to chase the rainbow until they learn this truth. For truth about the purpose of life cannot be learned from statistics, from experiments, from science. Neither philosophy alone, nor science can give us a satisfactory answer on the true nature and destiny of man. Christ came to tell us how to live intelligently. Divine truth can be learned from a Person, not from some theory. The Truth was actually in front of Pilate. He had heard philosophers discussing truth. To his practical, Roman mind it was all foolishness. He was what we call a skeptic. He made the same mistake that Americans make, who listen to professors or pseudo-scientists or popular writers and then, being muddled when they finish listening, imagine that there is no truth. He who will not listen to God speaking to us through the Church, through the priest, will never know how to live or why he is living. When young people say that life is futile, that there is no purpose in it; when they discuss religion or immortality, or the soul, or the nature of God, inform them that the answer may be had only by listening to this Person, Christ. Pilate missed his opportunity.

JOHN 18: 38. . . . And when he said this, he went out again to the Jews, and saith to them: I find no cause in him.

MATT. 27: 12. And when he was accused by the chief priests and ancients, he answered nothing. 13. Then Pilate saith to him: Dost not thou hear how great testimonies they allege against thee? 14. And he answered to him never a word; so that the governor wondered exceedingly.

LUKE 23: 5. But they were more earnest, saying: He stirreth up the people, teaching throughout all Judea, beginning from Galilee to this place. 6. But Pilate hearing Galilee, asked if the man were of Galilee. 7. And when he understood that he was of Herod's jurisdiction, he sent him away to Herod, who was also himself at Jerusalem, in those days. 8. And Herod seeing

Jesus, was very glad; for he was desirous for a long time to see
him, because he had heard many things of him; and he hoped
to see some sign wrought by him. 9. And he questioned him in
many words. But he answered him nothing. 10. And the chief
priests and the scribes stood by, earnestly accusing him. 11. And
Herod with his army set him at nought, and mocked him, putting
on him a white garment, and sent him back to Pilate. 12. And
Herod and Pilate were made friends, that same day; for before
they were enemies one to another.

The practical Roman realized that it was not true that Jesus was a criminal, a revolutionist against Rome's authority in Palestine. He had brought Jesus out before the priests again; and he was further astounded at the calm dignity, the silence of Jesus. He thought he saw a chance to get out of a tight fix by sending Him to Herod; for Rome had permitted Herod to have a certain amount of jurisdiction in Galilee. This Herod was one of the sons of Herod the Great, who was reigning when Christ was born.

Herod was much the sensualist; and he was superstitious. For more than a year he had been hearing of Christ, since he lived in Tiberias on the shore of the Lake of Galilee. Herod was a Jew trying to live as a Roman. He wanted to be amused with some magic tricks. He was like those moderns who assert that Christ had a superior personality and merely hypnotized the ignorant, gullible masses. Herod assembled all the hangers-on of his court and they were full of high jest at the prospect of some new thrill. But the gaiety soon turned into the silence of a morgue. Not a word, not a sign from those sacred lips, for Herod was dead of soul, and corrupt of heart. The silence of Christ stung him; he seems to have paid little attention to the attacks of the priests, but he would have his revenge — he would seek to advertise Christ as a fool. He sought to make sport of the King of kings, yet pass back to Pilate the responsibility for His death.

Luke 23: 13. And Pilate, calling together the chief priests, and
the magistrates, and the people, 14. Said to them: You have
presented unto me this man, as one that perverteth the people;
and behold I, having examined him before you, find no cause in
this man, in those things wherein you accuse him. 15. No, nor

Herod neither. For I sent you to him, and behold, nothing worthy of death has been done by him. 16. I will chastise him therefore, and release him.

The morning was dragging on; the whole city was in commotion. The persistent priests were pressing their advantage over Pilate, yet he seemed suddenly to become resolute. He was seeking a way out of a difficulty. Had he been a strong character he would not have argued with them. A chastising was a horrible thing. The victim was tied to a pillar. Leather thongs with sharp stones or lead on their ends were used as a whip. The flesh would be cut through to the bone. Pilate thought that such a punishment would satisfy the mob.

* *

What one accusation most interested Pilate and why? Show how Christ made an effort to enlighten Pilate. Why cannot science or man's own ingenuity solve the problem of the purpose of life? Why are we so sure we have the truth about God and about the destiny of man? What is the reason for the October feast of the Kingship of Christ?

* *

MATT. 27: 15. Now upon the solemn day the governor was accustomed to release to the people one prisoner, whom they would. 16. And he had then a notorious prisoner, that was called Barabbas. 17. They therefore being gathered together, Pilate said: Whom will you that I release to you, Barabbas, or Jesus that is called Christ? 18. For he knew that for envy they had delivered him. . . . 20. But the chief priests and ancients persuaded the people, that they should ask Barabbas, and make Jesus away. 21. And the governor answering, said to them: Whether will you of the two to be released unto you? But they said: Barabbas. 22. Pilate saith to them: What shall I do then with Jesus that is called Christ? They say all: Let him be crucified. 23. The governor said to them: Why, what evil hath he done? But they cried out the more, saying: Let him be crucified.

Pilate's second attempt to release Christ was shrewd, but he failed to reckon with the hatred of the priests, who circulated among the people and induced them to prefer an evildoer to One who had cured the blind and the lepers. The devil seems to have been in possession of the priests. It was they who turned the people against our Lord; theirs the responsibility. The pleading of a pagan unbeliever was of no avail. He showed weakness in thus seeking excuses. Moreover, the priests were crafty. The hidden reason for bringing Christ to Pilate now came to the surface. Crucifixion was a Roman form of punishment. It was more terrible than the Jewish method of stoning. The priests were afraid of what the people might do, for Christ had friends. But if Rome condemned Him, then the odium would not fall on the priests; they could justify themselves before the people by saying that Rome had found Christ guilty of treason. Their hatred and hardness of heart were now brought home to Pilate.

JOHN 19: 1. Then therefore, Pilate took Jesus, and scourged him.

MATT. 27: 27. Then the soldiers of the governor taking Jesus into the hall, gathered together unto him the whole band. 28. And stripping him, they put a scarlet cloak about him. 29. And platting a crown of thorns, they put it upon his head, and a reed in his right hand. And bowing the knee before him, they mocked him, saying: Hail, king of the Jews. 30. And spitting upon him, they took the reed, and struck his head. 19. And as he [Pilate] was sitting in the place of judgment, his wife sent to him, saying: Have thou nothing to do with that just man; for I have suffered many things this day in a dream because of him.

Sometimes the victims died in a scourging. The crimson mantle was an emblem of royalty. The thorns were perhaps those long and sharp-pointed thorns that grow around Jerusalem. Thus did the soldiers vent their hatred of the Jews on the innocent Christ. And all this time not a word of complaint, nor a cry from the Son of God. No apostle was there. Alone, and with love in His heart He bore that pain, those insults, for us. For only God realizes the full value of a single human individual.

One voice was raised in His behalf, that of Pilate's wife. Her tribute is eloquent — "that just man." In all the crowd, only the Prisoner could be called just. Judas had confessed His innocence; Pilate knew that He was not guilty; but the priests were hard.

JOHN 19: 4. Pilate therefore went forth again, and saith to them: Behold, I bring him forth unto you, that you may know that I find no cause in him. 5. (Jesus therefore came forth, bearing the crown of thorns and the purple garment.) And he saith to them: Behold the Man. 6. When the chief priests, therefore, and the servants had seen him, they cried out, saying: Crucify him, crucify him. Pilate saith to them: Take him you, and crucify him: for I find no cause in him. 7. The Jews answered him: We have a law; and according to the law he ought to die, because he made himself the Son of God. 8. When Pilate therefore had heard this saying, he feared the more. 9. And he entered into the hall again, and he said to Jesus: Whence art thou? But Jesus gave him no answer. 10. Pilate therefore saith to him: Speakest thou not to me? Knowest thou not that I have power to crucify thee, and I have power to release thee? 11. Jesus answered: Thou shouldst not have any power against me, unless it were given thee from above. Therefore, he that hath delivered me to thee, hath the greater sin.

Pilate had made a mistake in thinking that the sight of a bruised and bleeding man would melt the hearts of the mob. Whole pieces of flesh must have been torn from His back, or even from the chest. The face was bruised from blows, and blood was dropping from the holes caused by the thorns. Were Peter and Mary somewhere on the outskirts of that crowd, while a pagan, accustomed to cruelty, tried to move to pity the descendants of a people that had been shepherded, and guarded by God for two thousand years? He who had so often responded to the cry: "Jesus of Nazareth, have mercy on us," now received no drop of mercy from those who had physical sight and healthy bodies but who were blind of heart and leprous of soul.

The priests threw caution to the winds and shouted their religious accusation: "He made Himself the Son of God." Pilate had heard from pagan mythology about gods disguising themselves in human form. He recalled his wife's message; he lost his calmness. Pilate had no idea of the true God; but he was frightened. Christ did not at first answer His question because he had previously run away from inquiring into the truth. But Jesus now (and oh, how patiently and majestically He spoke!) taught a truth for every ruler, every president and judge to ponder — all civil authority is from God. The ruler, the judge is bound to justice in the name of God; he represents God. And Jesus would now even partly excuse Pilate. Caiphas had the greater sin for he abused spiritual authority.

He should have been the first to recognize Christ. Pilate was guilty in not standing for justice, but not so guilty as Caiphas.

> JOHN 19: 12. And from henceforth Pilate sought to release him. But the Jews cried out, saying: If thou release this man, thou art not Caesar's friend. For whosoever maketh himself a king, speaketh against Caesar. 13. Now when Pilate had heard these words, he brought Jesus forth, and sat down in the judgment seat, in the place that is called Lithostrotos, and in Hebrew Gabbatha. 14. And it was the parasceve of the pasch, about the sixth hour, and he saith to the Jews: Behold your king. 15. But they cried out: Away with him; away with him; crucify him. Pilate saith to them: Shall I crucify your king? The chief priests answered: We have no king but Caesar.
> MATT. 27: 24. And Pilate seeing that he prevailed nothing, but that rather a tumult was made, taking water, washed his hands before the people, saying: I am innocent of the blood of this just man; look you to it. 25. And the whole people answering, said: His blood be upon us, and upon our children.
> JOHN 19: 16. Then therefore he delivered him to them to be crucified. And they took Jesus, and led him forth.

Those subtle, hating leaders were too much for weak Pilate. Their final argument hit true, for Caesar had previously disapproved of some of Pilate's acts. Had Pilate been sharp enough he might have seized the opportunity to turn the case over to Caesar, for it was a custom to permit governors to take difficult cases to Rome. But he seems to have been afraid. And so the mangled, bleeding figure of the God-Man was brought forth again about noon on Good Friday. Pilate taunted the crowd. And in their frenzy of hate, the priests apostatized from God; that is, they chose Caesar in preference to the divine Ruler who had given glory to their nation. They who today are seeking to make the State a god are doing the same thing. We owe allegiance to the State, but God comes first. The sadness, the dreariness of modern trends is seen in thus making men to be slaves of the State.

A mob easily gets out of hand; Pilate feared its fury. His washing of his hands was meant to be symbolic of his own innocence in the matter; but we do not thus easily rid ourselves of responsibility. A Roman official permitted the killing of a

Man whom he knew to be innocent. And meanwhile the people were calling down upon themselves that terrible curse. (The Church wishes us to pray that it may be removed from them.) The priests had won in the battle, but little did they realize the cost to themselves and to their descendants. Pilate gave no official reason for the verdict.

1. Show how the leaders changed their accusations in the two trials.
2. Why did not the priests seek to stone Christ to death?
3. Describe the character of Pilate.
4. Show that Christ could not truthfully be accused either of blasphemy or treason.
5. When should an officer or an individual stand out against a mob?
6. How do we know that hate more than zeal for the truth moved the priests to murder?

Chapter 60

THE WAY UP TO THE THRONE

JOHN 19: 17. And bearing his own cross, he went forth to that place which is called Calvary, but in Hebrew Golgotha.
LUKE 23: 32. And there were also two other malefactors led with him to be put to death.

THE mocking, royal garments were removed, thus opening the wounds afresh; His own clothes were put on. Most likely the cross was in two pieces. We are certain that Jesus was forced to carry the burden at the start, perhaps the vertical piece, if the two pieces were separate. It is likely that the procession began at the hall or court where Pilate had judged Him, and went westward along the northern wall of the city, down into a deep valley, and then up a street of many steps and out through a gate to Golgotha, which was near by. The entire distance was about half a mile. The street of the way of the cross would be narrow and rough. That valley has been entirely filled up with debris; and the wall was destroyed centuries ago. Excavations have unearthed for us the place where Pilate probably judged Him. The flat stones of the pavement are still there. A guard of Roman soldiers went along and acted as executioners.

He who had often walked untouched in the midst of His enemies; He who just five days previously had ridden into the city in triumph to the shouts of hosannas, was now silent and utterly defenseless. He who had been resistless in argument answered nothing to the jeers of the crowd. Weak and mangled as He was, He took that wood which He was to change from a thing of ignominy and dread into a throne of glory and eternal triumph. He toiled and bled under its weight; He was in disgrace. At that moment neither soldier nor priest could see ahead to Easter Sunday; they could only see a beaten Man, who had mentioned something about being a king. The King was teaching us by example how to bear our crosses.

> MARK 15: 21. And they forced one Simon a Cyrenian who passed by, coming out of the country, the father of Alexander and of Rufus, to take up his cross.
> LUKE 23: 27. And there followed him a great multitude of people, and of women, who bewailed and lamented him. 28. But Jesus turning to them, said: Daughters of Jerusalem, weep not over me; but weep for yourselves, and for your children. 29. For behold, the days shall come, wherein they will say: Blessed are the barren, and the wombs that have not borne, and the paps that have not given suck. 30. Then shall they begin to say to the mountains: Fall upon us; and to the hills: Cover us. 31. For if in the green wood they do these things, what shall be done in the dry?

Hundreds of thousands of visitors were in the city at this time for the feast. Dense throngs either saw or were aware of the procession; and the soldiers must have had a hard task beating back the pressing multitude. Not all in the crowd were enemies. Christ was touched by the sympathy shown by these women who lived in Jerusalem. He broke His silence to warn them of the terrible days coming for Jerusalem. Since He who was innocent (green wood) was made to suffer such agony, much more prolonged would be the misery of those (dry wood) who would have to endure the siege of the city, especially the unrepentant ones.

The Gospels do not tell us that Christ fell a number of times, but that such was the case may be concluded from the fact that the Roman soldiers pressed Simon into service. He was one of the thousands coming into the city for the feast. He may never have heard of Christ. Even though he did it unwillingly, he performed a deed for One who never forgets. What sweet memories were his in the years to come! It is likely that his two sons became Christians. When we help suffering people to carry their burdens we are lending aid to Christ.

> LUKE 23: 33. And when they were come to the place which is called Calvary, they crucified him there; and the robbers, one on the right hand, and the other on the left.

Mark 15: 23. And they gave him to drink wine mingled with myrrh; but he took it not.
Luke 23: 34. And Jesus said: Father, forgive them, for they know not what they do. . . .

Crucifixions were not permitted inside the city walls. They were usually held at crossroads, where publicity would be given to the event. Calvary was a bald spot, an elevated knoll, outside the wall but near a gate.

It is likely that the wine was given to Jesus by those women of the city who had sympathy with Him. The myrrh, added to the wine, acted as a drug, to deaden the pain. Christ's refusal to take the mixture is an example for us to suffer patiently when death is near. There is nothing wrong in taking a drug to deaden pain that would be unbearable. Yet the practice of seeking to avoid all pain is not Christlike. Christ wished to die with His senses in their normal condition. His way up to His throne was one of indescribable pain. Suffering preceded the victory. If we rejoice in His victory, we should likewise suffer with Him.

We do not know the method used in nailing Him to the cross. The cross may have been placed flat on the ground and our Lord nailed to it, and then the whole raised up and slipped down into the hole; or, the upright piece was first fixed in a hole, and the arms nailed to the crosspiece and this latter lifted up and placed in a groove and then the feet nailed to the upright piece. Both methods were used. The nail for each hand was likely driven through the wrist, at the joint. On the upright piece a protruding spike or piece of wood may have helped support the body between the legs. Either method brought horrible suffering.

While the nailing was in progress Jesus prayed, not only for the executioners, but for the leaders who had contrived this outrageous crime. The heart of Jesus bore no hate. His first of the seven "words" spoken from His throne were words of mercy and forgiveness. He asks us to bear no hate even toward those who would kill us, who hate us because of our religion.

John 19: 19. And Pilate wrote a title also, and he put it upon the cross. And the writing was: Jesus of Nazareth, The King of the Jews. 20. This title therefore many of the Jews did read: because the place where Jesus was crucified was nigh to the city;

and it was written in Hebrew, in Greek, and in Latin. 21. Then the chief priests of the Jews said to Pilate: Write not: The King of the Jews; but that he said: I am the King of the Jews. 22. Pilate answered: What I have written, I have written.

There were three official languages in Palestine then, and the same number today. Hebrew (or a dialect called Aramaic) was spoken by the common people. In the educated and cultured circles Greek was supreme. The Greek lettering of the seats in an open-air theater that was built in the second century A.D. at Gerash, east of the Jordan, can be seen today. Latin was the language of Pilate and the governing power.

The priests had accused Christ of trying to be a king. In irony Pilate was glad to permit the accusation to fall back on the priests and thus make them the laughing stock of the world. The inscription was carried before Him in the procession. Yet, cynical as he was, Pilate must have felt that there was some truth in the statement. The God of heaven and earth had told a Roman that there is a Ruler above all earthly rulers, and a spiritual kingdom, a society of those who accept Christ. And the throne which would continue forever to draw men and women to this King was the Cross.

JOHN 19: 23. The soldiers therefore, when they had crucified him, took his garments (and they made four parts, to every soldier a part) and also his coat. Now the coat was without seam, woven from the top throughout. 24. They said then one to another: Let us not cut it, but let us cast lots for it, whose it shall be; that the scripture might be fulfilled, saying: They have parted my garments among them, and upon my vesture they have cast lot. And the soldiers indeed did these things.
JOHN 19: 14. And it was the parasceve of the pasch, about the sixth hour. . . .
MATT. 27: 36. And they sat and watched him.
LUKE 23: 44. And it was almost the sixth hour; and there was darkness over all the earth until the ninth hour.

The clothes of the crucified were usually given to the executioners. Is it not natural to feel that Mary had woven this tunic or coat? It was long and sack-shaped, having slits in the side for the arms. Mary saw them gambling for this garment which had been a work of love. Read psalm twenty-one for David's prophecy, made over a thousand years before the event took place.

It was about noon when Christ was raised on the cross. The soldiers were obliged to remain on guard. It was more than a coincidence that the divine Lamb should be sacrificed just at this feast of the Passover, which recalled the time when the blood of a lamb on their doorposts saved the Jews from the destroying angel in Egypt. Now blood was being shed to redeem the world. Unwittingly the priests had fulfilled the plans of God. The Passover had been intended as a symbol of Calvary.

This darkness was not due to an eclipse. It covered all Palestine. It was nature manifesting her sadness over the perversity of men who attempt to slay God, to kill religion in the hearts of the people. Darkness falls on him who kills God in his soul.

LUKE 23: 35. And the people stood beholding, and the rulers with them derided him, saying: He saved others; let him save himself, if he be Christ, the elect of God.

MATT. 27: 39. And they that passed by, blasphemed him, wagging their heads, 40. And saying: Vah, thou that destroyest the temple of God, and in three days dost rebuild it; save thy own self: if thou be the Son of God, come down from the cross. 41. In like manner also the chief priests, with the scribes and ancients, mocking, said: 42. He saved others; himself he cannot save. If he be the king of Israel, let him now come down from the cross, and we will believe him. 43. He trusted in God; let him now deliver him if he will have him; for he said: I am the Son of God.

Among those who remained silent were many friends of our Lord. The readiness with which those unfriendly to Him repeated His sayings shows that His words had become common property. The leaders gloated in their triumph. Their mocking indicates their cowardice. It was by not saving Himself that He was to save others. By enduring that crucifixion He won pardon for all sin, even the sins of the leaders if they would repent. Those moderns who ask why God does not work a miracle for them have the same attitude, the same heart as those who sneered: "Come down now from the cross and we will believe." The atheist brave? No, indeed. What would a champion prize fighter gain by knocking down a boy who dared him to do it? God does not work miracles for egotists, for they would not believe if they saw one. God wants in heaven those who believe out of free choice; He does not force anyone to go there. The atheist lacks a sense of humor. He takes himself and his ideas too seriously.

In every century many assert that religion is dying out, that educated people are dropping it. But the more they drop religion the more they go to psychiatrists and sanitariums for aid. Yes, the cause of Christ seemed lost on Good Friday. But in Christ we have not a losing Leader; we know whom we are believing. The loss is among those who take down the crucifix from their walls.

> LUKE 23: 36. And the soldiers also mocked him, coming to him,
> and offering him vinegar, 37. And saying: If thou be the king
> of the Jews, save thyself. . . . 39. And one of those robbers
> who were hanged, blasphemed him, saying: If thou be Christ,
> save thyself and us. 40. But the other answering, rebuked him,
> saying: Neither dost thou fear God, seeing thou art under the
> same condemnation? 41. And we indeed justly, for we receive
> the due reward of our deeds; but this man hath done no evil.
> 42. And he said to Jesus: Lord, remember me when thou shalt
> come into thy kingdom. 43. And Jesus said to him: Amen I
> say to thee, this day thou shalt be with me in paradise.

The true inner nature of a person is shown in a crisis. One thief was hard; the other must have observed Christ closely on the way up to Calvary. While all others were mocking, this man saw fit to proclaim Christ's innocence and to make a public act of faith. While the priests thought Christ defeated, this man believed that Christ would triumph. He believed when it was hard to believe. In the eyes of the world Christ had nothing to give at that time; even His clothes had been taken from Him. And yet, note the calm self-possession of His generosity. He gave salvation for that one act of faith. The paradise He mentioned was not heaven, but limbo, where the soul of Christ would go on that very day to announce to the souls of the just that redemption had opened heaven.

Anyone who clings to Christ when all seems lost will gain the same victory — the company of Jesus in eternity. This promise of Christ was the second of His seven "words" from the throne. True sorrow for sin, even at the last moment of life, can win pardon. If deathbed conversions seem to startle us, we should recall that there are always holy people who are doing penance for the conversion of sinners. Again, many sinners have done good deeds in their life which, perhaps, were not observed by the world but which God saw. And He can give extra graces which aid the sinner to be repentant.

JOHN 19: 25. Now there stood by the cross of Jesus his mother, and his mother's sister, Mary of Cleophas, and Mary Magdalen. 26. When Jesus therefore had seen his mother and the disciple standing whom he loved, he saith to his mother: Woman, behold thy son. 27. After that, he saith to the disciple: Behold thy mother. And from that hour, the disciple took her to his own.

In the last year of Christ's life we hear nothing of His mother. But now when others had abandoned Him she walks on the scene so quietly and courageously that we can be positive that she had been continuously in touch with Him and had been in Jerusalem suffering with Him during Holy Week. Mary, who silently pondered God's dealings with mankind, who never shirked responsibility, who never failed in a crisis, was now on hand — loyal to the end in her position as mother. Men might run away in fear; not so this woman of quiet, steady courage. There is no mention that she complained or shirked suffering and heartbreaking trials. Motherhood means sacrifice of self. With the eloquence of silent, sympathetic action Mary appeals to American girls and women to curb selfishness and to stand by Christ. No literary artist ever painted a more powerful argument than that penned by the eyewitness, St. John: "There stood by the cross of Jesus his mother."

Nor would Mary Magdalen, she of the great heart, fail in the test. And John, the "son of thunder," who had said that he would drink the chalice of suffering, said nothing; he just stood there in loyalty. The heart of Christ was consoled by these silent witnesses. His third "word" from the cross reveals how deeply the Son of God appreciated what Mary had done for Him and for us in consenting to be the mother of the Crucified. He would not leave her unprovided for. He would likewise show His trust in John. Religion is charity, is thoughtfulness of others. This domestic testament of Jesus means simply that He wanted a home and protection provided for Mary. It confirms our belief that Christ had no brothers or sisters. Earth's sole immaculate woman was entrusted to the most thoughtful of the apostles. And John signed the testament on his honor. The sword of sorrow had now pierced Mary's soul; but her courageous acceptance earned for her the capacity to guide youth to her Son.

As we look back over the Gospel accounts of the trial of Christ, over the journey to Calvary and the horrible enthroning on the cross, we are struck by the matter-of-fact manner in which the four Evangelists relate their story. There is no bitterness in their report, no misrepresentation, no effort to excite sympathy with Christ. They were guided by the Holy Ghost when writing, yet each gives in His own style facts which he thought would make us appreciate what Jesus did for us. The Gospels were intended to deepen our faith in Christ, to strengthen our hold on those truths of which the Church is the official guardian. By rereading this story often we are stirred to love of Him, who because He loved us resolved to mount up to His throne, which was in reality an altar of sacrifice, where He would pour out His blood that we might be redeemed.

1. What is the meaning of the words, *via dolorosa?*
2. What is the value in bearing one's crosses?
3. Why should each student have a crucifix in his or her room? Should there be one in each home?
4. How many of the Stations of the Cross are related in the Gospels? The others were added to help us visualize the scenes and to increase our devotion.
5. Write a composition on the impression you receive from the sentence: "There stood by the cross of Jesus his mother."
6. Does Christ forget when you help Him to carry the cross, that is, when you do something for Him, or practice your religion despite sneers from the crowd?
7. Show that a good deed done by a non-Catholic or a bad Catholic may earn the grace of conversion.
8. Have you ever prayed for those who have done an injustice to you?
9. What is wrong with the challenge of those who say: "Show me a miracle and I will believe in the Church"?
10. Why is it wrong for a sinner to say that he has no chance of forgiveness?
11. Why is a cross placed on top of so many Catholic buildings?
12. What action of Christ is a rebuke to those who drink to drown their sorrow?

Chapter 61

THAT THEY MAY HAVE LIFE

> MARK 15: 34. And at the ninth hour, Jesus cried out with a loud voice, saying: Eloi, Eloi, lamma sabacthani? Which is, being interpreted: My God, my God, why hast thou forsaken me? 35. And some of the standers-by hearing, said: Behold he calleth Elias.

IN THE lives of most of the saints there comes a period of trial in which all the future seems black. They are tempted to despair; God seems to have abandoned them; they feel that they are shut off from God. They persevere, however, and when the test is over God floods their souls with comfort. But no saint ever had to undergo the agony that Christ experienced. When His strength was about gone, He felt forsaken by His Father. It was a trial that the Father permitted to come to Him. We cannot understand it fully, but just as in the garden, so here it seemed to observers that the supporting strength of His divine nature withdrew, and that Jesus felt alone. In the crisis He had to prove His trust in His Father. The twenty-first psalm had been running through His mind since the night before. This fourth "word" is merely a quotation from that psalm. He was tempted; He was tormented; but He did not yield. The cry was not a cry of despair; but it tells us something of the mental sufferings of our Lord during those three terrible hours, even though the hypostatic union was maintained.

Knowing what God is like, He could feel bitterly the agony of separation from His Father. We find it difficult to realize what the loss of God means. Only after death shall we know what pain those souls feel that are deprived forever of God. The greatest pain in hell is the pain of the loss of God, for the soul was made for God. Christ, and the saints to a degree, realized here on earth what others learn only after death — the pain of separation from God after having known what the presence of God really is.

The devil may have again suggested that He yield to despair, that He break that resolution to suffer all torments for us. But the devil was unsuccessful. And, having felt in His human nature what it is to be tempted to despair, Christ knows how to be sympathetic with every form of human suffering. In one sense He had been a lonely Man because no human could rise to His thoughts. So, when we imagine that loyalty to Him, loyalty to the truth is a lonely path, we should recall that He trod that path before us, and His human will never yielded to discouragement. He is our Leader in affliction as well as in success.

> JOHN 19: 28. Afterwards, Jesus knowing that all things were now accomplished, that the scripture might be fulfilled, said: I thirst. 29. Now there was a vessel set there full of vinegar. And they, putting a sponge full of vinegar about hyssop, put it to his mouth. 30. Jesus therefore, when he had taken the vinegar, said: It is consummated.

It is impossible to describe the pain of that inhuman punishment of crucifixion. The three hours would seem an eternity. The wounds had swollen and the flow of blood would be impeded, causing a struggle in the heart. The body of Christ was not far above the ground; and dust and flies pestered Him. That thirst which so often drives men insane in the desert was His in full reality. Yet, the fifth "word" was more than an expression of physical thirst. Christ was fulfilling a thought predicted by David in another of the psalms (68: 22). He thirsts for our love, our gratitude, for more converts to the Church so that His sufferings will not have been in vain.

The sixth "word" is an announcement of a victory, of a triumph. God the Father had sent Him to earth as Man to offer His life in redemption for the sins of men. The new Adam could now say in all truthfulness that that work was finished (consummated). Adam had failed; not so our Leader. He was a Man who taught us to persevere, to finish the task that God has given each one of us to do, namely, to bring honor on God by the way we live, by the way we treat our neighbor, our fellow Americans both Catholic and non-Catholic. His example aids us to develop the habit of finishing well any duty that has been assigned to us, including our studies.

Personal appreciation of this act of redemption requires years of prayer and thought and action. All of our previous study of the life of Christ has been a preparation for an understanding of this greatest act of His earthly life. This act, in its results, reaches back to Adam and forward to all human sin. Let us glance at its meaning.

a) Redemption means satisfaction to God. God created man with the motive of sharing His life, His happiness with man. Man belongs to God and is dependent on God. Man owes God honor and gratitude. Sin is a refusal to obey God's direction on how to get ready for life with Him. Adam and Eve began that long story of rebellion. Christ came to be the new Adam, the new head of the human race. Being divine as well as human, His obedience and His offering of His life rendered atonement or satisfaction to God for all human sin. His death was a reparation; it gave honor to God. In His fidelity to God's will He gave infinite honor to His Father before all the world, and this honor outweighs the dishonor which all sin throws in the face of God. Being the God-Man, the acts of Christ had infinite value. Redemption, then, was satisfaction to God rendered by the head of the human race. He offered Himself in our name; He was our representative. He, the innocent one, atoned for our sins.

b) Redemption means a ransom. "To give his life a redemption for many" (Matt. 20: 28). Since He spoke of redemption, we must have been in debt; something was wrong with humanity; a weight bore men down. It may be said that so long as no human person could enter heaven the devil had the human race in his power. Christ bought back or earned for men a new right to enter God's presence. The death on the cross opened heaven and thus broke the hold of Satan.

c) Redemption stored up merit. By His obedience unto death Christ earned everlasting honor for Himself. And not only that, but He earned merits for us. To prepare for God's presence, to live a supernatural life on earth men need that divine life which only God can give. It is the supernatural equipment called grace. As head of the restored human race Christ earned this life which is the necessary preparative for heaven. It is up to us to obtain what He gained for us. Just as a trust fund is often built up for children, which they may obtain if they ask for it at the proper time, so we must seek our share of this infinite fund earned by our Leader, who died that we might have divine life. We must co-operate with the graces which God extends to us. We must do our share of suffering, of good works, of prayer and worship before this stored-up grace can be applied to us. Christ ransomed us without our co-operation; but He will not save us without effort on our part.

d) *The death on the cross was a sacrifice.* We have seen how thoroughly Christ as Man submitted His own will to the will of His Father. That is true religion — acknowledging our complete dependence on God and seeking to remain united to Him. A sacrifice is an external, public expression or profession of this interior submission of our whole self to God. A sacrifice is offered only to God; it is called worship. The death on the cross was an external, visible offering that was expressive of interior submission and dedication. In this sacrifice, which is the most perfect ever offered to God, Christ was both the Priest offering and the Victim offered. Acting as our Head, He paid homage to God for all creatures. Our redemption was accomplished on that afternoon of Good Friday, very likely April 7 of the year 30. That infinite sacrifice sufficed for all time; Christ died once and does not die again. But Christ arranged that what was accomplished on Good Friday should be extended into the future. In the Mass we reoffer, re-present to God the Lamb that was offered on Good Friday. The Mass is Christ in His humanity going to God the Father in our name. It is thus that the merits of Calvary are applied to us. The offering on the Cross was a sacrifice; the offering at Mass is a sacrifice — the greatest act that we can render to God.

> LUKE 23: 46. And Jesus crying with a loud voice, said: Father, into thy hands I commend my spirit. And saying this, he gave up the ghost.

This "loud voice" of the seventh "word" was a fitting farewell to the earthly career of Him who has shown men how to live their lives for God. And the fact that it was "loud" in an exhausted and dying Man would seem to show Christ's divinity and voluntary sacrifice. It was a voice of confidence in His Father, of complete faith that death is but a door through which He, and those who follow Him, enter into the reward exceedingly great. Death for Him was but a return to His Father's house where there are many mansions. The evil deed intended by His enemies was accomplished; and thereby was brought about the greatest good ever done, for while men propose God disposes. And they who have learned to follow Christ can likewise approach death with confidence; they can commend their souls to the loving Father who knows how to welcome them into His house.

> MATT. 27: 51. And behold the veil of the temple was rent in two from the top even to the bottom, and the earth quaked, and the rocks were rent. 52. And the graves were opened: and many bodies of the saints that had slept arose: 53. And coming out of the tombs after his resurrection, they came into the holy city, and appeared to many. 54. Now the centurion and they that were with him watching Jesus, having seen the earthquake, and the things that were done, were sore afraid, saying: Indeed this was the Son of God. 55. And there were there many women afar off, who had followed Jesus from Galilee, ministering unto him. 56. Among whom was Mary Magdalen, and Mary the mother of James and Joseph, and the mother of the sons of Zebedee.
>
> LUKE 23: 48. And all the multitude of them that were come together to that sight, and saw the things that were done, returned striking their breasts.

The sanctuary hall of the Temple was divided into two parts by this large tapestry which separated the Holy of Holies from the Holy Place. It may have been about sixty feet high and thirty wide. By the splitting of this veil the Temple lost its sacredness; no more would the Holy of Holies symbolize God's presence among His chosen people. The Jewish religion had been true; but it was a preparatory stage for the more perfect revelation of God that Christ brought to earth. In refusing to accept Christ this religion lost God's approval. No more was God to be worshiped in this Temple; henceforth sacrifice was to be offered to Him wherever there was an altar, a priest, and bread and wine.

Nature was torn asunder by this attempt of men to kill nature's

God. The quake broke open the tombs that had been cut out of the rock on the hillsides. But the dead thus exposed did not rise until after the resurrection of Christ.

The good thief and now this Roman soldier felt the presence in Christ of a divine power. In death He was to have new witnesses to His greatness. And today, men and women who have open minds acknowledge that there is something unique in the Catholic religion, for the Son of God carries on His work through the Church.

The mother of John now realized that the position of her son at the cross was far different from the place she had demanded in her dream of a worldly kingdom. And yet, she must have been proud of the stanch character of John. On the other hand, terror seems to have gripped many of Christ's enemies. It was a dread day indeed, with its darkness from midday until three, and its earthquakes. Sadness reigned in the hearts of Christ's friends, but that sadness is a joy when compared with the fear that froze the leaders at His crucifixion. The darkness of the afternoon matched the darkness of their souls.

JOHN 19: 31. Then the Jews (because it was the parasceve), that the bodies might not remain upon the cross on the sabbath day, (for that was a great sabbath day,) besought Pilate that their legs might be broken, and that they might be taken away.
32. The soldiers therefore came; and they broke the legs of the first, and of the other that was crucified with him. 33. But after they were come to Jesus, when they saw that he was already dead, they did not break his legs. 34. But one of the soldiers with a spear opened his side, and immediately there came out blood and water. 35. And he that saw it, hath given testimony; and his testimony is true. And he knoweth that he saith true; that you also may believe. 36. For these things were done, that the scripture might be fulfilled: You shall not break a bone of him.
37. And again another scripture saith: They shall look on him whom they pierced.

Mosaic law forbade that a corpse be left on a tree overnight (Deut. 21: 23). And, in their preparation of the paschal lamb the Jews were careful not to break a single bone (Exod. 12: 46; Num. 9: 12). This lamb was a figure of the Lamb of God. John, the eyewitness of these facts, desired that we might know those circumstances which would deepen our appreciation of prophecy. Love, likewise, is aroused by gazing on a crucifix.

> MARK 15: 42. And when evening was now come, (because it was the Parasceve, that is, the day before the Sabbath,) 43. Joseph of Arimathea, a noble counsellor, who was also himself looking for the kingdom of God, came and went in boldly to Pilate, and begged the body of Jesus. 44. But Pilate wondered that he should be already dead. And sending for the centurion, he asked him if he were already dead. 45. And when he had understood it by the centurion, he gave the body to Joseph.
> JOHN 19: 38. . . . He came therefore, and took away the body of Jesus. 39. And Nicodemus also came, (he who at the first came to Jesus by night,) bringing a mixture of myrrh and aloes, about a hundred pounds weight. 40. They took therefore the body of Jesus, and bound it in linen clothes, with the spices, as the manner of the Jews is to bury. 41. Now there was in the place where he was crucified, a garden; and in the garden a new sepulcher, wherein no man yet had been laid. 42. There, therefore, because of the parasceve of the Jews, they laid Jesus, because the sepulcher was nigh at hand.

It must have surprised Pilate to learn that Jesus had powerful friends as well as enemies. The official investigation as to the actual death helps to refute the childish arguments of those who say that Christ only swooned on the cross, and that the apostles took the body and later claimed that Jesus arose. The myrrh and aloes acted as embalming material.

The tomb belonged to Joseph. Even today people are buried outside the walls of Jerusalem. A person often prepared his tomb before he died. Many people of that day were more concerned about their burial place than the house in which they lived. As a result, Jesus, the poor Man, was to have the well-prepared tomb of a rich man. There was a dip in the land westward from the mound on which were the crosses. Then the garden rose on another mound. In this rise was the tomb, a little over forty feet west and north from where Christ was crucified. (The Church of the Holy Sepulchre covers both spots today.) There would be two rooms in the tomb, an outer one or vestibule, and in the inner one a stone bench along the wall for the corpse. A round stone, like a flat disk, fitted into a groove to the right or left of the vestibule entrance, and thus served as a door when rolled to the left or right.

Sadly the women looked on. The Mother of Sorrows was there. Quietly these two prominent men, who had been thinking about Christ for over two years, but who hesitated to show their faith in the open, now did honor to One in whom the rich may find their only true joy. Perhaps these men thought that all was lost. That voice that had called life and health into bodies was now stilled. Silently, John escorted Mary back into the city. Somewhere Peter was wandering about, undoubtedly still weeping. Hope had flickered low indeed. Was Lazarus there as they rolled the stone sideways and covered the entrance into the vestibule? Did they recall His words to Martha: "I am the Resurrection"?

> MATT. 27: 62. And the next day, which followed the day of preparation, the chief priests and the Pharisees came together to Pilate, 63. Saying: Sir, we have remembered that that seducer said, while he was yet alive: After three days I will rise again. 64. Command therefore the sepulcher to be guarded until the third day: lest perhaps his disciples come and steal him away, and say to the people: He is risen from the dead; and the last error shall be worse than the first. 65. Pilate saith to them: You have a guard: go, guard it as you know. 66. And they departing, made the sepulcher sure, sealing the stone, and setting guards.

On a Sabbath all were supposed to be quiet. Shops were closed; children's voices were subdued. But the law which forbade any activity did not hinder plotting priests from seeking to make their victory secure. Their precaution would turn out to be an added proof of the reality of the resurrection. A cord was drawn across the stone door and a seal made in clay at each end. Unwittingly they were contributing to the glory of Christ's victory. Four Roman soldiers were on guard and were relieved by four others, perhaps every six hours. Christ's soul had meantime left His body and had gone to Limbo, where He had promised the thief He would be.

1. Relate the seven last "words."
2. Study the twenty-first psalm.
3. Describe the location and nature of Calvary and the tomb.

4. Why did all men need a redemption? Cf. Rom. 5: 12.
5. Explain four aspects of the act of redemption.
6. What does Christ teach us about perseverance in any given task?
7. What is wrong if a Catholic is afraid to die?
8. What does the conduct of Joseph of Arimathea and Nicodemus teach us?
9. Show that Christ did not despair on the cross.
10. Explain the nature of the worst torment in hell.

Chapter 62

EASTER JOY

MATT. 28: 1. And in the end of the Sabbath, when it began to dawn towards the first day of the week, came Mary Magdalen and the other Mary to see the sepulcher.
MARK 16: 3. And they said one to another: Who shall roll us back the stone from the door of the sepulcher?
MATT. 28: 2. And behold there was a great earthquake. For an angel of the Lord descended from heaven, and coming rolled back the stone, and sat upon it. 3. And his countenance was as lightning, and his raiment as snow. 4. And for fear of him, the guards were struck with terror, and became as dead men.

THESE women did not expect the resurrection; they were bringing spices in order to complete the embalming. They had not even known about the placing of the guards at the tomb, for they had observed the Sabbath law of inactivity. As Jews, they had kept the Sabbath holy; but from now on, as Christians, they were to keep the first day of the week holy. The apostles did not alter the purpose of the third Commandment, but changed the time for worshiping God from the Sabbath to Sunday. God himself made Sunday holy by rising from the dead. Was it not natural for the apostles to decide to make it the day set aside for rest and worship of God; for reflecting on that sublime joy which the resurrection brings to us?

JOHN 20: 2. She ran, therefore, and cometh to Simon Peter, and to the other disciple whom Jesus loved, and saith to them: They have taken away the Lord out of the sepulcher, and we know not where they have laid him.
LUKE 24: 3. And going in, they found not the body of the Lord Jesus. 4. And it came to pass, as they were astonished in their mind at this, behold, two men stood by them, in shining

apparel. 5. And as they were afraid, and bowed down their countenance towards the ground, they said unto them: Why seek you the living with the dead? 6. He is not here, but is risen. Remember how he spoke unto you, when he was yet in Galilee, 7. Saying: The Son of man must be delivered into the hands of sinful men, and be crucified, and the third day rise again.
MARK 16: 6. Who saith to them: Be not affrighted; you seek Jesus of Nazareth, who was crucified: he is risen, he is not here; behold the place where they laid him. 7. But go, tell his disciples and Peter that he goeth before you into Galilee; there you shall see him, as he told you.
MATT. 28: 8. And they went out quickly from the sepulcher with fear and great joy, running to tell his disciples.

Mary Magdalen very likely reached the tomb ahead of the other women. She saw the stone rolled back. She became excited, and, without waiting to investigate, ran away, drawing a wrong conclusion. Notice to whom she went and who were together. While Mary was carrying her message, the other women ventured closer. There were many angels around. Sometimes one might be visible, at other times two. Christ's soul had been reunited to His body before the resurrection, and by divine power that body was changed into a glorified and spiritual body. Divinity cannot be caged by man. Christ lives forever in heaven in His glorified humanity. (New qualities will be added to our bodies at the resurrection.) Christ our Leader was the first to merit in His humanity this undying glory. He had passed through the tomb before the stone was rolled away. The angels were announcers of a divine event, as they had been at the birth. These women were to pass on the word, showing that Jesus was a true prophet, that He had fulfilled His promise of the resurrection. The chief apostle was singled out by name. The appearances in Galilee took place later. They were the solemn public appearances for the sake of founding the Church. The appearances on the first day were private, to re-establish the faith of His followers.

Each Evangelist adds his own personal touch to the account of the resurrection. They vary in their treatment of details, but the four agree on the truth — Jesus arose through His own divine power. It is a tremendous, a startling fact; but it is the historical truth. Although the excitement and the shock were enough to make them live a thousand days in one, yet the Evangelists do not exaggerate or overdraw the picture. They do not attempt to give all the facts. We know from St. Paul (1 Cor. 15: 5–8) that there were other appearances. And we notice that the Evangelists make no effort to describe the resurrection itself, which no human person saw. Appreciation of how reliable and truthful are these writers may be deepened by reading the fantastic descriptions of the resurrection itself, which are found in the apocryphal writing called the Gospel of Peter.

> LUKE 24: 11. And these words seemed to them as idle tales; and they did not believe them. 12. But Peter rising up, ran to the sepulcher, and stooping down, he saw the linen cloths laid by themselves, and went away wondering in himself at that which was come to pass.
>
> JOHN 20: 3. Peter therefore went out, and that other disciple, and they came to the sepulcher. 4. And they both ran together, and that other disciple did outrun Peter, and came first to the sepulcher. 5. And when he stooped down, he saw the linen clothes lying; but yet he went not in. 6. Then cometh Simon Peter, following him, and went into the sepulcher, and saw the linen clothes lying, 7. And the napkin that had been about his head, not lying with the linen clothes, but apart wrapped up into one place. 8. Then that other disciple also went in, who came first to the sepulcher; and he saw, and believed. 9. For as yet they knew not the scripture, that he must rise again from the dead. 10. The disciples therefore departed again to their home.

The reception given to the report of the woman shows clearly that the apostles were in neither an expectant nor a believing mood. They had seen miracles; they had been intimate associates with the most entrancing Person ever to walk the earth; but their slowness to believe, which they so honestly report, makes it easier for us to see that we are dealing with historical facts, not with an invented story. They were men, and, like many men, inclined to disbelieve supposed nonsense spread by women.

Peter had been a heartbroken man since Thursday night. Now his spirit was returning. He acted in his usual impetuous manner — his heart ahead of his brain. He rushed in; and his brain found the fact too big, too miraculous for him to grasp immediately.

John was more reverent; he hesitated to enter, yet he comprehended more quickly than Peter. The apostles were not dried up, bloodless men. Picture those two racing through the narrow, crooked streets. They were really unselfish and truehearted. As man with man they had walked with Jesus; and now their faith in their Leader as very God was gradually recovering from the terrible shock it had received. Faults they had, but soon they were to be saints. Faith in His divinity, strengthened now, would be dimmed no more. Easter joy would remain with them forever.

JOHN 20: 11. But Mary stood at the sepulcher without, weeping. Now as she was weeping, she stooped down, and looked into the sepulcher. 12. And she saw two angels in white, sitting, one at the head, and one at the feet, where the body of Jesus had been laid. 13. They say to her: Woman, why weepest thou? She saith to them: Because they have taken away my Lord; and I know not where they have laid him. 14. When she had thus said, she turned herself back, and saw Jesus standing; and she knew not that it was Jesus. 15. Jesus saith to her: Woman, why weepest thou? Whom seekest thou? She, thinking that it was the gardener, saith to him: Sir, if thou hast taken him hence, tell me where thou hast laid him, and I will take him away. 16. Jesus saith to her: Mary. She turning, saith to him: Rabboni (which is to say, Master). 17. Jesus saith to her: Do not touch me, for I am not yet ascended to my Father. But go to my brethren, and say to them: I ascend to my Father and to your Father, to my God and your God. 18. Mary Magdalen cometh, and telleth the disciples: I have seen the Lord, and these things he said to me.

Mary Magdalen had returned to the tomb, but Peter and John must have departed before her return. Grief had overwhelmed her. The resurrection did not occur to her as a possibility. She could not rid herself of the thought that the body had been stolen and perhaps hidden by His enemies. Not even the presence of angels could remove that thought from her mind. Not even the sound of a step behind her could force her to dry her tears and to look carefully. But the change in the tone of the voice when it carried her name caused her to leap. Could it be true! The first appearance was granted to one who knew how to be grateful for the cleansing influence of Christ. However, now that the redemption had been accomplished, undying faith in Him was to replace the strengthening effect of His visible presence. "Do not touch Me" probably means: "Cease touching Me." We do not seek to touch Christ; we believe.

MATT. 28: 11. Who when they were departed, behold some of the guards came into the city, and told the chief priests all things that had been done. 12. And they being assembled together with the ancients, taking counsel, gave a great sum of money to the soldiers, 13. Saying: Say you: His disciples came by night, and stole him away when we were asleep. 14. And if the governor shall hear of this, we will persuade him, and secure you. 15. So they taking the money, did as they were taught: and this word was spread abroad among the Jews even unto this day.

The group of women who had accompanied Mary Magdalen to the tomb were likewise hurrying back to the city. Jesus had met them and told them to tell the brethren to depart for Galilee. Meanwhile the guards had run away in fear. The first attempt to deny the resurrection came on the first Easter Sunday. It was a case of hush money that failed in its purpose. The guards themselves must have laughed at the arguments proposed by the priests, for, as Augustine says, how could men who were asleep give testimony on what occurred while they slept? The truth about the resurrection made headway despite all opposition. It could not be a story invented by the Christians because it was first successfully preached in the very city of Jerusalem. Notwithstanding all their precautions the priests and the elders found that they had been foiled. And from Jerusalem the truth spread, to change the tide of history and to make us Catholics nineteen centuries after the event.

LUKE 24: 13. And behold, two of them went, the same day, to a town which was sixty furlongs from Jerusalem, named Emmaus. 14. And they talked together of all these things which had happened. 15. And it came to pass, that while they talked and reasoned with themselves, Jesus himself also drawing near, went with them. 16. But their eyes were held, that they should not know him. 17. And he said to them: What are these discourses that you hold one with another as you walk, and are sad? 18. And the one of them, whose name was Cleophas, answering, said to him: Art thou only a stranger in Jerusalem, and hast not known the things that have been done there in these days?

19. To whom he said: What things? And they said: Concerning
Jesus of Nazareth, who was a prophet, mighty in work and word
before God and all the people; 20. And how our chief priests
and princes delivered him to be condemned to death, and crucified
him. 21. But we hoped, that it was he that should have redeemed Israel: and now besides all this, today is the third day
since these things were done. 22. Yea, and certain women also
of our company affrighted us, who before it was light, were at
the sepulcher. 23. And not finding his body, came, saying that
they had also seen a vision of angels, who say that he is alive.
24. And some of our people went to the sepulcher, and found it
so as the women had said, but him they found not. 25. Then
he said to them: O foolish, and slow of heart to believe in all
things which the prophets have spoken. 26. Ought not Christ
to have suffered these things, and so to enter into his glory?
27. And beginning at Moses and all the prophets, he expounded
to them in all the scriptures, the things that were concerning him.
28. And they drew nigh to the town, whither they were going:
and he made as though he would go farther. 29. But they con-
strained him, saying: Stay with us, because it is towards evening,
and the day is now far spent. And he went in with them. 30. And
it came to pass whilst he was at table with them, he took bread,
and blessed, and brake, and gave to them. 31. And their eyes
were opened, and they knew him: and he vanished out of their
sight. 32. And they said one to the other: Was not our heart
burning within us, whilst he spoke in the way, and opened to us
the scriptures? 33. And rising up the same hour, they went back
to Jerusalem: and they found the eleven gathered together, and
those that were with them, 34. Saying: The Lord is risen indeed, and hath appeared to Simon. 35. And they told what
things were done in the way; and how they knew him in the
breaking of bread.

These two had been friendly toward Christ. Just why they could not recognize Him is unknown to us. He could change His appearance in some manner. The fact that they were at first surprised that this Stranger seemed unaware of what all Jerusalem knew, shows that the whole city had been talking of the affair. A serious yet playful joy seemed to radiate from Him as He questioned them. Then He set about showing them how the Bible needs an infallible interpreter. They had read the Old Testament, but their craving for a worldly leader led them to misinterpret the meaning of the prophecies. Some non-Catholics continue to think that private interpretation of the Bible will give them the true Christ. As a matter of fact they read their own interpretations into the Bible. Like these two on Easter Sunday, they cannot see what is really in the Bible because they do not want all that is there. They pick only what pleases them. The living Church is now the official teacher of religion.

The Bible was intended to strengthen our faith in and love of Christ. Our Faith becomes personal and more real to us if we open the book with the desire of learning more about the qualities of Christ. What appears hard and uninteresting at the start becomes filled finally with undying attraction. Our hearts will burn to know more of Him as we become acquainted with the contents. Just as Jesus would have passed on, had not these two invited Him to stay, so likewise, if He sees that we wish to learn more of our Faith, if we wish to have Him near us, He will reveal Himself more clearly to us. We never finish learning our religion; it is old, yet ever new.

It is probable that Christ did not offer the Mass at Emmaus. He simply did what would be done by a host at any meal. He may have changed the shape of His countenance. This dawning on them of the great realization is like those sudden flashes which light up our minds and convince us that what we have been following all our lives without full appreciaion is in reality the inestimable privilege of being in the company of Jesus. God grants this joy of realization to true Catholics.

All doubt about the resurrection had been dispelled when the two got back to Jerusalem. Sometime during the day the Lord appeared to Peter. Simon's prestige was such that the story could not be denied. Would that Mark had told us something of that meeting! Peter felt that he did not deserve it; but no one of us deserves Christ. And Jesus had said that once Peter was converted he would strengthen the others. From henceforth for thirty years and more did Peter preach Christ.

Thus far we have noted four appearances on Easter Sunday. Faith in Him was, for the most part, now restored. What then, does the resurrection mean to us?

a) The apostles (and we also) believed in the divinity of Christ before the crucifixion. For us the resurrection is not the main proof; it may be taken as one of the proofs. Faith is the acceptance of the word of another in things we cannot see. We accept the word of Jesus because we know that He is truthful. God is truth. The basis for our belief that Jesus is God as well as Man is His life and character and deeds taken as a whole. His personality is of such a nature that we ought to believe Him to be God just because of what He is. The resurrection is a confirmation, a strengthening of the faith we have in Him.

b) The resurrection showed that Christ was a true prophet. He had definitely and publicly stated that He would rise from the dead the third day. His enemies had asked for a sign, a proof; He gave it to them. He kept His word.

c) The resurrection is a confirmation of our belief that our bodies will one day rise from the grave in a new form. By coming forth from the grave and appearing at various times and places during forty days (perhaps on eleven occasions), Christ convinced us that He can fulfill His promise to raise us up also.

d) The difficulty Christ found in convincing His friends of the reality of the resurrection refutes, for all fair-minded people, the absurd claim that the apostles longed so earnestly for the resurrection that they imagined they saw Christ alive again.

No mention is made of our Lord's appearing to His Mother because she did not need to have her faith re-established. She had believed without any confirmatory evidence. She knew His divine origin. Would that we might know her joy on that first Easter! For us, the resurrection strengthens what we already know, namely, the divinity of Christ; He is God. Knowing that, faith in the fact that the Church is God's messenger to us becomes easy. Christ is God today as well as yesterday.

1. When did Christ arise, before or after the opening of the tomb?
2. What qualities do risen bodies seem to possess? (Cf. 1 Cor. 15: 42–44.)
3. Is our attachment to Jesus due to His physical bearing or to the qualities of His character?
4. Show that the Bible needs an infallible interpreter.
5. Christ was a prophet because ———.
6. What value for us has the resurrection of Christ?
7. Show that the apostles were not in an expectant mood for the resurrection.

8. Why should we develop the habit of reading the New Testament?
9. What impression do you receive from reading the Emmaus incident?
10. Show why a conviction of the divinity of Christ makes acceptance of the Church easy.

Chapter 63

WHO WILL SHEPHERD THEM?

JOHN 20: 19. Now when it was late that same day, the first of the week, and the doors were shut where the disciples were gathered together for fear of the Jews, Jesus came and stood in the midst, and said to them: Peace be to you.

LUKE 24: 37. But they being troubled and frighted, supposed
that they saw a spirit. 38. And he said to them: Why are you
troubled, and why do thoughts arise in your hearts? 39. See
my hands and feet, that it is I myself; handle, and see: for a
spirit hath not flesh and bones, as you see me to have. 40. And
when he had said this, he shewed them his hands and feet. 41.
But while they yet believed not, and wondered for joy, he said:
Have you here anything to eat? 42. And they offered him a
piece of a broiled fish, and a honeycomb. 43. And when he had
eaten before them, taking the remains, he gave to them.

THE first Easter Sunday began with excitement, rumor, and doubt. The day was to close with the settled peace of conviction. The priests were busy spreading the lie that the apostles had stolen the body. Hence these latter had reason to fear. The priests would try to have Pilate prosecute them for robbing a grave. However, the divine High Priest would protect His own. With no warning, no noise, no opening of a door a Figure suddenly stood among them. "He presented Himself triumphant before those who had basely abandoned Him." The victorious Christ came to hearten the ten (Thomas was absent). He whose love and mercy for us is inexhaustible spoke peace to shamefaced men — the peace of forgiveness because their hearts were right.

The strongest of men tremble when face to face with the supernatural. Any one of us would have been unnerved. With the exception of Peter, this must have been the first sight that the others had of a glorified body. It took time to get over the fright of seeing a real person, with a visible body, come from nowhere. What a sensation for a man to touch the holes in those hands and the hole in the side (John 20: 20). Mary Magdalen had not doubted and had to be restrained. These men were slower mentally. He wanted to convince them that corporal life will be renewed on our day of resurrection. Just as there was no possibility for an illusion in His presence there, since they could touch Him, so there is no reason for us to doubt His word that He can reassemble all the dead at the last day and give them a new kind of body.

Gradually joy replaced fear in the hearts of the apostles. Imagine Peter's beaming face, the deep peace of John, the happy heart of timid Philip, the solid contentment of James the stern, the thankful soul of Matthew, the high delight of Nathanael, who had learned that the world's greatest good had come from Nazareth. As they saw Him eat, and thereby exclude any possibility of His being a ghost or a spirit, the old note of familiarity returned; the at-homeness which they had always felt with Him was theirs again. The eating was like a family reunion.

> John 20: 21. He said therefore to them again: Peace be to you. As the Father hath sent me, I also send you. 22. When he had said this, he breathed on them; and he said to them: Receive ye the Holy Ghost. 23. Whose sins you shall forgive, they are forgiven them; and whose sins you shall retain, they are retained.

This is the origin of the sacrament of Penance, which restores spiritual life to those who have sorrow for sin. He solemnly commissioned the apostles to forgive sins. He is God; God alone can forgive sins. But acting as Man He had forgiven sins, and He wanted the work to go on, for He knows the need for such a sacrament. Christ wants His followers to have His peace of mind. Every human being is subject to sin. And he has difficulty in knowing whether or not he is at peace with God. Suspense, doubt, and worry are always hard to bear. The man who is sick continually asks the doctor: "When will I get better?" Some, indeed, imagine they are not ill. Hence, for our spiritual life, Christ, the wise Physician, provided in the sacrament of Penance, an answer to that "when," for the mind needs to know the definite time at which forgiveness takes place: and, furthermore, an arrangement to prevent us from deceiving ourselves by imagining that we are not in sin. People who reject the sacrament of Penance easily fall into the habit of imagining that they are all right when in reality they need the Physician.

Confession is natural, and healthy. The doctor draws a boil to a head and then lances it in order to get the poison out of the body. It may hurt to do so, but it is the only way to regain health. Misinformed people do a lot of talking about not lowering themselves to tell their sins to a priest. However, in every city there are numbers of clinics, and in colleges there are psychiatrists. The patients are required to "open up," to tell their troubles and their complexes. Modern society has found it necessary to devise all sorts of bureaus and clinics to take care of the mental problems of people, thus showing how natural and modern is the sacrament which Christ instituted on Easter Sunday—the sacrament of peace, of restoration to spiritual health. And Christ would not have told the apostles that they had power to retain sins unless He thereby implied that people were to be obliged to tell their sins to the priest.

> JOHN 20: 24. Now Thomas, one of the twelve, who is called
> Didymus, was not with them when Jesus came. 25. The other
> disciples therefore said to him: We have seen the Lord. But he
> said to them: Except I shall see in his hands the print of the
> nails, and put my finger into the place of the nails, and put my
> hand into his side, I will not believe. 26. And after eight days
> again his disciples were within, and Thomas with them. Jesus
> cometh, the doors being shut, and stood in the midst, and said:
> Peace be to you. 27. Then he saith to Thomas: Put in thy finger
> hither, and see my hands; and bring hither thy hand, and put it
> into my side; and be not faithless, but believing. 28. Thomas
> answered, and said to him: My Lord, and my God. 29. Jesus
> saith to him: Because thou hast seen me, Thomas, thou hast be-
> lieved: blessed are they that have not seen, and have believed.

Thomas is the one who, before Lazarus was raised from the dead, had said that the apostles should go up to Jerusalem and be willing to die for Christ (p. 289). Thomas was no weakling. He resembles those who are hard to convince of the truth of the Church; but once convinced, they are pillars of strength. Asking for proofs is all right, provided the inquiry is sincere. God expects people to investigate, to study, and to become persuaded before they join the Church. But there is another kind of questioning which is based on conceit. It implies that God must bow down before modern man. The young are often told to accept nothing that cannot be proved by the senses, or by scientific experimentation. Human attempts to size up God, to measure God are as old as the human race. Honest scientists know that it is not the function of science to tell us why God created us; and they know that science could not do so if it tried. Human thinkers leave us in a muddle when they attempt to give an explanation of life that is not based on what God has told us about life. Now, Christ is not a merely human leader. Hence, fortunate are they who believe Him without asking for visible proofs that touch the senses. In taking Thomas at his word and showing him the holes, Christ not only delicately rebuked the apostles but also taught the principle that once we are sure God has spoken to us, our duty is to believe.

JOHN 21: 1. After this, Jesus shewed himself again to the disciples at the sea of Tiberias. And he shewed himself after this
manner. 2. There were together Simon Peter, and Thomas, who
is called Didymus, and Nathanael, who was of Cana in Galilee,
and the sons of Zebedee, and two others of his disciples. 3.
Simon Peter saith to them: I go a-fishing. They say to him: We
also come with thee. And they went forth, and entered into the
ship: and that night they caught nothing. 4. But when the
morning was come, Jesus stood on the shore: yet the disciples
knew not that it was Jesus. 5. Jesus therefore said to them:
Children, have you any meat? They answered him: No. 6.
He saith to them: Cast the net on the right side of the
ship, and you shall find. They cast therefore; and now they were
not able to draw it, for the multitude of fishes. 7. That disciple therefore whom Jesus loved, said to Peter: It is the Lord.
Simon Peter, when he heard that it was the Lord, girt his coat
about him, (for he was naked,) and cast himself into the sea.
8. But the other disciples came in the ship, (for they were not
far from the land, but as it were two hundred cubits,) dragging
the net with fishes. 9. As soon then as they came to land, they
saw hot coals lying, and a fish laid thereon, and bread. 10. Jesus
saith to them: Bring hither of the fishes which you have now

caught. 11. Simon Peter went up, and drew the net to land,
full of great fishes, one hundred and fifty-three. And although
there were so many, the net was not broken. 12. Jesus saith to
them: Come, and dine. And none of them who were at meat, durst
ask him: Who art thou? knowing that it was the Lord. 13. And
Jesus cometh and taketh bread, and giveth them, and fish in
like manner.

A proof of the reliability of the Gospels, that they were actually written by the four men to whom they are ascribed, is the manner in which they describe local, rural conditions. These descriptions fit into the scene of the life that was lived in Galilee and Judea in the first century. Here is an example. After a week in Jerusalem the apostles went north to Galilee, in obedience to the word of the angels and of our Lord Himself. Seven of them were now together, and John, the author of this Gospel, was one of the seven. Their fishing may have been listless, for they could not get their minds off the events of Jerusalem. Moreover, on the early morning, limpid blue of the lake of Galilee they recalled the day, over two years previous to this, when they had left their boats in answer to His "Come." Moreover, they thought of the night that He had walked on the turbulent waters.

About eight o'clock in the morning fishermen usually come ashore after hours of night labor. Often a man on shore can detect movements in the water which are not observed by those in the boat. This custom explains why the apostles so readily obeyed the Stranger. While Peter was busy and excited at the haul, John took time out to think. He glanced toward the shore, about a block away. He leaned over to Peter and communicated his inference. Peter stopped working. Christ meant more to him than any amount of fish. He pulled his long tunic down over his head and swam for the shore, like a little child running to meet his father as the latter comes home from work. Catholics who are anxious to learn more about their religion are like Peter. Nearness to Christ is preferable to rich catches in the world. And Jesus provides for those who come to Him. This shore breakfast that He had miraculously prepared illustrates His goodness. He so fills the soul of a genuine Catholic that that person does not need to inquire, or to reason, about who Jesus is.

He knows intuitively that his Leader is divine; and he receives Communion with the same reverent joy that the apostles had in partaking of the meal. On this occasion Jesus had something else also in mind.

> JOHN 21: 15. When therefore they had dined, Jesus saith to
> Simon Peter: Simon, son of John, lovest thou me more than these?
> He saith to him: Yea, Lord, thou knowest that I love thee. He
> saith to him: Feed my lambs. 16. He saith to him again: Simon,
> son of John, lovest thou me? He saith to him: Yea, Lord, thou
> knowest that I love thee. He saith to him: Feed my lambs. 17.
> He said to him the third time: Simon, son of John, lovest thou
> me? Peter was grieved, because he said to him the third time:
> Lovest thou me? And he said to him: Lord, thou knowest all
> things: thou knowest that I love thee. He said to him: Feed my
> sheep. 18. Amen, amen I say to thee, when thou wast younger,
> thou didst gird thyself, and didst walk where thou wouldst. But
> when thou shalt be old, thou shalt stretch forth thy hands, and
> another shall gird thee, and lead thee whither thou wouldst not.
> 19. And this he said, signifying by what death he should glorify
> God. And when he had said this, he saith to him: Follow me.

About a year previous to this time, and just twenty or thirty miles north of the lake (p. 226) Jesus had promised to establish His Church on Peter the rock. Peter had not yet shown himself to be much of a rock. He had publicly disgraced himself, but he was always man enough to admit his mistakes. Since he was to be the first pope, he must now be publicly reinstated before the rest of those future bishops. On three occasions had Peter denied His Master. Gently to test his humility, Christ now three times asked the same question; and it was asked in the presence of the other apostles. Peter and his successors did not usurp or create the office of pope. It is God's arrangement. The pope has supreme authority in the Church. This is known as the primacy of the pope. Peter was not merely one among twelve; he was picked out to head the twelve, just as a captain is chosen to head a team, or a president to have executive power. Mark, who was Peter's secretary, does not tell us about the office; but manly Matthew and John tell us of the selection of Peter. And John wrote this account about a quarter of a century after Peter's death, while the fourth pope, Clement, was reigning in Rome. Hence, in the eyes of John the position of pope was more important for the Church than was he, the beloved disciple. This is an evidence of the honesty of Matthew and John.

Man belongs to God. But human nature is so weak that false teachers easily deceive the people. Since the truth and the grace which Christ brought to earth are so important and so necessary, would we not naturally expect Christ to take some means of protecting truth and grace, some means of seeing that the people are not fed adulterated religious truth. The United States government has a Pure Food and Drug Law which protects people from poisonous food. Infallibility, therefore, becomes a necessity, for infallibility is a protection from error.

The verb, *to shepherd,* means "to rule." Christ is *the rock,* the *holder* of the *keys,* and the *shepherd.* We see now that He transferred this threefold power to Peter. But the pope is only the visible representative of Christ; he is the vicar of Christ on earth. Christ is the invisible Head of the Church. He said: "My lambs; My sheep." When we obey the pope in spiritual matters we are obeying Christ. All those of our day who are confused learn only more confusion from self-styled leaders. Who is to lead seekers for truth into safe pastures if not he who was told by Christ to do so?

Peter poured out his soul to Christ, but he was more modest now than at the Last Supper. Having once fallen, he could be more sympathetic, more merciful. The heavy responsibility of being pope would soon be his. He would go to Rome about A.D. 41, then return for the council in Jerusalem about 50, and be martyred in Rome about 67. Vaguely Christ predicted Peter's crucifixion. And today, at the end of each year's religion course, Christ would ask just one question of each student: "Lovest thou Me?" Faults and mistakes can be forgiven; knowledge is important; but one thing is essential—personal love of Jesus, abiding loyalty to Him, our Leader.

1. Why do we believe that after the general resurrection bodies will be enabled to pass instantaneously anywhere and through anything?
2. A young person claims that he does not need peace of mind, or that he does not need the sacrament of Penance because he is afraid of nothing. Where is he wrong?

3. If an unbeliever laughed at the idea of resurrection, what would be your answer?
4. Show that Christ implied that people should tell their sins to the priest.
5. Show how confession is mentally healthful and therefore not unnatural.
6. Show that Christ fulfilled His promise to make Peter the head of the Church.
7. What students stand the best chance of remaining loyal to Christ?
8. In the works of Macaulay there is found an essay on Ranke's *History of the Popes*. In that essay look up the "London Bridge" paragraph on the papacy.
9. In how far is the practice of asking for proofs good and when is it bad?
10. What three things are necessary in the penitent for the sacrament of Penance?
11. What three positions held by Himself did Christ transfer to Peter?
12. What one question would Christ ask of students at the end of a course in religion?

Chapter 64

CHRIST IS REACHED THROUGH THE CHURCH

MATT. 28: 18. And Jesus coming, spoke to them, saying: All power is given to me in heaven and in earth. 19. Going therefore, teach ye all nations: baptizing them in the name of the Father, and of the Son, and of the Holy Ghost: 20. Teaching them to observe all things whatsoever I have commanded you: and behold I am with you all days even to the consummation of the world.

THERE were other meetings in Galilee besides these mentioned in the Gospels. St. Paul records one at which five hundred were present (1 Cor. 15: 5–7). This solemn appearance on a hill, possibly the slope on the western shore of the lake, is memorable because it is the constitution and commission of the Church to carry on His work. He reserved this powerful statement until the end, until His character, deeds, and teachings would set Him off from every other man who has walked the earth. This statement deserves examination.

a) Recall the devil's false promise to put tremendous power in His hands (p. 76). Recall His refusal to permit the people to make Him king (p. 211). Picture His submission on the cross as He heard the insult: "Let Him now come down from the cross, and we will believe Him." Neither success nor failure had turned Him from His purpose. He who had so mercifully restrained His power during His earthly life now repeats to His apostles that they had actually shared companionship with the God of heaven and earth. He now speaks as God. Divine, eternal, all-embracing power is His, not only in heaven but on earth. He rules by right because men belong to God. Their souls are received from God. The privilege of entrance into the inner life of the Trinity, which is infinitely more exhilarating than the delight we feel in the presence of a mind of scintillating thoughts, is due to His redeeming sacrifice. The Church did not make Him divine; He is such by His very nature.

b) As the world rates greatness, the country of Palestine was insignificant in that day. Eleven weak men in that country heard their Leader say: "Going — teach." The commission is clear and evident. The Church speaks in God's name. She fosters education because all men, the young and the old, have a right to learn about the soul, about the Incarnation and the Trinity, about their duty of getting ready for life with God. This Light from the East has penetrated the world. The nature of the Light cannot be learned from science but from those commissioned to represent the Light.

The Church is universal (catholic), reaching out to "all nations," all types of men and women, all races, all ages. Christ looked out beyond the hills of Galilee. He saw St. Peter's in Rome, St. Patrick's in New York, the Catholic universities of Washington and Peking, China. He saw American missionaries in Africa, Alaska, and Japan. (Our contributions to the missions aid in that work.) The apostles could not live to reach all nations, therefore their commission to teach was to pass on to their successors, the bishops.

c) We have seen that Baptism is adoption and the imparting of supernatural life. The baptized are Christ-bearers; they are dedicated to Christ, and not to Christ as Man merely but, in fact, to the three Persons in God. Our Lord's use of the phrase, "in the name," shows the unity in the Trinity. There is a difference between nature and person. Three human beings have the same nature and are three distinct persons. God is one in nature but three in person. There are not three Gods, but each Person is God. Christ Himself taught us this mystery. He wanted us to know that those baptized in the name of the Trinity are intended to enjoy the inner life of the Trinity, hence the Catholic insistence on Baptism and on the supernatural life, which prepares and equips one to comprehend something of the beauty of this ineffable mystery when eternity is reached.

d) "Teaching them to observe." The purpose of instruction in religion is that one may better fulfill the obligations of a friend

I AM WITH YOU ALL DAYS

of Christ. Too frequently religion is regarded as something to be learned but not practiced. We are to do what our Leader told us to do: first, to have His aim — so to live as to bring honor on our Father, to do things that please Him; second, to maintain union with God and to worship Him; third, to do good to our neighbor because he belongs to God.

It is sometimes hard to do what the Church commands, but we need to recall that her official commands come from Him who first walked the path He bids us tread. Each bishop in the United States can trace his authority back to the apostolic group. There has been no break in the chain. That is why the Church is called apostolic. The apostles were the first bishops. Hence the authority of the Church to teach, govern, and sanctify was not built up without good reason; it comes from this divine Leader who has "all power" to delegate authority. Christ is reached, the whole Christ is learned and enjoyed only by those who listen to what the Church officially has to say about Him. They who reject the Church and yet assert that they belong to the group who accept Christ, who have an invisible unity without external organization lack this commission from Christ to teach. The truth and grace brought by Christ are too precious to be entrusted to those who would choose what they like and reject what does not appeal to them. That is why there is chaos among scholars who imagine that they know Christ. Without authority there is only individualism; and individualism wrecks more than football teams and political parties.

e) "I am with you all days." Just as an electric current is said to make a live wire, so this unseen presence of Christ in the Church gives her a power that cannot be naturally explained. Just as the character, words, and deeds of Jesus make Him unique, so there is something about the Church that makes her unique among the institutions of the world. The answer to the problem why more people do not see the power of Christ in the Church is partially found by analyzing the failure of the Pharisees and of Pilate to see truth in Christ. On the other hand, if a child were removed from its parents at an early age and brought up by someone who filled it with hatred against its parents, it would be difficult for the child ever to overcome that emotional bias against its parents. So it is with many of our day.

But they who look beneath all the human weaknesses in Catholics finally come to see that the Church is actually alive with a divine energy. They see that the Church cannot misrepresent Christ because He is hiddenly with her. One must first become hooked up with this divine wire before he realizes the tremendous force in the Church's inner life. The baptized may walk with Him in invisible companionship just as truly as did His Mother and Peter and John.

> MARK 16: 15. And he said to them: Go ye into the whole world, and preach the gospel to every creature. 16. He that believeth and is baptized, shall be saved: but he that believeth not shall be condemned.
>
> LUKE 24: 48. And you are witnesses of these things. 49. And I send the promise of my Father upon you: but stay you in the city, till you be endued with power from on high.

The closing words of St. Mark's Gospel re-emphasize the necessity of accepting Christ. It is our duty and privilege to inform young people and old just what the true purpose of life is, to show them that while there are good people in all religions, yet one religion cannot be as good as another. The effort of unbelievers to show that the Catholic religion copied its beliefs from pagan religions is futile. Moreover, it cannot excuse people from accepting Christ. They who seek to modernize God presume that no one had the truth about Christ until they came along. Their theories break down in face of the fact that the founders of the Catholic religion on the human side were witnesses of the divine Founder's greatness. They saw Him in the flesh; they are our ancestors in the Faith.

The Church began officially on Pentecost Sunday. To await the coming of the Holy Ghost the apostles were told to return to Jerusalem. It is the Holy Ghost who brought from on high that divine guidance which had such visible effects on Pentecost and which still works in the Church.

> LUKE 24: 50. And he led them out as far as Bethania: and lifting up his hands he blessed them. 51. And it came to pass, whilst he blessed them, he departed from them, and was carried up to heaven.

The scene of the final appearance of Jesus shifts from Galilee down to Jerusalem. It was in this city that He had so often repeated that He had come from the Father. Now, forty days after the resurrection, the ascension back to the Father took place on the outskirts of that very city where His heavenly origin had been denied. It was from the top of Olivet, or from one of its slopes on the eastern side, where lay Bethania, that Jesus majestically raised those pierced hands in benediction over His friends and slowly mounted into the air. By His own divine power He, who had come as a helpless Babe, now departed as only God could leave. His visible presence on earth was ended. It was hard to part from One so true, so good and attractive (Cf. Acts 1 : 9–11) ; and yet the ascension was but a fitting climax to a career that had been devoted to the raising of men to God.

They who teach that man is but an animal would have us keep our gaze downward toward the earth, like the animals. Human nature rebels against such a view because by the nature of his thoughts man was made to look upward. The very desire for a heaven here on earth shows that man was made for something better than the earth can give him. In reality it is animalism or materialism that acts as an opium on human beings. People who reject God have no right to speak about the brotherhood of man because the very word supposes a common Father who is in heaven. That sense of the futility of life that is so common among those who have tried to live like animals, that willingness to worship for a time the absolute State or the vague idea of Society in general indicate that man was made for the true Absolute, God. That unseen world to which Christ has directed the gaze of all mankind is the only hope that makes life livable. The materialist can deny that world but he cannot remove from the human heart the desire for it; he cannot stifle anxiety about it.

> JOHN 20: 30. Many other signs also did Jesus in the sight of his disciples, which are not written in this book. 31. But these are written, that you may believe that Jesus is the Christ, the Son of God: and that believing you may have life in his name.

We began our story of Christ with the words of St. John as he traced the eternity of the Son of God. We end our study with the words of the same eyewitness. Our Leader, our Redeemer, our invisible Head of the Church is not a mere philosopher, not a superman nor a religious genius. *HE IS GOD.* No other answer fits the facts. Since He is God all is well with those who accept His leadership through the Church.

The four Gospels which we have studied do not give us all the facts about Jesus. They were written from the viewpoint of arousing in us a more personal love of Him whose heaven-brought truth and grace have been transmitted to us through the Church. There are, of course, some people who persist in calling the Gospels myths. They deny that Christ ever worked any miracles or ever claimed to be divine. They would probably deny Christ if He appeared visibly today. Back of all discussion about religion or about Christ or the Gospels is that everlasting problem — is the person willing to submit his mind to God or not. Some people prefer to worship their own ideas. Since they lack a humble sense of humor, it will always be difficult to show them that God will always be God — infinite, supreme, and beyond the complete comprehension of human intelligence, yet supplying the greatest thought for human meditation. Man will always be man, limited, dependent, changeable, not self-sufficient and never so ludicrous as when he imagines that his dictum about God is the final word. Even the pope and bishops cannot originate ideas about God or Christ. They are, however, protected, and infallibly guided agents in passing on to us what Christ revealed to the world about God and also in explaining the deeper insight that the Holy Ghost supplies to the Church concerning what Christ revealed. To one group of men in the world and to their legitimate successors Christ said: "I am with you all days." Modern man must seek to find that protected and guided group through which Christ is reached.

There are multitudes who yearn for the truth. But they are confused by so much talk about modern discoveries overthrowing ancient beliefs. They must realize that what has been learned through human effort is one thing and what has come from God through Christ is another thing. The two must be kept distinct. Men have grown so accustomed to criticize and to distrust one another that they have carried this same method over into the Gospels. They forget that, because human beings change and are influenced by their environment, it does not follow that God changes. Pseudo-intellectuals are merely reflecting their own background of materialistic evolution when they assert that there is no absolute or unchangeable truth. That is why they cannot see facts; that is why they are claiming that Christ was limited in His outlook and conditioned by the scientific ignorance of His day. Being conditioned themselves they think that Christ ought to be. Their very contradictions in explaining Christ make them ridiculous.

Likewise, honest people must realize that calling a soul electricity or a chemical compound does not solve anything. The point is that Christ gave an answer, an explanation of the purpose of life. Modern discoveries and new names do not make us any wiser on what life is for. Experimentation and science are good and necessary in their own field, but it is not their function to tell us the reason for man's being here on earth. The new discovery that many Americans have to make is that God actually became Man to save us from the guesses of those who, having never been in eternity and having never seen God, yet profess to tell us all about God. The solution is not found in any theory of evolving man but in this *divine Person.* The crystal-clear statements of the timeless Master on the nature of God and on the certainty of immortality save us from the muddy views of the materialist and the chaos of the intellectualists who reject divine knowledge.

Every written life of Christ can only drive us back to the original Gospel portrait of our Leader. Since He bids us walk the earth confidently as He did; since He said: "Learn of Me," we must seek to carry that Gospel-sketched picture in our hearts and minds. No investment brings a higher reward than this tireless and thrilling search to appreciate the portrait. Like the facet of a diamond, any angle of approach will reveal the attractiveness of our Leader. His childlike reverence for the will of His Father, His persistence in revealing God as the Father of mankind, His treating all men as brothers, His aim to have that Father honored show the utter unselfishness of His life. Daily we see Him doing good, refusing to crush or to force human beings by a display of power hidden in Him, generous yet practical, willing to fail but never becoming sour or pessimistic, possessing an inner joy and serenity, loyal always to His own, meek but never weak, fearless in condemnation of injustice and hypocrisy, terrific in indignation yet infinitely patient and approachable by all, alert and quick to see the needs of others, commanding nature for the benefit of others yet having not where to lay His head, delighting in goodness and humility wherever found, seeing God's handiwork where men saw only nature, testing those whom He loved, tenderly touching sinners yet never sinning, finding men low and raising them high, proving Himself equal to God yet serving the outcasts, refusing to be a sycophant yet gripping men to His heart, reaching down to the illiterate yet staggering the learned, constantly mingling yet constantly withdrawing to pray, captivating the young and rejoicing the old, reproached with being a carpenter yet revealing with master strokes the mind of the divine Architect, infinitely above men yet calling them friends, so concerned about getting His truth and grace to us that He promised divine guidance to His organism the Church, steadfast and unfaltering in holding His course until the divine love of His heart shed its last drop of blood in the redeeming sacrifice, and then departing to send the strength of the third Person of the Trinity to His friends — such are some of the facets in that divine Diamond, a Leader whose program shows no weakness after nineteen centuries of attack.

There is an American sense of fair play. It is unfair to admire the thoughts and character of the new Adam and reject His deeds; for the three are inseparable. They who are blindly searching for the truth have but to open their minds and hearts to Him and He will touch the spring that releases the goodness inherent in every man, for:

"Never did man speak as this Man speaketh."

INDEX